LANGUAGE AND POWER
IN THE MODERN WORLD

Mary Talbot, Karen Atkinson and
David Atkinson

EDINBURGH UNIVERSITY PRESS

© Mary Talbot, Karen Atkinson and
David Atkinson, 2003

Edinburgh University Press Ltd
22 George Square, Edinburgh

Typeset in Sabon and Gill Sans
by Bibliocraft Ltd, Dundee, and
printed and bound in Great Britain by
The Cromwell Press, Trowbridge, Wilts

A CIP record for this book is available from
the British Library

ISBN 0 7486 1539 3 (hardback)
ISBN 0 7486 1538 5 (paperback)

CONTENTS

ACKNOWLEDGEMENTS

We would like to thank Núria Borrull and Shaun Moores for reading and commenting critically on parts of the book; Angela Smith for her support and especially for offering interesting examples of call centre talk; Chris and Sylvie Toll for their tolerance in having their oral narrative scrutinised in Chapter 3.

SOURCES

Extract 2.4: from Janet Holmes (2000), 'Doing collegiality and keeping control at work: small talk in government departments', in Justine Coupland (ed.), *Small Talk*, Essex: Pearson Education Ltd, pp. 32–61.

Extract 2.5: from Deborah Cameron (2000), *Good to Talk? Living and Working in a Communication Culture*, London: Sage, pp. 99–106.

CHAPTER 3 LANGUAGE AND GENDER

Extract 3.1: from Amy Sheldon (1996), 'You can be the baby brother, but you aren't born yet: preschool girls' negotiation for power and access in pretend play', *Research on Language and Social Interaction*, 29: 1, 57–80.

Extract 3.2: from Deborah Cameron (1998), 'Is there any ketchup, Vera?': gender, power and pragmatics', *Discourse and Society*, 9: 4, 437–55.

Extract 3.3: from Elinor Ochs and Carolyn Taylor (1995), 'The "Father Knows Best" dynamic in dinnertime narratives', in Kira Hall and Mary Bucholtz (eds), *Gender Articulated: Language and the Socially Constructed Self*, New York: Routledge, pp. 100–17.

Extract 3.4: from Peter Adams, Alison Towns and Nicola Gavey (1995), 'Dominance and entitlement: the rhetoric men use to discuss their violence towards women', *Discourse and Society*, 6: 3, 387–406.

CHAPTER 4 LANGUAGE AND YOUTH

Extract 4.1: Geneva Smitherman and S. Cunningham (1997), 'Moving beyond resistance: ebonics and African-American youth', *Journal of Black Psychology*, 23: 3, 227–32

Extract 4.2: from Signithia Fordham (1998), ' "Speaking standard English from nine to three: language as guerrilla warfare at Capital High', in Susan Hoyle and Carolyn Temple Adger (eds), *KidsTalk: Strategic Language Use in Later Childhood*, Oxford: Oxford University Press, pp. 205–16.

Extract 4.3: from Les Back (1996), 'Parodying racism and subverting racial meanings', *New Ethnicities and Urban Culture: Racisms and Multiculture in Young Lives*, London: UCL Press.

Extract 4.4: from Les Back (1996), ' "White identities" and dominant definitions', *New Ethnicities and Urban Culture: Racisms and Multiculture in Young Lives*, London: UCL Press.

Extract 4.5: from Mary Bucholtz (2001), 'The whiteness of nerds: superstandard English and racial markedness', *Journal of Linguistic Anthropology*, 11: 1, 84–100.

CHAPTER 5 MULTILINGUALISM, ETHNICITY AND IDENTITY

Extract 5.1: from Keith Morrison and Icy Lui (2000), 'Ideology, linguistic capital and the medium of instruction in Hong Kong', *Journal of Multilingual and Multicultural Development*, 21: 6, 471–86.

Extract 5.2: from R. Schmidt Sr (2000), *Language Policy and Identity Politics in the United States*, Philadelphia: Temple University Press.

Extract 5.3: from Nancy Hornberger (1998), 'Language policy, language education, language rights: indigenous, immigrant, and international perspectives', *Language in Society*, 27: 439–58.
Extract 5.4: from Joan Pujolar (2000), *Gender, Heteroglossia and Power: A Sociolinguistic Study of Youth Culture*, Berlin: Mouton de Gruyter

INTRODUCTION

This book is about language and power. But what is power? How should we go about studying it in relation to language? And for that matter, why? These are not easy questions to answer. Our aim in writing this book is to get you thinking about them, and to get you thinking about the way power 'works' in the linguistic practices that people engage in. Power in language is certainly not just about what we might initially think of as 'powerful language' (drowning out the voices of others by shouting a lot, for instance). Consider the claim that:

> power is more than an authoritative voice in decision making; its strongest form may well be the ability to define social reality, to impose visions of the world. Such visions are inscribed in language and enacted in interaction. (Gal 1991: 197)

Taking this further, add the view that:

> Language is the place where actual and possible forms of social organization and their likely social and political consequences are defined and contested. Yet it is also the place where our sense of ourselves, our subjectivity, is constructed. (Weedon 1997: 21)

From this perspective, language is where forms of social organisation are produced, and disputed, and at the same time where people's cultural identities come into existence. In effect, language constitutes realities and identities.

Our view in this book is that 'power' is constituted in many different locations, in many different ways. Language is crucial in articulating, maintaining and subverting existing relations of power in society, both on global, national and institutional levels and on the local level of interpersonal communication. Power, then, has multiple locations and valences. This perspective on power views it as productive, as deployed in **discourse** (all terms in boldface can be found in the glossary). It is basically a critical discourse analysis view, an approach to the study of language and power which is strongly influenced by the ideas of Michel Foucault (see, for example, Fairclough 1992). According to Foucault, positions of institutional power are bestowed on some to the exclusion of others. Power is deployed by those who are in a position to define and categorise, to include and exclude.

Many cultural analysts, including linguists, draw on Foucault's conceptualisation of power. Consider, for example, the following:

> Power, in Foucault's view … is a force and an effect which exists and circulates in a web of social interaction:
>
>> Power is employed and exercised through a net-like organisation. And not only do individuals circulate between its threads; they are always in the position of simultaneously undergoing and exercising this power. They are not only its inert or consenting target; they are always also the elements of its articulation. In other words, individuals are the vehicles of power, not its point of application. (Foucault 1980: 98)
>
> The point that power is not monolithic – that is, it does not emanate from one fundamental source such as the barrel of a gun or the ownership of the means of production – is important to Foucault with his metaphor of the 'net-like organisation', but it has also been echoed by many other contemporary theorists (large numbers of feminists, for example). More and more, such theorists are insisting that there are many simultaneous dimensions of power – for instance class, 'race', 'ethnicity', gender, generation, sexuality, subculture – and that theories which privilege one dimension (most commonly, class) as the 'ultimate' source of power are inadequate to capture the complexities of social relations. (Cameron et al. 1992: 19)

Central issues in Foucault's theorisation of power are that it is not monolithic and it is not one-way. Resistance, contestation and struggle are accompaniments of power.

There are two other particularly useful theorisations of language and power that are highly relevant to what we cover in this book. These relate to the concepts of **hegemony** and **symbolic capital**. Hegemony implies a hidden or covert operation of power. It refers to control through consent; or, more accurately, to the attempt by dominant groups in society to win the consent of subordinate groups and to achieve a 'compromise equilibrium' in ruling over them (Gramsci 1971). This winning of consent is achieved when arrangements that suit a dominant group's own interests have come to be perceived as simply 'common sense', such as, for example, whose language we should speak and write. The **dominant dialects** of British and American English (so-called

Standard British and Standard American English) are virtually the only varieties of English to be seen in print or, indeed, to be heard in broadcasting. The hegemonic status of these two national 'standard' varieties is overwhelming. Their use is seen as simply 'right and proper'; the idea of promulgating other varieties is largely perceived as scandalous. This is not to deny contestation and struggle as other varieties vie for some sort of acceptance, as will be seen in Chapter 4 on 'Language and Youth' in this volume. Consider, for example, Robin Tolmach Lakoff on the controversy surrounding the Oakland Schools Board (OSB)'s decision on the teaching of **ebonics** in the United States:

> As I bent over to pick up my San Francisco Chronicle the next morning my eye was caught by a typically florid Chron top-of-page-one headline:
>
> OAKLAND SCHOOLS OK BLACK ENGLISH
> Ebonics to be regarded as different, not wrong
>
> Worthy of note is the presupposition in the subhead: the normal way Ebonics is 'regarded' is as 'wrong': what's newsworthy is the OSB's proclamation that it is only 'different'. (From? We don't even need to mention the standard explicitly.) (Lakoff 2001: 228)

The concept of symbolic capital presents another way of accounting for the dominance of standard American English. Using the analogy of economic capital, Pierre Bourdieu (1991) argues that different ways of speaking carry different 'capital' in the 'symbolic marketplace'. Mainstream American English pronunciation is a symbolic asset in the US news media, whereas the local Brooklyn variety is most emphatically not. Similarly, in the British context, received pronunciation (RP) is the voice of authority. RP speakers are commonly perceived as being intelligent, having authority. Other accents do not carry the same capital, as a barrister with a strong Liverpool accent was made aware on being measured for a formal suit in his hometown. He reports being asked by the tailor: 'You work in the clubs, do you?' To spell this out, the tailor who was measuring the barrister for a suit assumed he was kitting himself out for a job as a nightclub bouncer. In other words, she assumed his occupation and social standing were considerably less prestigious than a barrister's, simply because of the way he was pronouncing standard British English (LINC 1991). Of course, in Britain, RP also connotes negative attributes; being 'snobby' and most definitely 'uncool'. An RP accent would not go down well in TV programming aimed at contemporary youngsters, whereas the Liverpudlian barrister might find himself in possession of an asset in that context, in Bourdieu's symbolic sense. Chapter 5, on 'Multilingualism, Identity and Ethnicity', deals in detail with issues around the symbolic capital of English, exploring, in particular, the status of English in Hong Kong and the 'English Only' Campaign in the USA.

LANGUAGE AND POWER IN THE MODERN WORLD: OUR APPROACH

This book is about both theory and practice. It is about theory in the sense that it describes systematic ways of understanding language. Its basic standpoint in this sense is that, in studying language in the modern world, we need to recognise that language use is simply not characterised by free, equal parties engaging in discourse on some sort of level playing field. In order to understand how language works and what it does, it is necessary to go beyond texts themselves and also to take into account aspects of the social conditions in which language is produced and interpreted. The book is practical in the sense that it is also about applying theory to the analysis and understanding of particular instances of spoken and written language, particularly through the activities which each chapter provides for you to work through. There are, of course, many overlapping themes across chapters; media issues are taken up in the chapter on youth, for instance, and gender arises in the chapters on the media and on multilingualism. These provide productive links across the five areas covered in the book.

Much of the book is about revealing and challenging aspects of the intense socialisation to which we are all subjected, not only through language but also about language. In this sense, its concerns, far from being obscure or removed from daily life, could not be more central to aspects of power which are vital to all of us. It comprises five main chapters, each with several readings and activities mediated by a substantial introduction. The readings in each of them have not been chosen to promote one approach over another, rather to illustrate a variety of approaches to the study of language and power.

Directions taken in the past few decades which share a focus on power are often grouped under the terms critical linguistics, critical sociolinguistics and critical discourse analysis or, more generally, simply critical language study. The word 'critical' is being used in a specific sense here, indicating a focus on power as it relates to issues of gender, 'ethnicity', class and so on and making its hidden workings visible. These orientations form the theoretical backbone of this book and, although they are quite diverse, they have certain features and starting points in common.

For instance, one basic assumption that all the above critical perspectives share is that language is part of society, and not in any way distinct and separate from it. The expressions 'language and society' and 'language in society' can be misleading (these are common titles for introductory courses and textbooks on sociolinguistics). Language is not a phenomenon independent or disconnected from society; rather it is itself a 'social institution, deeply implicated in culture, in society, in political relations at every level' (Cameron 1997a: 66).

Language plays a vital role in constituting what people perceive as reality

Another common perspective is that language plays a vital role in constituting people's realities. This insight has evident implications for the power and influence of media language. The media are particularly important in the modern world for a variety of reasons. For instance, for many people they have become increasingly accessible and often dominant in daily life, partly or wholly substituting more traditional sources of information such as the church, trade unions, and so on. They make powerful contributions to our under-standing of what is public and what is private in contemporary life and they tend to naturalise these distinctions so that they appear as 'common sense' (see Chapter 1, on 'Language and the Media').

That language is constitutive has important implications elsewhere – for instance, for issues of language and gender. It has been argued that socio-linguistics must go beyond describing patterns of use and how they correlate with social variables (such as gender) to accounting for how these correlations come about and are constantly negotiated and contested (Cameron 1995, 1997a). Chapter 3 ('Language and Gender') of this book discusses how this recognition has led to a rejection of simple contrasts between supposedly competitive 'male' and cooperative 'female' interactional styles in favour of a more nuanced analysis which recognises the crucial roles of societal and institutional power.

> *Power is exercised through language in ways*
> *which are not always obvious*

Much power in the modern world is unseen in the sense that it becomes 'naturalised'. It is exercised not through direct coercion but through the creation of 'common sense', by a process of hegemony. It isn't necessary to subscribe to a 'conspiracy theory', for instance, in order to accept that media reporting ideologically frames stories to favour and represent the views of dominant groups. Any text, any use of language, represents the world in particular ways, whether these serve the vested interests of a multinational corporation, the perspectives of an independent publication, or an individual journalist. An example is the way processes of globalisation are presented as 'natural' and 'inevitable' by, for example, the US network, CNN. Moreover, the North American and European-dominated media industries impose a particular view. As Fairclough observes:

> Despite their global pretensions, the version of the world which appears on the screen is an extremely parochial one – one indication of this is that 'global news' on for instance CNN consists largely of US news, including items which would seem to be of interest mainly within the USA (e.g. scandals affecting US politicians). The parochialism of these channels includes their language. What people see world-wide is predominantly 'North Atlantic' discourses of advertising, news, politics, sport, fashion, and so on. These channels contribute to a globalization of a 'North Atlantic' (and centrally US) way of life and way of language. (Fairclough 2001: 205)

Language moulds people's identities, but this
process can be and is resisted

In our daily lives we are constrained by 'subject positions' (e.g., Fairclough 2001) – our social roles are created for us through language. However, this does not mean that we are automatons or passive dupes. Imposed identities and statuses can be and constantly are being discursively negotiated, contested and resisted. This dynamic view is evident in every chapter. For example, Chapter 2 on 'Language and Organisations' describes how this process of contestation takes place in institutional contexts, such as that of welfare claimants in the USA. Both here, and in Chapter 4 on 'Language and Youth', 'resistance' is explored as an active process. It is articulated in many different ways and is every bit as complex as 'power'.

Resistance is not simply a matter of articulating oppositional discourses

We need to bear in mind that resistance does not always take the form of open challenge and opposition, but can be enacted more subtly through, for example, strategic practices of accommodation in talk. Chapter 4 discusses how this operates in an educational setting. In order to progress academically, African American Vernacular-speaking students opt to 'rent' the language of institutional power (Standard American English) in class but return to speaking their own variety outside this context. Their critical language awareness in merely 'leasing' SAE (as opposed to 'owning' it) enables them to distance themselves socially from mainstream American English and, at the same time, articulate their commitment to their own community language and culture. We also need to be aware of forms of counter-resistance. For many men, for example, recent transformations in the social relations between men and women pose a huge challenge. Chapter Three concentrates on patterns of gendered behaviour in modern societies, where the hegemonic status of traditional roles is no longer secure. As Cameron (1998) points out in one of the extracts provided as a reading, it is in such societies that claims about 'male–female miscommunication' are articulated. A miscommunication model of date rape, for instance, can be heard in courtrooms; it provides men accused of rape with a resource to challenge the accusation: an assertion that the 'signals ... between men and women are not being read correctly' (Ehrlich 2001: 121). Since rape trials in criminal courts are contestations of sexist practices, this resource is used as a form of counter-resistance to social changes effected by feminism. Another focus in Chapter Three is on the predicament of violently abusive men, whose partial recognition of their need to change leads to a rhetoric of denial and justification.

Power is the central dynamic of language change

Language changes, like other forms of social change, take place in the context of conflicting interests. As far as multilingualism is concerned, for example, the principal dynamic which determines the status of any given language is that of power. This view contrasts with early work in the sociology of language, which tended to see bilingual or multilingual communities as characterised by a neat, consensual and stable distribution of two or more languages according to norms of 'appropriacy'. However, more recent work shows that multilingualism and **diglossia** are much more fluid phenomena in relation to which groups and individuals act out their conflicting interests against the historical backdrop of the circumstances in which they find themselves. Susan Gal, for instance, wrote of her study of a Hungarian-speaking minority in Austria:

> A few weeks of observation in Oberwart made it clear that no single rule would account for all choices between languages. Statements to the effect that one language is used at home and another in school-work-street, would be too simplistic. (1979: 99)

A new orientation developed which had its origins partly in what is sometimes described as the 'sociolinguistics of the periphery', a reference to contexts in which the researchers themselves were committed to resisting the domination of a 'minority' language by a more powerful one. Some of the most prominent of these researchers in the 1970s were Catalan sociolinguists in Franco's Spain committed to saving the Catalan language from disappearance (see, for example, Martin-Jones 1989). Chapter 5 on 'Multilingualism, Ethnicity and Identity' illustrates the issues involved through discussion of aspects of language planning and policy and attitudes towards language in a number of contexts, including Hong Kong, the USA and, indeed, the case of Catalan in Spain.

ACTIVITY

At the time of writing, a controversy is building in the UK concerning the possible introduction of 'identity cards' and this is attracting some international attention, not least because of the UK government's attitude to linguistic aspects of the controversy.

A member of a civil rights group, writing in *The Guardian* of 1 July 2002 said:

> There can be little doubt that the government is seduced by the idea of 'entitlement' cards as spin doctors now wish to call them. So worried are they about the possible scale of parliamentary opposition, adverse media coverage and public backlash, that the term 'ID card' has been removed from the New Labour lexicon.

The main Spanish daily, El País, was critical and blunt about such language engineering by New Labour (2 July 2002):

> Following this government's golden rule of playing with words in order to confuse the public, they use the term 'entitlement card' rather than 'national identity card'. (author's translation)

Look at a variety of newspaper and magazine articles and/or television news items and programmes over the period of a week and see how many of them relate to issues of language and power in one way or another.

1

LANGUAGE AND THE MEDIA

This chapter considers the extent to which verbal interaction through the mass media differs from other kinds, such as the face-to-face interaction of individuals, and its consequences in terms of power relations. It examines the power of the media in its assertions of shared values and opinions and works through how such constructions of 'common sense' can be critically investigated, drawing for examples on work on racist discourse in the press. It then takes up issues specific to the mediated talk of television and radio, attending to the structuring of 'live' talk and to mediatised political language. This involves a shift of attention from articulations of a discourse to a variety of media genres.

WHAT'S DISTINCT ABOUT MEDIA LANGUAGE?

In a communicative event, there is always an addresser and an addressee. In face-to-face interaction, both are physically present. This is not the case in the mass media, however, where there are major spatial, and often temporal, disjunctions:

> Alongside other technological systems and institutional mechanisms in the modern world, they have served to 'lift' social relations out of face-to-face contexts and 'stretch' them across potentially vast distances, dislocating space from place. For instance, it has become possible for us to witness far-away events 'live' as they unfold in time, or to engage in dialogue with a distant interlocutor. (Moores 1999: 222)

A distinguishing characteristic of media language is the distance between addresser and addressee, in space and, frequently, also in time. This means that there is a sharp division between addressers and addressees. The addressees of a mass media text such as a television programme or a newspaper article (that is, its audience) are in a very different relationship with their addressers from, say, the audience in a theatre. An obvious but fundamental observation to make about such media texts is that the time and place of their production is different from the time and place of their consumption (Fairclough 1995: 36). A theatre performance is 'here and now'; performers and audience are all physically present, in the same place at the same time. Everyone present is in a position to affect the communicative event; someone in the audience could start heckling, for instance. Heckling has no effect whatever on a television broadcast or a newspaper. *interrupt by questions etc.*

A second point about mass media text and distance relates to globalisation. The vast majority of mass media production takes place in the developed world. The media are dominated by North American and European conglomerates. First-world texts are consumed by third-world audiences, but rarely the other way around. A third point about distance is that mass media texts are involved in highly complex chains of communicative events (ibid.: 37). Their production is disjointed. A documentary might be filmed in six countries over eighteen months, for instance. They are put together from a range of sources, which might include interviews, speeches and so on. The actual broadcast of the documentary is just the tip of the iceberg.

The matter of distance leads on to issues of access and power. Mass media communication is one-sided. Because of the spatial and temporal disjunctions between addressers and addressees, participation in the communication does not take place on an equal basis. In one sense, it takes place on the audience's terms and the audience is in control; a television viewer may not be listening, may choose to switch channels, etc. But in terms of output, the media are under professional and institutional control. Producers of media texts are professional practitioners, whereas audiences are not. The best access to the media is available for those who already have other forms of power: economic, political or cultural (ibid.: 40). There is no technical reason why this should be the case.

Unlike in most face-to-face communication, the addresser is a composite being, not a single individual. Mass media texts have multiple producers. If you traced the path of a single news story from its first draft to broadcast or publication, the most striking characteristic would probably be the number of people involved in its production. In face-to-face interaction, for the most part, language is produced by single individuals. The language of mass communication tends to be very different. Television newsreaders are not the source of the news. What they read has probably been produced by dozens of people: journalists, editors, sound technicians, camera operators. News is produced on an assembly line (Bell 1991).

In examining language production of this kind, it is useful to be able to specify the different roles involved. Adapting sociological work on speaker roles

(Goffman 1981), Allan Bell (1991) distinguishes four language-producing/addresser roles among news workers and newsmakers. The *Principal* is the originator of what is being reported, the one whose views are being expressed (for example, a government minister). The *Author* is the person who generates the form in which the content is encoded. In the production of news, this role could be taken up by many people. A government minister's speech writer is an author, in this sense; so is a journalist, the person who compiles the news copy, but also the various people whose job it is to tidy up the journalist's copy. The *Editor* coordinates the process of copy production. Finally, the *Animator* is the physical speaker, the mouthpiece. This role too is likely to be taken up by many people. A government spokesperson is one kind of animator; a newsreader is another. They are not the originators of the language they speak; they merely animate it. Others animators are technicians of various kinds. However, it must be noted that blurring of these different voices is very common, and this is probably a tendency that is increasing (see Walsh 2001 for detailed discussion in terms of **dialogism**).

Mass communication, then, has particular properties distinguishing it from other kinds of communication. These are partly attributable to the technologies employed, but not entirely. With contemporary recording and storage technologies, permanency and reusability have become inherent properties of many media genres. Media texts may be produced, distributed and consumed as commodities. Everyday language is transient, but media language is forever. Another property relates to the division of public and private. Gunther Kress argues that the media define these domains: 'the media do not so much perform the function of regulating access to either domain, as to ensure the constant reproduction of both domains' (1986: 397). The media constantly assert the existence of two domains and assign events and activities to each. So, for example, domestic violence is private whereas football hooliganism is public. These are clearly highly gendered activities. Domestic violence is overwhelmingly a crime against women (see Chapter 3), but it is perceived as a private matter, not a public one. As Kress makes clear, this is also a power issue:

> To assign an event to the sphere of the private is at once to declare it devoid of power, and to assign responsibility to individuals . . . To classify an event as belonging to the public domain is to assert that it is beyond individual responsibility and within the domain of social control. (ibid.: 400)

The division is sustained in newspaper genres. For instance, the front page is public; the letters pages (especially the 'agony columns') are private.

However, even while the boundary between the domains of public and private are constantly asserted, they are blurred and intermingled. Public events are made accessible for private consumption. Mass media texts may be produced from public domain source materials (such as political speeches, Royal funerals, demonstrations), then consumed in the private domain (in people's homes). They *mediate* between public and private. Conversely, private events may acquire public status as news. For instance, the anguish of bereaved parents may be presented as a newsworthy event, with cameras dwelling on their private behaviour (crying, flooding out with grief) for the public's consumption. Fairclough argues further that, through the course of the twentieth century, the mass media have attempted to bridge the gulf between the domains of public and private and in the process have restructured the boundaries between them. This restructuring is visible in the development of a distinct style of communication, a 'public colloquial' language (Leech 1966; Fairclough 1995). Broadcasters, in particular, have to be aware of the communicative dynamics of radio and television broadcasting. As Paddy Scannell has noted, they have had to learn how to address their audiences. While the context of broadcasting production is the public domain, most people listen or watch in the private domain, where they do not necessarily want to be lectured, patronised or otherwise 'got at':

> The voices of radio and television . . . are heard in the context of household activities and other household voices . . . It is this that powerfully drives the communicative style and manner of broadcasting to approximate to the norms not of public forms of talk but to those of ordinary, informal conversation. (1991: 3)

There are striking differences between the styling of contemporary broadcasting and early recordings of British radio broadcasts. Perhaps the most striking change is in the range of accents used these days. In the early years of British broadcasting, received pronunciation was chosen as the appropriate voice of authority to address the nation. We now frequently hear other accents, though RP is still used by newsreaders for the most 'serious' genre: the national news. Another change is towards 'chattiness', the simulation of a private kind of talk in broadcast media genres. In contrast with the stiff formality of early BBC broadcasting, a huge amount of effort goes into giving an impression of informality and spontaneity in much contemporary programming. People apparently having an 'ordinary' conversation on a television 'chat show' are in fact, of course, performing in front of the cameras and therefore about as much in the public domain as can be. We return later on to the creation of 'ordinariness' in broadcast talk.

When we talk to one another face to face, we take into account who we are speaking to and fashion our talk accordingly. However, the distance built into mass communication means that addressers do not know who their addressees actually are. Addressing a mass audience imposes on mass media producers the need to construct an imaginary addressee. Any text can be said to have an implied reader, an imaginary addressee with particular values, preoccupations and commonsense understandings. In having to construct an imaginary person to speak to, media producers are placed in a powerful position. They are in a position to attribute values and attitudes to their addressees, presenting them in a taken-for-granted way. For example, these are headlines from two advertisements:

> Are you doing enough for your underarms?
> You too can stop biting your nails!

The first is from an advertisement for hair-removing cream that appeared in a magazine for young teenage girls. Since 'enough' entails 'some', the headline expects you to be doing something 'for your underarms'. In fact, it is likely that it introduced the target audience to the notion of removing underarm hair, before they had even grown any. The second was targeted at a similar audience and presupposes, rather obviously, that its addressee is a habitual nail biter. Taken-for-granted elements can often be less easy to perceive. An actual reader who has a great deal in common with the imaginary addressee inscribed in a text is likely to take up the positions it offers unconsciously and uncritically. **Presuppositions**, and assumptions more generally, may tend to go unnoticed, unless they are totally misdirected. Conversely, of course, distance enables a reader to be more aware of the positioning and perhaps more critical of it. However, even if misdirected, such background assumptions still create or reinforce ideas. I return to media and the construction of common sense in the next section.

At the same time as constructing an imaginary addressee, a media addresser must create a persona for themselves. In the extract selected for Reading 1.1 in this section, the addresser-persona examined is a friendly older sister in a magazine for young teenage girls. The extract is taken from 'A synthetic sisterhood: false friends in a teenage magazine' (Talbot 1995). It takes up the notion of **synthetic personalisation** (Fairclough 2001: 52) to examine the way a feature on lipstick sets up a friendly relationship between magazine producers and readers. It details the linguistic means by which this close relationship is simulated: the construction of a 'synthetic sisterhood' on the printed page. The text is modern, but it is worth noting that the 'roots of synthetic personalization as a gendered capitalist strategy lie in the history of women's magazines ... developed in the context of patriarchal and capitalist social relations' (Talbot 1995: 148–9). The aim of achieving an active and 'intimate' relationship is by no means new; indeed it was explicit editorial policy in a new publication in 1910 (Talbot 1995, White 1970).

Media producers are also placed in a powerful position in that they can create imaginary groups for their audiences. These are communities based on patterns of consumption: Pepsi drinkers, *Time* magazine readers. To belong to the consumer group of Pepsi drinkers, all we have to do is buy and consume the commodity. Being a certain kind of consumer does not in itself form relationships, although at times it may have a perceivable spatial dimension (for example, at a football ground). In the article in the extract, the consumption community offered to readers is based on cosmetics. The extract frames its **dialogic** approach to analysis as scrutiny of the 'text population' that the reader associates with in reading the advertorial text. Part of that 'population' is the reader herself.

CONSTRUCTIONS OF COMMON SENSE: THE CASE OF RACISM

We are now going on to some fairly detailed examples of how media discourse constructs commonsense attitudes and opinions. What we take to be matters of common sense are largely ideological. Since 'ideological common sense' contributes to maintaining the status quo, we can view it as 'common sense in the service of sustaining unequal relations of power' (Fairclough 2001: 70). A particular perception of the world comes to be accepted as simply 'the way things are'; that is, it becomes naturalised. Racist discourse is to a large extent naturalised, though at the time of writing (soon after the events of 11 September 2001) the press are rather careful. For examples of writing about race issues we shall mainly be drawing on some studies of far less cautious reporting in the 1980s in Britain and Holland (van Dijk 1991; van Dijk et al. 1997) and in Australia in the mid-90s (Teo 2000). The former are based on material collected during a period of widespread disturbances (the most well known probably being in Brixton, London and in Toxteth, Liverpool). The latter, reproduced in part in Reading 1.2, is based on coverage in Sydney newspapers of violent activities among Vietnamese drug dealers in the city, centring on a 'gangland-style' execution. It is taken from a journal article entitled 'Racism in the news: a Critical Discourse Analysis of news reporting in two Australian newspapers' (Teo 2000). It begins with a short account of its theoretical background, providing a useful reflection on the principles of critical discourse analysis. We shall be focusing on aspects of style and rhetoric: journalists' choices of words, phrases and sentence structure when writing about minorities, and on verbal ploys used to persuade readers to their own view.

'Ethnic' topics

As Teun van Dijk remarks, 'perhaps the most obvious common-sense property of discourse is its overall meaning or topics' (van Dijk et al. 1997: 168). A good place to begin, then, is choice of topic: what do journalists write about when they write about 'them'? Van Dijk's studies show that there is a restricted range of 'ethnic' topics. The major 'ethnic' topic is crime. Typical 'ethnic crimes' involve drugs, mugging and rioting. Here is a selection of news headlines from his corpus of data:

> POLICE BLAME RIOT ON DRUG DEALERS (*Guardian*, 16 Sept 1985)
> SECOND BLACK ON MURDER CHARGE (*Daily Telegraph*, 14 Dec 1985)
> BLACK BRIXTON LOOTERS JAILED (*Daily Telegraph*, 14 Dec 1985)
> BRITAIN INVADED BY AN ARMY OF ILLEGALS (*Sun*, Feb 1986)
> (ibid.: 168–9)

'Ethnic topics' identified by van Dijk include crime, cultural differences and deviance, immigration and discrimination. 'Ethnic topics' have generally negative implications; he observes, for example, that 'immigration is never topicalized as neutral, or as a contribution to the economy' (ibid.: 168), but as a major problem, as fraud, invasion, etc. 'They' are a problem, even a threat. In contrast, 'our' crimes against 'them' tend to be mitigated or associated with deviant individuals or fringe groups (the National Front, skinheads). Van Dijk concludes:

> Systematic research of more than 4000 headlines in the British and Dutch press has shown that ethnic events and minorities are seldom defined in a way that is positive for them or negative for us, and conversely in a way that tends to attribute blame to us while denying or mitigating theirs. It is thus how the press, through its topical headlines, defines the 'ethnic situation', in which 'they' are a problem, if not a threat. (ibid.: 169)

This sort of content analysis is revealing, but rather superficial. We can go in more closely by focusing on lexical and syntactic choices and on rhetorical devices. Fairclough (1992a, 2001) both contain useful checklists for further detailed analysis.

Lexical and syntactical choices

First of all, it is worth considering the use of the term 'ethnic' itself. Only minority groups are so labelled. Majority groups do not talk about themselves as 'ethnic'. The way this term is used in Britain illustrates the point. In Britain, we would not refer to the Women's Institute as an 'ethnic group', to fish and chips as 'ethnic food', or to a bowler hat as 'traditional ethnic headgear'. The expression 'ethnic riot' would never be used in the press to describe civil disturbance caused by white middle-class people in the home counties, though the white middle-class of the home counties are just as much an ethnic group as the black community in Brixton, or any other. The white middle-class unself-consciously occupies the neutral, 'non-ethnic' centre.

In the right-wing press, van Dijk found that references to ethnicity are often irrelevant. They usually occur in a negative context, as in the identification of a crime suspect in British papers as black or Irish (the issue of 'ethnic' news and negativity is also raised in Chapter 4). However, a black person in a non-controversial, positive role is likely to be identified as English, as the writer of this letter to the editor points out:

> Can you explain why black Englishmen and women who win Olympic medals or excel at games are described as 'English' while those who riot and throw petrol bombs are almost invariably 'West Indian'? (*Telegraph*, 13 September 1985; quoted in van Dijk 1991: 212)

Use of **dysphemism** is a common characteristic of racist discourse. In van Dijk's corpus, the right-wing press routinely referred to the people participating in urban disturbances with terms like 'thugs', 'hooligans', 'mobs', 'packs', 'rioters'. Frequently used pre-modifiers were 'crazed', 'raging', 'monstrous', 'rampaging'. Such negative terms are hardly surprising, as van Dijk notes, for people engaged in a criminal activity such as murder; 'such terms are, however, also used for perfectly legitimate actions, such as demonstrating or protesting' (ibid.: 214). He discovered a distinctive style of invective that the right-wing press used to vilify leftist and anti-racist demonstrators. Dysphemistic expressions included:

> The hysterical 'anti-racist' brigade . . . the Left-wing anti-racist mob (*Sun*, 23 Oct 1985)
> Bone-brained Left-fascism (*Telegraph*, 30 Nov 1985)
> Mob of left-wing crazies (*Mail*, 24 Sept 1985)
> Blinkered tyrants (*Sun*, 6 Sept 1985)
> These dismal fanatics, monstrous creatures (*Telegraph*, 26 Sept 1985)
>
> (ibid.: 214)

The metaphors behind these invectives characterise the demonstrators in terms of mental illness and irrationality, or ideological intolerance and political oppression, or as threatening beasts. More recently a journalist in Dover, England, railed against the presence of asylum seekers using a grotesquely dysphemistic metaphor of 'human sewage': 'We are left with the backdraft of a nation's human sewage and no cash to wash it down the drain' (*Dover Express*, 1 October 1998). Establishing the boundaries of 'us' and 'them' through labelling is not, however, a straightforward matter of selecting abusive terms. In September 2001, the Muslim Council of Great Britain complained to the BBC about its repeated identification of Osama bin Laden as an Islamic Fundamentalist, insisting that he should be referred to simply as a terrorist:

> The BBC is planting an association in the minds of many people, the notion that ordinary peace-loving Islamic Fundamentalists are no different to bin Laden. We fear that this can cause unrest the type of which we have seen in Britain recently. The BBC should call bin Laden a terrorist, which is what he is. The BBC is not even-handed. It never refers to the IRA as a Catholic extremist organisation or IRA members as Catholic extremists. (*The Times*, 19 September 2001)

Reading 1.2 provides other examples of lexical and syntactical choices involved in positive us-presentation and negative them-presentation, or the 'rhetoric of othering' (Riggins 1997). The notion of **generalisation** deals with sweeping, reductive stereotypes. **Over-lexicalisation**, in this context, is about obsessive preoccupation with labelling of minority groups as such. For a rich account of the discursive construction of 'the other', see Jasinski (2001).

As well as looking at choices in wording we can also examine choices in clause and sentence structure: the way meaning is realised syntactically. In the reporting of civil disturbances in Brixton, the actions of the police were often placed syntactically in a non-prominent position in the sentence, or by keeping the agency implicit. In this way, negative acts of 'us' or in-group members can be downplayed. For example, a press report in a Sunday paper – about the police shooting an innocent woman in her home the previous evening – began as follows:

> Rioting mobs of youths set Brixton ablaze last night in an outburst of fury at the police for accidentally shooting a black woman. (*Sunday Times*, 29 September 1985)

The report does not begin 'police shot woman'. The the matised element (that is, the first one) is 'Rioting mobs of youths'. The response of the demonstrators is foregrounded; the police activity that triggered it is not. Rather, it is placed in an embedded clause and located at the end of the sentence. The second report, on the Monday, began like this:

> On Saturday, police were petrol-bombed, shops looted and cars burned after the shooting of a West Indian woman. (*The Times*, 30 September 1985)

The police activity that triggered the disturbances is now presented in a **nominalisation**: 'the shooting of a West Indian woman'. It is now just an event and there is no way of knowing who did the shooting. Unless already familiar with the story from the Sunday papers, we would have to read well into the article to find out that the police were responsible. We could readily assume that the agent was the same as those responsible for the burning, looting and petrol-bombing. **Passive** constructions also occlude the agent, as in 'police were petrol-bombed, shops looted and cars burned'. Here unspecified agents did things to the police, to shops and to cars. However, in the context of an 'ethnic riot' this information is readily retrievable. (Contrast this with Teo's analysis of the Australian newspaper articles in Reading 1.2, where the power and agency of the police is being stressed in the news coverage.)

Rhetoric

British newspapers, especially the tabloids, are fond of rhetorical devices like alliteration to drive a point home. They are most frequent in headlines and lead paragraphs, which tend to be crammed with such **expressive** and **poetic** elements. They function as attention-getters. Here is one example from van Dijk's corpus:

> BOMBS, BULLETS, BLOOD IN BARRICADED BRITAIN (*Mail*, 27 December 1985) (1991: 217–18)

Van Dijk found that they were predominantly used in allegations of 'ethnic' aggression, or other accounts of negative situations for which ethnic minorities were held responsible.

Another frequently used rhetorical device involving repetition is **parallelism**. In the following, taken from two *Sun* editorials, the patternings of repeated clause structure and vocabulary serve the argumentation:

> Now it is not merely sticks and stones and petrol bombs. Now it is shotguns and knives. Now it is not merely cuts and bruises. Now it is murder. (*Sun*, 8 October 1985)

> We have tyranny in Britain. We have intimidation. We have a sinister attempt first to curb and then to destroy freedom of speech. We have racism too – and that is what is behind the plot. It is not white racism. It is black racism. (*Sun*, 24 October 1985)

The first is accompanied by alliteration and repeated negation; the second contains a contrast. Van Dijk observes that 'parallelism and alliteration seem to have similar functions of emphasizing negative properties of opponents. Whereas alliteration . . . focuses on negative news actors and events, parallelism underscores argumentative steps made in evaluating such events (ibid.: 219).

Another rhetorical device is **metaphor**. Social unrest is commonly represented as disease, as in the following report:

AS THE CANCER SPREADS

As the riots of rampaging youths spread from the south, even the most optimistic have fears for the future, afraid worse is yet to come. How far will the trouble spread? If it comes to Scotland, where will it strike?

Conceived in this way, social unrest undermines the health of society, from which the rioters are, by implication, excluded. As Fairclough observes, the 'ideological significance of disease metaphors is that they tend to take dominant interests to be the interests of society as a whole, and construe expressions of non-dominant interests (strikes, demonstrations, "riots") as undermining (the health of) society per se' (2001: 100). He suggests that an alternative metaphor might be that of argument or protest: 'Different metaphors imply different ways of dealing with things: one does not arrive at a negotiated settlement with cancer, though one might with an opponent in an argument. Cancer has to be eliminated, cut out' (ibid.). Similarly, metaphors of water and war have functioned to dehumanise Kurdish refugees in Austrian newspapers (El Refaie 2001). The metaphors behind the invectives looked at earlier (characterising demonstrators in terms of mental illness, irrationality and so on) clearly have a rhetorical function.

Another way of persuading your addressee to your own point of view is to present it as taken-for-granted, as shared background knowledge. In 2000, some Afghan asylum seekers arrived in Britain on a hijacked aeroplane; as an emergency measure they were accommodated in a hotel in London. A reporter, claiming that he had been staying at the same hotel before the event, began his news coverage of it like this:

The needs of paying guests were suddenly deemed as insignificant as those of the British taxpayer yesterday as a flood of freeloaders began piling off the plane. (*Sun*, 11 February 2000)

There are three presuppositions in this opening sentence: that *paying guests have needs* (cued by definite description), that *the British taxpayer has needs* (cued by another definite description) and that *these needs are deemed insignificant* (cued by a comparative construction). This lead paragraph also contains a flood metaphor.

Reading 1.2 attends to more rhetorical devices, including in particular patterns of quotation, which are crucial in that they add 'facticity' to news reports. It is generally the voices of the powerful that appear in quotations. Voices, and hence perspectives, of the powerless are unlikely to be found. On rare occasions they are woven into news. In such cases, as Teo demonstrates in Reading 1.2, they tend to be turned against them

In conclusion to this section on racism, a news story about immigrants is never just that. At the same time, it may also be part of the complex social practice of communicating ethnic stereotypes. This may in turn contribute to reproducing the racist social system.

BROADCAST TALK

In this section our attention shifts from articulations of a discourse to a variety of media genres. We now take up issues specific to the mediated talk of television and radio, attending first to disputes on talk radio and the impact of its technologically mediated nature and then to aspects of mediatised political language.

Radio phone-ins

The radio phone-in provides a public space for private citizens to air their views on social issues. In the case of 'open-line' programming, callers are invited to raise a topic and are given the conversational floor. However, as Ian Hutchby found in his research on the genre, this does not appear to put the caller in control:

> Although it may seem that the caller, in setting the agenda for the call, is in a position of control over what might count as an acceptable or relevant contribution to their topic, in fact it is the host who tends to end up in that position. (1996: 41)

Hutchby's study is a conversation analysis account of how this comes about. He suggests that phone-in argument sequences have a built-in generic feature that means it makes a big difference whether you 'go first' or 'go second'. Callers, in setting the agenda, always 'go first'. This is an example of a phone-in opening sequence from Hutchby's data:

```
 1  Host:    It's Ka:y next from: Islington:, good morning.
 2  Caller:  Yes guh morning. Um:: (.) I: want to talk about
 3           thee- thee report on L.B.C. this morning about
 4           Diana's visi:t to::, America:? h [.hh
 5  Host:                                     [The Princess
 6           of Wa:les.
 7           (.)
 8  Caller:  Princess of Wa:les, yah. .hh E::r the- her stay
 9           in a thou:sand pou:nds a night hotel plus V.A.T::,
10           an' on her schedule she's visiting a home-p-
11           place for the homeless. .hh A:nd there's going
12           to be a ba::::ll, .hh where they're uh- the
13           Americans are clamouring for tickets at a thousand
14           pounds a ni- er the- a thousand pounds each,=
15  Host:    = [Mm hm,]
16  Caller:    [I:     th]ink it's obsce:ne.
17  Host:    .pt Which:, part is obsce:ne.
```

(ibid.: 44)

The host announces the caller; a greeting exchange follows. Then the caller immediately introduces the topic 'Diana's visit to America'. It is a structured sequence that can be represented as follows:

Host: Introduction of caller (1)
          Greeting (1)
Caller: Greeting (2)
Caller: Topic introduction (2–4)
Host: Check (5–6)
Caller: Confirmation (8)
          Position statement: description (8–14)
Host: Acknowledgement (15)
Caller: Position statement: assessment (16)
Host: Challenge (17)

The interaction is asymmetrical at the outset. It puts the host in the favoured second position:

> This means that the host can find it relatively easy to go on the offensive in disputes, whereas the caller finds him or herself in a defensive position with regard to the agenda they began by introducing ... going second actually means having the *first* opportunity for opposition. (Hutchby 1996: 47–8)

The speaker in first position has to put together a defence for their argument. The speaker in second position is able to pick and choose; whether to set out their own stance, and if so at what point, or whether to just oppose the other using, for example, 'validity challenges' ('So?' 'What's that got to do with it?' etc.) (ibid.: 50).

Hosts can also make challenges by using what Hutchby calls 'the "you say (X)" device' (ibid.: 66). Just like tactics used to cast doubt on witnesses' testimonies in court, hosts often use this device to undermine a caller's argument, finding fault with small details as a way of casting doubt on the caller's overall stance. In the following example, the caller's presentation of 'a lot', 'most' or 'the majority' as 'ninety per cent' gives the host an opportunity to mount a challenge:

```
1   Caller:   Ni::nety per cent of people, (.) disagreed with the
2             new propo:sals for thee N.H.S: in the White Paper.
3             (0.8)
4   Host:     You're- you're quite sure about that
5             You say ni:nety per cent of the people disapprove
6             uh- .h as if you have carried out your own market
7             rese:arch on this.
```

(ibid.)

As Hutchby remarks, the host uses 'his citation of the caller's claim to effectively turn it against itself by way of the commonsense inference that ordinary citizens do not do market research in order to test public opinion: the "you say (X)" device thus enables the host to pick on the caller's chosen way of putting her claim' (ibid.). Interruptions are other notable features in phone-in disputes. Hutchby examines their use as a part of disagreement moves, hence in a confrontational way (rather than cooperatively to support an interlocutor's point). Reading 1.3 elaborates on two further aspects of phone-in talk: formulations and closings. Reading 1.4 examines the 'power of the last word' in some confrontational closings. According to Hutchby, whatever the private outcome of phone-in disputes, the public outcome is that the last word is always the broadcast word. (For coverage of three-party interaction – between host, caller and a guest – see Thornborrow 2002.)

Not all radio phone-in talk is confrontational, however. In the radio genre that Crisell (1994: 194) calls 'the confessional phone-in', callers go on air to disclose personal problems, rather than to engage in debate. There are sometimes quite remarkable occurrences of intimacy on air, breaching the public-private divide. In such cases, social closeness is achieved, to some extent, despite the institutional power imbalance built into radio talk. This imbalance is very much apparent from the confrontation talk studied by Hutchby, but in confessional talk the host may work to minimise it. On a British radio programme called *Live and Direct*, the presenter, Anna Raeburn, elicits troubles-talk from callers:

> Raeburn has to present herself to dispersed audiences as being dependable and 'trustworthy', in order for people then to call up and disclose their

problems in the first place. The relationship with callers is ... intended to be 'reciprocal' – 'you give me your trust (.) I give you mine' (Atkinson and Moores in press).

Using the concepts of **face, negative politeness** and **positive politeness**, Atkinson and Moores examine Raeburn's presentation of self as 'ordinary' and 'sincere' and how she deals with the tension between 'ordinariness', 'sincerity' and broadcasting constraints.

Mediatised political language

Political discourses are articulated in a wide range of media genres. As Fairclough observes, the traditional genres of politics – parliamentary debates, party conferences and international conferences – are now also media genres:

> they are represented within the formats and genres of the media – news, documentary, and so forth – so that their representation is always a selective recontextualization ... according to the requirements of these formats and genres. At the same time, genres for political discourse that the media themselves generate are increasingly important for politicians – most notably the political interview, but also, for instance, phone-in programmes. (1995: 188)

He goes on to consider the further blurring of boundaries brought about by the appearance of politicians as guests on talk shows and even, on occasion, as programme hosts themselves.

One particular media genre in which political discourses are articulated is the party political broadcast. This is actually a genre hybrid, since such broadcasts may be a mixture of political speech, current affairs programming, advertising, soap opera, documentary. In a detailed study of a single Conservative Party political broadcast, the authors argue that the genre hybrid's salient genre is advertising:

> They rest upon a more or less direct injunction to vote for the party which figures in the broadcast. It is this feature which marks their resemblance most clearly to the televisual commercial with its injunction to buy. Indeed, party election broadcasts are often referred to dismissively as political advertising. This label usually implies criticism on the grounds, first, that they are not as good as 'real' commercials ... and, second, political parties should in any case not be presented to the public like commodities for consumption. (Allan, Atkinson and Montgomery 1995: 372)

Politicians and their speechwriters resort to many of the same rhetorical devices that we looked at in examining racist discourse. Particular points of interest in political rhetoric in the media relate to the 'sound bite': a short extract taken from a recorded interview or speech. Like advertising slogans, they are written for their impact; they are selected by broadcasting journalists for the same reason. Repetition and contrast are frequently used together as a rhetorical device. British Prime Minister Tony Blair vowed to be 'tough on crime, tough on the causes of crime' in his first election campaign. More recently, in his statement after the start of military strikes on Afghanistan (7 October 2001) he stated that 'The Taleban were given the choice of siding with justice, or siding with terror. They chose terror.' In his first election campaign, he also made good use of another device often to be heard in sound bites: the three-part list, as in the Labour Party slogan, 'Education, education, education'. Several rather more elaborated three-part lists could be heard in Blair's military strike statement; this is one of them:

> The world understands that whilst of course there are dangers in acting as we are, the dangers of inaction are far, far greater – the threat of further such outrages, the threats to our economies, the threat to the stability of the world.

Sound bites sometimes combine listing with use of pronouns or possessive articles to indicate group membership or otherwise (that is, 'us' and 'them'), as in election promises about 'our schools, our forces, our police'. Pronoun usage in politics can sometimes be a source of amusement. Margaret Thatcher's celebrated (and thoroughly mystifying) pronouncement that 'we are a grand-mother' has had her audience speculating ever since about exactly which group she thinks she belongs to. It is often suggested that she is using the royal 'we', giving rise to speculation among some commentators that she was under the impression that she had acquired the states of royalty.

Like Anna Raeburn, politicians have to present a persona. Some observations by Andrew Tolsen (1991) about the construction of 'television personalities' are interesting in this regard. He points to the shift in genre from interview to chat in this extract from a (rather old, but nevertheless worth looking at) current affairs interview:

Robin Day:	Mrs Thatcher do you intend to lead the Conservative Party into the next election in say '87?
Mrs Thatcher:	I hope so.
Day:	Because if you do that and let's say that the next in the autumn of 1987 do you realise then that you would have been, held the office of Prime Minister for a longer, for the longest continuous period this century and possibly long before that?
Thatcher:	Yes.
Day:	Eight-and-a-half years, and you'll be six-
Thatcher:	Not very long.
Day:	Eight-and-a-half years.
Thatcher:	Yes it's not very long if you look back to other times.
Day:	And you'll be sixty-two. You still think you want to go ahead at the next election?

| Thatcher: | Yes. I shall be a very fit sixty-two. You might be a little bit nearer that than I am, but you feel all right? |
| Day: | (chuckles) Forgive me if I don't answer that question Prime Minister, towards the end of this interesting interview. (*Panorama*, April 1984) |

There is a topic shift from public to personal here, which brings about a shift from interview to chat. This shift has transgressive potential, in which 'personalities' are born. As Tolsen remarks:

> Chat does not simply reproduce norms and conventions, rather it flirts with them, for instance, it opens up the possibility of the interviewee putting questions to the interviewer. Certainly, in the context of a *Panorama* interview, Robin Day must appear to 'manage' this behaviour; but at the same time (as this example shows) it is not simply disavowed. For in this momentary transgression of convention, both Mrs Thatcher, and in his response Day himself, are constructed as 'television personalities'. (Tolsen 1991: 180)

According to Tolsen, televised chat is central to the construction of **synthetic personality**.

Reading 1.5 is taken from a chapter in Fairclough's *New Labour, New Language?* that homes in on the rhetorical style of Tony Blair. Arguing that 'Blair's political identity is anchored in his personal identity' (Fairclough 2000: 98), Fairclough examines Blair's language use, gestures and expressions in a television interview and in several political speeches. The extract focuses on the conversational style of 'Blair the normal person' and how he incorporates into it a more authoritative style of a leader, requiring displays of assertiveness (through slow delivery, **modality** choices and so on). It goes on to explore his political persona as, in contrast with Thatcher, a non-confrontational politician and then examines various contrasts and similarities with Thatcher as a conviction politician.

ACTIVITIES

- Read Reading 1.1, then choose a magazine article and identify as many linguistic features in it as you can contributing to synthetic personalisation.
- Are newspapers still racist? Look through a newspaper for articles in which people are labelled in terms of their ethnicity. Are the details about ethnic identity relevant to the stories they occur in? Are there particular 'ethnic topics' (as claimed in van Dijk 1991)?

If you found coverage of 'ethnic topics', examine the way they are articulated. What lexical and grammatical choices have been made? What rhetorical devices are used? You may also find it useful to look for generalisation, over-lexicalisation and use of quotation (for examples of these, you will need Reading 1.2).

● Download the transcript of a political speech (for example, President George W. Bush's statement given after the start of the US and British military strikes on targets in Afghanistan on Sunday, 7 October 2001). Examine the rhetorical devices in it. Does it contain any particularly 'good' sound bites?

READINGS

Reading 1.1

Feminist criticism with a poststructuralist perspective, as outlined by Chris Weedon (1987), takes language as the site of the cultural production of gender identity: subjectivity is discursively constituted. An individual's identity is constructed at every moment through subject positions. These positions are taken up by the language user in the enactment of discourse practices and are constantly shifting. From this view of subjectivity as a process, it is evident that a person's sense of identity is an 'effect of discourse,' which is therefore changeable: 'A poststructuralist position on subjectivity and consciousness relativizes the individual's sense of herself by making it an effect of discourse which is open to continuous redefinition and which is constantly slipping' (Weedon 1987: 106).

This poststructuralist perspective on identity, combined with a dialogic, or intertextual, view of actual texts, is what Julia Kristeva (1986a, b) proposed in her work in the late 1960s and early 1970s. According to Kristeva, a text consists of a mesh of intersecting voices. These voices can be viewed as an indeterminate 'text population' (Talbot 1990, 1992, 1995). The metaphor is intended to capture the way any text is 'populated' with a heterogeneous array of voices through which a language user's identity is built up. A text is therefore not the product of a single author; instead, the author her/himself is multiple, fragmented, and part of the population of the text. The same can be said of the reader. In reading a text, s/he is drawn into a complex of intersecting voices.

My intention is to examine the mass media's contribution to the construction of a kind of femininity based on consumption. The material I focus on is a two-page consumer feature from a British magazine for teenagers called *Jackie* (which ceased publication in 1993). I outline the notion of women's magazines as a 'synthetic sisterhood.' [...] I concentrate specifically on one aspect of how this imaginary community is established: the simulation of a friendly relationship.

From: Mary Talbot (1995), 'A synthetic sisterhood: false friends in a teenage magazine', in Kira Hall and Mary Bucholtz (eds), *Gender Articulated: Language and the Socially Constructed Self*, New York: Routledge, pp. 143–65.

[…]

Synthetic personalization and friendship in a magazine for teenagers

How do we establish friendship? In part, by communicating, 'I know what you're like, and I'm like that too.' This kind of friendly behavior, the signaling of closeness and interest in another person, is sometimes known as being 'positively polite' (Brown and Levinson 1987). It involves the participants' attention to 'positive face': their need to be liked, approved of, flattered, or thought of as interesting. It is referred to as positive politeness, not in an evaluative sense, but to distinguish it from the kind of politeness, used predominantly among strangers and to superiors, that attends to 'negative face' needs: participants' need for freedom from imposition and harassment. Positive politeness is probably central to the well-documented cooperativeness of women. For example, Janet Holmes (1990, 1993) presents a detailed picture of New Zealand women's use of politeness strategies. These are mostly positive (affective tags and other hedges, boosting devices, compliments), but some are negative (e.g., apologies).'[1]

Positive politeness is very much in evidence in the mass media, and magazines are no exception. Certain kinds of linguistic features that are common in advertising and the mass media in general contribute to synthetic personalization and the establishment of an informal friendly relationship between the producers of mass-media texts and their audience. I concentrate on the mass-media producer's persona as a friend and the synthesized friendly relationship set up between producer and audience in a single sample of mass-media discourse, a consumer feature from *Jackie*. I shall briefly present two examples of synthesized positive politeness: the simulation of friendship and the simulation of reciprocal discourse.

The simulation of friendship

Aspects meriting attention in examining the producer's construction of a friendly persona for herself are the use of the pronouns *we* and *you*, relational and expressive values of lexis and punctuation, the setting up of shared presuppositions and projected facts (beliefs attributed to the reader, to 'us,' or just to common sense),[2] and, a variant of this, negating the reader's supposed assumptions. In focusing on these specific linguistic features, I attend to the way the producer realizes her simulation of friendly interaction with her audience, how she shows she knows who the reader is and how she establishes herself as a member of the same social group. The entire consumer feature is reproduced in Figure 1.1. The column of text on the history of lipstick reads as follows:

> Ask any clever advertiser how to suggest femininity with a product, and he'll probably tell you 'a kissprint.' Lipstick on a collar, a glass, his cheek—they all suggest that a woman was there. When men think of make-up, they think of lipstick.

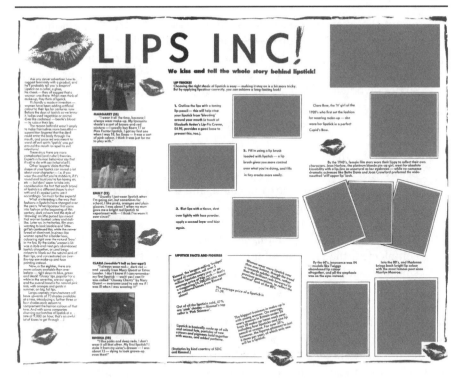

Figure 1.1 The Consumer Feature

It's hardly a modern invention—women have been adding artificial colour to their lips for centuries now. Before the days of lipstick as we know it, ladies used vegetable or animal dyes like cochineal—beetle's blood—to colour their lips.

The reason behind it wasn't simply to make themselves more beautiful—superstition lingered that the devil could enter the body through the mouth, and since red was meant to ward off evil spirits 'lipstick' was put around the mouth to repel his evil intentions!

These days there are more complicated (and ruder!) theories. Experts in human behaviour say that it's all to do with sex (what else?!).

Other 'experts' claim that the shape of your lipstick can reveal a lot about your character—i.e. if you wear the end flat you're stubborn, if it's round and blunt you're fun-loving etc. etc.—but don't seem to take into consideration the fact that each brand of lipstick is a different shape to start with and it's easiest just to use it accordingly. So much for the experts!

What *is* interesting is the way that fashions in lipsticks have changed over the years. When lipcolour first came into fashion at the beginning of this century, dark colours and the style of 'drawing' on little pursed lips meant that women looked cutesy and doll-like. Later on, in the forties, film stars wanting to look lovable and 'little-girl' ish continued this, while the newer breed of dominant, business-like women opted for a bolder look, colouring right over the natural 'bow' in the lips. By the sixties 'women's lib' was in style and most girls abandoned lipstick altogether, or used beige colours to blank out the natural pink of their lips, and concentrated on over-the-top eye make-up and face painting instead.

Now, in the eighties, there are more colours available than ever before—right down to blue, green and black! 'Glossy' lips, popular for a while in the seventies, are out again, and the overall trend is for natural pink tints, with oranges and golds in summer, on big, full lips.

Large cosmetic manufacturers will have upwards of 70 shades available at a time, introducing a further three or four shades each season to complement the fashion colours of that time. And with some companies churning out batches of lipstick at a rate of 9,000 an hour, that's an awful lot of kisses to get through...

Pronouns. In the column there is an example of the inclusive *we*, referring to both producer and audience together: *lipstick as we know it.* Elsewhere in the feature, use of exclusive *we* (i.e., the editorial we) contributes to setting up the producer as a team, the anonymous group voice is a friendly gossip in the orientation beneath the title (see Figure 1.1).

Pronominal reference to the reader as if she were an individual addressee is quite frequent. An example of it occurs in the first sentence in the column of text: *Ask any clever advertiser how to suggest femininity with a product and he'll probably tell you a 'kissprint.'*

Relational and expressive values of lexis and punctuation. The informality of some lexical terms contributes to the construction of a youthful female identity for the writer, matching the targeted audience by approximating the sort of vocabulary that teenagers might be supposed to use among themselves (e.g., *awful, cutesy,* in the column). The frequent exclamation marks add expressive value, attributing to the writer a friendly, enthusiastic emotional state. They seem to be the strongest boosting devices in this particular magazine feature. (Other boosting devices in this and similar magazines include *really, brill, well-trendy, mega*). The use of scare quotes contributes to setting up the familiar and the normal for the reader: the writer makes out that she knows what is and is not normal usage for her readers.

Common ground: projected facts and presuppositions. In the column of text in Figure 1.1, the writer negates an assumption attributable to the reader concerning the modernity of lipstick: *it's hardly a modern invention.* Similarly, in a set of instructions (reproduced below; see Figure 1.1 for the accompanying photographs), the writer challenges the reader's assumed pessimism about using lipstick successfully: *you* can *achieve a long-lasting look*!

LIP TRICKS!
Choosing the right shade of lipstick is easy—making it stay on is a bit more tricky. But by applying lipcolour correctly, you can achieve a long-lasting look!

1. Outline the lips with a toning lip-pencil—this will help stop your lipstick from 'bleeding' around your mouth (a touch of Elizabeth Arden's Lip-Fix Creme, £4.95, provides a good base to prevent this, too).

2. Fill in using a lip brush loaded with lipstick—a lip brush gives you more control over what you're doing, and fills in tiny cracks more easily.

3. Blot lips with a tissue, dust over lightly with face powder, apply a second layer and blot again.

The writer is represented as the reader's friend and as knowing what the reader thinks. She minimizes the social distance between herself and her readership, claiming common ground and a social relation of closeness. With her implicit claims to common ground in presuppositions and projected facts, she sets herself up as a member of the same social group as her readers. So, for example, two agreed-upon and interesting facts in the column are that each brand of lipstick is a different shape, and that fashions in lipstick have changed over the years. These are projected by the fact-nouns *fact* and *way*, respectively. The writer assumes shared knowledge that relates to historical details about 'breeds' of women, kinds of 'looks,' fashion changes, choice and ownership of lipstick, details relating to lipstick as a commodity that is subject to fashion change, the dullness of experts, and so on.

The simulation of reciprocal discourse
Various features that are used to simulate reciprocal discourse contribute to constructing relationships on the advertisement page: response-demanding utterances (commands and questions in particular), adjacency pairs, and interpolations.[3]

Producer-audience. Response-demanding utterances directly addressed to the reader occur notably in the instructions text. These commands requiring action as response are highly conventional in instructions scripts.

[stage 1]	'Outline the lips with a toning pencil...
[stage 2]	Fill in using a lip brush...
[stage 3]	Blot lips with a tissue, dust over lightly ... apply a second layer ... blot again'

In the column, the writer begins with a command addressing the reader: *Ask any advertiser* ... In the same text, she interpolates her own statements twice:

| Statement: | '...ladies used animal dyes like cochineal |
| Interpolation: | —beetle's blood— |

(Statement):	to colour their lips'
Statement:	'These days there are more complicated
Interpolation:	(and ruder!)
(Statement):	theories.'

Another interpolated remark occurs in the caption of a testimonial in the same feature: *CLARA (wouldn't tell us her age!)*

Representations of dialogue. The opening sentence of the column places the reader in an imaginary dialogue with a male advertiser. This dialogue consists of a two-part question-answer exchange, in which the reader asks the advertiser for information and he provides it:

| Question: | '. . . how to suggest femininity with a product |
| Answer: | "a kissprint." ' |

Although reciprocal discourse is commonly constructed between writer and audience, in the sample I have chosen, the simulation of two-way discourse is most striking between the writer and various characters set up in the text. The effect is an impression of overhearing gossip. Simulation of reciprocal, two-way discourse is particularly noticeable in the testimonial section of the *Jackie* consumer feature. These testimonials are reproduced below (see Figure 1.1 for the accompanying snapshots):

MARGARET (15)
'I wear it all the time, because I always wear make-up. My favourite shade's a sort of brown-and-red mixture—I usually buy Boots 17 or Max Factor lipstick. I got my first one when I was 10, for Xmas—it was a sort of pink colour, I think it was just for me to play with.'

EMILY (12)
'Usually I just wear lipstick when I'm going out, but sometimes for school, I like pinks, oranges and plain glosses. I was about 7 when my mum gave me a bright red lipstick to experiment with—I think I've worn it ever since!'

CLARA (wouldn't tell us her age!)
'I always wear red—dark red—and usually from Mary Quant or Estee Lauder. I don't know if I can remember my first lipstick—wait! yes I can! It was called "Choosy Cherry" by Mary Quant—everyone used to ask me if I was ill when I was wearing it!'

RHONA (18)
'I like pinks and deep reds. I don't wear it all that often. My first lipstick? I stole it from my sister's drawer—I was about 12—dying to look grown-up even then!'

To make any sense of these statements at all we need to postulate a set of questions or first pair-parts that were asked by an interviewer but that do not appear on the page. They are interviewee responses to three reconstructable questions: *How often do you wear lipstick? What's your favorite shade? When did you get your first lipstick?* Notice the echoing repetition of the question in the fourth testimonial.

Interestingly, although the whole consumer feature establishes a friendly relationship between apparently like-minded people, as I have indicated, it is particularly in these testimonials that positive politeness strategies of the kind used by women in face-to-face interaction are prominent. The high proportion of hedges (*sort of, I think, about*) contrasts sharply with the authority of the editorial voice in the other sections. The editorial voice is that of the expert with special knowledge. The interviewees do not always use the modality of categorical certainty, as the editorial voice does; in fact, the only things they are not tentative about are their color preferences. But of course the interviewees' supposed 'own words' have been structured by the interests of the editor-as-interviewer (present only as the shadow cast by her questions), who has set the agenda and constructed these interviews with 'ordinary' people. The hedging presumably contributes to the simulation of informal speech.

Conclusion

In concluding, let me emphasize that I am not presenting the readers of publications for women as passive receptors and ignorant dupes. This simplistic view of readers as gullible consumers has been most determinedly and effectively challenged by ethnographic work on readers of romance novels (Owen 1990; Radway 1987), which has shown us that readers are not simply taken in by the fiction they read, at least not in any straightforward way. Romance readers use fiction strategically—to escape family demands, for instance—and are quite capable of spotting poor writing and of challenging stereotypes. The readers of *Jackie* magazine cannot be dismissed as fools, either. As McRobbie (1991) demonstrates, the magazine was used oppositionally, as a challenge to teachers and parents. Such publications for teenagers, along with other elements of nonschool culture, provide strategies of resistance for low achievers in school. Like Radway's romance readers, teenagers use reading deliberately to cut themselves off from the rest of the world and the obligations it tries to impose on them. Actual readers of the sample text analyzed in this chapter would have taken up multiple, and almost certainly contradictory, subject positions. At most, one can say they may have been simultaneously both duped and not duped, so to speak.

Perhaps I had also better make it quite clear that lipstick per se is not under criticism here and no disparagement of lipstick wearers is intended (or indeed of practitioners of any of the other feminizing practices available to us). It is not a matter of repressing the pleasures of self-beautification. What I have been investigating are some of the mechanisms by means of which consumer femininity intrudes into the subjectivities of women. Women actively construct their own femininity, but this frequently means drawing on resources supplied by the magazine, clothing, and cosmetics industries. The femininity available to women is articulated principally in commercial and mass-media discourses. This very fact has certain consequences that are not beneficial to women and girls.

The audience of the feature analyzed here is offered sisterhood in consumption. Synthetic personalization and the need for adult femininity catch readers up in a bogus community, in which the subject position of consumer is presented as an integral part of being feminine. Members of this community other than the reader and her friendly editorial big sister are media celebrities, the testimonial givers, and other wearers of lipstick.

In the beauty feature, womanhood is a pattern of consumption Teenagers aspire to adulthood. What girls aspire to be as women is presented for them as a matter of what kind of look they will opt for. The beauty feature is not a piece of sisterly advice or an exchange of sisterly secrets; it is covert advertising: a consumer feature. Its producers' aim, apart from filling two pages in the magazine inexpensively, is to promote lipstick as a commodity. The advice that it does provide for readers—that is, the instructions for professional application of lipstick—is curiously inappropriate for the age range. These instructions seem to be calculated to encourage experimenters to consume extravagantly by playing at being movie star and beautician rolled into one.

Girls need peer-group membership; they turn to other girls for friendship and to learn how to behave like teenage girls. Consumer femininity is a real part of adolescent patterns of friendship. The consumer feature, however, offers no real human relationship. The testimonials are an example of how at puberty, girls are drawn into synthetic consumption communities of commodity users. Whether based on actual interviews or invented altogether, they are manipulative. Cosmetics use is presented as a natural part of a woman's identity, making demands on her discernment, her creative energies, and her time. In reading the feature, girls 'associate' with business people. Fashion and beauty alone are newsworthy. The only practices cultivated relate to being a competent consumer; in fact, readers are encouraged to ridicule the scientific and analytical.

The sisterhood offered in the consumer feature is also unsisterly because it is patriarchal. The feature makes a small contribution to the shaping of the 'paradigms for women's production of appearances' (Smith 1988:43) that are formed for women by the manufacturing, advertising, fashion, and magazine industries. In the opening paragraph of the column, in which the kissprint is presented as a symbol of femininity, this symbol is provided by a male character. It is a man who is the authority on femininity. The same passage goes on to present lipstick smudges as indices of a woman's presence. These are located on a man; to be feminine is to be (hetero)sexual. Feminine identity is achieved in consumption and in relationships with men. The friendly older sister writing for *Jackie* magazine (who could perfectly well be a man, of course) betrays her young readers, tying up the self-definition with external patriarchal standards of femininity. Given the poststructuralist vision of identity with which I opened, however, we need not view these readers as deterministically positioned in the act of reading this feature. Identity is not fixed but constantly in flux, being constructed moment by moment in the complexes of intersecting voices, or text populations, with which we engage in reading.

Notes

1. Hedging and boosting devices are kinds of modals, that is, elements that modify the force of a statement (Holmes 1984, 1993). Hedges (e.g., *sort of*, *kind of*, *rather*, *about*) are used to avoid making categorical statements by adding an impression of tentativeness. Tags (e.g., *isn't it?*, *don't you?*) sometimes function as hedges. Boosters, in contrast, serve as intensifiers and are used in expressions of interest or enthusiasm (e.g., *I'm so glad we came, we had a really good time*).
2. Projected facts and presuppositions are both kinds of external, prior text embedded in another text (Talbot 1990, 1995), but whereas projections are formal metalinguistic devices (Halliday 1985), presuppositions cannot be accounted for as formal features because they may be triggered by a wide variety of textual elements (Levinson 1983). Both projected facts and presuppositions tend to be backgrounded ideas that are noticeable only when assumptions of shared knowledge are erroneous.
3. Adjacency pairs are utterances that occur in pairs, forming small two part exchanges such as question-answer (Schegloff 1968; Schegloff and Sacks 1973). The first pair-part sets up an expectation of the second pair-part. In simulations of interaction in written discourse, a first or second pair-part may be present without its partner.

   In a study of the language of a disc jockey on BBC's Radio 1, Martin Montgomery (1988: 94) notes how frequently the DJ uses utterances requiring responses and observes that these utterances are contributing to a 'sense of reciprocity' in the one-way discourse of the radio. Other features he observes contributing to this sense of two-way talk are short shifts in speaker role, which he refers to as *interpolations*. They are often response-demanding or expressive utterances. *Jackie* frequently contained bracketed remarks that seem to be simulations of such interpolations.

REFERENCES

Brown, Penelope, and Stephen Levinson (1987). *Universals in language usage: Politeness phenomena*. Cambridge: Cambridge University Press.

Halliday, Michael A. K. (1985). *An introduction to functional grammar*. London: Edward Arnold.

Holmes, Janet (1984). 'Hedging your bets and sitting on the fence: Some evidence for hedges as support structures'. *Te Reo* 27: 47–62.

—— (1993). 'New Zealand women are good to talk to: An analysis of politeness strategies in interaction'. *Journal of Pragmatics* 20: 91–116.

Levinson, Stephen (1983). *Pragmatics*. Cambridge: Cambridge University Press.

McRobbie, Angela (1991). *Feminism and youth culture: From Jackie to Just Seventeen*. London Macmillan.

Montgomery, Martin (1988). 'D-J talk'. In Nikolas Coupland (ed.) *Styles of discourse*. London: Croom Helm. 85–104.

Owen, Mairead (1990). 'Women's reading of popular romantic fiction: A case study in the mass media. A key to the ideology of women'. PhD diss., University of Liverpool.

Radway, Janice (1987). *Reading the romance: Women, patriarchy and popular literature*. London: Verso.

Schegloff, Emanuel (1968). 'Sequencing in conversational openings'. *American Anthropologist* 70: 1075–95.

Schegloff, Emanuel, and Harvey Sacks (1973). 'Opening up closings'. *Semiotica* 8: 289–327.

Smith, Dorothy (1988). 'Femininity as discourse'. In Leslie G. Roman and Linda K. Christian-Smith (eds.), *Becoming feminine: The politics of popular culture* New York: Falmer Press. 37–59.

Talbot, Mary (1990). 'Language, intertextuality and subjectivity: Voices in the construction of consumer femininity'. Ph.D. diss., University of Lancaster.

—— (1992). 'The construction of gender in a teenage magazine'. In Norman L. Fairclough (ed.), *Critical language awareness*. London: Longman. 174–99.

—— (1995). *Fictions at work: Language and social practice in fiction*. London: Longman.

Weedon, Chris (1987). *Feminist practice and poststructuralist theory*. Oxford: Basil Blackwell.

Reading 1.2

Introduction

The subject of this study is 'racism'. But it is not racism of the sort that is overt and often violent, involving verbal or even physical abuse on the ethnic group that is being victimized. Such blatant discriminatory acts could take the form of physical assaults, lynchings, racial segregation as in South Africa's Apartheid policy or even genocide as we saw in Nazi Germany. That is the old racism. The 'new racism' (Barker, 1981) with which this study is concerned is a form of racism that is much more subtle, covert and hence insidious. This term is being used to refer to the changing nature of racism and ethnic domination in modern and increasingly cosmopolitan societies such as the United States of America, Western Europe and Australia.

[...]

The aim of this article is to show how the discursive strategies of two influential newspapers in Australia work to obfuscate, legitimate and naturalize the dominance of a group of Vietnamese migrants living in Sydney. The two newspapers – *The Sydney Morning Herald* (henceforth referred to as *Herald*) and *The Daily Telegraph* (*Telegraph*) – have been chosen because they have the largest circulations in Sydney, which is the largest city in Australia. I have chosen to focus on news articles about the *5T*, a gang of young Vietnamese drug-dealers who operate openly in the Sydney suburb of Cabramatta. One of their leaders, Tri Minh Tran, was killed in a 'gangland-style' execution on 8 August 1995. His violent death sparked media interest in the *5T*[1] and their drug-dealing and violent activities in Cabramatta. By examining the news reports/articles on the *5T* before and after the killing of Tri, an attempt was made to piece together a coherent picture of the *5T* as depicted by these two Sydney newspapers. Table 1 summarizes the source and content of the newspaper reports under analysis.

Through a systematic and principled analysis of this small corpus of newspaper discourse, I hope to unravel and 'demystify' (Fowler et al., 1979) the way

From: Peter Teo (2000), 'Racism in the news: a Critical Discourse Analysis of news reporting in two Australian newspapers', *Discourse and Society*, 11: 1, 7–49.

in which racial prejudice against the Vietnamese is imbricated within the structure of newspaper reporting in Australia. Before this can be done, it is necessary to lay down the theoretical framework within which the entire analysis is undertaken.

Theoretical background

This study adheres to the analytic paradigm of Critical Discourse Analysis (CDA) employed by Fowler et al. (1979), Fowler (1991), Van Dijk (1993, 1996)

Table 1. *Summary of news reports under analysis*

S/N	Date	Source	Summary
1	2 May 1995	*Herald*, p. 6	A key witness who allegedly saw an Asian gang bash a schoolboy to death was placed under protection when a Cabramatta gang threatened to kill anyone who talked to the police.
2	16 July 1995	*Telegraph*, p. 8	Asian youths brazenly peddle drugs at the Cabramatta train station area, seemingly oblivious to the police patrols and crowds of commuters nearby.
3	16 July 1995	*Telegraph*, p. 9	Cabravale Park has become the new drug haven for Cabramatta's heroin abusers, where syringes and other Implements litter the park.
4	8 August 1995	*Herald*, p. 2	Police believe that the three men who were gunned down in Cabramatta were victims of a power struggle in the *5T* gang, notorious for heroin trafficking and extortion of Asian shopkeepers.
5	8 August 1995	*Telegraph*, p. 11	Piers Akerman, a columnist writing in response to the spate of violence involving Asian gang members in Cabramatta is advocating bringing back capital punishment for those who profit from the drug trade as a final cure to the problem.
6	9 August 1995	*Herald*, p. 6	Tri Minh Tran, the leader of the *5T* gang, together with one of his henchmen were killed by a hail of bullets in his Cabramatta home.
7	12 August 1995	*Herald*, p. 2	In the wake of the brutal slaying of the leader of the *5T* gang, a news reviewer examines the cult of extreme violence among the gang youths and the anger and alienation which drive it.
8	13 August 1995	*Telegraph*, p. 9	Police hope that the underworld execution of sleazy Cabramatta gang boss Tri Minh Tran may produce a vital lead in their efforts to nail the killers of local MP John Newman.
9	6 October 1995	*Herald*, p. 1	Police have achieved a dramatic reversal in the war against the drug-lords of Australia's busiest heroin bazaar in Cabramatta by using cadres of undercover police.

and Fairclough (1992, 1995). CDA has its roots in *critical linguistics*, which is a branch of discourse analysis that goes beyond the description of discourse to an explanation of *how* and *why* particular discourses are produced. The term 'critical linguistics' was first used by Fowler et al. (1979) and Kress and Hodge (1979), who believe that discourse does not merely reflect social processes and structures, but affirms, consolidates and, in this way, reproduces existing social structures. In a similar vein, Fairclough (1992) attempts to articulate a vision of discourse that is at once socially constituted and socially constitutive, against the synchronic backdrop of socio-cultural and political forces. To Fairclough and other critically minded discourse analysts, discourse is not only a product or reflection of social processes, but is itself seen to contribute towards the production (or reproduction) of these processes.

Though a relatively young discipline, the roots of CDA can be traced as far back as Marx, whose ideas on social theory and organization have had a tremendous impact on latter-day social thinkers. For instance, Gramsci (1971) and Althusser (1971) have both stressed the significance of ideology for modern societies to sustain and reinforce their social structures and relations, while Habermas (1984) has focused upon the 'colonization of the "life-world" by the "system" of the economy and the state'. Neo-marxist in orientation, these views on social theory converge on the role of an abstract system of socio-political ideology in the construction and indeed reproduction of modern-day society. As a pre-eminent manifestation of this socially constitutive ideology, language becomes the primary instrument through which ideology is transmitted, enacted and reproduced (Foucault, 1972; Pecheux, 1982). Thus, by analysing the linguistic structures and discourse strategies in the light of their interactional and wider social contexts, we can unlock the ideologies and recover the social meanings expressed in discourse.

The social theories of Habermas, Foucault and others have in turn influenced, albeit to varying degrees, the work of linguists like Fowler, Kress and Hodge and, more recently, Wodak, Van Dijk and Fairclough, who share a common vision of the centrality of language as a means of social construction. Working independently but united by this common vision, they embark upon various investigatory studies designed to unmask and make transparent the kind of socio-political or socio-cultural ideologies that have become entrenched and naturalized over time in discourse.

The word 'critical' is a key theoretical concept in CDA that bears some explanation here. The word signals the need for analysts to unpack the ideological underpinnings of discourse that have become so naturalized over time that we begin to treat them as common, acceptable and natural features of discourse. In other words, ideology has become common belief or even 'common sense'. Adopting 'critical' goals would then enable us to 'elucidate such naturalisations, and make clear social determinations and effects of discourse which are characteristically opaque to participants' (Fairclough, 1985: 739). The word 'critical' in CDA also signals a departure from the purely descriptive goals of discourse analysts (Sinclair and Coulthard, 1975; Stubbs, 1983) who are commendable for their methodical approach to the analysis of everyday talk but whose method suffers from an inherent weakness of explanatory power. In other words, the attention to describing and detailing structural realizations is done at the expense of interpreting and explaining how and why such realizations come to be produced. CDA, on the other hand, moves from this surface attentiveness to a recognition of the crucial role played by deeper, larger social forces which exist in a dialectical relationship with the discourse: discourse both shapes and is shaped by society.

A *critical* approach to discourse analysis typically concentrates on data like news reporting, political interviews, counselling and job interviews that describe 'unequal encounters' or embody manipulative strategies that seem neutral or natural to most people. For instance, Trew (in Fowler et al., 1979) shows how two British newspapers portrayed the same event in vastly contrastive ways that reflected their differing ideological standpoints. Similarly, in an analysis of an interview with Margaret Thatcher, Fairclough (1989) describes and explains how the discourse which combines authority with popular solidarity is able to create an 'authoritarian populism', which effectively persuades Thatcher's audience over to *her* vision by making it *their* vision. More recently, Brookes (1995), working within a critical linguistic paradigm, exposes the neo-colonial racism evident in the portrayal of Africa and Africans in two British newspapers. Thus, we often see in CDA a need to broaden the social context to embrace the socio-political conditions that shape discourse, in an analysis aimed principally at revealing how power structures are constructed through discourse.

One of the earliest works that argues for a *critical* approach to understanding racism in the media is by Hartmann and Husband (1974), whose study on black racism in Britain reveals that:

> prejudice cannot be regarded simply as a matter of misinformation or wrongheadedness ... This is because racial prejudice serves a function, among other things, of maintaining whites in an advantageous position relative to blacks. Prejudiced attitudes cannot be changed significantly, independently of the structural relationships to which they relate. (Hartmann and Husband, 1974: 41)

Van Dijk (1984) adopts a similar stance in his treatment and analysis of racial prejudice in Holland, where he systematically argues that racism is a cognitive and social phenomenon that has the social function of protecting the interests of the in-group. Thus conceptualized, racism becomes pivotal in maintaining the power relationships and structures that historical or other forces might have emplaced in a society. It is this more *critical* approach to racism which locates it within the construction of modern society meshing it with socio-economic and socio-political power structures that is of interest in this study.

In sum, the approach that this research study adopts is a critical, multi-disciplinary approach to discourse analysis which focuses on issues of prejudice, power, dominance and hegemony, and the discursive processes of their enactment, concealment, legitimation and reproduction in the domain of newspaper reporting. While CDA may have 'passed through the first flush of youth' (Fairclough, 1995: 20), there is still much consolidatory work to be done to give it a conceptual and analytic unity and coherence, and it is hoped that this study can in some way reflect and contribute to this ongoing process.

Analysis

[...]

A general characterization of the newspaper discourse

NEWSPAPER HEADLINES AND LEADS

A definitive feature of news reporting is the use of the headline and/or lead to express, in a highly concise form, the crux of the news event and to orient the reader to process the text in a pre-determined direction. In fact, as pointed out by several news discourse analysts (including Tuchman, 1978; Cohen and Young, 1981; Van Dijk, 1983; Bell, 1991), news in the daily press is organized by the principle of relevance or importance, along a dimension of decreasing prominence with respect to the macro-structure. This means that a reader need only to glance at the headline or lead to obtain a fairly accurate idea of what the whole report is about. In fact, the lead has sometimes been referred to as the 'story in microcosm' (Bell, 1991: 174). This is commonly referred to in journalistic parlance as the 'inverted pyramid', where the most important or newsworthy information is located at the top and the least important at the bottom. The function of the headline or lead, then, is to form a cognitive macro-structure that serves as an important strategic cue to control the way readers process and make sense of the report. Part of this involves the activation of relevant background knowledge from our long-term memory that is needed to contextualize the meaning of the text. A case in point is the headline (*Herald*, 6 October 1995) *Got you . . . police hit back in the heroin war*, which recalls past reports of the flourishing drug-trade in Cabramatta, where gangs like the *5T* operated in broad daylight in flagrant disregard of the police (see, for instance, the summary of the two *Telegraph* reports on 16 July 1995 in Table 1). Thus, the words 'hit back' in the headline are meaningful only if set against this 'background knowledge' that the news report presumes readers to have. Likewise, the lead (*Herald*, 12 August 1995):

> The young leader of the 5T Vietnamese gang was shot dead this week in Cabramatta. Philip Cornford looks at the cult of extreme violence among the gang youths and the anger and alienation which drive it.

while recalling a recent news event (the fatal shooting of the *5T* leader) presupposes the *5T* to be a gang of extreme violence. What is significant is how the writer has made the 'cult of extreme violence' not only a defining but inalienable trait of the *5T* by embedding the presupposition that the *5T* is an extremely violent gang within the lead. In so doing, even if the proposition ('Philip Cornford looks at the cult of extreme violence among the gang youths and the anger and alienation which drive it') is negated (Philip Cornford does not look at ...) or questioned (Does Philip Cornford look at ...?), the presupposition that the *5T* is an extremely violent gang remains intact. The way the lead is constructed therefore suggests that the writer is interested only in looking at the reasons *why* the *5T* has become so violent rather than examining the issue of *how* they have been violent or *whether* they are indeed violent in the first place. This inevitably colours the readers' perception of the *5T*. Thus, the subsequent references to violence that recur throughout the report only serve to reinforce this presupposition, leaving little room for the reader to challenge this 'cult of extreme violence' that the *5T* supposedly embodies. In this respect, the macro-structure that is manifest in headlines and leads encapsulates an ideology that biases the reader to one particular reading, thereby subjugating all other possible interpretations of the news story. Typically, then, news reporting not only provides information for readers to interpret but often comes packaged with the interpretation as well.

In a genre of discourse where space is a premium, news headlines have to be crafted in such a way as to employ the minimum number of words to package maximum information. Thus, every word in a headline is carefully chosen and structured so as to maximize the effect of the headline. In this way, headlines often encapsulate the newspaper's ideological values and attitudes, and analysing the lexical choices and syntactic structures of newspaper headlines as well as the captions of photographs that may accompany some reports would allow the critical discourse analyst a peek into the underlying ideological meaning behind newspaper reporting.

Even a casual glance at the headlines summarized in Table 2 points to a motif of violence suggested by the lexical choices used in the headlines. What we have is a series of news headlines that highlight the murder, shooting (both in its literal and figurative senses), drug-dealing, fighting and other violent and unlawful activities of the *5T*. The lexical choices betray an explicit association of the *5T* with serious crimes like 'murder' and 'drug deals'. The headline 'Street gang's culture of murder' (*Herald*, 12 August 1995) is particularly telling in its association of murder with the gang's sub-culture, suggesting that killing is perhaps a way of life for these youngsters. Thus, the prevailing atmosphere is one charged with fear and insecurity, arising from the seeming brazenness of the *5T* in defying the law on the one hand and the ineffectualness of the law-enforcers to cope with the situation on the other. In light of this, the 6 October headline, 'Got you ... police hit back in the heroin war' is strategically timed to re-assert the authority of the police, a face-saving strategy to restore public faith

Table 2. *News headlines, leads and captions under analysis*

Source	Headlines/Captions
Herald (2/5/95)	**Murder witnesses threatened, court told**
Telegraph (16/7/95)	**Drug deals on the heroin express:** Kids make bucks feeding misery of suburban addicts.
Telegraph (16/7/95)	**The shooting gallery;** Caught in the act: Outside Cabramatta station, heroin dealers brazenly accost commuters. The passing of a police van scatters them temporarily. Minutes later it's back to business.
Herald (8/8/95)	**Two gunned down in heroin gang war**
Telegraph (8/8/95)	**Drugs – a final cure**
Herald (9/8/95)	**Killing ends reign of young 5T boss**
Herald (12/8/95)	**Street gang's culture of murder;** *The young leader of the 5T Vietnamese gang was shot dead this week in Cabramatta. Philip Cornford looks at the cult of extreme violence among the gang youths and the anger and alienation which drive it.* Face of the 5T . . . murdered gang leader Tri Minh Tran; street scenes in Cabramatta; an Asian inmate of Minda juvenile correction centre with the 5T gang tattoo on his left arm.
Telegraph (13/8/95)	**$10,000 to kill Newman:** *new lead from Tran slaying*
Herald (6/10/95)	**Got you . . . police hit back in the heroin war**

Main headlines are represented in bold type to distinguish them from leads (in italics) and captions of accompanying photographs which are in regular script.

in them. Furthermore, the syntactic structure of this headline is deliberately manipulated to emphasize the active role the police are taking in the 'war' against the 5T by juxtaposing the free direct speech in 'Got you' with the reported speech in 'police hit back in the heroin war'. The effect of using the free direct speech is to portray the police in a personal and palpable manner, giving the impression that the police are speaking directly to the readers (or, more specifically, the 5T). This sort of syntactic manipulation is also evident in the caption beneath the photograph showing five burly looking undercover policemen pinning an alleged drug-dealer to the ground: 'Without warning . . . undercover men trap another alleged drug dealer on a street in Cabramatta as police take on the violent gangs'. The manipulation becomes apparent if we re-write the caption as either (a) Alleged drug-dealer trapped by police on a street in Cabramatta; or (b) Alleged drug-dealer trapped on a street in Cabramatta. Both the passivization in (a) and the omission of the agent in (b) considerably diminish the significance and puncture the power of the police. In contrast, the frontal positioning of '*police*' and 'undercover men' foregrounds the police and is consistent with enhancing their visibility and credibility in their 'war' against the drug-dealers, which is what the news report is about after all. It is only in this light that the incongruity between the news of the arrest of a lone, alleged drug-dealer in Cabramatta and the front-page headline position that it occupies in a major newspaper in Sydney can be rationalized. Thus, what is newsworthy is not the arrest of an alleged criminal but the '*dramatic reversal*' of the power-relations between the police and the drug-syndicate in Cabramatta. This '*reversal*' contrasts with the headlines and captions of earlier reports where it is either the crime or the criminal, rather than the police, that occupies the informationally significant frontal position. In sum, we see how the active choices made in the way newspaper headlines, leads and captions are couched can have a very powerful ideological effect on readers' perception and inter-pretation of people and events.

GENERALIZATION *Conclusion ??*

Generalization refers to the extension of the characteristics or activities of a specific and specifiable group of people to a much more general and open-ended set. On one level, generalization offers reporters a convenient means to ascribe certain key qualities to the main participants of the news discourse without encumbering the reader with tedious details; on another, the selection and repetition of a particular generalizing attribute also hints at an underlying ideology that might have motivated the choice in the first place.

In the newspaper discourse under analysis, we observe a *generalization* of the crimes of the *5T* in Cabramatta to a progressively wider group of people (Vietnamese, Southeast Asians and Asians). References to 'Vietnamese' and 'Asian' appear so consistently and frequently in relation to criminal activities of the *5T* that it becomes almost an endemic part of the drug culture in Australia. Examples of such generalizing references abound (Table 3).

The homogenization of the drug-dealers as 'Vietnamese', 'Southeast Asian' or 'Asian' parallels the kind of categorical generalization that is often symptomatic of stereotyping or cognitive prejudice (Van Dijk, 1987); the larger the category, the more sweeping the generalization and hence the more 'severe' the stereo-typing. People who stereotype others tend to see them not only as less variable but also as less complex than themselves. They tend to simplify and chip away at the individual and often unique characteristics of the out-group, resulting in Asians appearing as people with yellow skin, black hair and slant eyes to a Caucasian, in the same way as Caucasians appear as white-skinned, blue-eyed blondes to an Asian.

More significantly, categorizing someone into a particular social schema also tends to colour the perception of the *meaning* of what that person does. Thus, a child taking an eraser from another may be seen as aggressive if he is black but assertive if he is white (Sagar and Schofield, 1980). Similarly, while a yellow-skinned youth seen loitering around Cabramatta may be perceived as a drug-dealing gangster out to create trouble, a white youth in the same situation is not likely to be perceived as such. Stereotypes are the cognitive culprits in prejudice and discrimination (Fiske and Taylor, 1993). Hence, the stereotyping of the *5T* as Vietnamese or Asian is not just a means of slotting them into a particular ethnic compartment; it also affects our attitude and behaviour towards them

Table 3. *Generalizations related to the 5T*

Source	Reference
Herald (6/10/95)	Vietnamese gangsters
Herald (12/8/95)	Vietnamese gang
Herald (8/8/95)	other Vietnamese criminals
Herald (8/8/95)	three Vietnamese men gunned down
Telegraph (16/7/95)	Groups of youth, many of South-East Asian appearance
Telegraph (16/7/95)	five other youths of Asian appearance
Telegraph (16/7/95)	the tall youth of Asian appearance
Telegraph (8/8/95)	two young Asian gang members
Herald (2/5/95)	an Asian gang
Herald (12/8/95)	Asian inmate of Minda juvenile correction centre
Herald (8/8/95)	heroin is being imported from Asia

and their actions. Put simply, how we categorize a social group affects the way we perceive and relate to them. The ideological significance of this is that the less evaluative and more factual generalizations appear, the less questionable and more naturalized they become. In this way, the generalizing references to the *5T* in the news reports not only reflect but reinforce the social schemata into which we have categorized people. Taken to its logical conclusion, the notion of being Vietnamese or Asian can become permanently imbricated into the social schemata not only of the Cabramatta drug-dealers but of *all* gangsters and drug-dealers alike. This kind of stereotyping only serves to perpetuate an unhealthy Us-versus-Them mentality between the dominant white majority and the ethnic minority of Australia. This phenomenon is consistent with Van Dijk's (1991) conceptualization of media racism: the professional socialization of predominantly white journalists contributes to the development of social cognitions and schemata that tend to favour the in-group (the white, Anglo-Saxon majority) and, consequently, to disfavour the out-group (the ethnic, Asian minority in this case).

QUOTATION PATTERNS

A third characteristic of the newspaper discourse under analysis is the reliance on various sources of information on which the news report is constructed. Hence, quotes – both direct and indirect – are frequently woven into the fabric of the news discourse to give it a semblance of 'facticity' and authenticity: a quote from the newsmaker's own words renders it as incontrovertible fact (Tuchman, 1978: 96). But, as Scannell (1992) notes, this dependence on legitimized sources of information results in a predominantly establishment view of the world, in which lay people are only entitled to their experience but not their opinions. In this way, the use of quotation becomes a gate-keeping device that admits only those in positions of power and influence while shutting out the opinions and perspectives of those deemed by society to be powerless. Thus, while the powerful are further empowered through quotation patterns that enhance their status and visibility, the systematic silencing of the powerless – the poor, the young, the uneducated, etc. – only further disempowers them.

Thus, it is hardly surprising that one of the 'properties' of racism in the press, according to Van Dijk, is that minorities are largely silent and are hardly quoted or quoted with suspicion or distance in newspaper reporting. Table 4 shows clearly that the ethnic minority is quoted, whether directly or indirectly, less than one-quarter of the time compared to the white majority. In the report about the 'gangland-style' execution of Tri Minh Tran (*Herald*, 8 August 1995), for instance, the only person quoted directly was a Detective Inspector Allan Tayler, a member of the white elite group. In contrast, one of the quotes attributed to the ethnic minority is from the 'neighbours of the dead man', anonymous (the neighbours are not named), indirect (reported speech is used) and placed at the very end of the news report, indicative, presumably, of its low-value status. It is no coincidence, either, that these nameless neighbours represent the only sympathetic voice about the deceased throughout the report: '*they were just "ordinary kids" out of work who gave them no trouble*', compared to the police who say that '*the 5T factions have fallen out the sale of rock-heroin, which has been responsible for a wave of overdose deaths this year*'. While the neighbours of the deceased portrayed the dead men as basically harmless, the police portrayed them as highly dangerous and directly responsible for 'a wave of overdose deaths'.

In the discourse under analysis, while the activities of the police are reported in elaborate detail and often quoted verbatim from a high-ranking officer, the activities of the criminals are often told only from the perspective of the police or some 'expert'. For instance, it is surprising that a news review that purportedly probes into the sub-culture of the 5T gang (*Herald*, 12 August 1995) quotes only from figures of authority or expertise from the white majority and not from (either present or former) members of the 5T or even the general Vietnamese community who would probably have a more intimate knowledge of the psychology and sociology of the Vietnamese gang. The people quoted are supposedly representative of the expert, authoritative voices and, more significantly, members of the 'in-group'. Although what they say about the 5T is not particularly derogatory, the point is that the newspapers seem to be interested in seeking the opinions and perspectives of only the elite majority, as though it is only they who have anything valuable or insightful to say about the 5T, thereby denying the ethnic community a chance to be heard and understood from *their* perspective.

An apparent exception to this is found in a *Telegraph* article (16 July 1995) in which the 5T is given ample voice and visibility as they 'work' the streets in Cabramatta peddling their illicit ware. The preponderance of direct quotes from members of the 5T, however, has quite a different effect compared to a

Table 4. *Quotation patterns of news reports under analysis*

		Source of quotes	
S/N	Reference	Ethnic minority	Elite majority
1	Herald (2/5/95)		The police prosecutor, Sergeant Colin Kennedy
2			Mr Warwick Anderson, a defence lawyer
3	Telegraph (16/7/95)	The tall youth of Asian appearance	
4		A male youth	
5		The 16-year old youth	
6	Telegraph (16/7/95)		Superintendent Allan Leek
7			Cabramatta MP, Reba Meagher
8	Herald (8/8/95)		Detective Inspector, Allan Tayler Police
9			
10		Neighbours of the dead man (Tri)	
11	Herald (9/8/95)	Ms Huong Tran (Tri's sister)	
12		Ms Gerry Trimarch, (Tri's wife)	
13			A detective who arrested Tran twice Police
14			
15			Detective Inspector, Allan Tayler
16	Herald (12/8/95)		Clinical psychiatrist, Dr Marie Bashir
17			High-school headmaster, Mr Geoffrey Darling
18			Mr Grahame Kidd, headmaster in Cabramatta High School
19			Inspector Bob Barnes
20	Telegraph (13/8/95)		Detective Inspector, Don Brown
21		Vietnamese community leader Andrew Nguyen	
22			Councillor Chapman
23			Police Commissioner Tony Lauer
24			Assistant Commissioner Alf Peale
25			Ken Marslew, executive manager of the Homicide Victims Support Group
26	Herald (6/10/95)		Patrol Commander Inspector Geoff Cavanagh

direct quote from a member of the elite majority. Apart from injecting a sense of 'live' drama, the series of pithy and pointed exchanges between the drug-peddlers and the reporter (masquerading as a potential customer presumably) – 'You want something?'; 'What have you got?'; '$35, $40 and $50 rocks'; 'Heroin?'; 'Yeah!'; 'Well, you want some or not?'; 'I'll think about it' – is calculated to highlight the *5T*'s brazenness in dealing drugs in broad daylight, and not so much to give voice to their opinion or perspective. In fact, it can be argued that the liberal use of direct quotes from the *5T* not only does not enhance their status and power as would be the case in a similar quotation pattern involving the elite majority, it in fact disempowers them further by alienating them from mainstream society by the shock-effect created by the knowledge that these exchanges take place openly during peak-hour 'as dozens of people walk on and off the ramp . . .'. This attempt to distance the *5T* from mainstream society is also manifest *syntactically* in the contrast between the drug-dealer's non-standard English ('You want something?' and 'Well, you want something or not?') and the reporter's more standard usage.

Quotation patterns, as we have seen, can become a powerful ideological tool to manipulate readers' perception and interpretation of people and events in news reports. The generalization of the ethnicity of the *5T* referred to earlier creates an association of the *5T* with Asians and of Asians with the *5T*. Denied of a voice to resist and challenge this stereotype, the association of the Asianization of Cabramatta with its criminalization 'naturalizes' over time, becoming resistant to challenge and change.

OVER-LEXICALIZATION

Lastly, we look at what Fowler et al. (1979) call 'over-lexicalization as a pragmatic strategy of encoding ideology in news discourse'. Over-lexicalization results when a surfeit of repetitious, quasi-synonymous terms is woven into the fabric of news discourse, giving rise to a sense of 'over-completeness' (Van Dijk, 1991) in the way participants in the news discourse are described. It is characteristic, according to Fowler et al., that powerless people are over-lexicalized: hence, a lawyer might be termed a 'female lawyer' whereas a male lawyer is just a 'lawyer'. Similarly, there is a certain stigma or markedness attached to 'male nurse' since nurses are presumed to be female. Seen in this light, over-lexicalization often has a pejorative effect as it signals a kind of deviation from social convention or expectation and reflects perceptions and judgements from the essentially biased standpoint of such cultural norms or social expectations.

Let us first of all examine the pervasive use of lexical cohesive devices to construct a profile of the *5T* as mere 'Kids' (*Telegraph*, 16 July 1995). The most direct and obvious form of lexical cohesion is the *repetition* of a lexical item such as 'youth' or 'young'. The use of synonymy in 'Kids' and 'lad' and other direct references to the age of the drug-dealers also contribute to the co-referentiality of youthfulness and the drug-dealers in Cabramatta. These are summarized in Table 5.

The question then is: what is the motivation behind this over-lexicalization of the 5T, emphasizing their youthfulness in such an explicit, repetitive and overt manner? While it may be typical for reporters to provide factual information such as the age and occupation of the main participants in a news event, it is fairly obvious that the intention behind these explicit references to age is not only to provide factual information but to orient the readers' perception of the 5T in a particular way. Being young is arguably a mitigating factor to the crimes of these drug-dealers, but it is evident that the purpose here is to evoke not sympathy but condemnation. The implicit argument is not so much that, 'They are young, fallible and susceptible to bad influence, so please excuse them', but rather 'Look, they are so young and are already "brazenly" and "openly" committing such heinous crimes, what more will they be capable of when they become adults!'. Evidence for such an antipathetic reading of youthfulness are as follows: '*As they grew older, they grew bolder*'; '*For all their arrogance ...*'; '*It's quite obvious the older people are glad to see them* [referring to members of the 5T] *go: you can see them smiling quietly to themselves*' (Herald, 12 August 1995). These references to a less-than-sympathetic view of youthfulness of the Gang are consistent with the use of over-lexicalization as a means to disfavour and even derogate. Further evidence in the same news article include: '*the cult of* **extreme** *violence*', '**extreme** *youth and* **extreme** *violence*', '*hacked and stabbed* **11 times with machetes**'. These instances of over-lexicalization (highlighted in bold type) suggest the 'extremeness' and brutality of the crimes committed by these 'kids'. The juxtaposition of the 'young' 5T against the very 'adult' crimes

Table 5. *Lexical cohesion I – the juvenilization of the 5T*

Source	Reference to youthfulness
Telegraph (16/7/95)	**Kids**; tall **youth**; five other **youths**; A male **youth** ... looks and sounds like he is **about 13**; Groups of **youths**; The **16 year old youth**; **lad**; **juvenile** detention centre
Herald (8/8/95)	Ordinary **kids**
Telegraph (8/8/95)	two **young** Asian gang members
Herald (9/8/95)	Tran first came to the attention of police **aged 11**; spent six months in a **children's** institution; **At 13**; including another **juvenile**
Herald (12/8/95)	The **young** leader; the gang **youths**; homeless **young** men; their **young** sons; extreme **youth**; **juveniles**; Tri Minh Tran was their leader at **13**; had beaten two murder charges by **17**; at least two of the accomplices were of the same age (i.e. **13 and 14**); **Too young**; other **young** Vietnamese; **adolescents**; other **teenage** gangs; Some are **as young as 12**; the **kids**; **children**; these **kids**
Herald (6/10/95)	5T dealers, some as **young as 12**

like drug-dealing and murder creates in the mind of the reader an image of extreme youth and extreme violence that is the *5T*.

Besides signalling youthfulness, over-lexicalization also draws attention to some rather derogatory characteristics of the *5T*. Table 6 lists the range of epithets used to refer to the *5T* members or its activities.

As can be seen, the *5T* has been ascribed with a plethora of epithets ranging from unfathomable, cruel, vicious, evil, frenzied and animal-like, in ascending order of negativization. This has the effect of dehumanizing and hence further alienating the *5T* sub-culture from the mainstream Australian culture. The over-lexicalization of the *5T* parallels their powerlessness to articulate an identity for themselves, submitting therefore to the public caricature of them not only as violent or dangerous criminals but as evil and vicious animals.

SUMMARY
It is useful at this juncture to attempt to summarize the findings of my analysis so far:

Table 6. *Lexical cohesion II – Negativization of the* 5T

Source	Epithet	Reference
Herald (12/8/95)	angry, resentful unfathomable and mystifying	angry, hurt, full of resentment and lonely Australians have great difficulty understanding why, having found sanctuary in this wonderful land, some of these kids just can't make it
Telegraph (13/8/95)	sleazy	sleazy Cabramatta gang boss
Herald (6/10/95)	precocious and violent	the young and violent *5T* gang rules Australia's busiest heroin bazaar brazenly touting for business
Telegraph (16/7/95)	brazen	
Telegraph (13/8/95)	notorious	the suburb's notorious heroin trade
Herald (12/8/95)	ruthless cruel and arrogant	the pawns of bigger, more ruthless criminals success made the *5T* cruel and arrogant
Telegraph (8/8/95)	corrupt and corrupting	Those who chose to go into the drug business go into it for its high illicit profits … a reality that corrupts our police, our children and society
Herald (9/8/95)	vicious	the vicious *5T* gang
Telegraph (8/8/95)	evil	Let's start taking the evil lives of those who prey upon the innocents of our society
Herald (12/8/95)	frenzied, ferocious, animal-like	The *5T* attacked in a pack and in frenzy, screaming insults, sharing the kill … They were ferocious, attacking in numbers

(1)   The analysis of lexical choice and syntactic structure of the newspaper headlines and leads reveals an ideology that depicts the police in a position of power and control while the minority *5T* is consistently associated with crime and mayhem. In other words, there is lexical and structural evidence of what Van Dijk sees as positive Us-presentation and negative Them-presentation in the news headlines.

(2)   The crimes of the *5T* are extended via generalization to the entire Vietnamese community in Australia, and even Asians in general are sometimes implicated. This represents stereotyping in its most naked and ugly forms. The often irrelevant reference to the perpetrators as Vietnamese or Asian, repeated often enough, gives the impression that being Vietnamese or Asian is synonymous with crime.

(3)   Analysis of the quotation patterns and information sources points to an overwhelming disproportion of white majority voice against ethnic minority voice. This silence and silencing of the minority group are symptomatic of their powerlessness and disempowerment by the 'expert', 'authoritative' white community.

(4)   While the powerless are silenced, they are over-lexicalized with a wide but largely unsavoury characterization. As they are not given a voice to speak for themselves, they are literally at the mercy of those who do to say whatever they will of them. This creates a stereotype of the *5T* not only as a highly dangerous and predatory sub-culture but also an alienated enigma. This deliberate 'othering' reinforces the 'Us versus Them' dichotomy and widens the gulf between the predominantly white community of Australia and the ethnic community.

[. . .]

REFERENCES

Althusser, L. (1971) *Ideology and Ideological State Apparatuses: Lenin and Philosophy and Other Essays*. London: New Left Books.

Barker, M. (1981) *The New Racism*. London: Junction Books.

Bell, Allan (1991) *The Language of News Media*. Oxford: Blackwell.

Brookes, Heather Jean (1995) 'Suit, Tie and a Touch of Juju – The Ideological Construction of Africa: A Critical Discourse Analysis of News on Africa in the British Press'. *Discourse & Society* 6(4): 461–94.

Cohen, S. and Young, J. (eds) (1981) *The Manufacture of News*. London: Constable.

Fairclough, Norman (1985) 'Critical and Descriptive Goals in Discourse Analysis', *Journal of Pragmatics* 9: 739–63

Fairclough, Norman (1992) *Discourse and Social Change*. Cambridge: Polity Press.

Fairclough, Norman (1995) *Critical Discourse Analysis*. London: Longman.

Foucault, M. (1972) *Archaeology of Knowledge*. London: Tavistock Publications.

Fowler, R., Hodge, R., Kress, G. and Trew, T. (1979) *Language and Control*. London: Routledge and Kegan Paul.

Fowler, R. (1991) *Language in the News: Discourse and Ideology in the Press*. London: Routledge.

Gramsci, A. (1971) *Selections from the Prison Notebooks*. ed. and trans. Q. Hoare and G. Nowell Smith. London: Lawrence and Wishart.

Habermas, J. (1984) *The Theory of Communicative Action*, Vol. 1, trans. Thomas McCarthy. Boston: Beacon Press.

Hartmann, P. and Husband, C. (1974) *Racism and the Mass Media*: London: Davis-Poynter.

Kress, G. and Hodge, R. (1979) *Language as Ideology*. London: Routledge & Kegan Paul.

Pecheux, M. (1982) *Language, Semantics and Ideology: Stating the Obvious*, trans. H. Nagpal. London: Macmillan.

Scannell, P. (1992) 'Public Service Broadcasting and Modern Public Life', in P. Scannell, P. Schlesinger and C. Sparks (eds) *Culture and Power*. London: Sage Publications.

Sinclair, J. and Coulthard, M. (1975) *Towards an Analysis of Discourse*. Oxford: Oxford University Press.

Stubbs, Michael (1983) *Discourse Analysis*. Oxford: Blackwell.

Tuchman, Gaye (1978) *Making News: A Study in the Construction of Reality*. New York Free Press.

Van Dijk, Teun (1984) *Prejudice in Discourse*. Amsterdam: John Benjamins.

Van Dijk, Teun (1993) 'Principles of Critical Discourse Analysis', *Discourse & Society* 4: 249–83.

Van Dijk, Teun (1996) 'Discourse, Power and Access', in Carmen Rosa Caldas-Coulthard and Malcolm Coulthard (eds) *Texts and Practices: Readings in Critical Discourse Analysis*, pp. 84–104. London: Routledge.

Reading 1.3

Formulations

Conversation analysis has proceeded on the premiss that conversational inter-action is a *self-explicating phenomenon*: 'A member may treat some part of the conversation as an occasion to describe that conversation, to explain it, or characterize it, or explicate, or translate, or summarize, or furnish the gist of it, or take note of its accordance with rules, or remark on its departure from rules. That is to say, a member may use some part of the conversation as an occasion to *formulate* the conversation' (Garfinkel and Sacks, 1970: 350). Such for-mulations, of course, occur in a wide variety of mundane talk; and some of their properties have been investigated empirically by Heritage and Watson (1979). However, Heritage (1985) has isolated some specific classes of formulations occurring with marked frequency in the particular *institutional* context of the news interview. Institutions are themselves 'self-explicating phenomena' (see Pollner, 1979; Sharrock and Anderson, 1987); that is to say, in their observable organization are *displayed* the requirements of given bureaucratic practices: and one such radically observable locus of organization lies in the common bureaucratic requirement for 'successful' *processing* of lay members passing through the institutional machinery ('cases', 'patients', 'interviewees', 'defen-dants', 'callers'). In this respect talk radio broadcasts are no different to any

From: Ian Hutchby (1991), 'The organisation of talk on radio', in Paddy Scannell (ed.), *Broadcast Talk*, London: Sage, pp. 119–37.

other institutional phenomenon: callers must be 'processed' ... that is, have their topic, once introduced, dealt with, assimilated (or rejected) in so far as it makes (or fails to make) 'some sense' of an issue-in-question, and their call terminated in order to make way for another caller. And this processing must be directed, in a necessarily ad hoc, rule-of-thumb manner, by the individual who is the 'visible' organizational hub of the entire institution, and who operates *at the interface* of lay member and institution, namely the host.

Formulations produced by news-elicitors in an institutional setting like the talk radio broadcast can be seen to 'work' on a number of levels. In an immediate sense, formulations of gist or upshot work to focus or 'pare down' the 'meaning' of the news offered prior to their production. At the same time they recognize the 'public' and the 'private', the 'institutional' and the 'interpersonal' dimensions of talk radio. As summaries of callers' calls-so-far, they are directed both towards 'assisting' the caller in developing the 'sense' of his/her call and towards 'clarifying' that 'sense' in an overarching manner *for the overhearing audience.*

Fragment [1] displays adequately the focusing/refocusing qualities of the formulation:

[1]
10. *M.* ((...)) I think we should be working at breaking do:wn that separateness I think these (.) telethons actually increase it
11. *H.* [how/]
12. *H.* well (.) what you're saying is that charity does
13. *M.* .hh charity do::es ye:s I ⌈think it's-
14. *H.* ⌊ok so you're .h so you're going back to that original argument we shouldn't have charity
15. *M.* well (.) no I um I wouldn't go that far = what I would like to- ⌈see is-
16. *H.* ⌊well how far are you going then
17. *M.* well I would- what I would like to see ((...))

Here, two formulations are evident: one involving *gist* at T12 and one involving *upshot* at T14. At T12, in formulating the gist of M's prior newsproducing utterance(s), H clearly not only *focuses* M's 'point' concerning the contradictory effects of 'telethons' (which, while rhetorically encouraging wider concern with problematic features of our social structure, in fact, M claims, promote a passive altruism and exacerbate the 'separateness' between donor and donee), but *refocuses* it, expanding its field of reference from telethons alone – the restrictive topic of M's call – to charity in general. It is the case that, throughout the course of the call so far, M had made no attempt to generalize his point in this way; hence it might be said that H's T12 formulation of gist presents an example of what Heritage (1985; 108) labels the 'inferentially elaborative probe'. H here infers, and verbally proposes, that M's restricted critique is in fact, and in this specific way, generalizable and, as is visible at T13,

M acquiesces in the proposal by restating the inferred elaboration, somewhat emphatically, himself (we might call this an *inference reinforcement*).

H's second formulation, at T14, links itself to, and builds upon, this acquiescing utterance at T13, attempting to relate the inferred 'underlying sense' of M's contribution, formulated by H at T12, to another call, aired earlier in the broadcast, whose contribution (centring around the argument that, as H states it, 'we shouldn't have charity') had instigated an ongoing debate within this broadcast on the question of the overall validity of organized charities. M, at T15, responds negatively to this attempted extension with 'no I um I wouldn't go that far', which utterance, shaped as it is as a 'weak' declination (as opposed, for instance, to an outright rejection of H's formulation of upshot), provides, in the first instance, for a further, clarifying utterance from the caller; or, in the absence of such a clarification, a requesting of it by the host in next turn. In fact, as is visible at T15 and T16, both these provisions are realized, with M moving directly from his declinational unit into a proposed clarification; and H, at T16, having 'anticipated' the sequential relevance of this clarification, producing his request for it even though M has, pre-emptively, entered into the task of accomplishing it.

In this sequence, therefore, are visible what Heritage (1985) identifies as 'cooperative' and 'uncooperative' features of formulations as conversational phenomena in institutionalized news-generating settings. Formulations project for the caller the alternative responsive strategies of *acceptance* (in which case the formulation and its response may be characterized as 'cooperative') or *rejection* (in which case the formulation and its response may be characterized as 'uncooperative', and further talk pertinent to the declination may be judged relevant and requested). Thus the formulation, while in an obvious sense serving the overhearing audience by 'parcelling' the overall gist, or some particular aspect, of the news produced within the call, may also serve the caller by allowing him/her either to accept the pared down version of their reporting and so take up in further talk the direction proposed by the formulation, or to reject this version and so take up in further talk their account of the grounds for this rejection. In either case, the formulation serves simultaneously as 'newsmark' and 'further-news-elicitation', and so intrinsically operates as a mechanism facilitating the interactive management and collaborative production of news or 'sense' in talk radio talk.

Closings

As Schegloff and Sacks (1973: 289) observe: 'the unit "a single conversation" does not simply end, but is brought to a close'. The 'closing' of a conversation in everyday life is not something which occurs randomly due to an unaccountable decision by one party to cease conversing and engage in other activities, but something which is, like every other feature of conversational activity, a negotiated, interactively produced, accountable, accomplished, *self-explicating* practice. Members' work in closing conversations has been analysed at length in, for instance, Schegloff and Sacks (1973) and Button (1987): the specific issue being that, 'while conversational openings regularly employ a common starting point – with greetings etc. – and then diverge over a range of particular conversations, conversational closings converge from a diverse range of conversations-in-their-course to a regular common closure with "bye bye" or its variants' (Schegloff and Sacks, 1973: 291, Note 3). Clearly, the same circumstance holds for talk in the setting of the talk radio broadcast; notably, however, the technical problematics of the accomplishment of a call's 'closing' exhibit a radical dissimilarity from those observable in mundane talk: a dissimilarity emanating, once again, from the talk's 'institutional' colouring, and gravitating around one pervasive characteristic, namely that conversational closings in talk radio talk are not required to be, and overwhelmingly are not in practice, *negotiated* in any overt respect between host and caller. Given the host's institutional siting as organizational 'hub' of the broadcast, as processing agent both accessing callers to the air and removing them from the air, it is in a very basic sense the host's task not only to 'open' calls (as we have already seen) but also to 'close' them.

Note that it is not being claimed by this that hosts may or must, consistently, unilaterally and *arbitrarily* close off callers' air-access, but that it is consistently the *host's task* to discern 'some' point in the organization of turns structuring a given call at which a relevant and/or necessary *bid for closing* might be made. As I show below, such a bid for closing may be accepted or rejected by the caller in question; but the point remains that ordinarily no exchange of 'ritual' closing utterances (e.g. 'goodbye' or 'see you') is required or offered in talk radio talk, and that, by virtue of both bureaucratic and technological siting, the host is not 'compelled' to pay regard to the caller's response to any closing bid, as might be the case, for example, for an accountable participant in everyday conversation.

In facilitating closing a mechanism sometimes employed is the summarizing formulation.

[2]

28. M. ((....)) I mean (0.3) .h it- it is it's really it is the poor: the poorer pensions that've had it taken away from them (0.4) because of this: er money that's been e:r the means uh th- the needs allo:wance money

29. H. so you don't think the government's being all that marvellous and generous ab ⌈out this

30. M.   ⌊I think they're dis:gusting (.) ⌈I really do

31. H.   ⌊thank- thank you Margaret

H's T29 formulation here pares down M's critique of the government's restructuring of the state pensions system into a simple, parcelled statement of opposition to the legislation, allowing M, at T30, to reinforce this negative summarization, after which H, having thus fashioned an appropriate possibility for withdrawing the caller from the air, closes the call with a peremptory (and commonly occurring) 'acknowledgement token' ('thank you Margaret') at T31. An alternative strategy involves the projection of some *isolated aspect* of the call, as in [3]:

[3]
22. *E.*　but *a*ll we saw was a woman's
　　　　grief ⌈ (.) and an ordinary ⌈ young man who ⌉ =
23. *H.*　　　⌊ok well erm　　　　⌊y-y-yeh　　　⌋
22a.*E.*　= w*a*s in the ⌈boy scouts and who: was whatever
24. *H.*　　　　　　⌊right I understand (.) I understand Eva and er understand m- the point you're making particularly fr- from the your st*a*rting point which was that .hh you will s*ee* .hh controversial programmes from .hh a part*i*cular (.) point of v*ie*w .hhh and we've had tw*o* of those particular points of views .h er yours and earlier R*i*chard's thank you very much indeed for calling us

Here, H's closing formulation at T24 involves an explicit *selection* of a *certain* point made by the caller ('particularly ... your starting point') which the host cites here as the newsworthy content to be preserved (for the overhearing audience) from this call. Noteworthy in this fragment are two features distinguishing it from fragment [2]: first, that the host, on his first attempt at instigating the closing – with 'ok well erm' at T23 – retracts the attempt when it becomes clear that the caller's turn is not yet completed, and tries again a moment later ('right I understand' at T24), whereupon E, finishing her utterance rapidly, withdraws; and second, that once the closing formulation is entered, there is no further response from E, and indeed H, unlike the host in [2], fashions no space *for* a response by the caller. Thus the closing summary in [3] exhibits greater *selectivity* and *finality* than that offered in [2].

A closing of a different type, but illustrating another *retraction* of a closing bid by the host, is exemplified in [4]:

[4]
28b.*K.*　= it gives people the choice as to whether they w*a*nt to shop on a Sunday
31. *H.*　t ok*ay* .h ⌈thank-
32. *K.*　　　　⌊I mean th*o*se who want to keep Sunday special by all means l*e*t them I'm not against th*a*t ⌈ (.) ⌉ those that d*o* =
33. *H.*　　　　　　　　　　　⌊yes⌋
32a.*K.*　= but I mean we must move wi- with the t*i*mes I think (.) in my opinion=
34. *H.*　=mm h*m*=
35. *K.*　⌈anyway I (.) ok*ay* Brian　　　　⌉
36. *H.*　= ⌊ok thank you very much uh　⌋　(.) thank you very much K*ei*th

Here, no formulation is involved: H appears to opt, at T31, for what might be called a 'simplest' closing bid, namely one constituted solely by an acknowledgement, thanking the caller for his/her call. K, however, interrupts this attempt with a further elaboration of his point concerning Sunday trading at T32, with the result that H, as in example [15], withdraws his attempt. Subsequently, however, at T35, K himself acknowledges belatedly the closing attempt made by H, allowing, with 'anyway' (a unit identified in Button (1987), as, thus sequentially located, a *first or second close component* – i.e. a component indicating that the speaker is seeking to move, or is acknowledging another's attempt to move, into a closing sequence), a space for H to reinstigate his closing; although, as is clear, at T36 H has pre-emptively reinstigated closing himself, in an overlapping utterance.

A final closing strategy considered here, and perhaps the most radical, is the 'explicit dissension', wherein, quite simply, the host appears to override the caller *in the course of their speaking* in order to produce, as the closing turn of the call, a summarization of his own, usually dissenting, view as regards the topic addressed in the call. An example is given in [5]:

[5]

36. *M.* well no I what I th*i*nk is that these telethons are <u>e</u>ducating people
  but they're educating them in a certain wa:y they're educating
  them to give m<u>o</u>ney what they sh<u>ou</u>ld be doing is educating
  them to take an <u>i</u>nterest in their community .hh instead of
  just giving m<u>o</u>ney which can in f<u>a</u>:ct .h stop them being
  interested ⌈because –

37. *H.*   ⌊well I d<u>o</u>n't think the job of the telethon is to <u>e</u>ducate
  people to do <u>any</u>thing .hh er it gives them an opportunity .h er
  throu:gh a kind of entertainment if you like .hh er to give money
  now you may not l<u>i</u>ke that and so th<u>e</u>refore you don't have to
  w<u>a</u>tch it .hh <u>I</u> don't find it (.) terribly entertaining or interesting to
  wa:tch .hh but I c<u>e</u>rtainly wouldn't pr<u>eve</u>nt people who d<u>o</u> enjoy
  it .hh er from s<u>ee</u>ing it .h b<u>e</u>ing enterta:ined <u>a</u>nd at the same time
  giving money .h whether it salves consciousnes- consciences or
  n<u>ot</u> .hh thank you M<u>a</u>rtin

Plainly, in this fragment, H's lengthy utterance at T37, interrupting R's T36 summarization of his 'point', itself produced in response to an earlier elicitation from H (data not shown), both: (a) *explicitly dissents* from the viewpoint elaborated by R in the body of the call; and (b) in itself *closes* the call, allowing no space for any responsive utterance from the caller. Notably, H's dissension here addresses itself not merely to the point raised in R's immediately prior turn (i.e. the *educative significance* of telethons), but also to two major points broached earlier in the call: that involving the possible 'prevention' or 'banning' of telethons, and that concerning the suggestion that televised charity events operate in some way to 'salve consciences'. So that, in this example at least, the explicit dissension of the host operates on a quite comprehensive level: at T37, H systematically articulates the three major points raised by this caller to his own *critical* point, namely that 'I certainly wouldn't prevent people who *do* enjoy it, .hh er from seeing it .h being enterta:ined and at the same time giving money'.

In sum, then, whether the closing is effected by means of a summary formulation, a selective summarization, a 'simplest' acknowledgement, or an explicit dissension, we see that the 'leading party', the occupant of what might be termed 'dominant speaker locus' within the bounds of the sequence, is the host. Although hosts may frequently *defer* to callers, at least momentarily, withdrawing closing bids in face of offerings of further news by their inter-actants, the bureaucratic processual imperatives implicit in the structuring of the talk radio broadcast *as a broadcast*, as 'that kind of phenomenon', and the interactional constraints generated by the context in which talk radio talk *suigeneris* is brought into being, endow the host ultimately with the task of 'organizing' the passing of the caller through the machinery of the broadcast, of 'directing' the processing of each individual call. And I want to suggest that it is, therefore, in the routinely self-explicating work of the *closing* of conversations on talk radio that the operation of the broadcast as a *bureaucratic phenomenon*, and of the host as the *organizing agent at the interface of the 'public' and the 'private' in talk radio talk itself*, is at its most immediately visible.

[...]

REFERENCES
Button, G. (1987) 'Moving out of Closings', in G. Button and J. Lee (eds), *Talk and Social Organisation*. Clevedon.
Garfinkel, H. and H. Sacks (1970) 'On Formal Structures of Practical Actions', in J. C. McKinney and E. A. Tiryakian (eds), *Theoretical Sociology*. New York.
Heritage, J. (1985) 'Analysing News Interviews: Aspects of the Production of Talk for an Overhearing Audience', in T. van Dijk (ed.), *Handbook of Discourse Analysis*, Vol. 3. London.
Heritage, J. and D. R. Watson (1979) 'Formulations as Conversational Objects', in G. Psathas (ed.), *Everyday Language*. New York.
Pollner, M. (1979) 'Explicative Transactions: Making and Managing Meaning in Traffic Court', in G. Psathas (ed.), *Everyday Language*. New York.
Schegloff, E. and H. Sacks (1973) 'Opening Up Closings', *Semiotica*, 8(4).
Sharrock, W. and R. Anderson (1987) 'Work Flow in a Paediatric Clinic', in G. Button and J. Lee (eds), *Talk and Social Organisation*. Clevedon.

Reading 1.4

Confrontational closings: the 'power of the last word'

Arguments may end on a note of opposition rather than assent between the participants. In these cases, the pattern is that the host's negation of the caller's

From: Ian Hutchby (1996), *Confrontation Talk: Arguments, Asymmetries and Power on Talk Radio*, Mahwah, NJ: Lawrence Erlbaum, pp. 102–7.

stance comes in a position-taking utterance of his own, which occupies the entire terminal segment. This is illustrated by extract (1), in which the final turn of the call shows the host first dissenting from the caller's view, then directly moving to a terminal acknowledgment:

(1)
```
 1  Caller:   ... what I think is that these telethons
 2            are educating people but they're educating
 3            them in a certain way they're educating
 4            them to give money. What they should be
 5            doing is educating them to take an
 6            interest in their community. .hh Instead
 7            of just giving money which can in fact,
 8            .hh stop them being interested ⌈because-
 9  Host:                                    ⌊Well I
10            don't think the job of the telethon is to
11            educate people to do anything, .h er it
12            gives them an opportunity, .mhh e:r
13            through a kind of entertainment if you
14            like, .hhh to give money. Now you may
15            not like that, .hh I don't find it,
16            terribly entertaining to watch, .hh but I
17            certainly wouldn't prevent people who do
18            enjoy it, .hhh er from seeing it, .h being
19            entertained and at the same time giving
20            money, .h whether it salves consciousnes-
21            uh consciences or not. .hh Thank you
22            Philip, .hh it's: er twelve minutes to
23            eleven ...
```

The host's turn begins as a straightfoward disagreement with the caller's position that telethons are 'educating people' in the wrong kind of way: 'Well I don't think the job of the telethon is to educate people to do anything.' Subsequently, he puts his own dissenting view on the matter, before ultimately closing the call with a terminal 'Thank you,' leaving no space for a rejoinder from the caller. In this kind of case, the sense of confrontation is promoted in terms of both the relationship between the final turns of the call and the disputatious nature of the call's conclusion itself. In having the last say in the call, the host thereby gains the last say in an ongoing dispute over the issue.

Clearly, hosts are in a very powerful position for having the last say in their disputes with callers. In an important sense, that power is connected to the technological framework within which hosts and callers interact. By virtue of the technologically mediated nature of talk radio disputes, the host has at his disposal a specific resource for not allowing the caller an opportunity to respond to his last word. That is, he can close off the caller's channel of access to the argumentative arena while retaining full access to that arena himself.

But as I have argued before, the power that is attached to the interactional and technological arrangements of talk radio does not come into play as an automatic effect. It exists only as potentialities that must be instantiated in actual talk. The way in which the 'power of the last word' can be instantiated as an interactional resource is illustrated particularly clearly in the examples that follow.

In the call from which the next extract was taken, the caller has complained that a TV program about the death of a suspect in police custody was 'biased' against the police. The host has developed the position that the program had a particular perspective on the subject and so was inevitably selective in its presentation of the 'facts.' In the extract, the host's attempts to take a counter-position are repeatedly overlapped by the caller doggedly pursuing his own line (lines 6, 8, and 15). The host responds by verbally closing down the caller's channel of access using a terminal acknowledgment in order to put his own point forward (line 20):

```
(2)
1   Host:    But you do have to come to your own
2            conclusion when you watch things, .hh erm
3            quite often things are biased the other
4            way, .phh e:r you know the–the the -(,)
5            .ph consta⌈ -ntly put opinion-⌉ that=
6   Caller:        ⌊I:    just     fail-⌋
7   Host:    = ⌈⌈ the police are⌉ won⌈derful⌉
8   Caller:   ⌊⌊ u:h a:-absolu ⌋     ⌊I   fai⌋l to see
9            what–what 'is antecedence in the church
10           'ad anything to do with it. Or or⌈ or I⌉s=
11  Host:                              ⌊Well,⌋
12  Caller:  =it in the Boys Brigade
13           movemen⌈t.
14  Host:           ⌊Yeh ⌈but that's understandable.⌉
15  Caller:              ⌊.hhh an they kep' show⌋in'
16           you the funeral the mother cryin' .hh th-
17           the everybody wallin' over the grave I mean
18           i- was totally unnecessary.
20  Host:    Okay Steven thank you very much indeed,
21           erm:, it is understandable how-however if
22           you, bi- have the ki:nd of view that
23           you're suggesting that programme (.) had,
24           .hhmhh e::::rm, that they should e:rm, .bh
25           (.) talk about thee- the character, of the
26           victim. .thh Thank you Steven, a::nd
27           Gerald, good morning . . .
```

In line 6, the caller interrupts the host's attempt to argue against his line that the program was biased against the police and, having gained the floor (line 8), pursues his line of complaint. The host then appears to make another attempt at arguing (line 11), but the 'Well' that signals this attempt is overlapped as the caller adds yet another sentence onto his complaint. A further attempt is made in line 14, but this too is overlapped by the caller as he adds yet more points to his complaint. In his final attempt to put his view forward, however, the host precedes the resumption of his argument with a terminal acknowledgment, 'thank you very much indeed' (line 20).

We thus see how, faced with a recalcitrant caller with whom he wants to disagree, the host may deploy the strategy of getting in the last word *after* he has closed the call. The significance of this is that no comparable strategy is available to the caller. Although callers may elect to terminate a call unilaterally, they can do so only by withdrawing from the interactional arena, and therefore withdrawing from the argument. Vuchinich (1990) has shown that withdrawing is one among a small number of strategies by which participants in conversational arguments terminate disputes. By physically leaving the arena, a participant may seek to kill the dispute by effectively leaving his or her codisputant no one to argue with. But when the dispute takes place in public, as on talk radio, withdrawing can be a disadvantageous strategy, because the up shot is not that one gets the last word oneself, but that the last word is thereby ceded to one's opponent.

On talk radio, this feature is compounded by the asymmetry in the participants' levels of technical access to the public arena. The host's institutional status is supported by a technological positioning which enables him, if he so chooses, to have the last word in a dispute by expressing his opinion in a public space that is not available to the caller: the space occurring after the caller's channel of access to the host and the audience has been closed down, either by the host himself, or by the caller hanging up on the host.

Although this claim sounds quite plausible, a possible empirical problem is that the recorded data on which these analyses are based do not in themselves provide evidence that would allow us to say at what point the caller's access to the air may actually have been closed off. In other words, in the absence of additional ethnographic data, it is not clear to what extent callers may be complying with the host's getting the last word by remaining silent, as opposed to *being* silenced by virtue of being cut off.

That lack of ethnographic data may be seen as a significant absence, given the concern of this chapter with the endings and outcomes of arguments on talk radio. However, the data at hand – recordings and transcripts of the actual broadcast talk – can in fact provide their own kind of evidence that allows us to see how the asymmetry in channels of access is used as a resource by the host in accomplishing the termination of calls and of arguments. One sort of evidence for this is provided by the previous extract, in which we saw the host using the routine closing device of 'Thank you, [Name]' *before* putting forward his own position. In that call, the technological asymmetry between host and caller is actively utilized by the former to win out in a dispute.

A second type of evidence we can look at consists of cases where callers remain on the air during the host's closing move, and attempt to resist that move. In these cases, the host unilaterally closes the call on an oppositional note by overriding the caller's objections and pushing through to a termination. In extract (3), the caller had earlier proposed a system aimed at superseding charitable donations, based on a personal tax levied by the government that would then be distributed to the various organizations currently reliant on charitable giving. As the extract begins, the caller has moved on to complain about the number of mailed requests for donations that he claims to receive from such organizations:

```
(3)
 1  Caller:   But then a'course y- you do get eventually
 2            you find yourself about thirty or forty
 3            different charities comin' through your
 4            post an' you can't donate to all of them.
 5            .hhh It's such an expense isn' it when
 6            people .hhh ⌈ these (    ) send out
 7  Host:                 ⌊Well you don't haff- n-a- hold
 8            o:n, a m- a moment ago: you were saying we
 9            should give to all of them, now you're
10            saying .h it's too difficult to give to
11            them, .h e⌈r the s:-
12  Caller:             ⌊N-   no  ⌈the-
13  Host:                         ⌊the system that you
14            introduced ⌈ was still ⌉ charity It makes no=
16  Caller:              ⌊ It (    ) ⌋
17  Host:     =difference. .hh Thank you Charlie, Jim::::
18            now good morning.
```

In lines 7–10 the host begins by arguing that the caller's line has become incoherent: 'a moment ago: you were saying we should give to all of them, now you're saying it's too difficult to give to them." Notice, however, that the caller begins to take issue with this characterization of what he is saying (line 12). But the host holds the floor through this attempted objection, going on to state his opposition to the caller's principal point. In the process, he talks over a second apparent objection by the caller (line 16), and ultimately, terminates the call on this expression of his opposing line (line 17).

Similar features can be seen in extract (4):

```
(4)
 1  Host:   I see you- you- you're going back to the
 2          ol:d- the old argument that people have too
```

```
 3              many children and therefore that
 4              impoverishes them are you?
 5              (0.3)
 6  Caller:    .hh Well ⌐I think-
 7  Host:           ⌊Not a very enlightened view I
 8              would've thought, ⌐but perha-per⌐ haps=
 9  Caller:                      ⌊.hh  No   no:.⌋
10  Host:      =perhaps you come from the fortunate
11              minority Marjorie=th ⌐ank you very muh-⌐ =
12  Caller:                         ⌊No:   I    do:n't,⌋
13  Host:      =.h Thank you very much we go to Mabel…
```

The host attributes a position to the caller in the first turn of the extract. But once it is clear that the caller is about to take issue with some aspect of that attribution (as signaled in lines 5 and 6 through the slight pause and the disagreement marker, 'Well'), he interrupts her (line 7), again overriding further objections from the caller (line 9 and line 12), before ultimately terminating the call.

In sum, asymmetries in participant status that are connected to the techno-logical asymmetries of talk radio become a resource available to the host for accomplishing confrontational closings. Even in the absence of additional data that tell us whether or not callers' lines of access have actually been closed down, we find empirical evidence of hosts utilizing that access asymmetry in order to determine the public outcome of a dispute. In examples where hosts observably work to blot out objections from callers, strong evidence is provided of how the potential power dynamic in this context is actually instantiated in the local practices of talking.

Conclusion

The observations made in this chapter serve to highlight the relevance of the public arena in which talk radio disputes are carried out. The asymmetries outlined here arise as a result of the participants' unequal access to that public arena, populated by the overhearing audience. This adds a further dimension to my analysis of power relations in talk radio discourse, because it illustrates that power, on talk radio, is not just a phenomenon linked to and produced through the sequential details of talk, but is also connected in significant ways to the mediated nature of the interaction. The outcomes of talk radio disputes, the determination of which we have observed in this chapter, are public outcomes, in the sense that the last word is a *broadcast* word. Clearly, there is a sense in which callers could have the last word on their own terms, by continuing to argue with the host's voice on the radio after their call has ended. But the relevance of arguments on talk radio is precisely that they take place in the public sphere of broadcasting, and this represents a principal reason for callers to place a call in the first place (Rancer et al., 1994). […]

References

Rancer, A., Miles, T. and Baukus, R. (1994 April). 'Communicative predispositions and demographic characteristics of listeners and non-listeners to talk radio'. Paper presented at the Annual Meeting of the Eastern Communication Association, Washington, DC.

Vuchinich, S. (1990). 'The sequential organization of closing in verbal family conflict'. In A. D. Grimshaw (Ed.) *Conflict talk* (pp. 118–38). Cambridge: Cambridge University Press.

Reading 1.5

As contemporary politics has become increasingly centred in the media, the prominence of leaders in the political process has increased. Political parties and governments are now more strongly identified in terms of the individuals who lead them than ever before – Thatcher and Blair in Britain, Reagan and Clinton in the USA. This public visibility can certainly give a misleading impression of what goes on in politics and government. Nevertheless, no political analysis can ignore the political identity and personality of the leader; and identity and personality centrally involve language, rhetorical style.

Politics is a social practice which sets up a range of positions for people involved. Party leader and, in government (depending on the political system), Prime Minister or President are such positions. Much of what particular politicians do and much of the way they behave follows from the positions they occupy. Having said that, there is considerable variation in how people perform in these positions. Indeed, it is these differences in performance that are decisive for political success or failure – parties do not need leaders who perform the role in a textbook fashion, they need leaders who perform the role distinctively, and are perceived to be distinctively better than others. People perform differently as political leaders depending upon their social identity (their social class, the cultural or regional community from which they come, their gender, etc.), but also depending upon their particular life history and experience. It is thus partly a matter of the social identity and personality they bring to the leadership position, but it is also partly a matter these days of how their attributes are honed and inflected on the advice of the political communications industry.

Political identity is constructed, built. Here is one of Blair's key advisers, Philip Gould, writing about a memorandum he wrote in 1994 called 'Consolidating the Blair Identity':

> First I spelled out the strengths and weaknesses of Blair's position. His strengths were 'freshness and a sense of change; confidence and self-assurance; that Tony Blair is a new kind of politician; that Blair changes what it means to be Labour'. His weaknesses were that he could be perceived as 'over-smooth', 'too soft and not tough enough', and

From: Norman Fairclough (2000), *New Labour, New Language?*, London: Routledge, pp. 95–112.

'inexperienced'. In response to this, 'Tony Blair should not be what he is not. This will not work and will be counter-productive. He should not try to avoid the problem of youth by behaving with excessive gravitas. Nor try to avoid looking soft by behaving with excessive aggression. What he must do is build on his strengths, and build an identity as a politician that is of a piece with the political positions he adopts. He must be a complete, coherent politician who always rings true.'

Gould writes in rather general and indeed vague terms, but he is partly alluding to Blair's language and rhetorical style, envisaging a process of development and construction certainly, but one that 'builds on' what is already there rather than attempting incompatible add-ons (such as an aggressive communicative style) which will prevent him 'ringing true'. Notice also that he envisages a process of 'building', which seeks coherence between political identity and political positions, a point I return to below.

A rhetorical style is not an invariable way of using language; it is rather a mixture of different ways of using language, a distinctive repertoire. Tony Blair does not always speak in the same way, but he has a distinctive repertoire of ways of speaking which he moves between in a recognisable way. Part of the variability of his style is to do with the variability of the genres within which he operates. For example, a political speech at a Labour Party conference or in Parliament entails a different use of language from that of a radio phone-in programme, television interview, Fabian Society pamphlet, or an article in the *Daily Mail*. Even within any one of these genres – let us say a political speech – Blair uses language in different ways to do different things, for instance to spell out Government policy, or to argue a contentious issue, or to establish a rapport and intimacy with his immediate audience.

My approach to Tony Blair's style in this chapter will be to show how he moves through different ways of using language, focusing on two examples in different genres: his speech at the 1997 Labour Party conference, and an interview he did in January 1999 on the BBC1 television programme *Breakfast with Frost*.

The speech was given at the first Labour Party conference after New Labour won power. The conference slogan was 'New Labour, New Britain', and Blair summarised his objective in the speech as follows: 'Today I want to set out an ambitious course for this country: to be nothing less than the model 21st century nation, a beacon to the world.' The interview was framed within the crisis of late 1998 and early 1999, which I referred to in the Introduction. It begins with questioning about ministerial resignations (especially Peter Mandelson's), as well as a scandal involving the Foreign Secretary Robin Cook, then it takes on the character of a broad review of major aspects of policy. I shall also discuss more briefly his style as a 'wartime leader' during the NATO attacks on Yugoslavia. This will allow me to say something about another important aspect of the variability of Blair's style – how it is changing over time.

Blair's rhetorical style is not purely a matter of language. It is a matter of his total bodily performance, of which what he says is just a part. It is a matter of how he sounds, how he looks, the shifting expressions on his face, the way he moves his head and other parts of his body. While it is highly important to try to capture this total bodily performance, it is very elusive, difficult to describe, and particularly difficult to describe in print. Ideally, we (author and readers) should be watching and discussing a video together, if not Blair in person.

Blair the 'normal person'

Leader identity in contemporary politics is generally built upon a tension between the public office and the private individual, the extraordinary position of the leader and the 'ordinary' person who holds it. In terms of language, this means a tension between the public language of politics and everyday language. Politicians differ not in whether they show this tension – they virtually all do – but in the particular forms it takes. According to his political biographer, 'a central component of Blair's appeal in the two years before he became leader was that he was recognisably a human being, that he did not sound like a politician . . . an impression he sought to reinforce when he became leader'. Blair himself wrote:

> I feel like a perfectly normal person. I look at politicians who are older than me and I wonder when was the last time they had their own thoughts to themselves in their own way without feeling they had to programme their thoughts to get across a message . . . I don't actually feel much like a politician.

With the passage of time, Blair has come to be seen increasingly as a politician like others, and there is a certain irony about the way he dismisses programming 'their thoughts to get across a message' in the light of New Labour's preoccupation with being 'on message', as well as Blair's reliance on focus group research in determining how to move politically. Nevertheless, the tension between the 'normal person' and the politician remains, in a form which is an important part of Blair's style and of his apparent continuing popularity (at least according to opinion polls).

[. . .]

In my view, Blair's political identity is anchored in his personal identity; or, more accurately, in how his personal identity is constructed in his public performances. Whatever public abilities and qualities he has built up – including, for instance, a capacity to be 'tough' which Gould saw as lacking in 1994 – it is a crucial part of his political identity (and his apparent continuing popularity) that the 'normal person' regularly emerges from the public figure. He rarely fails to 'touch base', so to speak. What this means in terms of language and the overall 'bodily performance' that constitutes Blair's rhetorical style is that Blair's political performances are inflected by the language and communicative style of Blair 'the normal person'. In this section I will trace some of the forms which that inflection takes.

So what is 'base'? What sort of 'normal person' does Blair come across as? Not only relatively young, but youthful. When he suddenly grins in the course of a political interview, the impression is of irrepressible youthful vitality and enthusiasm, and, as Gould notes, 'confidence and self-assurance': Blair comes across as a relaxed, firmly anchored and well-adjusted personality in a generally rather sordid political world. I should add that he comes across as middle class – more specifically, northern middle class as shown by certain details of the accent he shifts into at these more personal moments. We are virtually all cynical about politics these days but, for many, the repeated evidence of an engaging 'normal person' with an infectious smile redeems Blair's unavoidable political manoeuvring. This is likely to wear thin eventually and is already perhaps doing so – cartoonists and satirists (such as the television satirist Rory Bremner) are already getting the measure of Mr Blair. But my impression at the time of writing is that it still has considerable potency. Let me emphasise that what is at issue is a public construction of normalness: we should not assume that Blair in his private life is necessarily the 'normal person' he seems to be in public. Inevitably, there are parts of his private personality that will be different from what we see in public.

An interview is more like a conversation than a political speech, more interactive more dialogical, and therefore a genre in which the 'normal person' is more likely to be prominent. But there are parts of the interview in which Blair speaks in a public, authoritative and essentially monological way convention- ally associated with politics. Here is one example, where Blair is responding to a question about the European Union and its new currency, the euro:

> and it is as I said in the e:m Wall Street Journal it is essential for our country not to end up walking away from Europe or believing there is any future at all in being on the sidelines in key debates in Europe there's no future in that for Britain . and even though I know I've got a large part of the media against me on this and even though I know I've got a lot to do in convincing the country on this it would be the biggest failure of leadership imaginable if I failed to point out to the British people the consequences of walking away from Europe and leaving ourselves without influence in it Europe matters to Britain and in or out of the euro we have got to be positive constructive engaged shaping the debate about Europe's future

Part of the authoritativeness is in the language and specifically in the modality, the degree of assertiveness Blair makes a number of categorical, authoritative assertions (e.g. 'it is essential ... not to end up walking away', 'there's no future in that for Britain', 'it would be the biggest failure of leadership imaginable'); but part of that authoritativeness is also in the way he says it. Three of the assertions are delivered in a slow, emphatic way in which he stresses each word separately ('it is essential for our country not to end up walking away from Europe', 'it would be the biggest failure of leadership imaginable', 'Europe matters to Britain'). Each assertion is accompanied with sharp emphatic vertical movements of the head and/or hand. Slowing down and using body language in this way is how Blair makes important points in his political speeches too.

But even here the 'normal person' is not entirely absent. There is a shift towards speaking in the first person singular in the middle of this extract ('even though I know I've got a large part of the media against me on this and even though I know I've got a lot to do in convincing the country on this'). What is also important and characteristic here is Blair's capacity to stand back from and comment upon the position he is in, the difficulties he faces – the 'normal person' reflecting on the politician. Furthermore certain details of Blair's accent vary according to whether he is speaking more publicly or more personally, and one of them is the pronunciation of 'I': either rhyming with 'eye' (more public) or with an 'a' sound (more personal – a part of his northern middle-class accent). 'I' is pronounced in the latter way twice in this extract – in 'I said' and the second time Blair says 'I know'. Otherwise it is pronounced in the former way. This may seem trivial, but such minor details are important in conveying the message that even when Blair is being most public and political, the anchorage in the 'normal person' is still there.

The interview continues as follows:

> FROST: and how do you deal with that problem of that problem which you rightly mentioned of the of the way some of the strongest elements of the press are ranged against this policy on Europe I mean . the Murdoch press e:m the Telegraph Group the Mail Group I mean right there you have a huge prependerance e:m how does that affect your policy making or does it just affect your policy presentation or does it just affect the fact that you don't read those papers?
>
> BLAIR: ((*laughs*)) no it means that you've got to go over their heads to a large extent . and and reach the people . and let's have an honest debate . about the euro I mean before Christmas we had some of the most ludicrous stories about what Europe was planning to do with our taxes and our lifestyle and all the rest of it there is a big big question . about Britain's future . and the future direction of the country and . I believe that Britain cannot stand apart from Europe Britain has got to be part of Europe I believe that . as I say the test on the euro is that it has to be . in our national economic interest . but what we cannot do . is stand aside as a matter of principle

In this extract there is a more marked movement between the public and the personal. First of all, Blair responds to Frost's joke at the end of the question with the sort of engaging grin (as well as a laugh) I referred to above, strongly conveying a sense of the 'normal person'. This is sustained in what he goes on to say. The pronoun 'you', used in a non-specific way (where 'you've got to' is an informal equivalent of 'one has to'), belongs to everyday language, and Blair's use of it brings the perspective of everyday life into government. Other politicians do similar things, but what makes Blair's style distinctive is a whole set of features – some of which taken singly are not at all distinctive to him). Blair also pronounces 'got to' in a conversational way with the 't' sound replaced by a glottal stop (a feature of what has recently been referred to as 'Estuary English', a fashionable style of pronunciation based upon cockney).

The part with the most sustained conversational style is: 'I mean before Christmas we had some of the most ludicrous stories about what Europe was planning to do with our taxes and our lifestyle and all the rest of it'. Blair uses 'I mean' (as well as 'you know') frequently in his more conversational talk. This is a feature of his style, which has been widely noticed and picked up by satirists. Its presence here marks the shift of style. 'Ludicrous' is a conversational word rather than a political one, and 'all the rest of it' is a conversational way of saying 'and so forth' or 'etcetera'. At the same time, both the delivery and the body language shift to being conversational – for instance, Blair expresses his contempt by elongating the first syllable of 'ludicrous', and his head movement, instead of being vertical as it was earlier, is a rather idiosyncratic oscillation from side to side. From 'there is a big big question . about Britain's future', the style shifts back – to authoritative assertions underlined by shifts in the pace and rhythm of delivery and emphatic vertical head and hand movements.

Summing up on this example, it shows first of all that Blair has developed the capacity to speak with authority, he has acquired the public, political language to do so; yet he has retained the capacity to portray himself as a politician who is redeemed by an engaging normalness – a capacity which shows itself communicatively in the inflection of the political language with a personal language.

Frost raises the issue of the peace process in Northern Ireland – the search for a political settlement of the differences between Republicans and Unionists:

FROST: Northern Ireland. Today is it on schedule?

BLAIR: – yes I think it is e:m . e: I mean partly because of the e: the strikes in the in the Gulf e:m there was an overshadowing of of the huge breakthrough before Christmas in the agreement of the e: cross-border bodies e:m and also the agreement of the the new departments in the Northern Ireland assembly . we literally have this . thi– this one last . part . e:m of the jigsaw to put in place now e: which is getting the new executive set up and dealing with the issues like decommissioning which are a problem in respect of it . but e:m I mean I jus– I can't believe we've come this far. to go back now . I mean if you think back eighteen months people would never have believed we could have come this far in Northern Ireland . you've got a whole . new situation there and I just hope there exists the imagination and vision on all sides to to bring it to fruition

Blair's response is not the conventional, bland, reassuring political response. He gives the impression of being open and honest (whether he is or not is of course another matter), and that impression depends on a rather substantial presence here of the language of the 'normal person'. He begins by cocking his head on one side in a gesture which indicates that he is thinking before he replies – there is quite a long pause – and when he does reply the intonation (his voices rises rather than falls on the word 'is') indicates only a qualified judgement that the peace process is on schedule. Notice that there are three instances of 'I mean', a favoured feature of Blair's conversational style as I indicated above. The hesitations ('e:m', 'e:') and repetitions ('of of', 'the the', 'this . thi– this') are further conversational features which are markers of a person responding in a thoughtful way rather than a politician reeling off prepared answers. When Blair says 'thi– this one last . part . e:m of the jigsaw to put in place now', he opens his hands and looks down at them (as he says 'part') as if physically trying to grasp the missing part, and then smiles broadly at Frost. Shortly afterwards he shifts to speaking in the first person: 'I mean I jus- I can't believe we've come this far, to go back now'. What comes across is a genuine, heartfelt conviction which is conveyed by the body language as well as the language – he vigorously shakes his head and smiles slightly as he says 'I mean I jus-', and 'can't believe' is delivered with heavy stress on both words and a downward movement of the head. At the end of the extract he expresses hope that the necessary vision and imagination exist. Overall, Blair gives the impression of being deeply committed to the peace process and optimistic about it, but open about its uncertainties – a frankness and degree of personal involvement which has been unusual in politics and which again is an effect of the communicative presence of the 'normal person'.

[...]

A consensus politician

There is a significant absence in Blair's style both in his political speeches and in his interviews – an absence of polemic. [...] The point is perhaps best made by a comparison between Blair and Thatcher. Thatcher's style is highly polemical and oriented to combating enemies. Here, for instance, is Thatcher speaking about trade unions:

> If some unions continue to act as an engine of inflation, and a drag on improvements in industrial efficiency, they will go on alienating themselves from the people, including those whom they represent. ... It is a patent contradiction for [them] to urge the Government to treat pensioners more generously, when it is the inflation which they have helped to create that diminishes the value of the pensioners' money. To claim social conscience in these circumstances can fairly be described as humbug.

Blair seems to avoid such polemic where possible. Inevitably, there are circumstances in which the Government does take a position against particular groups of people, and Blair can be 'tough' in such cases, as we have just seen, but he tends not to polemicise against them, but rather to seek consensus around the need to be tough. Blair might have been 'tough' in the above extract through polemicising against those whose failings he is alluding to – teachers, head teachers, educational authorities, parents. But characteristically he doesn't do that. He avoids confrontation in various ways while still being 'tough'. The failings he alludes to are alluded to through nominalisations which do not identify explicitly who failed ('failure, 'muddling through', 'second best') – hence the list of phrases without verbs I referred to above, rather than for-mulating the injunctions explicitly. Ways of acting in response to failure are formulated as passives ('will be set targets', 'will be taken over') so that the interventions of Government are backgrounded. The most contentious Govern-ment action, sacking 'poor teachers', is referred to intransitively ('poor teachers will go') as if the teachers would leave of their own accord. The focus is generally on the positive, action to overcome failings, rather than the failings themselves. Blair thus manages to be 'tough' and authoritarian towards parti-cular social groups – be it 'poor teachers', those 'dependent' on welfare, or criminals – without explicitly demonising them. The myth of 'one nation' is sustained while treating certain of its parts in sometimes draconian ways.

The contrast between the styles of Thatcher and Blair carries over into interviews. Thatcher was notorious for her combative interview style, inter-rupting interviewers, rejecting their attempts to change the topic, challenging their questions, and so forth. Blair by contrast tends to be a model of politeness in his political interviews, listening attentively to questions, being careful not to start speaking before the question is complete, giving ground to interviewers when they interrupt him. Here is one small example from the *Breakfast with Frost* interview where Frost asks a question ('what about you?') while Blair is talking, and Blair compliantly shifts from whatever he was about to say next to answer the question:

> BLAIR: and again let's just be honest about this if you look at parts of the Liberal Democrats they're modern social democrats. I mean the- . you know the- there's there's lots in common
>
> FROST: what about you?
>
> BLAIR: well I think the- if I was to sit down and say the ideological differences between myself and some of the . Liberal Democrats they're pretty small

Avoidance of polemic is an important feature of Blair's political style. It accords with the New Labour commitment to 'one-nation' politics oriented to building consensus around policies, which are represented in a value-neutral way as 'modernisation'. In that sense it meets Gould's recommendation that Blair's identity as a politician should be 'of a piece with the political positions he adopts'. It also accords with an intolerance of dissent within the ranks of the

Labour Party, and a focus on promotion and the management of consent when it comes to public consultation on policy, rather than debate and dialogue.

[...]

The conviction politician

Blair often formulates policies of the Party and the Government in a personal way as if it were simply a matter of his own commitments and aspirations. An example from the speech:

> it's pretty simple you know the type of country that I want it's a country . where our children . are proud and happy to grow up in feeling good not just about themselves . but about the community around them . I don't want them living in a country . where some of them go to school hungry . unable to learn because their parents can't afford to feed them . where they can see drugs being traded at school gates . where gangs of teenagers . hang around street corners . doing nothing spitting and swearing abusing passers-by . I don't want them brought up in that sort of country . I don't want them brought up in a country where the only way pensioners can get long-term care . is by selling their home . where people who fought . to keep this country free . are now faced every winter with the struggle for survival skimping and saving cold and alone waiting for death to take them ((*applause*)) and I will not rest . until that country is gone . until all our children live in a Britain where no child goes hungry the young are employed and the old are cherished valued till the end of their days ((*applause*))

The personal focus is sustained through this extract, beginning with 'I want' . then the three occurrences of 'I don't want', and finally 'I will not rest'. The values of the Party are transposed into the aspirations and commitment of the leader who comes across (in the Thatcher vein) as a 'conviction politician'.

But there is more than speaking personally to being a 'conviction politician'. One characteristic element of Blair's style, both in interviews and in political speeches, is that when he argues for a position, often a contentious or disputed one, he often appears to do so with real personal conviction. Again, the 'normal person' inflects the politician. This style is in contrast with the more authoritative style identified above – where Blair is setting out his own or the Government's established position rather than arguing a case. One rough-and-ready visual indicator of a shift between the styles is whether or not his forehead is furrowed – once he moves into arguing his forehead tends to become more frequently and more deeply furrowed.

An example of his argumentative style is the following answer to Frost's question on the sensitive issue of the relationship between the Labour Government and the Liberal Democratic Party. Blair has supported various forms of involvement of the Liberal Democrats in government which have given rise to fears in his own party of a coalition or even a merger:

FROST: What about the subject of the Liberal Democrats? e:m there was a story yesterday in one of the papers and other stories about the fact that three of your Cabinet are not, are not keen at all on e: getting close to the Liberal Democrats and on the idea of a e:m referendum on PR and so on. Do you plan to still proceed with that – near-marriage shall we say?

BLAIR: ((*laughs*)) well I'm still proceeding with the cooperation yes because it's it's right and it's in our interests to do so and again I . say to people just discount those type of stories. I mean this is something we've agreed ages ago . and I think it's sensible . if for example in areas like e:m . the constitution or indeed in respect of e:m education it may be or any of the issues which matter to the country you can work with another political party because there are lots of things we have in common with the Liberal Democrats why not do it? I mean what's the point of sitting there and saying we just have our own tribal positions and ((*inhales and shakes his head, smiling*))

There is a shift in style from 'and I think it's sensible'. First of all there is a change in grammatical mood – instead of making statements, Blair is now asking questions ('why not do so?', 'what's the point of sitting there . . .?'), more specifically, rhetorical questions whose answer is assumed in asking them. The formula used in the second question ('what's the point of . . .?') is very much a conversational one. But he is also speaking in a way that signals personal involvement and commitment. He stresses the word 'I' when he says 'I think that's sensible'. The pitch of his voice rises as if he was involved in a heated argument, and he also talks faster. He keeps glancing at Frost and then away from him until he asks the questions, when he keeps his eyes on Frost, simultaneously furrowing his brow and reaching his highest pitch. His face is serious and earnest until he reaches the questions, then he has a bemused slight smile, which turns into a full smile at Frost after each question. What is difficult to convey in a written description is the appearance of authenticity – Blair gives the impression (to this viewer at least) of bringing a real personal commitment to the political issue. An important aspect of it is 'common sense'. He significantly uses the word 'sensible', and the rhetorical questions, leaving the second question incomplete, and the bemused smile when asking the questions – all suggest that this is a matter of common sense, and that Blair is struggling from his commonsensical position to see what problems people could possibly have with 'cooperation'.

[. . .]

Conclusion

I have focused in this chapter on different ways in which Blair uses language, and how he moves between them, how they are brought together in his speeches and interviews. A central theme has between the tension between the public figure, the politician, and the 'normal person' – the particular form which this tension takes in the case of Blair.

Recall Philip Gould's judgement that Blair is 'a new kind of politician'. Is there perhaps finally something enigmatic about Blair, something that is difficult to pin down, which constitutes his novelty as a politician, and which centres upon the relationship between the 'normal person' and the public figure? The way in which the public figure is always anchored in and, in a sense, redeemed by the 'normal person'? In so far as that is so, sustaining the power of the enigma depends upon a continuing sense of the authenticity of Blair the 'normal person', a continuing trust in Blair as a person. But that itself is difficult to sustain in the relentless exposure he is subject to in the media, not to speak of the attentions of satirists and cartoonists. What seemed to be his distinctive personality tends to be revealed as performance. It is partly a generational matter, the transposition into a new domain of a new mix of elements, a new style, which is commonplace elsewhere. Blair's generation (and the same is true of Clinton's, though British and American versions of the style are somewhat different) handles power differently, be it in business (for instance, Richard Branson), education, or politics. They are more laid-back, and rather than drawing a line between the public person and the normal person, they build upon the latter to constitute the former. It is a matter of a change in taste, a new aesthetic, a new mood. Perhaps Mr Blair after all is not that special.

Commentators will differ in how critical they are of Blair. His political persona is clearly a crafted one, based upon calculations of what will work, fed by focus group research. His constructed personality reassures those who are able to see themselves included within it – the white, middle-class, young, successful and confident. On the other hand, it implicitly excludes those who can't, including the substantial body of losers in this increasingly polarised society. Blair's political identity gainsays his claimed concern to 'tackle social exclusion' and achieve an inclusive society. More harshly, this pretence, this extension of the marketing of commodities into the marketing of politicians, makes the claimed concern with values and morality look decidedly hollow. But is Blair really to blame for such distasteful features of contemporary public life? Does he have any alternative to going along with them? Perhaps not, but the question remains: Is the gap between what Blair claims to be and what he inevitably is consistent with his moral stance?

2

LANGUAGE AND ORGANISATIONS

This chapter explores the relationship between organisational discourse practices, power and resistance. It is concerned with the ways in which language is used to create and shape an organisation, to carve out an internal structure with circumscribed roles, responsibilities and rights for its different members, and for others with whom they interact. Covering institutional documentation, work discussions and routine talk, it also explores the discursive patterns of control and challenge as struggles for identity occur. We are interested in what has been defined as 'institutional language' (Thornborrow 2002; Drew and Heritage 1992) – talk that has pre-inscribed participant roles; is explicitly task-oriented and framed within institutional contexts, as well as other types of discourse. For instance, talk about organisations, along with employees' social chat is seen as just as significant in the construction of institutional culture and identity. There exists an extensive and quite varied literature on the language of organisations (see Thornborrow 2002; Walsh 2001; Wodak 1996; Boden 1994; Drew and Heritage 1992). The readings selected here have been chosen because they are useful in developing particular theoretical themes of this chapter, and do so in a way that advances understanding of how power and discourse may function in specific organisational settings. The first three readings that are discussed all touch on contexts of social welfare of one kind or another; the fourth concerns itself with staff interaction in government departments; and the final reading focuses on communication in call centres.

After initially discussing why discourse is key to the way an organisation is defined, we look first at how the language of UK social security literature constructs and steers claimants in ways that are bureaucratically convenient.

From here, we switch attention to spoken discourse, to consider how the everyday talk of US public assistance workers categorises recipients of state aid as, by and large, 'undeserving', 'manipulative' and 'indolent'. Attempts made by some women on welfare to rework this 'spoiled' (Goffman 1963) image reveal how entangled such resistance is with dominant ideologies – how the redefining of their selves intertextually draws on conventional discourses of motherhood and work ethics. We look further at intertextual processes in relation to the emergence of new linguistic registers in the workplace. In the contemporary world of organisations, those in authority have seized on the discursive tool of **conversationalisation** (Fairclough 2001) – a talk strategy of apparent friendliness and informality that gets exploited by managers as a powerful resource to define and direct. Yet employees, too, can tactically take up small talk for their own instrumental goals by using it, for instance, as a lead-in to request a day's leave. The transactional function of small talk is also seen in our focus on call centres where workers are given communication training in making their telephone manner more approachable, personable and polite – to follow a standardised script that helps brand the organisation they are working for. As language is used to renegotiate identity dynamically, exert and resist authority, and parade as friendly for marketing reasons, we start to understand how complex and multifaceted the relationship is between power and discourse within organisational contexts.

WHAT'S LANGUAGE GOT TO DO WITH ORGANISATIONS?

In recent years, organisations and how they function have attracted the interest of those working in the field of sociolinguistics. Analysis of what an 'organisation' is has taken a linguistic turn and moved beyond Giddens's (1989: 276) definition of it as a 'large association of people run on impersonal lines, set up to achieve specific goals' (quoted in Iedema and Wodak 1999: 10). Understanding the discourse of an organisation is now considered central to appreciating how power, identity, conflict and resistance interrelate within work settings. Language plays a central role in the everyday life of an organisation: the greetings and conversations people have in the corridors; debates that occur in meetings; verbal warnings given to employees; telephone calls; letters; or the advertising jingles of a sales promotion. Moreover, organisations are not merely 'out there' but are constructed by this very language that routinely takes place between people. Mumby and Clair pinpoint its significance:

> Organisations exist only in so far as their members create them through discourse. This is not to claim that organisations are 'nothing but' discourse, but rather that discourse is the principal means by which organisation members create a coherent social reality that frames their sense of who they are. (Mumby and Clair 1997: 181)

Accordingly, an organisation, its workers and others with whom they come into contact are continuously being constructed and reconstructed as daily interaction occurs.

A primary concern of one branch of sociolinguistics – that of critical discourse analysis (CDA) – is how the organisational context functions as a site of struggle over meaning and identity. CDA explores the textual expression of power, conflict and resistance and relates this to broader social structures and change. Bourdieu (1990: 137) notes that the power to construct categories or groups is the power of 'worldmaking'. As people strive to secure the identity they want, to determine a social reality which best fulfils their needs, what serves the interests of some may not serve the interests of others. An organisation's literature – its application forms, memos, mission statements and such like – positions people and affords them different degrees of power. Critical discourse analysts are interested in the linguistic processes by which this occurs. Moreover, since routine spoken interaction is just as crucial in determining who people are, CDA also examines everyday talk as a negotiation of identity. Language is not just a place where all this happens, but it is also used by speakers as a tool – Fairclough (2001: 73) calls it a 'stake' – in the battle to constitute perceptions of the world, their selves and each other.

THE LANGUAGE OF SOCIAL WELFARE

The context of social welfare is one area in which discursive struggles of identity occur with very real consequences for those with least economic capital (Bourdieu 1977). People requesting social security payments encounter a system that institutionally positions them as powerless in a variety of ways. As Reading 2.1 discusses, access to state resources or public assistance is largely contingent upon how claimants 'fit' pre-existing categories and classifications of a bureaucratic organisation designed to filter out fraud. From the very beginning, the filling in of forms narrowly circumscribes identity by asking people to tick a box describing the type of client they are. Define themselves outside these boxes and they risk their chances of securing money on which to live. In fact, a degree of institutional literacy is required in order to complete documentation like this successfully. What's more, those asking for support have to sign declarations of truth and can be asked to provide photocopied evidence to back up their claim. This climate of suspicion also contextualises spoken interactions between applicants and officials. Interviews are held against a backdrop of 'beat-a-cheat' campaigns which encourage neighbours to telephone the Benefit Fraud Hotline to tell on those they think are making disingenuous requests for welfare aid. So, how claimants represent themselves through talk to those charged with 'gatekeeping' state assistance plays a significant part in their economic survival. Given that benefit officials hold the purse strings, their construction of a claimant's identity may have significant consequences too regarding the help that's eventually offered. What discursive strategies then do officials use to categorise those asking for assistance? Against these, what linguistic resources can claimants possibly draw upon to contest and reconstruct spoiled identity? How can pejorative discourses be reworked to offer alternative, more positive accounts of self? It is to these questions that Reading 2.2 and Reading 2.3 attend.

Institutional categories and constructions

The first reading, by Sarangi and Slembrouck, focuses on the bureaucratic nature of official documents. In particular, it discusses how, until fairly recently, the layout and language of application forms for incapacity benefit and income supplement required literacies that claimants might lack. The authors initially map some general properties of forms and comment on their design to service institutional needs rather than those of claimants. For instance, to an outsider, form names and numbers do little to reveal how an organisation is structured. How client information works to enhance or jeopardise a claim is not transparent, and spaces on the form entitled 'for office use only' record details that applicants typically do not see. The quantity and type of information a client is allowed to give is determined by limited space, dotted lines, multiple choice questions and such like. Claimants are forced to remould their selves, abilities and needs, as the categories demand. State benefit forms presuppose an 'implied client' as institutional assumptions are made about those applying for help. Indeed, this reformulation of client identity is ongoing as the application form is channelled through the bureaucratic machinery of welfare aid. Located within discourses of suspicion, those requesting public assistance are, at times, perceived negatively and blamed personally for their dependence on welfare. Later, Reading 2.2 documents this happening in practice as benefit workers' everyday talk constructs images of applicants as 'deceitful', 'lazy' and 'unclean'. As claimants rarely have access to these subsequent processes or conversations, at this level, they are clearly excluded from decisions and definitions made about them.

Fairclough (2001: 176) argues that as it categorises, classifies, shifts and processes people in the modern world, bureaucracy functions as a form of state control. He argues that the growth of capitalism has meant greater intrusion into people's lives, and that this is especially evident as the welfare state has evolved. Without a doubt, for those reliant on means-tested benefits, rights to privacy often do not exist and their lives are turned into what Sarangi and Slembrouck term 'open books for bureaucratic gaze'. This raises an issue that will be discussed later regarding the defining and dichotomising of 'public' and 'private' spheres of interaction. Certainly, for some groups of people the difference between the two is academic to their own experiences. Hurtado explains how, in the US, the 'distinction is relevant only for the white middle and upper classes since historically the American state has intervened constantly in the private lives and domestic arrangements of the working class' (1989: 849). In the UK, a single mother requesting benefit may be required to disclose information regarding intimate relationships, insofar as they relate to current cohabitation status and parentage of her children. Research conducted into the discourses of lone motherhood in the 1990s (Atkinson & Oerton 1996; Atkinson, Oerton & Burns 1998; Oerton and Atkinson 1997, 1999) verified how intimidated and powerless claimants felt in interviews with welfare state officials. One lone mother, Jemma, was called in to her local office to answer charges of fraud after a neighbour had inaccurately advised the Department of Social Security (DSS) that she was cohabiting with a boyfriend:

> You've gotta go down (.) DSS and (1.0) tell them everything that's gone on (.) nightmare (.) it's dreadful down there you go down there and (1.0) well they make you feel so small (.) it's just their attitude down there (.) they look down at you (.) I've had it done to me (.) someone phoning up and saying oh she's got so-and-so living with her (.) and I mean they weren't living with me (.) but I mean you know it's really frightening (laughs nervously) go into this little room you know (.) desk (.) chair (.) sat down (.) be interrogated (.) of course they're only allowed to stay (.) was it about three nights a week and it can't be on consecutive nights (.) or something like that (.) they said someone's been to visit you and this is his [car] registration number (.) and you go in there and they ask you this and that and the other and you have to give them a description of your ex (.) in case maybe they're going to watch your house and they're going to see if he is living there or if he has moved out (.) it's just really embarrassing (.) you've got nothing to hide and you could feel yourself blushing. (Atkinson and Oerton 1996)

Here, bureaucratic definitions of what it meant to be a 'lone mother' extended beyond the filling in of forms to invade the private lives of individuals. From this account, if she was to remain eligible for state help, personal relationships had to be defined in accordance with institutional rules and regulations (whether lone mothers chose to attend to these in practice was a different matter). The organisation of social welfare 'boxed' Jemma into a category that prescribed how often she could have her partner to stay. Another lone mother, Caroline, commented on the definitional inflexibility of the category she was forced to slot into:

> I'm classed as a single parent in one respect but in another I'm not because we both bring her up (.) he's [father of her daughter] always been there every step of the way (.) I don't actually live with him but (.) we bring her up together (.) in the eyes of the state I'm a single parent. (Atkinson and Oerton 1996)

Given the rigidity of bureaucratic definitions, lone mothers who were economically disadvantaged found themselves having to 'round up square pegs' (Sarangi and Slembrouck 1996) in order to survive materially. In other words, to access benefits, their accounts of self were designed to fit the pre-existing categories of welfare aid.

Accusations that inaccessibility and disempowerment characterised welfare aid encounters has led to a change in the way some benefit literature is designed. Family income supplement forms and leaflets, for example, have undergone what Fairclough (2001: 181–4) calls a process of 'easification' – a manipulation of style and structure. Purportedly to help democratise the relationship between provider and recipient of state aid, they now draw upon the discourses of advertising. User-friendly vocabulary is employed along with less complex syntax and clearer layouts. **Synthetic personalisation** positions prospective claimants as individual consumers, who are, accordingly, directly addressed and textually placed on an equal footing with those providing the service. The tone is friendly and informal. The use of advertising hooks is not uncommon. In detailing what entitlements are available, school meals, milk, vitamins, pre-scriptions and so on are all listed under the catchy statement of 'And these things free'. Yet to what extent do such changes reattribute authority and status to claimants who are economically disadvantaged? On the surface, less jargon and a simplified design may mean such forms and leaflets are easier to read but a more critical interpretation of the use of consumerist discourses is needed if we are to interrogate the dynamics of power here.

Fairclough argues that the appropriation of such language is part of a wider tendency of **discourse technologisation** in modern society. In the last decade or so, there has been an increased general awareness of language and how to use it for particular effect. For example, these days, there is greater knowledge surrounding the discourse of political spin. Expert 'discourse technologists' have emerged to offer guidance ('social skills' training) in the linguistics tools best used to persuade, inspire confidence and court popularity. Furthermore, the techniques on offer are defined as being relatively context free and, as such, can be applied to a variety of settings. As certain language strategies become transferable, textual **hybridisation** results as discourses traditionally associated with specific areas start to colonise other domains of interaction. So, as we've seen, the language of sales is now often used to sell public services as products; 'friendly' conversational talk is currently adopted by managers to mask their authority (more of this later) and therapeutic discourse has begun to pervade a good deal of our everyday lives from discussions on the radio to the pastoral care of university students and staff. Businesses draw on the language of 'self development'. The 'mission statement' of Mary Kay Cosmetics – one of the largest direct sellers of skincare products in the United States – reads, 'We will also reach out to the heart and spirit of women enabling personal growth and fulfilment for the women whose lives we touch' (Mary Kay Cosmetics 2002).

The technologisation of discourse typically involves simulation of some kind. For instance, the setting up of a relationship of apparent equality between those with different degrees of power is clearly disingenuous. However 'democratic' benefit forms appear to be, and however genial the commodified language sounds, ultimately clients have to complete such documentation according to the script of a bureaucratic institution. Moreover, the power to judge claims as

ate or not rests with someone other than the applicant. Given the
chical nature of the welfare aid system, the construction of affable
lliness between provider and claimant cannot be sustained beyond the
stic informality of the form. In addition, Fairclough notes how:

> synthetic personalisation may strengthen the position of the bureaucracy
> and the state by disguising its instrumental and manipulative relationship
> to the mass of the people beneath a façade of a personal and equal
> relationship – but only so long as people do not see through it! (2001: 184)

This caveat is important as it points to an issue to which we shall return later –
that the negotiation of identity is not inevitably all one-way, not solely in the
hands of people with organisational authority. The defining of self is more
complex than this, more dynamic and fluid, so that even those with seemingly
few resources may resist, or accommodate and rework the roles that bureaucratic procedures prescribe.

So, specifically then, what are these roles, and how are they linguistically
realised in the spoken discourse of welfare aid? The next two excerpts, from
Pelissier Kingfisher's research into women on welfare, explore benefit workers'
and recipients' discursive constitutions of their world. We have already seen
how social security forms are styled in an attempt to control clients – how
applicants are recast into category types that suit the bureaucratic demands of
the organisation they encounter. Set against a backdrop of unequal power
relations and social structures of modern US society, Reading 2.2 attends to the
way in which officials' reformulations of claimant identity function in everyday
conversation.

Pelissier Kingfisher (1996a) argues that in order to understand why workers
may opt to define clients in pejorative ways, an appreciation of how they are
occupationally positioned is needed. Assistance Payments (AP) employees,
working at the forefront of the US welfare system, are largely women – in
keeping with the stereotype of caregivers as female. In executing benefit aid to
those in need, they are placed at the bottom of the organisation's hierarchy,
attributed low status, offered few promotional opportunities and overburdened
with caseloads. As the author comments, 'AP work reflects the gendered
organisation of many government bureaucracies', and the women Pelissier
Kingfisher interviewed felt 'resentful', 'trapped', 'frustrated' and 'powerless'
(1996a: 84). To lessen the unremitting pressure of heavy and demanding work,
they developed coping strategies – one of which involved the assessment of
claimants. In the Kenyon County welfare office on which she focused, the
defining of client eligibility for aid became a powerful resource in the struggle to
handle hefty workloads – fewer 'eligible' clients meant less bureaucracy to
process. Pelissier Kingfisher comments on the complex interplay between
discourse, organisational hierarchy, local task management and the power to
construct identity:

AP workers are in the business of constructing clients out of otherwise significantly more complicated human beings ... Once they have transformed people into 'clients', workers can respond by providing (or not providing) particular services, depending on what type of client the applicant now is, if indeed they qualify as a client at all. Stereotypes provide a useful short-cut in this process insofar as they simplify the social world: the range of people who should receive assistance is narrowed, and, among that narrow group, the number of people who should receive good service is further limited. (ibid.: 98–9)

At the time that this research was being undertaken, New Right Republican discourses were proposing cuts to medical services for those claimants with dependent children, and young unmarried mothers were being condemned as a burden on state resources. In the UK, similar sorts of vilifying public discourses were circulating. In the early 1990s, the then Home Secretary, Michael Howard, argued that it would be a good thing if more unmarried mothers gave up their children for adoption. As the press jumped on the moral panic bandwagon, more stringent state control was called for to force women into conventional modes of motherhood:

you can have as many babies as you want – if you don't ask the Government to take care of them. But when you start asking the Government to take care of them, the Government ought to have some control over you. (*Daily Mail* 11/5/93)

With a local need to cut caseloads, AP workers readily drew upon the prevailing negative public discourses about welfare claimants. As those requesting aid were discursively constructed as 'deceitful', 'lazy' and 'unclean', they were actively defined as 'undeserving' – of time, considerate treatment and even, on occasion, of state help.

On a day-to-day level, the conversations that AP workers engaged in clearly articulated their perceptions of clients as a very different group of people. However, the stories and anecdotes that were told were just as much about creating their own subjectivities – their own sense of selves as a cohesive unit of like-minded employees – as they were about constructing negative images of claimants. Narratives were, significantly, jointly produced, as support and empathy for each other were linguistically realised through a matching of anecdotes, laughter, jokes and **minimal responses**. These expressions of solidarity accompanied accounts of clients behaving 'badly', which interestingly were often represented as insults to the workers themselves than as desperate measures of economic survival. For instance, the use of first person pronouns in one anecdote reveals how a worker (called Fran Knight) perceives an applicant's 'lies' as a personal affront, with damaging consequences to the claim for state aid ('I'm empathetic to all my clients 'til they lie to me. Once they lie to me I hate them and I won't give them anything'). The power to give or withhold public assistance here seems very much interwoven with a discursive conceptualising of identity and relations. As Pelissier Kingfisher comments, 'in their own phrasing, *they* were the ones who paid clients' rent, processed their food stamps, and stopped the gas company from turning off their utilities'. At other times, claimants were represented as recalcitrant children needing the discipline of a firm parent. So, an eighteen year old woman is referred to diminutively as a 'little girl' and, in narrating particular anecdotes, workers often **double-voiced** clients, recalling, in a whiney, childish tone what they had apparently said. The implications for power and status here are clear: those asking for help were afforded little respect or consideration as responsible adults. The narratives also evidence how the behaviour of a few was generalised and applied to the client population as a whole. The discussion of a local stabbing which involved only one known claimant is extended into a longer conversation in which the categories of 'client' and 'criminal' overlap, and are, at times, conflated and used synonymously.

In discursively locating clients in an illegal and dangerous underworld, the reading describes how they are routinely characterised as antagonistic to norms of good conduct. The depiction of claimants as hostile and aggressive is developed further in the final account of workers' talk in which the author analyses the narrative construction of a female client as a child abuser. Here, in the transcribed exchanges between welfare officials and an African American woman (Lana Tucker), Pelissier Kingfisher shows how definition of claimants intersected with broader discourses of sexism and racism. It seems that when workers dealt with female clients, they frequently called into question their lack of moral fitness or mothering skills. This is evidenced by the analysis of officials' talk to Lana and to each other. For Harriet, the employee centrally involved in the case, Lana's cultural identity (being a black woman) worked against her as it was pejoratively equated with 'irresponsibility, shiftiness, sloppiness and laziness'. In tracing the sequential development of the worker's dialogue with both client and colleagues, we see how Harriet progressively offers increasingly detailed and elaborated accounts of Lara's child apparently being hit by her. To bolster the credibility of her construction of Lana as abusive to her children, Harriet selectively pulls into play particular pieces of information, which she recontextualises to fit her own framing of the story. For instance, the disclosure that this client had previously lost custody of a child is used to situate her as a 'bad mother', despite this having happened, for unknown reasons, seven years earlier when she was sixteen years old. In the retelling of her interview with Lana to another colleague, Harriet's version of events, and character assassination of her client, is supported by her co-worker. The mother's refusal to co-operate with questions about what happened is interpreted as evidence of her guilt.

Accommodation and resistance

Overt resistance to institutional discursive practices by recipients of state assistance is uncommon, if not just for reasons of economic survival. However, in contexts where less is at stake, there is evidence that some clients are prepared to question strategies that narrowly prescribe identity or invade personal space. Fraser (1989) discusses Rains's sociological study of black teenagers who were being counselled by social workers to self-reflect on the circumstances that led to their becoming pregnant. She notes how they resolutely defended their private lives from state intrusion:

> The young black women resisted the terms of the psychiatric discourse and the language game of question-and-answer employed in the counselling sessions. They disliked the social worker's stance of non-directiveness and moral neutrality – her unwillingness to say what *she* thought – and they resented what they considered her intrusive, overly personal questions. These girls did not acknowledge her right to question them in this fashion, given that they could not ask 'personal' questions of her in turn. Rather, they construed 'personal questioning' as a privilege reserved to close friends and intimates under conditions of reciprocity. (quoted in Fraser 1989: 179)

As a group, these teenagers developed a variety of discursive strategies to counter institutional reformulation of their identities. For instance, they responded to a therapeutic elicitation that asked how they felt about getting pregnant with carnivalesque humour ('everybody started mimicking questions they supposedly had had put to them'). As Fraser (1989: 180) points out:

> they were keenly aware of the power subtext underlying their interactions with the social worker ... In effect these young Black women blocked efforts to inculcate in them white, middle-class norms of individuality and affectivity. They refused the case-worker's inducements to rewrite themselves as psychologized selves ...

Houghton's (1995) research on adolescent Latina women also uncovered strategies of explicit challenge as they resisted therapy that attempted to address their contraceptive 'problems', reliance on welfare aid and apparent disregard for work. McElhinny further discusses these teenagers' discursive struggles to determine their own identities. She points out how they marked their dissociation from these encounters by 'mimicking almost to the point of parody' the linguistic strategies used by the therapist. In this context, they also strategically adopted a solidary interactional style with each other that was typically employed in free-time periods. As McElhinny observes, the 'use of "ordinary" talk in "institutional" settings was a form of resistance' (1997: 118).

For those who are not part of a group but on their own, open contestation such as this is, arguably, more difficult. Given the power of institutional reformulations, it is understandable why clients like Lana (discussed above) prefer not to engage with welfare officials. Claimants are clearly aware that the content of what they say can be recontextualised and used against them. When economic survival is the priority, a strategy of silence may be the best option – although, as discussed earlier, even this can be read as culpability. For the same reason, women on welfare tend not to contest publicly the derogatory discourses made about them. However, lack of a direct and explicit challenge does not necessarily mean that pejorative categorisations are accepted as legitimate. Alternative, more positive accounts of self might be constructed in safer contexts, 'backstage', away from those with institutional authority – and, as such, constitute what are known as 'hidden transcripts' (Scott 1986: 22). Moreover, as Pelissier Kingfisher argues, 'accommodation may be strategic, "a choreographed demonstration of co-operation" (Faith 1994: 39) that is in fact a form of resistance'. In certain instances, 'co-operation' can be 'contestation' (Pelissier Kingfisher 1996a: 7). A client's language can both acquiesce and challenge the negative images that welfare aid organisations articulate. Elsewhere, Pelissier Kingfisher develops this further, pointing out that in talk, '"mixed forms" may occur, comprising both accommodation and resistance. Each is often present in the other: resistance to a dominant discourse of necessity partakes of that discourse, while apparent accommodation may be a tool of subversion' (1996b: 540).

An example of this in practice can be seen in research done by Oerton and Atkinson (1999). They report an account from one UK lone mother, Emily, who, in interview with a welfare aid official, was required to reveal the identity of her daughter's father in order that he be assessed by the Child Support Agency for financial support of his child. Although separated, they remained on good terms, and her ex-partner already helped in other ways with his daughter's care. Concerned with protecting him and their healthy rapport as well as successfully securing state money on which to live, Emily represents herself in a way that risks being judged as morally lax and careless:

> with Mary her father I just made up a name (.) a place a first name a place was it (.) I and that was it I said it was just a one-night stand and that was it (.) cause I mean I get help off Mary's father I could never (.) he's not working now he's a carer (.) he cares for his mother's elderly aunt (.) he can't get a good job either so he could never afford to pay what the child support agency actually want (.) I couldn't do that to him
>
> (Oerton and Atkinson 1999)

With few options open to her, Emily reconstitutes her identity as someone who is prepared to have sex outside a stable relationship and careless of contraception. In so doing, she both draws on and perpetuates pejorative mainstream views about the behaviour of lone mothers. Clearly here, when the alternative means economic vulnerability, being seen as promiscuous is the lesser evil. The colloquial phrase 'one-night stand' – with all its likely connotations of immorality – is used to subvert the assessment criteria that would determine her ineligibility for state benefit. Emily's accommodation of derogatory discourses undermines a bureaucracy intent on narrowly prescribing the relationship she could have with the father of her child. In this regard, it constitutes resistance.

In theorising contestation, Pelissier Kingfisher also draws on the notion of **reverse discourse** (Foucault 1981) – where speakers use the language of dominant discourses to their own advantage. Reading 2.3 documents how both 'mixed' and 'reverse' discourses work in a US context, tracing the negotiation of identity by those in receipt of public assistance. Elsewhere, the author contends that women in the welfare system are often portrayed as powerless and given little credit as active agents struggling to define and improve their worlds (Pelissier Kingfisher 1996a: 3–4). In attempting to readdress this, she details their 'engagement in producing, reproducing, and contesting identity, ideology, institutional arrangements, and policy' as it 'manifests itself in language'. She adds that 'recipients and workers are in continual struggle with themselves, one another and the welfare system in their attempts to impose their view of reality; particular interpretations, stereotypes, ideologies and policies are the site of these struggles'. Pelissier Kingfisher conducted interviews with women from Low Income people for Equality (LIFE) and the Madrid Welfare Rights Organisation (MWRO) which were supplemented by audio-recordings of their everyday conversations. As relatively 'safe' environments away from institutional eyes, this data documents, she argues, the complex processes of 'social construction in action'.

The claimants in the study drew on a range of strategies to contest their stigmatisation. By and large, they appropriated for their own ends dominant ideologies of one kind or another. The most commonly used tactic – what Pelissier Kingfisher calls the 'bad-people-exist-but-I'm-not-one-of-them' strategy – entailed the women giving credence to the notion of an 'undeserving poor' but discursively positioning themselves (as 'deserving') outside of this. Upholding this distinction allowed them to attack a policy that advocated more widespread adoption of punitive measures against all women on welfare. Reformulating themselves as reluctant claimants ('the MAJORITY of us out there on it is NOT like that I bust my ass trying to get off [welfare]') and keen to work, they constituted a very different group from 'welfare degenerates' whose curtailment of reproductive rights (through forced sterilisation) they supported. Espousing the work ethic, the women's reconstruction of themselves as separate from other claimants relied in part on the existence of these as a credible negative client group. Accordingly, mainstream views about welfare recipients being 'lazy' and 'work shy' remained unchanged. As such, their talk was 'mixed' – dominant discourses were resisted insofar as they disparagingly impacted upon the women themselves – yet perpetuated in that the validity of the stereotypes was not questioned.

The second most common response to stigma involved confessing to 'undesirable' behaviours, but adding a disclaimer regarding their cause. This strategy accommodated and resisted the prevailing view of benefit applicants as 'welfare cheats'. For instance, some women admitted making fraudulent claims but rationalised these to be the result of an unfair system that discriminated against them. They were left, they reasoned, with no option but to fabricate. The 'welfare-made-me-do-it' argument followed a typical pattern in which claimants reported how their initial candour in social benefit interviews worked against the securing of food, money and shelter. They framed unsuccessful claims as punishment for being truthful, and represented themselves as forced to practise dishonesty for survival. As such, they justified their actions. Significantly, the women's accounts were generally concluded with an evaluation of lying as an unfavourable mode of behaviour. Close examination of this strategy reveals a 'reverse discourse' at play. In defining themselves as essentially 'honest', they hold the makers of unfair welfare policy culpable for their fraud. They appropriate the discourse of their critics, turn it around and use it against them. Pelissier Kingfisher notes that as legislators were discursively constructed as 'irresponsible', the women 'reconstituted dominant notions of responsibility to reflect well on themselves and poorly on those who would portray them as immoral' (Pelissier Kingfisher 1996b: 552). This example is useful in moving us theoretically forward. Clearly, what it means to be 'dishonest', 'irresponsible' and so on isn't fixed or singular. Such terms can have multiple readings and uses, and this instability of meaning allowed the women to renegotiate their subjectivity. For them, 'dishonesty' meant 'survival' while 'irresponsibility' was characterised as the placing of economically vulnerable, otherwise 'honest' citizens in an impossible situation. The women's talk was both the site (place) and stake (weapon) in the contestation of definition and in the reformulation of their selves.

These welfare claimants also engaged in other positive reconstructions of identity. In reconstituting themselves as 'hard workers' and 'just ordinary people', they challenged the stereotype of women on state benefit as lazy and promiscuous. If women engaged in prostitution, it was argued, it's because, once again, the system doesn't provide them with adequate financial support. Rather than be castigated, the women asserted, they ought to be seen as victims of an uncaring and punitive public assistance policy. Appropriating the voice of 'human rights', they called for enough money upon which to live decently – as tax-paying Americans, they laid claim to economic security. In drawing on other mainstream discourses, they represented themselves as aspiring to conventional models of marriage and motherhood, at times depicting the nuclear family as ideal. As they talked, the women's interactive strategies jointly constructed their co-membership of a stigmatised group. Attending to each other's **positive face** (Brown and Levinson 1987), they employed minimal responses ('yeah', 'mm', 'huh'), and **simultaneous speech**, asserting common ground through the reiteration of values and opinions.

Pelissier Kingfisher's research offers a theoretically sophisticated view of language, identity and power. The discursive negotiation of self and others has been seen to be both complex and dynamic as the struggle for meaning takes place. Moreover, accommodation and resistance can function as part-and-parcel of the same text, working together to articulate views which in themselves are open to interpretation as hegemonic or not. As she points out:

A piece of talk does not have to be definitively – within all contexts and at all levels of interpretation – conservative *or* subversive, despite the analytic distinction between the two; nor does it have to be spoken with particular conscious intent by a unitary agent. Rather, accommodation and resistance are in constant struggle with each other, within power relations, by subjects who both constitute and are constituted by the discourses to which they have access and which they produce. (1996b: 553)

CONVERSATIONALISATION

The ongoing tension in the battle to define identity and determine meaning can be seen clearly in the next reading (2.4) which analyses how power is managed through the expression of small talk in four New Zealand government departments. Although this type of talk (sometimes described as 'phatic') is often regarded as peripheral, marginal or minor to the discourse of main business, Holmes (2000) maintains that to dismiss it as such ignores its centrality and importance in the everyday, ongoing construction of our selves and others. In initially focussing on how managers use small talk to assert authority and control over their staff, she links this with the emergence of informality in the workplace. As such, Reading 2.4 usefully ties together several of the theoretical threads we have discussed so far. Earlier, we noted how the use of synthetic personalisation in welfare aid literature disguised unequal power relations – how the friendly tone of benefit leaflets which textually positioned claimants as consumers actually masked bureaucratic control. The analysis of talk in the contexts that Holmes explores witnesses a similar process at play in the technologization of discourse: **conversationalisation** (Fairclough: 1995). On the surface, manager use of small talk appears to minimise status difference and foreground solidarity, yet a closer examination reveals it as merely another tool by which power is wielded.

According to Fairclough (1992b: 204), conversational discourses, at one time confined to the private domain, have increasingly been appropriated for use in the public sphere. So, for instance, UK morning television presenters are typically 'chatty' to their audience, addressing them directly as if talking on a one-to-one basis; health professionals are seen to adopt an amicable, relaxed and familiar style with their patients employing minimal responses and open-ended questions; and, in an effort to project themselves as less formal and distant, politicians use colloquial expressions to project the voice of ordinary experience (see Reading 1.5 of Chapter 1). As discourses from the private and public sphere start to move and intermingle, the ideological dichotomy set up between them becomes questionable, and accordingly their very definitions need reconsideration. We've already seen how the distinction between these two spheres has been blurred for recipients of state aid as their personal lives become public property under bureaucratic gaze. The appropriation of small talk as part of 'managerspeak' is further evidence of discourse colonisation – and, in this new context, what it means also needs to be interrogated. Although typically associated with interpersonal solidarity between equals, what is its function in professional settings between those of different rank? Are we to assume that its use signals a more equable relationship between managers and their staff? On the contrary, claims Holmes, 'doing power' has simply gone underground with small talk being the expression of what she calls 'subterranean power construction'.

In being contrasted with 'instrumental' or 'transactional' talk, small talk has traditionally been viewed as having less to do with tasks and information than it has to do with being sociable. It has generally been seen to consist of 'safe', neutral topics like 'the weather' (Coupland and Ylanne-McEwen 2000) and 'how are you?' utterances (Coupland, Coupland and Robinson 1992). So defined, it was considered useful in 'oiling the wheels' of interaction, establishing a rapport between speakers while reducing interpersonal distance. Yet in the last decade or so, more sophisticated analyses of small talk have emerged which have examined its functions in a wide variety of contexts ranging from family gatherings around the dinner-table (Blum-Kulka 1997, 2000) and the talk of close female friends (Coates 1989, 1996, 2000) to more institutional and occupational contexts involving communication between patients and health professionals (Ragan 2000).

Small talk as transactional in the world of work has already been researched in an analysis of young and old speakers. In a study exploring interactions between home care assistants and their elderly clients (Atkinson and Coupland 1988; Atkinson 1993), it was reported as significant in defining the occupational status of carers. Institutionally, their job description stipulated duties such as talking and listening to be as equally important as the more practical tasks of shopping and cleaning, as one carer reiterated during interview:

> If they [elderly clients] are very shut off from the world (.) you've got to really talk to them bring them out (.) I ask questions and I talk about the weather anything (.) as long as you get them talking to you. (Atkinson 1993)

Another home care assistant, in pinpointing how small talk was instrumentally useful in re-engaging 'socially-alienated' clients, noted that 'what you've got to do is to stimulate the conversation by talking about everyday things that is (*sic*) happening'. Yet another interviewee reported that if they didn't do this, 'you'd just be a cleaner then wouldn't you ... like a daily help sort of thing well we're not that at all we've got to be carers'. Clearly, small talk here plays an important role in the marking of professional status. Occupying a fairly central place in the communication between young and old, it is neither peripheral nor minor. For these carers, at least, it *was* the discourse of main business, although given the potential threat to face that perceived loneliness or social disengagement brings, in real-time encounters it might well have been glossed as interactional – as just 'ordinary chat' establishing friendly rapport. The multifunctionality of talk allows for this: small talk can mean different things to different people. For home care assistants, in being part of their formal job responsibilities, it can be read as an organisational discourse imperative, bolstering their identity as professionals engaged in some kind of social work. For elderly clients, it can be defined as friendly, everyday gossip about the familiar. While this might work for some, it is not surprising that for others the tension around what small talk means is undoubtedly problematic. Its definition – as discourse principally concerned with effecting solidarity – clashes with it being for some home helps just one of many work duties needing to be done:

> I find it often difficult er erm I find I'm watching the time a lot and saying that I can't stay and talk too long now I must do a little bit of [house]work for you ... but they [elderly clients] will try and keep you talking. (Atkinson 1993: 206)

Part of what is going on here is the struggle to determine the function of this talk; to ascertain who has the authority to decide when it should begin and end; to establish what interactional rights each speaker has in directing the way the conversation develops; and so on. In looking at communication between government employees in Reading 2.4, Holmes too addresses such issues. Her analysis reports initially on a number of manager conversational control strategies that constitute overt and obvious expressions of power. For instance, it was senior staff that set the agenda for talk; gave direct orders; evaluated the actions of others; and summarised decisions. Yet more subtle, indirect and covert expressions of organisational status were seemingly articulated through managers' use of small talk. Holmes found that while it *could* serve to reduce social distance between a superior and her staff, it was also used to foreground power difference and hierarchy. She notes that 'the senior participant generally determines how much small talk there will be at the beginning and end of an interaction' (2000: 52) and this is illustrated by transcribed examples of openings and closings in practice. So, in one extract, a manager signals to her personal assistant that their interaction is at an end by switching to small talk – a typical move towards conversational closure. In another, the brief responses of a different manager, followed by a marked topic-switch ('now how can I help you') express his reluctance to be drawn into a worker's social chat. He clearly assumes command of the exchange.

In being a site of negotiation, however, small talk also offers up space for employees with relatively less authority to challenge managers' conversational control strategies and direct the interaction in a way that suits them. The reading reveals its use by one worker as a lead-in to a disclosure of personal problems, obliging her boss to listen or else appear insensitive and rude. Other workers adopted it as a precursor to requesting time off, or as tactic to mark solidarity with a manager in the hope that this might enhance support for promotion. Holmes concludes that while 'management of small talk is one way in which superiors constitute their organisational control ... subordinates may challenge, resist or subvert the discourse' (2000: 57). Small talk, she adds,

fundamentally social kind of talk, can serve transactional as well as inter-
rsonal goals', and workers here exploit its multifunctionality in an attempt to
distribute conversational power.

'STYLING' THE WORKER

Small talk as transactional surfaces in other workplace contexts too. In the late
1980s, Eliasoph (1987) documented what Coupland calls its 'commercialisa-
tion' (2000: 12). This study examined the promotional techniques of the
'skincare company' Mary Kay Cosmetics, and showed how the training and
policing of employees' linguistic behaviour, illustrated discourse technologisation in practice. Eliasoph explains how:

> Mary Kay teaches her saleswomen to use 'warm chatter' to sell their
> products to 'casual' groups of 'friends' … [the] saleswomen typically
> explain that their sales pitches are more successful if they 'do some warm
> chatter' before making the sale, the friendliness has been completely
> instrumentalized.

Workers' talk is thus 'styled' (Cameron 2000) to be as affable and pleasant as
possible so as to maximise company profits. In order to establish rapport with
the customer, small talk is strategically employed to reduce interpersonal
distance, and do positive politeness by claiming common ground. The sales-
women promoted themselves as likeable and sociable – as 'friends' who could
be trusted.

   In an early study that looked at this 'selling of personality' in modern
capitalist society, Hochschild (1983) termed such interactional work 'emotional labour'. Focusing on flight attendants employed by two US airlines, she
noted how companies sought to control employees' appearance, morals,
behaviour and language. In 'communications skills' training, staff were told
to 'work the passenger's name' by repeating it ('Yes, Mr Jones, it's true the flight
is delayed'); if something went wrong, to use terms of empathy ('Whatever
happens, you're supposed to say, I know just how you feel') and not to forget
that 'Your smile is your biggest *asset*'. The talk of flight attendants was crafted
in such a way so as to appear to treat passengers as individuals within an
organisation designed to handle people en masse – a typical feature of synthetic
personalisation. Moreover, as Hochschild (1983: 97) found, in order to attract
customers, airline advertisements promised a 'human and personal' service.
Along with the typical promotional props of competitive ticket pricing, efficient
baggage handling and distinctive uniforms, flight attendants' talk too was used
to brand a particular image.

   Rather ironically, as synthetic personalisation is scripted into philosophies of
customer care, workers are trained and regulated in ways that attempt to
control variation in their encounters with 'the public', as Cameron points out:

Employees' behaviour is regulated by instructions to perform all communicative acts in a prescribed manner: smiling, making eye contact, using the customer's name, greeting him or her 'warmly' and selecting personalized formulas like 'how are you doing?' which incorporate direct second person address. These linguistic and paralinguistic preferences are designed to express particular dispositions, notably friendliness and sincere concern for the customer's well-being, and thus to construct a particular kind of interpersonal relationship between the customer and the employee. (2000: 75)

Of course, in practice, a stranger's over-familiarity – their non-negotiated camaraderie – can be equally irksome, functioning to distance potential customers rather than connect with them. Employees too can feel awkward in having to verbalise expressions of 'sincerity' and friendship to people they have never met before. Cameron reports more uncomfortable repercussions in her discussion of the 'superior service' programme set up by Safeway supermarket chain in the late 1980s which required staff to 'do courtesy' with their customers (2000: 74). As well as the usual tactics of synthetic personalisation (eye contact, smiling, greeting, thanking shoppers by name and so on), workers were also obliged to suggest other possible purchases. At a union conference, however, female employees complained that the policy exposed them to sexual harassment from male customers who interpreted their friendliness as flirtation. Customers didn't respond wholly positively either. There were complaints from foreign-born customers whose names were mispronounced, while others felt embarrassed by staff commenting on the contents of their shopping basket. Not surprisingly, the strategy itself lacked apparent authenticity. As Cameron comments, (one problem with "synthetic personalization" is that people may perceive it as more synthetic than personalized) (ibid.: 76). Even with the development of more sophisticated customer care programmes which avoid such scripted behaviour in favour of staff 'reading' customers to decide upon an appropriate response, emotional labour is still key. Both employees and customers still need to manage talk that might be perceived as disingenuous.

Standardising interaction through scripted talk is the theme of the fifth and final reading. Reading 2.5 focuses on UK call centres – or what Cameron calls 'communication factories'. In discussing the similarity of call-centre work to that of a production line, she draws attention to both being highly repetitive, with workers being subject to strict time schedules. As the conventional factory worker is expected to meet particular targets, so call operators have fixed temporal limits about how long they can spend with one customer on the line. In call centres, however, the 'product' – or what is being processed, is 'communication'. It is this that is made uniform in the bid to brand a particular image as well as maximise efficiency. As Cameron explains:

Call centre managers may set out to determine exactly what sequence of interactional moves is needed to accomplish a given transaction efficiently, and then institutionalise the preferred sequence in a model or script which all workers are required to reproduce in every transaction of the same type. (Cameron 2000: 95)

In order for such regulation to work, call operators are monitored carefully, and subjected to a high degree of control through surveillance. Supervisors can 'listen in' to customer calls at any time without an employee's knowledge. One ex-worker who was employed by a call centre in the North East of England told us how such checks worked:

> A supervisor would be keeping an eye – and an ear! – on the operators. She would frequently shout out observations of our behaviour, such as the length of time an individual had been on a particular call, or how long we were spending between hanging up on a call and indicating our availability to receive the next one. (personal communication, July 2002)

The surveillance that workers are subjected to records not only the volume of calls they process but also whether their interactional style fits the company's script. Interestingly though, even with 'silent listening', acts of resistance against such measures of control do occur. Cameron (2000: 99) reports on research by Tyler and Taylor (1997) who found that airline sales and reservations staff could tell when covert monitoring was taking place. If they felt sure that nobody was listening, and were faced with a 'difficult' customer, they would quite readily depart from the standard script, and even disconnect the caller.

The reading links organisational prescription ('styling') of operators' interactional routines with the modern managerial phenomenon of 'Total Quality Management' that promotes consistency as a key concern. Like a packet of breakfast cereal, Cameron notes, 'the behaviour of employees in service encounters is regulated in an attempt to make it as predictable and invariant' (2000: 100). As with airline companies, branding plays its part in the standardising of employees' encounters with customers. Indeed, given that this is the only contact most callers will have with a business, operators' talk is important in building the desired company image. The script does not allow individuals to express their own personalities. Rather, they become 'embodiments of a single corporate persona whose key traits are decided by someone else' (ibid.: 101), and certainly some call centre regimes finely tune the way their workers present themselves.

It is true to say that call centres can vary with regards to the extent to which they standardise operators' talk. There are those, for instance, that merely provide a checklist against which a worker has to self-monitor her own language behaviour. However, Cameron found several that regulated every possible interactional move that operators made during telephone encounters with customers. In these cases, the talk that was prescribed was designed to pay attention to the caller's **positive face**, as operators were told 'your telephone manner should convey the impression that you have been waiting for that call

all day'. Our own data from a call centre training manual reiterates this in stating 'To show the customer that you are effectively listening to them you need to frequently use "verbal nods" eg "um" when appropriate throughout the conversation'. Cameron also notes how workers were instructed to attend to the prosodics of their speech such as stress and tempo, and to paralinguistic features such as tone of voice so that they would not 'sound bored'. Workers were also told to smile when they responded to a call. Again, our own training manual data supports this ('Remember: Always smile on the telephone the customer can hear it!'). In situations where credit card authorisations were rejected, the reading points out how the script softens potential embarrassment by obliging operators to say: 'Unfortunately, this application has been declined but thank you for calling'. Cameron discusses how such a strategy follows what conversation analysts call the 'preference system' in language, where the preferred action, acceptance, is often articulated with no mitigation as in 'This application has been accepted'. The alternative, rejection is 'dispreferred' and, accordingly, requires **hedging** in some way so as not to threaten face and offend.

Whereas synthetic personalisation in earlier contexts tended very much to be associated with discursive informality, it is interesting to note that in call-centre work, a more formal style of language seems to be advocated. The reading describes operators working for a utility company being directed to 'ALWAYS USE THE STANDARD GREETING ... NEVER SAY ... HELLO!!!' Corporate branding demands a salutation that marks its telephone calls as 'professional', differentiating them from those that are 'personal'. It is as if, in this workplace context, there exists a definite policy to move away from 'conversationalising' interaction, but in doing so the talk sounds oddly formal. Utterances like 'I am unable to validate your PIN number' or 'I will connect you to X who will be happy to assist you in this matter' appear rather 'official'. When combined with the synthetic personalisation features meant to signal friendliness and excitement, as Cameron concludes, 'the result can be a strange hybrid'.

In styling and monitoring employees' talk to such an extent, call centres constitute institutional control at its extreme. Given heavy surveillance, there is commonly very little opportunity to contest or negotiate what the organisation prescribes as 'operators' talk'. In a job that offers very little (interactional or other) freedom, they suffer boredom, frustration and stress. As Cameron concludes, it is difficult not to see a 'communication factory as a deskilling and disempowering place to work' (2000: 124).

ACTIVITIES

- Analyse the discursive construction of corporate branding with specific examples downloaded from the internet.
- Find and analyse features of synthetic personalization in the promotional texts of public service organizations (for example, hospitals, universities, schools, etc.).

READINGS

Reading 2.1
Executing bureaucracy: application forms

[...] bureaucracy is all about processing people. Most of this processing takes place by examining information collected from clients through application forms, and turning this information into files on the basis of pre-existing categories which follow set institutional criteria. These categories inform institutional decisions.

Let us first discuss a few general properties of application forms.

(1)   Forms typically have names which reflect the subroutines, the labour division and the departmentalisation in an organisation in a way which is not transparent to clients (form names are there for the sake of bureaucrats).

(2)   The layout of forms heavily constrains the client's activity in that it does not allow clients to tell a whole story. Boxes, dotted lines, multiple choice questions, pre-formulated answers, limited space (e.g. six letter spaces to fill in date of birth) all contribute to the packaging of the client's case. From a bureaucrat's point of view, this is tied up with the efficiency of processing information. There is, however, a recent trend to provide a space where the client can state things not accommodated by the form. This may appear as a move to minimise clients' constraints, but it is a double-edged sword, because it increases the possibilities that clients may give away information which could jeopardise their case.

(3)   Forms have also temporal dimensions (deadlines and eligibility periods), which equally constrain the client's activities. Clients may be required to declare something ahead of a situation, whether or not it reflects the client's actual needs at that point in time.

(4)   Forms are also used to provide information to clients; they have a 'leaflet function' through the occurrence of explicit information about the procedure, entitlements, and so forth, and there is also the implicit 'leaking' of information when clients work out aspects of the procedure and the decision making from the nature of the form.

(5)   Forms also have sections for 'office use only' – boxes and diagrams which run parallel to the spaces used for clients' responses. This is where the decision making will leave its traces on the form and the categorisation of an applicant as 'a particular case' will become definite. This is usually done in a non-transparent way (with abundant use of abbreviations and non-transparent codes). This may explain why forms, once filled in and processed, remain the property of the institution and are seldom returned to clients.

From: Srikant Sarangi and Stefaan Slembrouck (1996), *Language, Bureaucracy and Social Control*, London: Longman, pp. 128–36.

The processing of information provided by clients by bureaucratic channels can be captured through the concept of '(re)formulation' [...]. To (re)formulate a state of affairs is an act of classification but it also amounts to the imposition of a particular interpretation which informs subsequent action. (Re)formulation thus links up with situational power. It also successfully captures the asymmetry and the 'translation' element involved. Bureaucrats' (re)formulations take priority over clients' characterisations. Although forms reduce clients to category-types, this also entails a form of protection in the sense that a legitimate claim does not require more than what the form caters for.

Forms have an information-seeking function. They are often after the same information (e.g. personal particulars, education) but they vary when it comes to the amount of detail needed. For instance, one embassy may require certain personal details not required by another embassy, or embassies may require certain details not required by banks. The wide difference in what information is sought suggests that different institutions regard different types of information as essential and thus assign values to their 'preferred' types of information. Clients are very familiar with such differential treatment, but they rarely make this an issue and deny information that they deem 'irrelevant' on the basis of their prior experience with similar institutional processing. In fact, this reconciliation points to the fact that clients occupy a compliant/ cooperative role and turn their lives in to 'open books' for bureaucratic 'gaze'.

From the bureaucrat's perspective, it is easy to rationalise why certain bits of information are asked for. This may depend on the following factors:

- immediate processing: 'more information is always better', so that the bureaucrat can act on it without having to send reminders or having to seek further information from other sources. A form may also have a number of sections to be filled in by other institutions before it can be submitted. This reveals the hierarchies between and within institutions;
- traditions in record keeping, background statistical research;
- forms of legitimation (e.g. a client may be entitled to something following a verbal promise, but a form needs to be filled in for the record);
- records of information exchange with an implicit claim of 'objective' treatment (it carries the assumption that clients will be treated in the same way);
- devices to apply for and/or deny entitlement;
- face-redressive functions: apparent distancing from the institution when bureaucrats claim they do what forms require.

One of the questions arising here is whether forms can be offensive in the way they probe and in the way they address a particular type of client. Or do they require of a client some understanding about their immediate functioning? The latter would mean clients must learn to 'distance' themselves from the information asked/provided in the form and not consider the forms as a 'moral grid'! But this also highlights the one-sidedness of information exchange and leaves clients with little power to 'challenge' bureaucratic practices. Forms can be described as a defence which bureaucrats use to protect themselves from accusations of partiality, bias and so on. An unsuccessful outcome is often blamed on the client, because the bureaucratic decision is taken in accordance with the information provided in the form.

The implied client in application forms

Institutions operate with certain assumptions about the clients they address and process. Institutional assumptions about client categories have implications for the kinds of application forms which are used and for the questions which are put to applicants in a particular form. Let us take the situation of claiming 'incapacity benefit' in Britain. An 'incapacity for work questionnaire' has to be filled in in order to claim this benefit. This questionnaire has various categories related to muscular activity, but there may not be room for people suffering from, say, a skin condition to be able to declare their situation. While client constructs have been built into application forms, the real clients may remain absent from the form.

The questionnaire elicits detailed information about everyday activities, such as 'getting up from a chair', 'walking', 'lifting and carrying' etc. Under 'walking' for instance, the form asks:

> **Example**
> You cannot walk, without having to stop or feeling severe discomfort, for more than
> * Just a few steps
> * 50 metres, this is about 55 yards
> * 200 metres, this is about 220 yards
> * 400 metres, this is about 440 yards
> * 800 metres, this is about half a mile

Questions such as the above objectify (in)abilities and require clients to measure and express abilities in numerical terms. Additionally, there is a tension between 'an activity one ideally should avoid doing because of medical conditions' and 'what one manages to do, even against the medical odds, simply because daily living becomes impossible without it'. The applicant here has to grasp that the objectified measurement is the bit which is going to count – rather than a statement of the difficulties one experiences in coping with these things in daily life. As the manager (Ma) and the deputy manager (DM) of a local Citizen Advice Bureau (CAB) explained to us [...]:

> Ma: we have difficulty with it [...] how far fifty yards is because if you ask me if I can walk fifty yards I have no idea – so this is a problem and the other thing is people tick that and if they tick it in ignorance if they cannot walk fifty yards then everybody is assessed – they have an assessment – they go to the assessment

and first thing the doctor says is you ticked fifty yards and you have just walked all the way – and I think that puts them in a position they are thinking they are worse than they are.

DM: I think there are words that are very difficult like walk – what does it mean when you say walk – does it mean can you walk fifty metres and that's not understood by the client from the stuff that explains it – does this mean could I actually get there given all that I get there comfortably – can I do that and I repeat that people don't understand what is meant by that expression – ok there is a box to expand the point if you don't understand what they are after anyway it doesn't occur to you to qualify the tick

Clearly, self-assessment constitutes an important dimension of the filling in of application forms and clients may not only be inclined to under-estimate their needs, they will also be held responsible for the subsequent outcome of the decision-making.

Self-assessment also bears directly on the ways in which certain clients are excluded. Although the incapacity questionnaire addresses a wide range of audiences, certain kinds of clients are excluded if one goes by the range of questions asked in the form, as can be seen from the following comment made by the CAB deputy manager:

DM: [...] the questions they are asked on incapacity they are descriptors – the difficulty is that for many people none of these actually fit their conditions – for example this week we had someone with psoriasis – a skin condition – none of the questions got skin conditions none of them are about [...] conditions and the only way you can fit people in with that severe condition of that type into those descriptors are – if for example their pain keeps them awake at night or if their skin condition is such that they have lost grip of their hands and their joints cause them problems – but the condition itself does not trigger anything.

Let us now look closely at a more widely used form (application for income supplement) to illustrate further how clients can be confused and are actually affected by the categories in the application form. One difficulty which clients commonly experience with the application form lies in the declaration of their marital identity in institutional terms. This is particularly the case for clients [...] who may not [...] understand what each category entails. For instance, cases have been noted where 'sharing a flat' was interpreted as 'living together' and communicated accordingly in the application form, without the client realising the consequences of such an interpretation. [...] Interpretative discrepancies of this kind are not restricted to groups who may or may not share the dominant cultural or linguistic conventions. To quote the CAB manager again:

DM: [. . .] there are some forms that ask questions about for example the relationship with people who live in the house where they don't perceive that one of the answers is correct because neither of them seem to fit and therefore they usually feel constrained to tick one of the boxes and they are then judged according to this

Let us concentrate on one particular case which involves a woman in her mid-fifties, who applies for income support. She is divorced after a violent marriage and takes in a man in his seventies as a lodger. Early on in the application form the applicant (in this case the woman) is asked about her marital status. She is required to 'tick the boxes that apply to you and your partner' [. . .]. We reproduce the relevant section here for our analysis:

Example
You

Married	[ ]	Separated	[ ]
Living together	[ ]	Divorced	[ ]
Single	[ ]	Widowed	[ ]

The applicant first ticks 'living together' and then strikes it out and ticks 'divorced'. The deputy director of the CAB recounts this instance as follows:

DM: [. . .] it's the lady who herself was divorced but had a lodger living there – she should have ticked that she was divorced and has nothing to do with a partner because she doesn't have one – but also she was thoroughly confused as to which bits she was ticking – because it wasn't clear to her where the boxes matched up [refers to form] I mean if you work from this side it's clear that box matches that but if you come over here that box goes with those questions – she ticked this box thinking she was ticking divorced but in fact of course she was ticking living together – you see what I mean [. . .] the boxes are nearer to the next question than to the question they have replied – she meant to tick divorced – but what she did was ticked living together because that box is answering living together not answering divorced – although it looks the other way round [. . .] she ticked it and then she crossed it out when she realised that that box was divorced – in fact the department read it wrong and they actually read it as she ticked living together – so it's their own fault that they've been misled – because the form is so badly designed they actually couldn't work out where the answer was anyway – it meant for these people that this woman had her benefits stopped because she had him there living which resulted in the man saying I can't give you this trouble I will move out – so we ended up with a seventy one year old man living in one unheated bed-sit while we sorted all this out – and this woman who had loads of mental health problems over the years was back on valium for the first time in ten years [...] we had to go to the tribunal which took several months to sort this out – he had to go and live in a bed-sit to leave her alone so that she could get her benefit back while we sorted it out – all because the form elicited the wrong information or wrongly interpreted

What we see here is two levels of confusion: the first is at the level of the layout and design of the form. The applicant and the institution associate the boxes and the categories differently. The second level of confusion pertains to the interpretation of the categories. Because 'living together' is a potential label to characterise this client (a divorcee, who shares her house with a lodger), the institution in fact applies the living together category to the client without hesitation [...]. In the appeal procedure which followed, the investigation department adopted the direct surveillance method to verify the applicant's movements, before the misreading could be rectified.

Several general points can be made here on the basis of how actual clients have perceived their information-giving role when filling in application forms:

* Clients may feel that not ticking a box is a risky strategy which could lead to an unfavourable categorisation and outcome. Even when they are confronted with several sections which do not apply to them, having answered the first question (and going by the instructions), they feel that they are expected to answer each of these questions.

* Application forms presuppose a client who is literate to understand the instructions contained in the form, who is prepared to provide the information required and who is in a position to judge whether or not s/he falls within a category. However, the institution denies clients' lived experiences and its associated interpretations, when, informed by notions of uniform and rational treatment, it upgrades certain 'factual' pieces of information (with fixed interpretations) to the central plane of decision making. This, in its turn, makes it easier for the institution to deny/withdraw an entitlement to a benefit or an allowance.

* Some clients assume that the department already knows from previous correspondence about their condition and that the crucial bits of information are already owned by the institution.

Questions in application forms not only presuppose that clients have a fair idea about organisation procedures, the applicants are also put in a difficult situation – deciding exactly what information to provide, but also worrying about how that information will be processed. There are bound to be mismatches between the institutional construction of client situations and the actual client conditions. As the deputy manager of the CAB notes:

DM: [...] I take a cavalier attitude to forms – and I think that the purpose of the form is to actually collect information but if you can't put it down the information in the box provided just scribble it anyway [...] even our workers have to have us to tell them to take that attitude – they feel so constrained by the form – they are attempting to answer something that doesn't really fit in the box – so I say well you know just write across the box what you want to tell them even if it's not answering the question because that way you can't be accused of not having supplied the information [...] that the purpose of the form is to collect information not to make it difficult to present it

[...] At the heart of application forms then is a presupposition of institutional literacy (cf. the ways in which clients are assumed to know which form number to turn to, know how other institutions play a role in their case, etc.).

Official forms reveal to a certain extent some information about the bureaucratic procedure that the client will go through, and about how the work is organised within a bureaucratic organisation (e.g., expert opinions sought from relevant professionals). When the initiating moves have been completed, the information provided by clients about their situation travels in 'files' from one desk to another within the institution. Looking at the type of information which forms seek of clients, one could argue that each form has an 'implicit client' built into it. Thus, forms construct clients in terms of a potential set of common denominators.

Reading 2.2
Negative constructions of clients

In the Kenyon County welfare office, 'bad' clients were assumed to be the norm: engaging in negatively evaluated behavior was part and parcel of being a client. Indeed, workers expected this from all their clients, and expressed surprise when they did not encounter it.

'I think a lot of them know what to say and what to do':
the maneuvering client

The most frequent claim that workers made about their clients was that they were deceitful and manipulative. In their view, dishonesty was a strategy clients used to intervene in the system. It took various forms, ranging from outright lying to playing by the letter, but not the spirit, of welfare policy. On one occasion, for instance, Sherry Nelson and Valerie Wood [benefit officials] discussed two women's attempts to manipulate information in order to increase their benefits. In both cases, the women cohabited with their male partners but maneuvered so that the men's incomes would not be included as part of the

From: C. Pelissier Kingfisher (1996), *Women in the American Welfare Trap*, Philadelphia: University of Pennsylvania Press, pp. 99–111.

household income by the welfare department. One woman claimed that she and her partner ate separately, thus excluding his income from the food stamp budget, and increasing her allotment considerably. As Sherry told the story:

> Well I had one little girl that came in—this one always makes me mad, Valerie's heard the story a Million times—I had this girl come in ... not too long ago and her ((cousin is)) a new case worker in Golden County, and she came in, she didn't even know how ... her cousin answered the appliCAtion,[1] she's living with a boyfriend and pregnant, and she says they don't prepare food together, which I think is a bunch of crApp but ... you know, I have to take it for what they say. THEN, HE's been living there in this apartment for four years, she's eighteen and just moved in, now they're claiming the rent's three fifty, they're claiming that she pays the full three fifty ... and that she pays completely for heat and utilities. Now he's been there for four years, now I KNOW that he's been, but, in this case she will get the full amount even though—and he's WORKing, he's got a good job, but we can't count his INcome or ANYthing, I think he was making like ... sixteen hundred dollars. ... SILLY, silly things, those are IRRitating sometimes, FRUStrating. [...]

Valerie was able to produce her own story:

> oh I hate that ... that's what this one that I was doing was closed for fraud, she claimed she paid FULL rent, she claimed she paid heat and utilities and the heat and utilities were VENdored in HER name, the WHOLE amount. [...]

In both stories, clients are constructed as cunning and deceitful. They know enough about how the system works to manipulate it, and have no scruples about accepting illegitimate benefits.

[...]

Because clients were viewed as devious, workers often approached them with more than a modicum of skepticism. On one occasion, for instance, Karrie Holmes [another worker] had asked an applicant about his assets, to which he replied that he had none. When he later mentioned that he had been living in his car, Karrie jumped in and asked, 'a CAR? I thought you said you didn't have a car?' She later told me that she had been 'burned' several times, and so was quick to be suspicious. [...] A week later, Karrie received a rental form from another applicant on which a man's name had been written in and then crossed out. She immediately called the landlord to inquire whether the man in question had actually vacated the apartment. Because the landlord could not verify the case either way, Karrie decided that things looked questionable and turned down the application on the basis of insufficient information. [...]

Like Karrie, most of the workers could produce a story of being 'burned,' or of someone they knew who had been. This contributed to an atmosphere in which an assumption of deceit was in operation, and in which very little evidence was required to interpret a client's actions as manipulative. Moreover, workers often reacted to a client's purported dishonesty as if it were a personal affront, rather than, for example, an attempt to make ends meet. As Fran Knight put it, 'I'm empathetic to all my clients 'til they lie to me. Once they lie to me I hate them and I won't give them anything' [...]. Fran's use of 'I' and 'me' is noteworthy, and is in keeping with general pronoun usage among the workers. In their own phrasing, *they* were the ones who paid clients' rent, processed their food stamps, and stopped the gas company from turning off their utilities. Given this attitude, one can understand how workers could feel betrayed and cheated by clients who appeared (or were) dishonest.

'Lazy' clients

In the workers' view, one of the reasons why clients lied and cheated was that they were lazy, wanting to get something for nothing. [They believed that] if it were not for such indolence, many clients would not have gotten on the relief rolls in the first place.

The following describes how Sherry Nelson approached one of her 'least favorite' clients, who was due to arrive at the office any minute for an appointment that she had rescheduled twice. The story, told to me and Valerie Wood, exemplifies workers' constructions of clients as lazy.

> ### 'Miss Nelson, Miss Nelson, Here's Another Excuse'
> Cindy Smith was due to come in for her yearly review appointment, during which eligibility for assistance is redetermined. Rather than keeping her appointment, however, she called Sherry, and, realizing the ramifications of failing to meet her obligation, pleaded, 'Miss Nelson, Miss Nelson, my case is going to close, I want a new appointment.' Sherry obliged, and set up a second meeting. Again, however, Cindy failed to keep the appointment. She also neglected to telephone Sherry until four days later, when she complained, 'Miss Nelson, Miss Nelson, I missed my appointment on THURSday ... and I just got a CLOSure letter and MY case is going to close.' Sherry told her that her case was indeed about to close and that she needed to bring the appropriate papers into the office so they could have their meeting. 'Well can't I mail the stuff in?' asked Cindy. Sherry's reply was clear: 'Cindy, you don't WORK ... you are COMing IN, you HAVE to come in for this appointment ... we only ask you to do it once a YEAR.' Cindy acquiesced, and a third appointment was scheduled. Sherry warned Cindy that, 'if you're not here at nine o'clock. I'm not gonna see you ... and I will NOT have an appointment.

Sherry meant what she said. Recently, for instance, another client, Barrie Teton, had also missed and then rescheduled two appointments. Sherry was flexible enough to schedule a third meeting, but she told Barrie that she expected her to 'be prompt.' Barrie, however, did not want to meet at the appointed time of 1:30, but at 2:30, and so failed to arrive at the welfare office until shortly after 2:30. In response, Sherry decided to punish her by leaving her in the waiting room for a while: 'So I made her wait 'till 3:30, and then she came in, she said, "MISS NELSON would you like to remind me what time my appointment was?" I said, "Yeah I would, your appointment was at ONE-thirty and you wasted an HOUR of MY time ... so I wasted an hour of YOURS."' In Sherry's view, clients like Barrie and Cindy were simply 'LAZY, lazy, lazy, lazy, lazy.'

[...]

In this conversation, Sherry and Valerie characterize as lazy anyone who misses an appointment, regardless of the reason. In their view, employment is the only viable excuse for canceling meetings; it is the only activity that constitutes 'work.' Even school ... let alone mothering ... doesn't count in this case. Valerie made this clear in her talk about a client who was attending community college:

> I HAD, one (appointment) scheduled for like the fourth, she (the client)) called me and said, 'well I have to change it because bla bla bla, and this and that,' so I changed it, to last week, and I said, 'I really do NOT like to see my appointments this late because, you know, if you don't get all your papers in, you know, and this and that, your case is gonna CLOSE.' So ... she said, 'Well, I have exams next week, and well ... can I come on Monday?' I just thought, 'oh boy.' [...]

Sherry and Valerie refer to these clients in a pejorative tone of voice, sometimes resembling that of a stern parent speaking to a naughty child. Indeed, when they imitate their clients, their voices take on the tone of spoiled, whiny children. Again, laziness is the reason why clients fail to fulfill their obligations, whether it takes the form of missing appointments, not completing paper work, not being employed, or—the focus of the next section—not showering before going into the welfare office. Indeed, after her appointment with Cindy Smith, Sherry commented that if she could take a shower before seeing her clients every day, her clients should be able to take showers before seeing her, rather than just tumbling out of bed and rolling into the welfare office any old time.

Clients as unclean
I remember putting rubber bands around my pant legs when I went to this one place ... because I didn't want any rats running up my pants. (Debbie Brown [a worker])

Although workers did not refer to slovenliness on the part of their clients as often as dishonesty or laziness, they found it particularly repugnant. It was also the subject of derisive jokes. One morning, for instance, I accompanied Karrie Holmes and Valerie Wood on a visit to Myra Goodwin's home; Myra [...] lived in a trailer with 30 cats. Not only did both workers change into old clothes for the visit, but Karrie brought along a can of spray disinfectant. She displayed the can to the other workers as we were leaving the building and on our return; the workers responded with jokes about the 'cat lady.' Although Karrie and Valerie repeatedly referred to the strong odor around Myra's trailer—indeed, Valerie refused to enter the trailer on the excuse that she couldn't stomach the stench— Karrie never actually used the spray. Fran Knight, however, did make occasional use of the disinfectant she kept in her desk drawer, spraying it around the chairs polluted by clients she considered dirty.

Uncleanliness often co-occurred with other traits, as pointed out in the above discussion of laziness. In the following, Nora Ryan [another worker] tells me about a couple who had come in for a conference with her and her supervisor. In this case, uncleanliness concurs with stupidity.

> Too bad you ... weren't here yesterday when we had a ... pre-hearing conference. Empty, absolutely empty. Vacuum. I mean ... they're both barely able, they smell, they had a very strong odor, and what they were complaining (about) had nothing to do with policy. [...]

Clients who appeared disheveled or unbathed, or who emitted an odor, were thus constructed by workers to be inherently lazy, stupid, or otherwise inadequate. The possibility that they might not have the resources to bathe properly or appear neat and tidy was not entertained. Nor was it possible that intelligent, competent people might choose to appear unkempt for political or lifestyle reasons.

The social construction of client's characters: two examples

The following cases display the processes involved in constructing particular types of clients. In both cases, the constructions are central to workers' decisions to intervene (or not) in specific ways: that is, they are part of workers' officially unsanctioned production of policy.

A general case: clients as criminals

One morning, Judy Reynolds, Becky Wright, Sherry Nelson [all workers], and I had a conversation about a local stabbing that had involved clients. In this conversation [...] the women moved back and forth between clients and criminals, often conflating the two.

As Becky described the stabbing, 'I thought they were probably down on the street, and he was just calling him names and then they, they said he stabbed him right in the heart with a kitchen knife.' As it turned out, the man who had been murdered was one of Judy's clients. He had been released from jail only one month ago, when Judy had added him on to his wife's AFDC case. In addition, the apartment in front of which the stabbing occurred belonged to one of Sherry's clients. When I asked whether the person who had committed the murder was also a client, Sherry and Judy responded, in unison, 'oh, probably.' Or, as Sherry put it, 'the one who did the MUrdering probably just got out of jail and is on SOme case load SOmeplace.'

The women expressed no sympathy for any of the people involved in the stabbing. Becky, whose son Ben had had an alteraction with the murdered man, reported that, 'the county cop told Ben to go down to the funeral home and spit on 'em ((laughs)), 'cause Ben said he was looking forward to kicking his ASS and, and now he's dead so he can't.' Judy shared Becky's disdain. Without clarifying whether she is referring to the murdered man's status as client or criminal, she states:

> As I SAY, they will all eliminate each other soon or LAter so just let 'em keep going TO it . . . he is JUST, he's just the SCUZ of the EARTH, and I mean, and there's no loss to ANYthing, not to ANYbody . . . I know it sounds really cold hearted, but you know THAT'S just like all those drug gangs [. . .]

Becky's response to Judy was to argue that such people should simply be done away with: '. . . too bad they [the police] don't know when they have these parties, then they could just BOMB the houses, you know ((laughs)), and just wipe out all the houses.' Judy agrees: 'if INNOCENT people didn't get killed . . . I don't want INnocent people getting killed, but if they just got, I mean, WHY BOTHER with the tax money for trying to STOP 'em? ((laughs)) Let them do it . . . they just kill each OTHER.' Sherry then went on to describe her ideal prison, in which the worst criminals would be locked up with no guards, and provided with food, water, and weapons. The criminals would no doubt kill each other off, and the prison could then be plowed over and a garden planted in its place. Although Judy comments on my possible reaction to this conversation ('boy, Catherine is going to wonder . . .'), both she and Becky go along with Sherry's description ('let 'em kill, kill each other,' 'like Lord of the Flies'). Shortly afterward, when Ester Dove, a supervisor, walks in, Becky and Judy explain to her what we have been talking about:

> B: we're discussing variables in clients
>
> J: we're discussing if all these clients just eliminated each other what a wonderful world we'd have, but then we'd have to look for another JOB [. . .]

Throughout their discussion, the women make little distinction between clients and criminals. Clients and criminals are indeed often the same people, and Sherry's story about encouraging incarcerated criminals to murder each other could be applied to clients as well as to convicted killers. Indeed, Judy refers specifically to the 'wonderful world we'd have' if 'all these clients just eliminated each other.' The movement from client to criminal and then back again is thus smooth and unmarked. Moreover, in her vehemence, Judy later declares that she will take steps against the murdered man's wife: 'and I didn't know he worked, so now I'm gonna charge his little wife and two children with a FRAUD.' The wife, tainted by her husband, is now also a criminal. As pointed out above, however, Judy felt compelled to comment on what I might be thinking of what they were saying. Both she and Ester again addressed my presence later in the conversation. In addition, after Becky told Ester that the murdered man had previously been involved in an assault on her son, and that her son and a local police officer had joked about going to the funeral home to spit on the corpse, Judy and Ester explained to me that joking was one of their coping mechanisms.

This conversation, then, is at the extreme of worker's negative constructions of clients. Nevertheless, it provides one example of workers jointly constructing the people with whom they interacted on a daily basis. In this particular context, the categories 'client' and 'criminal' overlap, and the behavior of several people is generalized to encompass an entire group. In the following case, rather than extrapolating from a particular case in order to make a generalization about all (or a large segment of) clients, the worker extrapolates from various pieces of evidence to construct one particular client as a child abuser.

A specific case: client as child abuser

The construction discussed above involves a male world of criminality and violence [set] against the norm of orderliness. When the workers turned their attention to families and women, the negative attributes they invoked related to women's (lack of) moral fitness, or, as in the next example, to women's neglect or abuse of children, in contrast with the norm of good mothering.

Harriet Eaton had been having trouble with her client Lana Tucker, an 'overweight' African American who wanted funds to move to a new apartment. The traits of overweight and African American identity seemed to work against Lana in this case, symbolizing for Harriet irresponsibility, shiftiness, sloppiness, and laziness. The trouble started, according to Harriet, when Lana was evasive about her current living arrangements and lied about having paid rent at her previous address. Harriet and Lana had several telephone conversations concerning these matters, during which hostilities were exchanged (Harriet accused Lana of lying, Lana expressed feelings of persecution). The trouble reached a peak when Harriet discovered a recording on her message machine that sounded to her like Lana telling someone to hit and kick one of her twin babies. Apparently Lana had been unaware that the machine had started recording. Harriet was extremely upset by the incident and felt obliged to write a referral to the child protective services unit.

The following talk all occurred on the same day, during the course of which Harriet, myself, Lana, Sherry Nelson, and finally Mike Smith, a social worker, were engaged in constructing or contesting Lana's identity as a child abuser.

I met Harriet in the coffee lounge first thing in the morning. She was visibly agitated as she poured herself a cup of coffee and told me about the distressing recording on her answering machine:

. . . it was in the afternoon, and I, I was gonna play ((a previous phone message from Lana)) back, you know, to be sure I had the right phone number, and when I played it BACK on my machine there was ANOTHER instance of her being on, apparently she had tried to call and my—'cause I asked her about it when I did get a hold of her, I said, 'did you try to call TWICE?' and she said, 'yes, they put me through but your machine didn't give any message.' Well, all there was was her and the, you know, I could hear a child crying in the background, and SHE was saying 'HIT 'EM! KICK 'EM! KICK 'EM! HIT EM!' Yes, and so, you know, later I . . . went to a protective SERVICE worker, to Mike Smith, and asked him to come listen to the tape. Think I could FIND it? I must have accidentally ERASED it, so . . . I talked to him though and, and I told him that. You know, he just kinda GLOSSED over it—'well the woman's under a lot of pressure'— and, and 'we don't know that it was an adult doing it,' you know, that she was talking to. I said, adult or CHILD, what kinda—what mother TELLS somebody to kick and hit, because this child was really really CRYING in the background, and when I DID talk to her, I said, uh, 'Lana, did you try to call me earlier?' and she—that's when she said yes [. . .] and I asked her what was going on and she didn't say, so, I, you know, I want to write OUT my protective service referral this morning. [. . .]

Harriet begins to make her case by establishing that it was indeed Lana's voice on the answering machine: as she points out twice, Lana admits to having called her. Harriet then describes what it was that she heard on the tape: a crying child and Lana's voice saying 'HIT 'EM! KICK 'EM!' Harriet proceeds to describe how the social worker, Mike Smith, had failed to take the situation as seriously as she would have liked. A key feature of Harriet's construction of Lana as a child abuser comes out when she asserts, 'what mother TELLS somebody to kick and hit.' Harriet invokes the category of 'mother,' complete with the attributes of caring and protectiveness, as something which Lana falls short of. By the end of her report, the child is not just 'crying in the background,' but is 'really really CRYING in the background.' Lana's refusal to tell her what was going on when asked about the message provides Harriet with additional justification for her child protective services referral.

Back in her office, Harriet again attempted to retrieve the message on her answering machine. She was unable to do so, although all the other messages she had received several days prior to and since were intact. She then repeated her claim that she must have accidentally erased Lana's message, and reiterated the distressing nature of what she had heard:

I don't see . . . I guess I ERASED it accidentally, you know, and . . . he [(protective services worker)] didn't sound all that interested in, hearing it either but I, I just thought it'd give him a better idea because it was, it was an AWFUL sound and it was not a chi—it didn't sound like a child crying because they're upset or because they're, ANGRY at something, it sounded like a child that was being hurt, and then to have her standing there saying 'HIT 'EM! KICK 'EM! HIT 'EM!' [. . .]

Harriet is now even more specific concerning the nature of the crying she heard. Whereas initially she described a child who was 'crying,' and, later, who was 'really really CRYING' (i.e., seriously crying, as opposed to crying over something trivial), here the crying sounds are like those of a child 'that was being hurt.' Harriet again expresses shock at a mother who could encourage someone to hit her child ('and then to have her standing there saying "HIT 'EM! KICK 'EM! HIT 'EM!"'). She is clearly distressed—'it was an AWFUL sound'—and is suffering genuine anguish over what she interprets as a child being beaten.

Shortly after providing me with a description of the telephone message, Harriet presented further support for her interpretation of Lana's comments on the answering machine by citing the fact that Lana had lost custody of a child before. Although this had occurred seven years previously, when Lana was 16 years old, and for reasons unknown to Harriet, she nevertheless concluded, 'so she's been abusive in the past.'

Harriet's conviction that Lana was a child abuser, well-established by this point, is manifested in the following interaction she had with Lana later the same morning, during which she tries to convince Lana to speak with the social worker. In so doing she encounters Lana's resistance, thereby, in her view, uncovering even more proof of Lana's guilt.

```
 1  H:  okay, and I, um, you ARE, I DID want you to talk to another
 2      gentleman in the office this morning
 3  L:  who?
 4  H:  okay his name is Mike
 5  L:  who IS he?
 6  H:  okay, he IS with protective services
 7  L:  I'm not talking to 'em
 8  H:  okay, the reason I—the reason I DID it is because of that phone
 9      message yesterday
10  L:  WHAT phone message?
11  H:  okay, when I played my tape
12  L:  oh, 'cause a something you heard in the background
13  H:  mm huh, right
14  L:  oh I'm not TALKing to him, I will NOT talk to him and you can't
15      make me, I REFUSE to talk to him, I will not talk to him
16  H:  okay, WHY would you refuse to talk to him Lana?
17  L:  because I REFUSE to talk to him, I will not talk to ANY
18      protective services worker, I have one child already gone and they
19      will NOT get the twins
```

20 H: okay well they would have no REASON to take the twins
21 L: I don't wanna TALK to him
22 H: okay, I guess TALKing to him would probably—
23 L: talking to him won't do any good, I will NOT talk to protective
24   services, I will not
25 H: mm kay, he'll assume that there's something to HIDE then
    probably
26 L: let him assume whatever he WANTS to assume, they have to
27   FIND me first if they wanna to talk to me I will NOT talk to him,
28   all he's going to do is say 'what did you—' what DIFFerence does
29   it make what you heard in the background of a conversation?
30 H: okay, well I guess he'd wanna KNOW what was happening
31 L: WHY is it his business 'what is happening'? WHY is it his
32   business 'what is happening'? You know TV, you know, some of
33   the kids were watching wrestling, people HAVE VCRs
34 H: mm huh
35 L: people LIKE wrestling, people LIKE boxing, people LIKE sports,
36   but NO, everybody assumes 'cause you have kids and they hear
37   somein' about kick and hit that somebody's abusing children, I
38   WISH I could go inside people's minds, and really find out where
39   they're coming from
40 H: I GUESS the reason I thought it was because it sounded like your
41   VOICE
42 L: it WAS my voice
43 H: saying the 'kick 'em' the 'hit 'em'
44 L: oh, I LIKE boxing, and I like wrestling I have, you know, friends
45   who have VCRs who watch, who tape you know, WWF DOES
46   tape their matches, I get very in to it
47 H: well, I just thought I should explain to you WHY I did it, WHY I,
48   made the referral [. . .]

Nothing that occurs during their meeting convinces Harriet that she should withdraw her protective services referral. In fact, Harriet and Lana are at loggerheads, with neither willing to entertain the other's point of view. When Harriet mentions that she would like Lana to talk to 'another gentleman in the office' (lines 1–2), Lana is immediately suspicious, and as soon as Harriet admits that he is a social worker, Lana cuts in to declare her refusal to speak with him (line 7). Lana reaffirms her position an additional 10 times by line 26, indicating her anxiety (she had, after all, had a child taken away from her before), and her need to pre-empt a protective services investigation. Lana is already aware of Harriet's 'evidence,' as she indicates at line 12 when she states, prior to any explanation on Harriet's part, ''cause a something you heard in the background.' In response to her anxiety about losing her children, Harriet assures Lana that protective services 'would have no, REASON to take the twins' (line 20), which is untrue since child removal is a clear option in cases of child neglect or abuse, the situation Harriet in fact suspected. At the same time, however, she construes Lana's refusal to talk to Mike as an attempt to hide something. This puts Lana in a difficult position, to which she responds by directly confronting Harriet. Although Lana had questioned Harriet's evidence earlier (line 12), the line of questioning she begins later is more forceful: 'what DIFFerence does it make what you heard in the background of a conversation?' and 'WHY is it his business "what is happening?"' Not only does she in effect accuse Harriet of being unreasonable, Lana also recounts her version of what it was that Harriet overheard. Harriet, however, has no response, despite her indication that an explanation from Lana was what was being sought. Instead, she summarily closes the topic.

Returning then to the official purpose of their meeting—funds for an apartment—Harriet gathered Lana's paperwork and left to go to the photocopying machine. While Harriet was gone, Lana asked me if I was planning on becoming an AP worker. When I responded in the negative and told her that I was trying to find out, among other things, what it was like to be on AFDC, Lana replied that, 'it's horrible ... and they treat you like dirt.' At this point, Harriet returned, finished Lana's paper work, and concluded their meeting by saying, 'I know you don't believe this, but I really do wish you the best. 'She then sent Lana to the reception area to wait for a bus pass to Madrid. It was at this time that Mike Smith approached Lana and insisted that she accompany him to his office. Prior to the following segment, Sherry Nelson, another worker, had been describing to Harriet and me the interaction between Lana and Mike; Harriet then reports to Sherry what Lana had claimed about the answering machine message:

```
 1  H:  she just, you know said that it, er, it was part of the TV in the
 2      background and so forth that I heard, which is a bull, you know
 3  S:  bunch a bull?
 4  H:  'I like, I like boxing'
 5  S:  that's what she said?
 6  H:  yeah, so
 7  S:  you shoulda said, 'you should like boxing, that's fine, but not on
 8      your KIDS'
 9  H:  well, she's trying to—
10  S:  you can't SAY that
11  H:  she was saying 'bit 'em, kick 'em, hit 'em, kick 'em' because of the
12      boxing thing, but (you know) the little kid was
13  S:  bull
14  H:  crying in the background, but, so, you know, I'm glad she ...
15  H:  didn't just get up and take OFF [...]
```

Sherry is clearly a co-participant in the construction of Lana as a child abuser. After clarifying Harriet's use of the word 'bull' (Harriet rarely used such words and thus tended to use them inappropriately) and listening to Harriet's version of Lana's story, Sherry suggests what Harriet might have said to Lana ('you should like boxing, that's fine, but not on your KIDS'; lines 7–8). While Sherry's self-correction at line 10—'you can't SAY that' – indicates a behind-the-scenes discourse that workers know they cannot employ in face-to-face interactions with clients, she is clearly in agreement with Harriet's evaluation of the situation. She shows her support for this assessment not only at lines 7–8, but also at line 13, when she gives her view of Lana's story: 'bull.'

Later in the morning Harriet spoke with Mike about his interview with Lana. Mike claimed that he found no evidence on which to base an investigation, and that all he could do was offer Lana voluntary access to counseling services. He did, however, state that she was 'an accident waiting to happen.' He then went on to characterize Lana's approach to the system:

```
 1  M:  you know, I'm saying that she's pretty savvy to the system, she
 2      KNOWS what she needs to say, and, uh, you know, I have no
 3      MEANS of DETERmining at this point if, you know, what she's
 4      telling me is what she feels I need to hear, or what, what, if she—
 5  H:  MY main concern was, that those children, the sound I heard
 6      yesterday was ((coughing in background))
 7  M:  and her RESPONSE to that
 8  H:  and you checked 'em even and you don't see any bruises, then you
 9      know, you, you are the one responsible for for THAT
10  M:  that's correct, that's correct
11  H:  but I . . . cannot get that SOUND in the background of that child
12      (out of my head)
13  M:  I understand that it DISTURBS you
14  H:  ((coughs)) I wish I WISH I could get that tape again because it
15      would disturb you also because that child was crying
16      HYSTERICALLY
17  M:  well I'm not . . . I'm not SAYing you know, I'm not saying, I'm not
18      saving it's not DISTURBING, okay, what I—
19  H:  but you don't really FEEL that there was any abuse going on at
20      then point
21  M:  even if I FEEL there was some abuse going on, okay, I DONT
22      have the RIGHT, the legal RIGHT to interVENE in a
23      circumstance where I cannot support a finding
24  H:  right, but if you looked a child over and you don't, you just did
25      not see any bruises at all
26  M:  right, right
27  H:  okay um [. . .]
```

Mike's characterization of Lana as someone who is 'pretty savvy to the system' and who 'KNOWS what she needs to say' (lines 1–2) does little to reassure Harriet. Harriet was unhappy with this outcome; she had wanted a full investigation. As far as she was concerned—and she seeks reassurance three times [...]—Mike had provided no evidence to contradict her assessment. Confused about the ability of an investigator to discern abuse on an African American child (at one point she wondered out loud if bruises would be visible on dark skin), only a thorough examination would have satisfied her. A cursory look was insufficient.

In the end, a lack of what Harriet considered concrete evidence indicating that Lana was *not* beating her children, Sherry's active support of Harriet's views, and the lack of challenge on my part and on the part of Mike Smith, all contributed to the construction of Lana as a child abuser. In keeping with the assumption that clients were bad in nature, Lana's guilt was clear to Harriet from the outset. All that remained was to intervene.

NOTE

1. Capitals indicate emphasis.

Reading 2.3
'It's not true—at least not in the way most people think': challenges to stereotypes

The women challenged negative stereotypes of welfare recipients in three ways: by admitting their reality, with the qualification that the stereotypes did not apply to *them*; by claiming that the negatively valued activities they engaged in were the outgrowth of relationships with a welfare system that taught—indeed, forced—them to behave in such ways; and by categorically denying their reality.

Bad-people-exist-but-I'm-not-one-of-them

[...] recipients themselves sometimes reproduced the distinction between the worthy and undeserving poor. The bad people-exist-but-I'm-not-one-of-them strategy entails precisely this kind of collusion and was the most common tactic employed by MWRO and LIFE participants in their challenge to negative stereotypes. In essence, the strategy entailed acknowledging the existence of 'bad' individuals who were lazy, who lied and cheated, or who were promiscuous or otherwise morally lax while simultaneously claiming that they themselves did not belong to this undeserving category. As well as providing a means to exempt themselves from negative stereotypes, the bad-people-exist-but-I'm-not-one-of-them approach provided grounds for arguing against

From: C. Pelissier Kingfisher (1996), *Women in the American Welfare Trap*, Philadelphia: University of Pennsylvania Press, pp. 57–71.

punitive policies which the women felt were inappropriately constructed on the basis of such stereotypes.

The following exchange on forced sterilization provides a good example of the working out of this position. The participants are Susan Harrison. Janet Burns and her mother Marge, and myself.

```
 1  J:  um. I'VE¹ heard it before, I've heard RUMORS of this before, of
 2      women who've had some—certain amount of kids
 3  S:  I have too
 4  J:  and been forced to have a tubal litigation [sic], NOW—
 5  S:  well, Ashley Potter, my, my uh, ex sister, well she's my sister-in-
 6      law, she had six kids and they MADE her tie HER tubes
 7  M:  who made her? welfare?
 8  S:  their welfare did, either she tied 'em or she didn't get benefits, and
 9      that's in Virginia. Six is enough for the welfare rolls, but THIS
10      woman literally DID, she IS a welfare (degenerate), when she was
11      fourteen, she started having BABIES, she never finished
12      SCHOOL, her MOM, it was generation, down
13  M:  you can unders—
14  S:  and HER kids is also gonna be welfare AGAIN, and that's how
15      they were raised
16  M:  well, THAT, they'll use THAT kinda instance to justify it
17  S:  yeah they do
18  G:  yeah EXACTLY
19  S:  they DO
20  M:  and ARE they justified in it then?
21  S:  no NO because the MAJORITY of us out there on it is NOT like
22      that. I bust my ass trying to get off
23  M:  yeah
24  S:  I don't want to be on it no no more, no more than I have to, but
25      when it, when I HAVE to be on it. I don't want to feel like some
26  M:  yes
27  S:  you know CRUD coming in the door
28  M:  I know
29  S:  or leavin' the door
30  J:  or feelin' like—
31  S:  or not being able to DO so—you know GET off of it. I don't LIKE
        that [...]
```

Susan's story about her ex-sister-in-law 'Ashley' brings to life the stereotype on which policies of enforced sterilization are potentially built. Not only is Ashley reproductively irresponsible, but, as Susan rhythmically lists them, she exhibits a range of negatively valued behaviors: she started having babies when she was only fourteen, she dropped out of school, and her mother was also a welfare recipient (lines 10–12). Ashley reproduces welfare dependency as well as human beings (note the phrase 'generation, down,' line 12).

In her comment 'Six is enough for the welfare rolls' (line 9), spoken slowly and in a low voice, Susan indicates agreement with the welfare system's ultimatum—*in Ashley's case*. By not calling into question the legitimacy of forcing Ashley to have a tubal ligation, Marge's comments immediately following the story (lines 13 and 16) support Susan's evaluation. No one questions that the system has the right to coerce a woman such as Ashley to be sterilized. What *is* challenged is the idea of transforming the legitimate application of forced sterilization in Ashley's case into a generalized policy applicable to all women receiving public assistance. As Marge points out at line 16, the welfare system will use cases like Ashley's to justify creating such policies: a position with which Susan and I agree. In her next turn, during which she asks 'and ARE they justified in it then?' (line 20), Marge provides the opportunity for rebuttal. Susan takes this opportunity, arguing that most women on welfare are not like her ex sister-in-law, that she herself has been working hard, and that she is not willing to accept the disgrace of being placed in the same category as Ashley. In making this argument. Susan invokes 'working' (as opposed to simply producing a lot of babies) as something to be respected and rewarded, and challenges not only a policy of forced sterilization, but also the stigma that would be attached to her and other 'good' recipients as the result of such a policy. Marge's comments ('yeah,' 'yes') help Susan along in this argument. Janet's bid [a bit later] although unsuccessful, also reinforces Susan's position insofar as she seems about to name another negative feeling to back up Susan's feeling like 'crud.'

Together, then, Susan, Marge, Janet and myself criticize both the inappropriate application of stereotypes and the construction of policies based on stereotypes. Simultaneously, however, we reinforce mainstream views of generational welfare mothers. There was no objection in principle to punitive policies. Indeed, the women sometimes suggested punitive policies that could be applied to other segments of the 'welfare' population, most notably men. Susan, for instance, reacted strongly to a television documentary (entitled *Stuck on Welfare*) describing a Wisconsin program that forced women on AFDC to work or attend school on penalty of losing their benefits. Susan, whose children had been sexually abused by babysitters while she was at work, felt strongly that women should be permitted to stay at home with their children. In her view, much of the problem rested with men who were delinquent on child care payments. Nothing was done to punish these men [. . .] the targets of punitive policies always seemed to be women. Therefore, to hold men accountable for the children they fathered, Susan proposed that they be placed in half-way houses, required to work, and forced to wear wrist bands that would alert the police if they wandered off. This strategy for resistance, then, was dependent on the construction of a category of individuals deserving of punishment.

Susan's response to one woman's view of welfare cheats provides another example of this strategy. At a LIFE meeting Dara DeLuca, a close friend of Susan's who had never received public assistance, voiced her disdain for people who abuse the system because they are too lazy to look after themselves [...]:

> I understand the people that have kids, and that can't get a job, yes I understand, but I (don't) understand people that CAN get a job and that are on WELfare ... you LOOK AROUND and you see these people driving these nice cars and you know damn WELL they're on welfare because of the way they LIVE you know damn WELL or they've TALKED about it with you, so how the hell'd you get this nice CAR if you're such a you know, on WELfare, who are YOU screwing ((laughs)) you KNOW, and I don't agree with that, hell NO, I don't ((laughs)). [...]

Susan's response to Dara was to concede that lazy people exist, but to claim—as in the discussion of forced sterilization—that they comprise only a small proportion of welfare recipients:

> But see that's, THAT'S just a FEW ... There's fifty percent working, working welfare moms, there's twenty-five percent I think that would LIKE to work but they don't have no HOpe and then we've got the twenty-five percent that just don't GIVE a damn, go out there and do it FOR me, you know type shit. [...]

Here Susan argues, in scientific parlance, that the ones who 'don't give a damn'—the undeserving—comprise only one quarter of all recipients. A full 50 percent of welfare recipients are employed; they are, moreover, also mothers ('working welfare moms'). Those who work, and those who want to work [...] are deserving, and should not be penalized for what the 25 percent who 'don't give a damn' do (or, more significantly, don't do). [...] Interestingly, Susan's figures were not questioned; the mere recitation of percentages lends an authority to her argument that Dara seems unwilling to contest.

In sum, the bad-people-do-exist-but-I'm-not-one-of-them approach involved simultaneous criticism of 'bad' people and of welfare policy. When the women deprecated individuals who purportedly engaged in stigmatized activities, they afforded validity to and thereby reproduced the stereotypes. However, the claim was that those who engaged in the stigmatized activities were a minority, and that to thus base policy on stereotypes was to punish innocent recipients. Just as the bad-people-exist-but-I'm-not-one-of-them argument did not question the validity of the stereotypes, so the critique of policy generated by the argument did not question the appropriateness of punitive policies per se; they just had to be applied to the right people. There are, therefore, elements of both mixed and status quo narratives in this talk—mixed insofar as the women seem to simultaneously reproduce and challenge certain ideologies, and status quo insofar as they are willing to participate in the perpetuation (and even the extension to new categories of people) of punitive policies that have their roots in such ideologies.

Welfare-made-me-do-it

The second most common way the women challenged negative stereotypes entailed admitting to 'bad' behaviors, with the proviso that such actions arose not from the women's personalities but rather from the nature of their relationship with the welfare system. The implication is that the responsibility for these behaviors rests with the welfare system, not the women.

For instance, a common belief about welfare recipients is that they are dishonest. 'Welfare cheat' is ubiquitous both in everyday conversation and in official debates about welfare reform. The presence of welfare fraud hotlines in many cities provides further testimony to the prevalence of this view. In response to the accusation of deception, MWRO and LIFE members routinely claimed that the welfare system itself generated dishonesty, a response which implies a latent structure of the welfare system: lying is required in order to survive. Susan Harrison explained the process in the following way:

> I don't lie to people, unless I ABsolutely HAVE to lie I don't lie. I just avoid the question or go around it another way ((laughs)), I don't actually LIE lie ((laughs)). If you're gonna pin me to the wall you better make sure you ask it JUST the right way, 'cause I'm gonna go AROUND it ((laughs)) if there's any way I CAN, but HELL, you learn that from welfare. Yep, my aunt told me that one time, years and years ago, 'cause I always wondered how could she get . . . you know, things that I couldn't get . . . and she said 'Susan Harrison, you don't go in there and tell them the truth, ya ASS-hole,' you know. [. . .]

Despite her aunt's advice, Susan continued in her honesty. She could only bring herself to break her habit of telling welfare workers 'anything they wanted to know' after she experienced homelessness. As she put it, 'I don't like to LIE. I was raised never to LIE.' Rita Moore, who was present at my interview with Susan, shared Susan's disposition: 'it goes against MY grain, I am NOT a liar' [. . .].

The argument, then, is that 'you learn that ((lying)) from welfare,' and that you have to lie to get the basic necessities, such as shelter, and the extra 'things' that Susan's aunt managed to finagle. What to lie about, and how to go about it, however, is not always clear: rather, because workers are unpredictable, recipients must develop skill in 'winging it.' As Rita put it, 'after so many times of going in there and talking to them you just sorta get a feel for the situation.' Once having been forced to lie, though, the strategy can be employed in trickster-like fashion to subvert the system. Again: 'if you're gonna pin me to the wall you better make sure you ask it just the right way, 'cause I'm going to go aROUND it ((laughs)) if there's any way I CAN, but HELL, you learn that from welfare.' Even this trickster element is attributed to the welfare system.

The stories about learning to lie (or engage in some other negatively valued behavior) usually followed the same format: when I first got on welfare. I told my worker everything (I was honest). Pretty soon, however, I figured out that that didn't pay (I was penalized for telling the truth), so I got smart (started lying). This was usually followed, or preceded, by some evaluative remark to the effect that the teller believed lying (or some other negatively valued activity) was wrong: 'It's a shame to have to do that, you know, it really is.' The narratives produced were clearly mixed, containing elements of both accom-modation (by admitting to lying, cheating, or whatever else was at issue) and resistance (in claiming that such behavior was in essence required by the welfare system).

A second area to which the 'welfare-made-me-do-it' argument was applied concerned spending habits. According to received wisdom on the right (see, e.g., Gilder 1981: Mead 1986; Murray 1984), recipients of public assistance do not budget wisely, they spend money on things they cannot afford, and, like children or 'primitives,' they are incapable of deferring gratification. The idea here is that public assistance creates dependency and poor spending and work habits. To some extent the women agreed with this assessment: when you don't know when you'll get your next welfare check (that is, if you get one at all), or how much it'll be for, you tend to spend money while you have it. There is a difference, however, in the underlying assumptions of the two positions. From the point of view of the right, the welfare system is lax, thus making it easy for recipients to avoid economizing. From the point of view of the women in this study, the system both fails to provide for basic needs and is unpredictable—in other words, it is *irresponsible*.

In sum, women who drew on the welfare-made-me-do-it argument trans-formed accusations against themselves as recipients into accusations against the welfare system. It was not they who were abusing the system; rather, by forcing them to engage in behavior which went against their principles, the welfare system was abusing them.

Denial: the convenient ideologies argument
A final discursive strategy for resisting negative stereotypes entailed a catego-rical denial of their reality. This approach was most clearly articulated by Louise Black [involved in Welfare Rights], who claimed that negative stereo-types of poor people were little more than convenient ideologies used by those in power to maintain the status quo. She argued that the priorities of legislators who determined the state budget did not include taking care of poor people, despite their awareness of the hardships suffered by their impoverished con-stituents. Claiming that 'there's no doubt in their mind what's going on.' Louise described the legislative agenda and its consequences as follows:

> ...they're deciding that the state of Michigan has some priorities and those priorities are increasing, and one of the things Wenger ((a Democratic politician considered friendly by MWRO)) talks about ((is)) increasing tax expenditures, increasing tax write offs for businesses, that is extremely important, that is what ((the priorities are)) gonna continue to be, and when they do that, they will let a certain number of at this point, black, primarily black youth between eighteen and twenty-five, die, there is no problem with that, they will have, a certain number of children who are born to poor people who will die, or who will be permanently disabled as a result of living in poverty, and that is acceptable to them, that's the choice they make. [...]

Later in the conversation, Louise describes legislators' claims that they are trying to provide opportunities for the 'underclass' through their JobStart program (which was designed to remove people from the welfare rolls by giving them steady employment) as a 'straight out lie.'

Not only were legislators aware of the fact that the poor would suffer and perhaps die as a result of budget priorities, but they used negative stereotypes of welfare recipients to make these facts more palatable to themselves and the general public. According to Louise, politicians justified leaving 'whole groups to die' by invoking a 'crisis of morals' – meaning a crisis in individual morals or in family structure – or distinctions between worthy and unworthy poor. The 'attack' on the poor is accomplished through division:

> the move is to ... picking some kind group that they think is deserving and protecting that group, which means that that it's okay to kill folks, that it's okay to leave whole groups to die, and that that has become okay and acceptable, and they call it, you know, being politically realistic, or something like that [...]

The false distinction between the deserving and undeserving poor was all the more salient for Louise, given her conversion, after her own experiences with AFDC and food stamps, from someone who had been unsympathetic to welfare recipients into someone fighting for welfare rights.

The accomplishment of the convenient ideologies approach to stereotypes is illustrated in the following exchange between Louise, Naomi Anderson, and Bobbie Bradford at an MWRO meeting. [...] Bobbie had been describing an encounter with an African American worker who had been 'real snippy with me,' to whom she had responded by asking, 'what the f((uck)) do I have to do? paint myself to be a nigger?' This remark was challenged by Naomi, who argued in favor of greater racial integration. Louise then interjects her claim that racism is a divisive tactic used by the powerful to keep the poor from uniting.

```
 1  L:  the way that they get OVER with trying to FEED us all these
 2      CUTS is trying to do EXACTLY that same THING, is trying to
 3      separate this BLACK-WHITE stuff
 4  N:  that's what they're doing and if you go into a big city like Chicago
 5      it IS RIDICULOUS, it is AWFUL, in Chicago
 6  L:  and they TRY to get us to BUY it, but we have to say, we HAVE
 7      to say, EVERYbody, EVERYbody needs enough money to live
 8      on, if YOU can't give us jobs
 9  B:  right
10  L:  WE have to live. WE have to feed our kids. WE have to have a
11      house to live in. NObody in this country needs to die in the street
12      and that means ALL of us
13  B:  right
14  L:  whether anybody's black white
15  B:  and green purple
16  L:  old YOUNG, WHO CARES
17  B:  yeah
18  L:  nobody needs to die in the street and WE need to be about
19      SAYIN' that [...]
```

Louise argues that when the poor agree that some people deserve more help than others—when they take a tack similar to bad-people-exist-but-I'm-not-one-of-them—they are serving the interests of those in power. As is made clear in the first half of the exchange, both Louise and Naomi have strong feelings about racism. Bobbie, the speaker to whom Louise and Naomi are addressing themselves, eventually voices agreement. Not only does she begin to respond, 'right,' 'right' (lines 9, 13), but she adds to the argument by producing some of the features typically listed when referring to the range of human variation (line 15). Louise and Naomi together produce an anti-racist message, then, in which Bobbie eventually participates by correcting herself.

The argument Louise makes at line 18 is a 'bottom line' argument: everybody has the same needs (food, shelter), and everybody has the right to have those needs met. To accept any of the stereotypes about people on welfare—or even to reinforce ideologies that ostensibly have nothing to do with welfare, like racism—is to collude with those in power in denying certain people the right to live. The talk produced in this exchange therefore counters the status quo. There was no place for accommodation to *any* feature of the dominant ideology, insofar as the claim was that the dominant ideology was 'ideology' in the sense of false, distorted belief erected and perpetuated to serve the interests of the dominant classes.

'I work harder than anybody I know of': the challenge of positive constructions
In addition to, and often co-occurring with, direct counters to stereotypes, the women produced positive identities that drew on mainstream values concerning

gender roles and the achievement of economic success and security. In so doing, they portrayed themselves as clearly something other than lazy, dishonest, and promiscuous. Rather, they constructed identities as good, ordinary, hardworking women and mothers trying to do 'the right thing.'

Hard workers

A very powerful counter-construction to the lazy recipient stereotype was that of a hard worker. All the women claimed that they worked hard, and that if they were unemployed, it was not by choice. [. . .]

In the following exchange. Susan Harrison, Meg Irwin, and Janet Burns discuss how the welfare system undermines people's efforts to succeed. Susan has just been recounting how she was homeless for five months because the welfare department would not provide her with any assistance. As the segment opens. Meg and Janet agree with her point that 'there's no right to live here ((in the U.S.)).' Janet then brings up the topic of work, which, along with the idea of being 'stuck' on welfare, provides the focus for the remainder of the exchange. The participants are Susan, Janet, Meg, and myself.

```
 1  S:  they are refusing us a right to LIVE
 2  M:  right to live
 3  J:  right to live, and that's not saying that we're not working
 4  S:  that's IT
 5  J:  you know, that's just IT you know
 6  S:  I work harder than anybody I KNOW of
 7  J:  uh huh
 8  B:  and to, to be on ADC ((laughs))
 9  J:  yeah
10  S:  I mean you know I pull some hellacious hours
11  J:  uh huh
12  C:  sounds like it
13  S:  there's no getting OFF of it
14  J:  exactly ( )
15  S:  if you get off it, what're you LOOKing for, there's no HELP out
16      there
17  J:  and and talk about, you know, that's just IT you know they think
18      well you're lazy this or that you know, like [. . .] where's my time
19      that I've gone out and partied all night? you know
20  S:  that's it, they think we have such a wild life you know
21  J:  yeah
22  S:  we're single moms we're hot in the ASS ((laughs)) I mean that's
23      what they SAY, we can get some money, you know, but yet we get
24      out there and try to MAKE money we get arrested, oh WOW
```

25		there goes our kids bye-BYE
26	J:	right, exactly
27	M:	mmm, huh
28	S:	you know, but you HAVE to do it, you have to
29	J:	((to child)) are you eating that?
30	S:	so you're breaking one law after another trying to make it.
31	J:	RIGHT
32	S:	and which is basically your right, as a tax payer if nothing else as a
33		human BEING
34	J:	well you know a lot of times people will say things like, well, this
35		person, you know, [...] like Vienamese and things like that
36	S:	yeah
37	J:	that come over and they start with nothing, and they work and
38		work and get things done—well YEAH, they work and they, GET
39		somewhere okay—
40	S:	they're also, quote, a minority
41	J:	yeah
42	S:	they get a lot a help me and you aren't even QUALIFIED for
43	J:	that's true and I DON'T even think they have to pay TAXES
44	S:	none
45	J:	not that I'm saying this is WRONG or anything, BUT, it's not
46		saying that we you know
47	S:	it's wrong in the aspect that they can get it and we're not eligible
48		for it and it's our own damn COUNTRY [...]

Early in the exchange, Susan states, 'I work harder than anybody I KNOW of' (line 6), claiming an identity as industrious rather than lazy. Janet participates in this construction by debunking the stereotype of 'lazy' welfare recipients: 'where's my time that I've gone out and partied all night?'. Susan then makes the transition from 'partying' to another negative stereotype: namely, that of the promiscuous welfare mother. Not only does she ridicule this stereotype (line 22); she also turns it against the welfare system by claiming that women receiving public assistance are forced to engage in prostitution in order to survive. The final topic of the exchange is 'foreigners.' Janet brings up the stereotypical hard-working Vietnamese for a reason that she is unable to voice immediately (later it comes out that she was trying to argue that she, too, is 'industrious'). Instead, Susan uses Janet's example to complain about 'minorities' who get more help than Anglo Americans do—a perspective that reinforces her claim that she and the others present are being oppressed. In sum, the interpretation that Susan and Janet produce is one that portrays women on welfare as victims: despite their efforts to fulfill the work ethic, they cannot extricate themselves from the system: and they continue to suffer from stereotypes that in no way represent their actions or desires.

Just ordinary people/women

Many of the women also stressed that they were just like anyone else: they had the same dreams and aspirations as other women, and did what anyone else would do to fulfill those dreams. The 'anyone' referred to was, as can be gleaned from the aspirations and dreams discussed, a middle class woman; and the dreams had to do with marriage, motherhood, and economic security.

The women often invoked cultural models of marriage, motherhood, and economic security when discussing claims that promiscuity is characteristic of women on welfare. Rita Moore refers to a legislative hearing during which a Senator had accused AFDC recipients—meaning women—of being reproductively irresponsible:

> The thing that got me at the hearing was, 'why do they have these children if they can't afford to raise 'em?' I was married. Sure my husband—he's 45 years old, 45 or 46—he ought to be working a decent job and making a decent living ... Well I figured I could work and he could work together, you know, we could raise a family, we could have, you know, the little nuclear family, and everything would be hunky dory. [...]

Rita claims to be pursuing the idea of the nuclear family. If the traditional arrangement of husband-as-breadwinner was not possible, then husband and wife could both work in paid employment to maintain the family. In either case, no one could accuse Rita of either irresponsibility or immorality. She was only trying to do what a good woman should, and only wanted what other women wanted.

Susan Harrison also drew on the model of the nuclear family when she testified at a legislative hearing on the welfare budget:

> ((People end up on welfare)) because something happens in their life, not because you wanna be, you have your kids—you meet your husband you get married you have your kids or whatever, you got the KIDS what'd ya wanna DO? Just, you know? It's, it's not like you're TRYing to have kids to stay on welfare, it's not like that. You GOT your percentage of some welfare people (that) that ARE lazy, okay? (but that's not your maJORity). [...]

The point Susan endeavors to make in her testimony is that women are not on the relief rolls because they choose to be, but as the result of unfortunate circumstances. At least, this is so in the majority of cases. [...] In summary, according to Susan and Meg, most AFDC recipients have their children the way women are *supposed* to have their children—through marriage. The majority of women on public assistance are, moreover, hard workers. In this view, welfare mothers are simply ordinary citizens, both hardworking and morally upright, who have suffered some set-back, such as desertion by a husband.

Summary

The women's talk explored [here] illustrates varying engagements with dominant views of welfare recipients. These engagements may be situated in the immediate contexts of their production, MWRO and LIFE meetings and the specific topics of discussion at those meetings. The task at hand—contesting forced sterilization, racism, or accusations of promiscuity—influenced the kind of argument produced. In resisting workfare programs, for instance, it may be useful to invoke the sanctity of motherhood, while a challenge to the charge of immorality, on the other hand, might call for an alignment with the values of hard work and responsibility.

The women's talk may also be situated in the wider context of the welfare system and society at large. This would provide insight into the connections between accommodation and resistance and reproduction and change at the level of culture and society. When read from this perspective, only the convenient ideologies argument is truly counter-hegemonic: it does not enter into conversation with dominant views but rather denies their validity altogether. The other strategies employed by MWRO and LIFE members are mixed in nature and all, to some extent, reinforce ideologies and stereotypes that contribute to the specific oppressions they are resisting. For example, the bad-people-exist-but-I'm-not-one-of-them argument reinforces and in effect reproduces received views of lazy, dishonest, and otherwise irresponsible welfare recipients. In using this strategy, the women did not question the validity of the stereotypes, as long as they were not included in the categories at issue: nor did they present any argument against the use of such stereotypes in the construction of punitive welfare policies (e.g., forced sterilization), as long as they were only applied to those who fit the stereotypes. Although extricating themselves from negative characterizations, the women left mainstream views of welfare recipients intact. The women's invocation of the work ethic may also be detrimental to their interests in the long run. As Abramovitz (1988) has pointed out, the work ethic is a crucial aspect of welfare ideology; welfare policy and efforts to deter people from seeking public assistance have been based, both historically and currently, on various aspects of this ethic (see also Katz 1986; Piven and Cloward 1971). While resistant to accusations of laziness, the women's constructions of themselves as hard workers reinforce the view that all able-bodied people should be gainfully employed, with the implication that those who are not (for whatever reasons, including motherhood in the case of poor people) are undeserving—a view, along with the need for cheap labor fundamental to workfare programs. The women also support the idea that mothering is not 'work.'

In appropriating dominant views, however, recipients were not simply reproducing them. What is culturally available to think with is enabling as well as constraining [...], and provides opportunities for resistance as well as accommodation. In their confrontations with the dominant system, LIFE and MWRO members used the words, categories, and values of the dominant system to their own advantage. Such acts are superficially accommodating, insofar as they partake of dominant views. Insofar as they appropriate dominant views for subversive purposes, however, they are acts of resistance. For instance, in the welfare-made-me-do-it argument, the women deployed mainstream values of honesty and frugality to claim that lapses in their honesty or financial responsibility were the direct outcome of welfare policy. Policy, not recipients, should be held to blame.

The women's positive constructions of themselves also drew on dominant ideologies and confronted the system with its own contradictions concerning, for instance, women's roles as mothers, workers, and dependents. Weedon (1987) following Foucault refers in this regard to 'reverse' discourses, discourses that draw on the very vocabulary or categories of dominant discourses in order to make a case for oppressed groups. In this case, the contradictions inherent in the welfare system concerning women's role as mother versus worker provide a discursive space within which recipients may challenge the system. This discursive space is perhaps where the struggle over 'worldmaking' to which Bourdien (1990) refers takes place.

In sum, in MWRO and LIFE talk, accommodation and resistance interact to produce views which may be read as complicit or counter-hegemonic or both depending on the interpretive perspective. Generally, however, the metamessage of much of the women's talk was something like the following: 'I'm doing my best to be a good woman and mother and to take care of myself and my family, but the welfare system will not allow me to succeed.' In other words, the women expressed belief in the American values of motherhood, the nuclear family, and the work ethic, but saw all their efforts to fulfill those values as futile in the face of the constraints of the welfare bureaucracy.

NOTE

1. Capitals indicate emphasis.

REFERENCES

Abramovitz, Mimi 1988 *Regulating the Lives of Women: Social Welfare Policy from Colonial Times to the Present.* Boston: South End Press.

Bourdieu, Pierre 1990 *In Other Words: Essays towards a Reflexive Sociology.* Stanford, CA: Stanford University Press.

Gilder, George 1981 *Wealth and Poverty.* New York: Basic Books.

Katz, Michael B. 1986 *In the Shadow of the Poor House: A Social History of Welfare in America.* New York: Basic Books.

Mead, Lawrence M. 1986 *Beyond Entitlement: The Social Obligations of Citizenship.* New York: Free Press.

Murray, Charles 1984 *Losing Ground: American Social Policy, 1950–80.* New York: Basic Books

Piven, Frances Fox and Richard A. Cloward 1971 *Regulating the Poor: The Functions of Public Welfare*. New York: Random House.

Weedon, Chris 1987 *Feminist Practice and Poststructuralist Theory*. Oxford: Basil Blackwell.

Reading 2.4

Doing power in the workplace

Discourse in the workplace involves the construction not only of collegiality but also of power relationships. Every interaction involves people enacting, reproducing and sometimes resisting institutional power relationships in their use of discourse [...]. Pateman (1980) examines power relationships from the perspective of 'oppressive' and 'repressive discourse, while Fairclough uses the term 'coercive power' (Fairclough 1989, 1995). 'Oppression' is the open expression of power, while 'repressive discourse' is a covert means of exercising 'top-down' or coercive power, in which superiors minimise overt status differences and emphasise solidarity in order to gain their interlocutor's willing compliance and goodwill [...].

Fairclough notes that it is the people in positions of power who decide what is correct or appropriate in an interaction. He comments that they also have 'the capacity to determine to what extent ... [their] power will be overtly expressed' (1989: 72), and that in recent years the overt marking of power has been declining. Along with this decline has gone a reduction in formality (Fairclough 1992), and a process of 'conversationalising' public discourses (Fairclough 1995). Similarly Ng and Bradac (1993: 7) discuss strategies for 'depoliticising' the message in order to exercise covert influence over the attitudes and behaviour of others. Power, it is suggested, is increasingly expressed covertly and indirectly; it is hidden.

Holmes, Stubbe and Vine (1999) describe a variety of ways, both overt and covert, in which people 'do power' in the workplace. One obvious means of directly expressing power or status is the use by senior staff of overt discourse strategies for controlling an interaction. So, for example, in our data the senior participants generally set the agenda, gave direct orders, expressed explicit approval of the actions of others and summarised decisions. But they also employed a variety of less direct, less overt and more subtle means of 'doing power', one example of which was the way they generally 'managed' the small talk. In many New Zealand workplaces, in response to an egalitarian work ethic, rather than being relinquished, power seems to have gone underground

From J. Holmes (2000), 'Doing collegiality and keeping control at work: small talk in government departments', in Justine Coupland (ed.), *Small Talk*, Essex: Pearson Education Ltd, pp. 32–61.

[...]. The management of small talk could be regarded as one example of subterranean power construction.

Apart from the first contact of the day, small talk is usually optional. But it is generally the superior in an unequal interaction who has the deciding voice in licensing it [...]. Except at breaks, there is often little or no small talk between people who are involved in an on-going work relationship: e.g. a senior policy analyst walked into the office of his administrative assistant saying *can you ring these people for me Joe*. Similarly a manager delivered a pile of papers to her PA saying *can you send these out, they need to go by this afternoon*. In such contexts these superiors did not use or expect small talk, and it did not occur. No overt flaunting of power is involved; the superior's definition of the situation simply prevails.

On the other hand, [...] those in positions of power may use small talk to ease the transition to work-related topics, or to develop or maintain good social relations between themselves and their subordinates. Hence small talk can be used to reduce the social distance between superiors and their subordinates. Small talk topics do not reflect expertise or specialist knowledge. Topics such as the weather, holidays, child care problems and problems with transport are mundane and accessible to all, and so lend themselves to an emphasis on equality. But the positive politeness functions of small talk may be manipulated as well as used for sincere and genuinely positive affective functions.

The management of small talk may thus provide insights into the ways in which superiors manage interaction with their subordinates. In unequal encounters, the senior person typically sets the agenda. Similarly the senior participant generally determines how much small talk there will be at the beginning and end of an interaction. The extent to which the discourse of work may be de-institutionalised, the extent to which the world of leisure will be permitted to encroach on the world of work is largely in the hands of the superior. In the following extract Carol, Ruth's PA, uses the topic of the tape recording, which has become routinised in this workplace, as a small talk token. Ruth, however, does not allow the topic to develop but instead moves quickly to business.

Context: Ruth walks in to give her PA some typing which needs correcting
1   R: hello
2   C: hello missus – Ms Tape [laughs]
3   R: huh?
4   C: I said hello Ms Tape
5   R: who's *Ms* Tate?
6   C: TAPE
7   R: TAPE oh yeah yeah I'll drive everyone up the wall
Pointing to the typing Carol has done for her
8   is that a space or not + it is a space
9   C: [quietly] no it's not a space it's not a space

The superior has the right to minimise, or cut off small talk and get on to business, and Ruth here resists attempts to use small talk as a bridge to an extended session of social talk. Because of the routine character of small talk it is possible to use it equally as a transition to work talk as well as to social or personal discourse. By responding formulaically and minimally, Ruth keeps the small talk to a ritual function.

It is also possible for those in more powerful positions to deliberately use small talk to 'manage' or influence the behaviour of others. So, for example, because small talk is associated with the peripheries of interaction, a senior person can use small talk as a strategy for bringing an interaction to an end.

> B: so no it was good I didn't have to worry about meals I didn't have to worry about hills or kids or um work or anything just me
> H: (just) a holiday for you
> B: yeah + [tut] it was UNREAL [laughs]
> H: now listen are you going to be wanting to take time off during the school holidays

By contrast, in a similar interaction with Jocelyn, an equal, the social talk is more extensive and the transition to a closing is carefully negotiated between the two women. Jocelyn's account of her 'time out' is not cut by Hana, and she responds to Hana's potential pre-closing *that's neat* by indicating she is ready to go.

> *Context*: Hana and Jocelyn, two managers, are finishing a planning meeting They have been chatting about Jocelyn's non-work activities.

> 1 H: excellent
> 2 J: it was good + very good
> 3 H: oh excellent oh
> 4 J: yeah
> 5 H: great Jocelyn that's neat
> 6 J: must go
> 7 H: mm okay
> 8 J: all right?
> 9 H: okay thanks

By suggesting that those in positions of power tend to manage and often to limit small talk, this discussion has assumed that subordinates have a greater vested interest in developing small talk with their superiors than vice versa. This interpretation is supported by American research using a questionnaire to study small talk in two business organisations (Levine 1987). The results suggested that, while employees appreciate the opportunity to engage in small talk with their bosses, the employers preferred to restrict small talk to non-personal topics. There was evidence in our data that subordinates tended to respond very positively to small talk initiated by superiors, and often endeavoured to extend it in the direction of more personal talk, while superiors tended to respond more circumspectly maintaining a degree of social distance.

The workplace data also provided evidence that subordinates in an interaction do not always accept their superior's construction of a situation. Talk is a potential site of resistance and challenge [...]; talk can be characterised as a 'resistant political activity' (Kingfisher 1996: 536). So there was sometimes a suggestion of resistance to a superior's repression of social talk, especially if the subordinate had reason to feel exploited or manipulated, a victim of 'repressive discourse'. The interaction between Kate and Anne below [...] illustrates this point. Kate, the superior, initiates the interaction pretty much head-on without any small talk to ease into her request for assistance (which is also an indirect complaint). Anne is faced with a problem when she has scarcely settled back to work after some time away. As mentioned above, Kate later apologises, but uses the apology as a licence to introduce a second problem. Once she has responded to both problems, Anne asserts her right to some consideration, and she uses small talk as a channel to social talk which enables her to air her personal problems.

> *Context*: Anne, computer adviser, and Kate, a more senior policy advisor

> 1   A: yeah it was a real bummer me not coming in yesterday
> 2   /but I was absolutely wrecked\
> 3   K: /oh don't worry I worked it out\ for myself and I didn't need to use it

Kate responds to the first part of the comment and overlaps the more personal discourse. Effectively, she focuses on the transactional aspect of the utterance. Anne persists:

> 1   A: I got up and I I just was so exhausted and I thought
> 2   gee I just wanted to cry
> 3   K: oh you poor thing

At this point Anne has moved from small talk to very personal self-disclosure. Kate is faced with the option of being overtly and explicitly rude or of listening to Anne – the price, perhaps, of trying to obtain advice more speedily than if she had booked Anne's time. She responds sympathetically to Anne's self-revelation. Anne then continues with her story of stress. She has effectively resisted Kate's attempts at repressive discourse and asserted her own interests. The interaction ends only when Kate's PA interrupts.

1	N:	would you like to speak to Mr D?
2	K:	oh yes I would
3	A:	okay
4	K:	thanks

The interaction then winds up with references back to Kate's problem and Anne offers to come round and check it later. Other similar examples involve small talk used by a subordinate as a precursor to a request for a day's leave, before requesting support for a promotion and before asking for permission to leave work early one day. The subordinate uses the small talk to reduce social distance and emphasise their good relationship with their superior, before requesting a 'good' that only the superior can bestow. Superiors vary in the extent to which they respond to such talk. Finally, they have the right to cut it short, and proceed to business [. . .].

Context: Tom enters Greg's office to request a day's leave

1	T:	can I just have a quick word
2	G:	yeah sure have a seat
3	T:	[sitting down] great weather eh
4	G:	mm
5	T:	yeah been a good week did you get away skiing at the weekend
6	G:	yeah we did + now how can I help you
7	T:	I was just wondering if I could take Friday off and make it
8		a long weekend

Tom's small talk (line 5) focuses on common areas of interest, reducing social distance and de-emphasising status differences, but Greg effectively resists the invitation to extend the small talk with his brief responses.

Though I have focused in this section on the relationship between differential status and the management of small talk, there are obviously many other relevant factors which account for the precise ways in which interactions progress, and the degree of explicitness with which people 'do power in interaction. So, for instance, the urgency of the task at hand may override all social niceties, or the closeness of the relationship between two people may override any status difference. Conversely, people may dispense with small talk when they are not concerned to nurture or develop the social relationship. Contextual factors must always be considered.

The analysis has suggested that the management of small talk is a clear but generally indirect and polite manifestation of workplace power relations. Superiors typically determine whether and to what extent there will be any small talk in an interaction, and they may explicitly use small talk as a means a managing a variety of aspects of an interaction. Subordinates use small talk to do power too, but the extent to which they are successful is finally determined by their superiors.

[...]

Appendix

ription conventions

ιes are pseudonyms.

YES	Capitals indicate emphatic stress
[laughs]	Paralinguistic features in square brackets
[drawls]	
+	Pause of up to one second
++	Two second pause
.../...\...	Simultaneous speech
.../...\...	
(hello)	Transcriber's best guess at an unclear utterance
?	Rising or question intonation
publicat-	Incomplete or cut-off utterance
...	Some words omitted

REFERENCES

Fairclough, Norman L. (1989) *Language and Power*. London: Longman.
Fairclough, Norman L. (ed.) (1992) *Critical Language Awareness*. London: Longman.
Fairclough, Norman L. (1995) *Critical Discourse Analysis: Papers in the Critical Study of Language*. London: Longman.
Holmes, Janet, Stubbe, Maria and Vine, Bernadette (1999) 'Constructing professional identity: "doing power" in policy units'. In Srikant Sarangi and Celia Roberts (eds), *Discourse in the Workplace: Communication in Institutional and Professional Settings*. Berlin: Mouton De Gruyter.
Kingfisher, Catherine Pélissier (1996) 'Women on welfare: conversational sites of acquiescence and dissent'. *Discourse and Society* 7 (4): 531–57.
Levine, Deborah Clark (1987) 'Small talk: A big communicative function in the organization?' Paper presented at the Annual Meeting of the Eastern Communication Association. Syracuse. EDRS. ED283228.
Ng, Sik Hung, and Bradac, James J. (1993) *Power in Language: Verbal Communication and Social Influence*. Newbury Park, CA: Sage.
Pateman, Trevor (1980) *Language, Truth and Politics: Towards a Radical Theory for Communication*. Sussex: Jean Stroud.

Reading 2.5
Standardizing interaction

It is characteristic of the 'communication factory' that emphasis is placed on standardizing the output, or 'product', talk. [...] The standardizing impulse [is related] to the notion of 'efficiency': standardized interactional routines are intended to ensure that information is elicited in the order the computer

From: D. Cameron (2000), *Good to Talk? Living and Working in a Communication Culture*, London: Sage, pp. 99–106.

software needs it to be input, that ongoing checks are made for accuracy, that the exchange is conducted with due regard to the customer's expectations of appropriate service, and that talking time is not wasted on inessentials.

[...]

But there are other reasons for standardization. Efficiency might dictate the number, sequence and general content of interactional moves, but it need not preclude some degree of individual variation in the actual words uttered. In many call centres, however, it is made clear to operators that even the most trivial variation will not be tolerated. The goal is to give customers a completely uniform and consistent experience of dealing with the organization, regardless of which employee they happen to find themselves talking to.

Here we see the influence of modern managerial ideas about 'quality'. In the approach known as 'Total Quality Management', *quality* does not mean what it usually means in everyday usage, namely an especially high standard, but rather refers to the consistent achievement of a specified, measurable standard – getting something right first time, every time. In relation to mass-produced goods, it is easy to understand the logic of this idea. When a customer buys a particular brand of breakfast cereal, say, s/he is entitled to expect that the packet will always contain the same amount of cereal, and that the cereal will look and taste exactly as it did the last time s/he purchased it. Quality control is not just about ensuring every packet reaches a certain minimum standard of acceptability, but also about ensuring packets vary from one another only within narrow limits. Increasingly, however, the same notions of quality that apply to mass-produced goods are also being applied to the provision of customer service. The behaviour of employees in service encounters is regulated in an attempt to make it as predictable and invariant as a packet of cereal.

The other consideration that lies behind the demand for uniformity in operators' performance is the company's concern about its 'brand image'. Branding – creating a consistent, distinctive and easily recognizable identity for your products and services – is regarded as one of the key marketing tools companies have at their disposal. But whereas a face-to-face operation can attend to this issue in a variety of ways – in its store layout, signage and decor, the packaging of its goods, the uniforms worn by its staff – a call centre has only one means of getting its brand image across, and that is the way operators speak to customers. Some manuals in my corpus of call centre materials explicitly remind operators that they 'are' the brand; specific instructions on how to conduct calls are prefaced by a formula such as 'remember: you are [name of company]'. 'Being' the company means behaving/speaking in accordance with the values it has chosen as central to its distinctive brand image. One centre which deals with insurance claims, for instance, encapsulates its 'brand values' in the acronym FISHES, which stands for *Fast-acting, Imaginative, Straight forward, Helpful, Expert, Self-assured.*

appreciation
&
beauty

When the notion of 'branding' is extended to the verbal and other behaviour of employees, the result is [...] 'styling', creating a uniform style of service encounter by regulating small surface details that have aesthetic value. In the case of call centre operators, this styling is exclusively linguistic: language is regulated to ensure operators function, not as individuals with their own personalities (or their own individually constructed on-the-job personae) but as embodiments of a single corporate persona whose key traits are decided by someone else. The parenthetical comment in the last sentence alludes to a distinction I take to be important, between allowing people to 'be themselves' at work and allowing them to *construct* themselves. It would be idle to criticize call centres simply for demanding that employees adopt a professional persona which is different from their non-professional self. This demand has been part of what it means to 'go out to work' since work itself became a distinct social domain: competent workers understand that they must behave in ways appropriate to the context of being at work (rather than at home or in a club, say), and this in itself is not generally seen as unreasonable – indeed, there is a certain amount of pleasure and satisfaction to be had from manipulating self-presentation in different situations. But [...] the difference between people's everyday styling practices and workplace regimes of styling is that in the latter case, the speaker is not the 'stylistic agent' and does not 'own' the style s/he adopts. By standardizing speech performance, and particularly by requiring the expression of 'standard' personality traits ('outgoingness') and emotional states ('excitement'), the call centre regime imposes on workers the demand to present themselves in a way the company determines, down to the last detail. This carries the risk that employees may perceive the prescribed way of speaking not just as 'inauthentic' in the manner of any professional persona, but more problematically, as alien and demeaning. The call centre regime is not alone here, of course. But the extent of scripting and the intensity of surveillance in call centres make them a particularly extreme case of institutional control over individuals' self-presentation.

The verbal production of a uniform and consistent operator-persona is often justified to call centre staff by managers as something the customer expects and indeed wants. This raises the question of whether customers in fact apply the same criteria of judgement to verbal interactions with other human beings as they do to packets of cereal. There is some evidence that they do not. In an OU [Open University] programme about empowerment, it was revealed that McDonald's had stopped telling its staff exactly what to say to customers when they entered and left the restaurant, after research had shown that customers disliked getting the same scripted greeting and farewell from every employee on every occasion. And in a survey of over 1000 call centre users, 'dealing with someone clearly reading from a script' was among respondents' 'pet hates'. Conversely, the main factor producing customer satisfaction was a positive perception of the individual operator.

From a sociolinguistic perspective these findings are hardly surprising. However banal an interaction, the mere fact of engaging in it creates a kind of temporary social relationship; consequently, the criteria we ordinarily use to assess the quality of social relationships (as opposed to the quality of packets of cereal) are brought into play. We do not expect people to be uniform; conversely, we do expect them to be (or at least to seem) 'sincere'. In that light, it is a curious assumption that the same high degree of personal involvement, deference, enthusiasm, and so on, should ideally be manifested in every transaction. Callers are more likely to expect, subconsciously and on the basis of long experience of spontaneous interaction, that performance will be tailored to the needs of the context: that a straightforward inquiry, for instance, will be processed with less deference than a complaint. By suppressing (at least in theory) contextual variation, the call centre regime inadvertently increases the likelihood that many routine exchanges will be so excessively deferential, or enthusiastic, as to convey an impression of patent insincerity. This is ironic, given that some materials in my corpus actually specify 'sincerity' as one of the qualities operators are required to project in their speech.

Call centres do vary in how far they go in attempting to impose linguistic uniformity. At one end of the spectrum, one call centre in my sample, dealing with technical enquiries about telecommunications, hardly regulated employees' communication strategies at all, nor did it record or systematically monitor calls (a manager told me he believed that would be 'devastating for morale'). Operators at this centre must acquire a certain amount of technical knowledge (they are not themselves engineers, but are often called upon to talk to engineers), and training focuses more on this than on the minutiae of interaction. At the other end of the spectrum, I found several call centres which provided employees with a script covering more or less any interactional move that could occur in the course of a transaction, imposed detailed style rules regarding how they should speak, and monitored compliance assiduously.

Where a high degree of uniformity is demanded, managers often include in guidance to staff some explanation of what motivates that demand. For instance, a 1996 memorandum headed 'Standard Call Speech' and addressed to teleprocessing staff in a financial services centre begins: 'You should all know by now that we intend to introduce a standard telephone speech'. It goes on:

> There are a number of reasons for standardizing the speech and improving call techniques. The most important of which is *Meeting and Exceeding Customer Expectations*. If we don't, someone else will.
> Some more reasons are:
>
> - Creating a professional image
> - Improves quality of processing
> - Allows you to manage the call sequence and pace.
>
> Every operator must use the speech, no exceptions!

An interesting (and typical) feature of this explanation is that it puts 'customer expectations' first. Considerations of efficiency – that is, the idea that standardizing calls will increase the speed and accuracy of processing – are placed below 'service' considerations. There is some reason to doubt that this is the management's true order of priorities. A further memo, addressed only to supervisory staff, notes that while the introduction of a 'standard speech' may initially slow down call processing, as operators struggle with unfamiliar scripts, in the longer term 'I expect talk times to actually reduce as we better manage calls'. This particular centre processes requests for credit authorization, and the 'standard speech' is therefore quite a complicated construct, with options covering a range of eventualities: the caller's application may be accepted, declined or referred for further investigation. There is also a scripted option for cases where the operator is 'suspicious of the customer'.

Customer care training materials for the directory assistance centre whose standard routine we examined earlier include a section explaining to operators why the company insists on what it terms 'salutations'. (In this case 'salutation' does not refer only to the prescribed greeting ('XYZ Directories') but to all those moves which are motivated by considerations of politeness rather than by the main business of eliciting and providing information.)

> *Why Have Salutations?*
> Salutations give the call structure and allow it to be handled in a polite and efficient manner. It also gives a professional standard of customer service which is consistent every time they call.

In this explanation, 'professional' service is explicitly equated with being 'consistent every time [customers] call'.

Another approach to the regulation of calls is to provide operators with a checklist of things they should do, but no explicit modelling of how to do them, except in the case of the opening move (which is scripted in all cases in my corpus). Here, for instance, is the checklist provided by a call centre belonging to a utility company:

- Quick response time
- Standard greeting
- Be polite and professional
- Use listening noises
- Take control
- Ask questions – don't demand information!
- Take notes
- Obtain reason for call
- Use customer's name
- Take appropriate action to defuse anger
- Make the customer feel important

- Treat the customer as an individual
- Know our products and services – promote them!
- Summarize the call
- Offer your name and extension
- Thank the customer for calling and finish the call with goodbye.
- ALWAYS USE THE STANDARD GREETING:
- GOOD MORNING/AFTERNOON, … SPEAKING, CAN I TAKE YOUR REFERENCE NUMBER?
  [*NEVER SAY… HELLO!!!*]

These instructions reflect the same considerations we have noted in cases where there is a script. Some are to do with the particularities of telephone interaction (for example, 'use listening noises' – while back-channelling is normal in all conversation, it is particularly important where there are no visual cues). Other instructions relate to efficiency. Since time on the phone is money (and one customer's call time is another's queuing time), operators must 'take control' and 'obtain reason for call' as quickly as possible. They must also minimize errors by summarizing information given by the caller.

Many of the checkpoints on the list, however, are concerned with 'polite and professional' behaviour. This is a subject for extensive discussion and detailed prescription in all the materials I have collected. Under the heading of 'politeness' I include not just instructions to use conventional formulas like 'please', 'thank you', 'sorry', and so on, but any instructions to use language in a way that displays attention to the caller's 'face wants', that is, their desire for approbation ('positive face') and their desire not to be imposed upon ('negative face'). One obvious area where politeness is important is in mitigating potential offence to the customer. Thus workers at the credit-authorizing call centre mentioned above are given the following script for rejections: 'Unfortunately this application has been declined but thank you for calling'. The script for acceptances by contrast is just 'This application has been accepted'. This difference formalizes an intuitive understanding that what conversation analysts call a 'preference system' is in operation: acceptance is the 'preferred' response to a request for authorization and can be produced without ceremony; rejection is 'dispreferred' and requires more elaboration. As Marion Owen has argued (1983), the moves conversation analysis (CA) has identified on formal criteria as 'dispreferred' (such as declining an invitation, disagreeing with an opinion, refusing a request – all of which are typically performed with pausing, hedging and/or additional justification) are also strongly associated with threat to the addressee's face. Not only call centres but also some shops – which rarely have scripts for 'ordinary' transactions – provide scripts for use in seriously face-threatening situations (when a customer's money turns out to be counterfeit or s/he presents an invalid cheque). Such scripting reflects the emphasis placed on handling these situations sensitively; organizations do not want to take chances by leaving the details of sensitive behaviour to the individual employee's discretion. As Robin Leidner observes (1993: 230), one function of scripting is to establish a 'floor of civility', that is, a minimum level of politeness; though the effect may be to establish a 'ceiling' as well, it is more important to ensure that a minimally acceptable standard is met consistently.

Positive face is also the object of attention in guidance for call centre workers. What the utility company's checklist alludes to under the heading of 'making the customer feel important' may be realized linguistically through a number of strategies, including using the customer's name but also and importantly through prosodic and paralinguistic features. The directory assistance materials advise, for example:

> Remember voice intonation is also very important as tone, pace and clarity convey your attitude to the customer. You must never sound bored on a call. *Your telephone manner should convey the impression that you have been waiting for that individual call all day.* To assist in this try putting a smile on your face when receiving a call. We acknowledge that this can be difficult, but at the very least you *must* sound professional (my italics).

It is extremely common to find the instruction to 'smile' being given to telephone workers (and other 'invisible' workers, such as those who make public announcements at airports and railway stations). It is also common for workers to be instructed, not only in how they should *not* sound (for example, 'bored') but also in the precise attitudes they should be trying to convey in their voices. The same company's employee handbook includes, under the heading 'Standards at Work', this paragraph:

> Voice Impression – It is amazing the impression you can give a person just by the way you answer the phone. Think of the impression you get from somebody just by the way they say 'hello' when you call them. Our commitment is to give an impression of excitement, friendliness, helpfulness and courtesy to every caller. Additionally you should speak clearly, professionally and at a proper pace.

Of course, it has to be borne in mind that 'sounding bored on a call' is a real danger where operators may be repeating their script for the 800th time that day. It is not the caller's fault that the operator has already said the same thing to 799 other people, and presumably the caller would just as soon not be made aware of the operator's *ennui*. Even so, what caller would really expect or want a directory assistance operator to sound as though s/he has been waiting for them to call all day, or to display 'excitement' at the prospect of finding a telephone number for them?

The word 'professional', which occurs in both the examples just cited, appears to cover several aspects of language-use, including politeness, consistency of response, and formality. It is noticeable that whenever operators are provided with scripts, these tend to be in a formal register. The utility company's stern injunction 'NEVER SAY HELLO!' is not simply a reminder that 'hello' happens not to be the company's standard greeting; more importantly it is a reminder that 'hello' – the salutation most people utter when they pick up their own phone at home – is not formal enough to be selected as a standard corporate greeting; the 'professional' choice is 'good morning/afternoon/ evening'. in other words there is a deliberate attempt to differentiate the 'professional' from the 'personal' call (though some businesses with a young or 'counter-cultural' customer base deliberately mark themselves out as 'cool' and 'laid back' by flouting this norm and prescribing an informal greeting like 'hi, trendy co'). the scripts given to operators often prescribe forms of words which seem almost perversely un-conversational, or even un-speechlike, such as 'i *am unable to* validate your pin number', 'what do you *require?*' 'i will connect you to *x* who will be happy to *assist* you in this *matter*'. the register these examples call to mind is that of the business letter. how far it is the result of a deliberate decision to mark the transaction as 'professional' by actually avoiding a conversational tone, and how far it just results from scripts being composed in writing, by people more used to writing letters than scripting dialogue, is difficult to say. when markers of professional formality are combined (as they often are) with markers of synthetic personalization, the result can be a strange hybrid. [. . .]

REFERENCES

Leidner, Robin (1993) *Fast Food, Fast Talk: Service, Work and the Routinization of Everyday Life.* Berkeley, CA: University of California Press.
Owen, Marion (1983) *Apologies and Remedial Interchanges.* Berlin: Mouton.

3

LANGUAGE AND GENDER

In this section the focus is on patriarchal power. It attends to how patriarchal power relations are maintained in and through language. To begin, it examines the well-known claim that men and women tend to use interactional styles based on power and solidarity respectively. The section then goes on to maintain that, in order to explore patterns of male dominance effectively, we need to go beyond this polarised view and attend to discourses and practices in specific situations, institutions and genres which may establish men in positions from which they can dominate women. Studies of the dynamics of dinner-table talk show fathers established in positions of dominance by other family members. The section concludes with attention to starker assertions of male authority. It examines violence and the rhetoric that denies, hides or justifies it, focusing particularly on men's talk about their own wife-battering.

MALE AND FEMALE INTERACTIONAL STYLES

Early claims about language, gender and power came out of the equal rights struggles of the 60s and 70s. The role of language in the maintenance of patriarchal power was something that was first addressed by feminist linguists in the 1970s. They identified the centrality of language in the routine main-tenance of social inequality. For example, an investigation of gender roles in private conversations among couples identifies an unequal division of conver-sational 'labour' in which women do a great deal of support work for men; women are pushed into low-status, routine maintenance work in interaction, just as they are pushed into low-status jobs (Fishman 1983). Pamela Fishman found, for example, that the women in her study made frequent use of minimal responses (*mm, yeah* and so on) supportively, encouraging their partners' development of topics in a co-operative conversational manner. In contrast, the men withheld or delayed minimal responses with the effect of curtailing topics, in an unco-operative way. Other explorations of male dominance through language have addressed issues surrounding women's silence and the silencing of women (for example, Spender 1980). The silencing of women in positions of authority, by talking over them, has been the subject of a range of studies; for example, male patients interrupting women doctors (West 1984), male employees interrupting women managers (Woods 1988). The earliest research on interruptions as ways of 'doing power' in interaction is now generally considered to be flawed, however, since it is based on a rather simplistic notion of what constitutes an interruption (Zimmerman and West 1975; West and Zimmerman 1983). They cannot be identified solely by mechanical means, such as by looking for where people are speaking at the same time. Simultaneous speech can be far from disruptive, as shown by studies of 'high-involvement style' (Tannen 1984) and of conversations among women (Coates 1988, 1996).

Feminist interest in language, then, lies in the part it plays in reflecting, creating and sustaining gender divisions in society. In what is often called the 'dominance' framework, language patterns are interpreted as manifestations of a patriarchal social order; asymmetries in the language use of men and women are thereby seen as enactments of male privilege, as in the studies mentioned briefly above. According to the 'difference' framework, by contrast, gendered language patterns are a consequence of distinct female and male sub-cultures. In this view, women and men behave differently because they are segregated in childhood. Boys, who tend to play in large groups with hierarchical social structure, learn to value status and become power focused; whereas girls, who tend to play in small groups of 'best friends', learn to value intimacy and become solidarity focused. In the process, children acquire different gender-appropriate behaviour. As its key populariser, Deborah Tannen is the best-known proponent of the 'difference' position (Tannen 1986, 1991, 1995).

It is by now a well-known claim that men and women use interactional styles associated with power and solidarity respectively. The existence of distinct female and male interactional styles has now gained widespread acceptance, to the extent that they have entered popular 'commonsense'. The claim that men are competitive and women co-operative is a familiar one; it has been cropping up in advertising, magazine articles, management training and elsewhere since the early 90s (see, for example, Cameron 1999, 2000; Talbot 2000). There is a considerable weight of evidence to support the view, including research on politeness (for example, Brown 1980, 1993; Holmes 1995) and on physical alignment and eye contact in conversations (e.g. Tannen 1990). In a detailed study of compliments and compliment responses, for example, Janet Holmes has found New Zealand women using compliments a great deal more than men do, with compliments between women being used to consolidate solidarity between the giver of the compliment and the recipient. Holmes found that men, in contrast, tend to find compliments threatening and may use mock insults and sparring to cement friendships instead. The overall picture is one of polarisation, of men's talk as power based and competitive, women's talk as solidarity based and co-operative.

There are, however, problems with this picture, as it stands. Put bluntly, it is an oversimplification. The first two extracts in this section help to explore the main problems with this polarisation and to underline how and why it leads to oversimplification.

'You can be the baby brother, but you aren't born yet': co-operating while competing

Reading 3.1 is a close examination of the talk of children at play. This material is taken from some research on conflict management among pre-school children, conducted by Amy Sheldon. As Sheldon demonstrates, co-operativeness and competitiveness are not mutually exclusive. This point has also been made by Deborah Cameron in a study of gossip among young, male American students (Cameron 1997b). Reading 3.1 takes a close look at some of Sheldon's data: three small girls in a conflictual play situation. It has been selected to provide a detailed example of discourse analysis, following an entire play scenario through from beginning to end. In it, the children use an impressive array of conflict management strategies in trying to get their own way. The article from which the extract is taken has an appealing title: 'You Can Be the Baby Brother, But You Aren't Born Yet'. Sheldon's claim is that the polarisation of competitive and co-operative behaviour is inaccurate and exaggerated. She makes a distinction between conflict that is power based and conflict that is solidarity based. Power-based conflict is about getting your own way very directly, probably involving physical intervention. Solidarity-based conflict is much more elaborate and less direct; it involves exploiting the **multifunctionality** and potential **ambivalence** of utterances. The girls – under pressure to be 'nice', even in conflictual situations – are using co-operative strategies to ultimately competitive ends. Sheldon names this kind of talk 'double voiced', since it is both competitive and co-operative simultaneously. (You may find it useful to go to the first activity here, before reading further, as it deals with the contrasting power-based and solidarity-based conflict management strategies). The first extract, then, presents evidence of small girls engaging in both competitive and co-operative behaviour at the same time, casting doubt on the validity of the simple polarisation of men's talk as power based and competitive, women's talk as solidarity based and co-operative. Conflict, as Sheldon argues elsewhere,

> is a contest of wills. Gender ideology in many cultures gives males the
> license to argue in direct, demanding, and confrontative ways, with
> unmitigated rivalry. Girls and women do so at the risk of being called

'bossy', 'confrontational', 'bitchy', 'difficult', 'big-headed', or worse for the same behaviours that boys and men can garner praise for being 'manly', strong', or 'assertive'. (Sheldon 1997: 221)

Misunderstanding, conflict and social change

The 'difference' position, with its notion of distinct male and female interactional styles arising from different gendered sub-cultures, is used to account for misunderstandings between men and women. Women interpret in a solidarity frame, men in a power frame; the outcome is often misunderstanding. A compliment may be heard as a friendly act by a women (solidarity) or as a patronising put-down by a man (power). So when men and women communicate they misunderstand one another, a miscommunication resulting from the different sub-cultures they have been socialised into. When this view was first articulated in the early 1980s, it set out to reinterpret existing findings about language, gender and dominance in the light of research on 'crosstalk': cross-cultural miscommunication leading to racist discrimination in workplace settings. As in research on cross-cultural miscommunication, different discoursal expectations among women and men were said to lead to misunderstanding of intentions (Maltz and Borker 1982). So, for example, the difference in use of minimal responses pinpointed by Fishman is reinterpreted in terms of mismatches of expectations about how they are used. Women have learned to use them as interested-listener noises; men have not. So women think: why do men never listen? And men think: why do women always agree with you?

Reading 3.2 critically explores this view. In contrast with Reading 3.1, it is more theoretical, though the discussion centres on three vignette-like examples of dialogue. In it, Cameron argues that the issue is not miscommunication at all but *conflict*; the alleged phenomenon of 'male-female miscommunication' has arisen in communities where gender roles are most contested: middle-class, non-traditional communities. Two of the vignettes she discusses involve alleged male-female 'misunderstandings' over ambivalent utterances in workplace settings; the third involves an **indirect request** by working-class husband to wife – 'Is there any ketchup, Vera?', quoted in the title of the article from which the extract is taken – which, though indirect, in the context of its utterance is not ambivalent at all.

Ambivalence (elsewhere in this chapter multifunctionality, relativity and ambiguity) is an important issue in the exploration of language, gender and power. As Cameron explains, we interpret others' utterances on the basis of our background knowledge. This background knowledge includes assumptions about social roles, rights and obligations that the context imposes. In a society where social relations – such as gender roles in the workplace – are undergoing change, there is likely to be considerable divergence in assumptions about them. So, in a setting where a man has a female employer, the two of them might entertain rather different ideas about *her* rights and *his* obligations. Cameron gives the example of a male employee 'misunderstanding' an indirect request to finish a report ('Would you like to finish that report today?') as an enquiry about his wishes.

Ambivalence and multifunctionality can be further illustrated with an example of a non-verbal act discussed later, in Reading 3.4: a bouquet of flowers placed on the doorstep by an ex-partner. This act is ambivalent; it has potential for different functions. Without knowing the ex-couple, we might expect the recipient to interpret this act as a conciliatory gesture. The point being made is this: the meaning of a bouquet on a doorstep is not fixed. Presented with 'bouquet giving' in a contextual vacuum, we would tend to assume a loving relationship. In the context of domestic violence, separation and a subsequent restraining order, however, the bouquet giving was not in fact a loving gesture but an act of terrorisation.

Reading 3.2 begins by critically engaging with Tannen's position as a 'difference' proponent, as presented in Tannen (1993). Tannen takes issue with the preoccupation with male dominance and female subordination and points out that, in identifying discourse features (interruptions, **hedges, indirect requests,** etc.) as indices of powerful or powerless behaviour, the 'dominance' approach disregards the multifunctionality of language. So, for example, from the 'dominance' position, an interruption always has the same function; it is always assumed to be a bid to dominate talk, ruling out the possibility that it may be functioning supportively. However, Cameron argues, while this criticism is well founded, Tannen herself does just the same in her preoccupation with gender. Tannen's interpretations of her anecdotal examples have none of the careful regard for potential multifunctionality that she advocates. As Cameron makes clear in her discussion of the vignettes, the polarisation inherent in the notion of distinct male and female interactional styles is an oversimplification in that it leads to gender overriding all else; it effectively decontextualises gender. Moreover, insofar as it disregards institutional and societal *power*, the difference framework that the notions of male and female interactional styles are set in leads to depoliticisation, that is, loss of contact with feminism.

In summary, there has been a great deal of research on gendered patterns of language use; much of it has been used to support a notion of distinct male and female interactional styles. There are problems with such an account, however. To set up competition and co-operation in simple binary opposition is an oversimplification. It is not particularly useful in accounting for the complexities of interaction, as the study of small children being 'co-operatively competitive' illustrates. Another shortcoming of the notion is an overriding preoccupation with gender to the exclusion of other crucial contextual factors: in particular, power differences and conflicts of interest. To ignore conflict suppresses power. This is a problem in general with the whole 'sub-culture' approach to language and gender (for more detailed critiques, see, for example, Cameron 1992; Talbot 1998; Uchida 1992). Attention to apparently 'neutral' difference in gendered styles loses its feminist objective; unless, that is, those different styles are grounded in their institutional and societal context (and therefore not neutral at all).

EXPLORING THE MAINTENANCE OF PATRIARCHAL POWER

So far we have been encountering problems. On a more positive note, in order to explore patterns of male dominance effectively, we need to attend to discourses and practices in specific situations, institutions and genres that may establish men in positions from which they can dominate women. Examples are provided in Readings 3.3 and 3.4 and in the remainder of this introductory section.

A few words about 'patriarchy' are in order here. Tracing it back to its Latin origins, the term referred initially to 'the rule of the fathers'. In her critical investigation of discourses in the public domain – organisations including British Parliament and the Church of England – Clare Walsh prefers instead the term 'masculinist' (Walsh 2001). Since women have traditionally been excluded from these institutions, their institutional structures and practices are historically associated with men, but not in a specifically patriarchal way. She argues that patriarchy 'carries connotations of paternalism that do not capture the subtle and varied ways in which women continue to experience discrimination in a range of public domains' (ibid.: 17). Rather, the discriminatory practices have come about as a result of practices of exclusion which now position women who have succeeded in gaining entry as 'outsiders within' (ibid.: 18). For what we cover in this section, however, 'patriarchy', despite its pre-modern origins, seems entirely appropriate.

'Father knows best': narrative roles in family dinnertable talk

Reading 3.3 is taken from a study of the dynamics of narrative activity at the family dinner table conducted by Elinor Ochs and Carolyn Taylor. In it, the focus is on the particular social roles taken up by women and men, girls and boys in the institution of the family, and in the genre of oral narrative. The research project examined narrative activity and child socialisation, especially how children learn gender roles in daily interaction at home. The extract in Reading 3.3 focuses on the functioning of everyday storytelling in the assertion and maintenance of the father's position of authority. He is established in a position of dominance, with the mother's collusion, being set up in an invulnerable position as the family judge.

The focus in this section then is on 'Father knows best'. There is an allusion here to a 1950s American situation comedy, with a cliched, rather old-fashioned father figure. In fact, according to Ochs and Taylor's extensive research findings, despite its antiquity this character is still very much alive. Reading 3.3 gives details of their approach to analysing narrative roles in family dinnertable talk, with numerous samples of their transcribed data. Conversational narratives are collaboratively produced in interaction; they are not monologues, but co-narrated. Using categories for narrative roles including **protagonist,**

introducer, primary recipient and **problematiser,** Ochs and Taylor present an asymmetical scenario of children and mothers narrating their lives before fathers, who are empowered to criticise. Ochs and Taylor liken it to a *panopticon* (Bentham 1791; Foucault 1979). The term refers to a construction (such as a prison with a watchtower) that enables one person to monitor a group without being observed themselves. Used for surveillance, panopticon-like structures bestow on the watcher a position of power over those being scrutinised. Like the figure in the watchtower, the father is scrutinising children and mother without being subject to scrutiny himself. Family narrative productions at dinner contribute to the socialization of children. At the same time as establishing fathers as authority figures, they position mothers as people who may be legitimately criticised.

Another study employing the same categories for narrative roles in family dinnertable talk has examined interaction in the home of an agoraphobic woman (Capps 1999). Agoraphobia – prevalent among women to the extent that it is thought of as a women's disorder – is generally viewed as an individual pathology. Lisa Capps offers an alternative view. She counters the psychiatric view of agoraphobia as solely clinical, by demonstrating the production of its fraught emotions in domestic discourse. Building on a range of research into narrative as a theory-building activity, she explores narrative interactions as activities that bring emotions and identities into existence:

> In narrating, interlocutors attempt to construct themselves from a particular point of view, both as protagonists acting and feeling in the past and as narrators acting and feeling in the present. Narrators describe a setting in which a protagonist encounters a problematic event of some kind and relate ensuing psychological and behavioral responses and consequences. By forging causal connections between emotions and events, narratives build theories about experiences. (Capps 1999: 85)

People reframe experiences in narratives; these experiences are ratified, or not, by the other interlocutors present. As in the households in Ochs and Taylor's research, Capps found an asymmetrical distribution of narrative roles. The woman diagnosed as agoraphobic, Meg, frequently narrates accounts of her own distressing experiences, which she directs to her husband, William ('the world's *nicest,* most *normal* guy', according to Meg):

> By routinely narrating her anxiety-provoking experiences in this way, Meg establishes William in a position to (de)legitimize her emotions and actions as protagonist in the narrated scenario, as well as her present concern over this circumstance. Meg, perhaps like others who feel themselves to be 'irrational', appears to seek validation (especially from 'the world's *nicest,* most *normal* guy') for her framing of events and experiences, particularly those that remain unresolved. In the process, William obtains the authority to confer or withhold a judgment that

Meg's feelings and behavior are rational, and his identity as – 'the world's nicest, most normal guy' – is instantiated. (ibid.: 88)

Capps conducted a lengthy **ethnographic** study of Meg and her family, involving observation in the home environment over thirty-six months. Capps (1999) examines a small part of it: a set of related narratives about pitbull terriers told over a period of weeks, focusing in particular on the husband's lack of responsiveness to his wife's narrative and its possible contribution to her distress. As she narrates an anxiety-inducing encounter she had with a pair of pitbull terriers, his gaze is elsewhere and he withholds feedback; he does not ratify her fears as justified and rational. This leads to escalation in the teller's bids for response and in her own anxiety. Capps speculates that William, as primary recipient, may withhold his ratification of Meg's expressions of anxiety in order to curtail her panic but, as Capps observes, it has the opposite effect. Meg's narrative production compounds her anxious emotions. Her mental illness comes into being in her narrations of her experiences and her interlocutors, particularly her primary recipient, contribute to its (re)production.

A study contrasting Israeli and Jewish American dinnertable storytelling and its role in the socialisation of children shows the importance of cultural differences other than gender (Blum-Kulka 1993, 1997). Shoshana Blum-Kulka does not use quite the same model in investigating narrative productions, but it is still possible to make comparisons. There are similarities in the narrative roles taken up in American families across the different sets of studies; the Israelis in Blum-Kulka's study are very different. Her American families engage in ritualised 'How was your day?' performances, with the children in the spotlight most and the father least. This is perhaps comparable to the parental panopticon. In contrast, narrative roles at the Israeli dinner tables are more evenly distributed. Both parents undertake more main telling of stories, though fathers do so less often than mothers; children are less likely to be grilled by their fathers and more likely to be active listeners (producing co-operative promptings, preemptive interpretations of story information, etc.). Overall, the narratives are more 'polyphonic', demonstrating a 'high-involvement style'.

None of this research reveals monolithic patriarchal power wielded by fathers over families. Instead, what emerge, in the context of white middleclass American two-parent families, are practices establishing fathers in positions of dominance much more subtly, including the collusion of mothers in manoeuvring fathers into invulnerable positions of control over other family members. In some cases at least, this is clearly not to women's advantage. However, assertions of male dominance are sometimes not subtle at all, as the next section goes on to consider.

Male dominance: rhetoric and violence
The starkest assertions of male authority involve physical violence, even murder. In Britain, a quarter of all assaults reported to the police involve

domestic violence (Mirrlees-Black, Mayhew and Percy 1996, 1998). The same survey estimates that only one in five cases are reported. Every week, in England and Wales alone, two women are murdered by their partner or ex-partner. According to Home Office Homicide Statistics, just under half female homicides are committed by partners or ex-partners, compared with eight per cent of male homicides. The most risky time is immediately after separation, though domestic violence often begins or increases in intensity during pregnancy. In the vast majority of cases, children are either in the same room or within earshot (Source: Wearside Domestic Violence Forum).

Earlier in this section we saw studies of the family as a hierarchical social institution in which a position of dominance is assumed by the father. Parents assume authority over their children; their rights to scrutinise, control and command obedience have a commonsensical quality. In social work these parental rights over children are widely recognised as at the root of child abuse; however, gender hierarchy is not similarly understood to underlie wife-battering (Tifft 1993: 90–1).

With Reading 3.4 we continue to attend to specific discourses and practices establishing men in positions from which they can dominate women. This last reading illustrates an approach to language analysis that is rather different from the one looked at in the last section. It is an extract from 'A Discourse of Natural Entitlement: Rhetorical Justifications of Male Dominance' (Adams, Towns and Gavey 1995) and presents a discursive psychology approach to discourse analysis, examining men's talk about their violence against their partners. The study examines articulations of a discourse of natural male entitlement, through which men assert patriarchal authority.

The extract focuses on rhetorical devices used in interviews by men who had recently been violent to their partners. The men interviewed had recently begun to attend a 'Men Stopping Violence' programme in Auckland, New Zealand. Their belief in the existence of a gender hierarchy is very evident:

Gavin:	You see another reason I wanna do this [stopping violence] course was I, I don't wanna bring my son up with the same macho image that I was brought up with, y'know. Like –
PA:	Macho image? Would you say that the macho image is quite important?
Gavin:	Um yeah. Yeah I think so.
PA:	how does the macho image work for you?
Gavin:	Well um [pause] just like I'm the <u>man</u> y'know. ((laughter)) Ah it's hard to explain
PA:	I'm a man?
Gavin:	(.) I dunno, I just get the attitude like, 'don't fuck with me', ((laughing)) type thing. Um I'm bigger and stronger than you and who are you to give me this sort of shit.
PA:	this is the woman you're talking to?

Gavin:	Yeah
PA:	So who is, who is it? How dare <u>she</u> try and challenge my, my position?
Gavin:	Yeah something like that. And like I'm the man of the bloody house. In the end what, when it comes down to it, what I say goes, y'know. In the end. Whereas it shouldn't really be like that.
PA:	I'm the man of the house. Can you tell me a bit about what that means, means for you?
Gavin:	Um (.) I rule the roost, y'know. Plain and simple. Um, what I say goes. This is my house, I pay the bills, I pay the rates. And you do as I fucken tell you, sort of thing. (ibid.: 399–400)

They had been invited to discuss their views on a range of issues related to violence, in interviews that were semi-structured around topic areas including ideal relationships, women's rights and causes of violence. The extract contains detailed analysis of samples of interview data. The rhetorical devices examined in it include **ambiguity** of reference, **axiom markers**, **metaphor** and **synecdoche**. Adams et al. also attended to **metonymy**, the main example of which is quoted above. Signs for masculinity can substitute metonymically for signs of authority and power, so that 'man' in itself functions as a term expressing authority. This link seems to be self-explanatory for the speaker, to the extent that he has difficulty articulating it.

This discourse of natural entitlement is a cultural resource men can use to make sense of their relationships with women; however, it seems clear from the samples of interview data that it is not securely hegemonic. The men articulating it appear to be aware that it is problematic or, at least, that it may be open to criticism in the interview context. As Adams et al. demonstrate, the men make very frequent use of ambiguity in making statements, making chauvinistic interpretations of them deniable. More overt articulations of the discourse, such as simple assertions of authority, are sometimes hedged with laughter (a point not mentioned by the researchers which is nevertheless interesting). The men interviewed are having to respond to social changes, and resisting them.

Meaningful acts such as utterances are interpreted in context; they only have meaning in context. Interestingly, Adams et al.'s own differing interpretations as researchers (two women with first-hand experience of domestic violence, one man without such experience) became a focus of interest in themselves. For example, they formed different views about how particular axiom markers were functioning. An example of this happening is where one of the interviewees prefaces a global statement about the nature of reality with the axiom marker: 'the bottom line is . . .' The male researcher interpreted this as indicating the speaker's commitment to his axiomatic statement. The women, more sensitive to the context of domestic violence (and therefore unequal relations of power), interpreted it as an assertion of authority and power. Rather than simply adding emphasis to a personal view, they heard it as intimidation: a proclamation of omniscience. An issue raised by the study is the impact of the discourse of natural male entitlement, and the rhetoric used to support it, on abused partners in relationships. The extract opens by reflecting on the disenfranchisement of abused partners from their own understanding of events.

At the same time that abusive men can distance their partners from their own experiences, they can also distance themselves from their actions. Frequent in men's accounts of their own violence are linguistic strategies of depersonalisation, minimisation and reduction of personal agency. For example, an investigation of the language of sexual assault trials in Canada details the defendant's extensive use of 'the grammar of non-agency' in his courtroom testimony (Ehrlich 2001). This ranges from outright denial of something to elimination of personal responsibility for it:

> mitigating responsibility by hedging: 'I perhaps might have taken my shirt off'
> diffusing agency by representing events as consensual: 'we were fooling around'
> obscuring agency by using agentless **passives**: 'our pants were undone'
> eliminating agency by using **intransitive verbs** with **nominalisations**: 'the sexual activity started escalating', 'the intimacy began'. (ibid.: 41–52)

In a similar vein, a British study investigates the way men convicted of assaulting their partners articulate and account for their violence. It details three main textual devices they use in describing their own violent acts:

> subject/object relation: 'I hit her'
> reciprocal process: 'We were fighting each other'
> an abstract life of its own: 'It just happened,' 'It boiled up.' (Hearn 1998: 86)

Often used in combination – as in 'she'd nag and nag until I just explode, headbutt her or something' – these devices are very frequently hedged with the minimising adverb 'just'. In the third kind, 'the violence is an "it" that is constructed as having an active agency that then *affects the man*, the doer of the violence, and the woman, the receiver of the violence' (ibid.). This often takes the form of a simple existential statement (for example, 'it was just something that happened') or a metaphorical construction (for example, 'I just snapped') used to present absence of control and diminished personal responsibility for the actions described. Hearn observes that the discourses available to articulate accounts of violence facilitate such depersonalisation:

> The idea of the incident is so widespread and dominant in both lay and professional accounts that one might reasonably speak of its hegemony. The word 'incident' is itself a convenient reduction, fitting neatly into, and perhaps between, several discourses, including those of medicine, law and

social work ... In each case, there is a possible circumscription of the violence.

...One man described his violence at the end of the relationship in a very matter of fact way: '...yes, there was some violence. The day she left I hit her. I think it was a bit late. It was the booze. There was no dispute.' (ibid.: 85)

To conclude, within the constraints of a single chapter, we have had to be selective in the coverage of language, gender and power. We have presented a range of material that has practical usefulness as well as theoretical interest. However, you will find that gender crops up throughout the book. In the last chapter, for example, the final reading of the book emphasises the significance of gender issues in the context of young people's codeswitching between Catalan and Spanish in Catalonia.

ACTIVITIES

- Read Reading 3.1. Then examine the conflict management strategies in the two samples of talk among children at play that follow (both taken from Sheldon 1997). Can you find evidence in these data to back up the claims that neither power and solidarity nor competitiveness and co-operativeness are mutually exclusive?

Sample 1
Tony (aged 4 years, 1 month); Charlie (aged 4)

1. Tony: I pushed two squares (giggles)) two squares like this ((pushes phone buttons))
2. Charlie: ((comes closer, puts his fist up to his ear and talks into an imaginary phone)) Hello
3. Tony: ((puts his fist up to his ear and talks back)) Hello
4. Charlie: ((picks up the receiver that is on Tony's chair)) No, that's my phone!
5. Tony: ((grabs the telephone cord and tries to pull the receiver away from Charlie)) No, Tha- ah, it's on <u>my</u> couch. It's on <u>my</u> couch, Charlie. It's on <u>my</u> couch. It's on <u>my</u> couch.
6. Charlie: ((ignoring Tony, holding onto the receiver, and talking into the telephone now)) Hi ((walks behind Tony's chair, the telephone vase is still on Tony's lap))
7. Tony: ((gets off the couch, sets the phone base on the floor)) I'll rock the couch like this ((he turns the foam chair on top of the telephone vase and leans on it as Charlie tries to reach for it under the chair)) Don't! That's my phone!
8. Charlie: ((pushes the chair off the telephone and moves it closer to himself, away from Tony)) I needa use it

9. Tony: ((kneeling, sits back on his heels and watches Charlie playing with the phone))

Sample 2

Arlene (aged 4 years, 9 months); Elaine (4 years, 6 months); Erica (4 years, 2 months)

1. Arlene: Can I have that- that thing? ((referring to the blood pressure gauge in Elaine's lap)) I'm going to take my baby's temperature

2. Elaine: ((looking up from talking on the telephone)) You can use it- you can use my temperature. Just make sure you can't use anything else unless you can ask ((turns back to talking on the telephone))

3. Arlene: ((picks up thermometer from a nearby table and takes her baby's temperature)) Eighty-three! She ain't sick. Yahoo! May I? ((she asks Elaine, who is still on the telephone, if she can use the needle-less hypodermic syringe))

4. Elaine: No, I'm gonna need to use the shot in a couple of minutes

5. Arlene: But I- I need this though ((asks in a beseeching tone, picks up the hypodermic syringe))

6. Elaine: ((firmly)) Okay, just use it once

7. Erica: ((whispers)) Arlene, let's play doctor

8. Arlene: ((to Erica)) No, I'm gonna give her a shot on the–

9. Elaine: Hey, I'm the nurse. I'm the nurse ((she puts down the phone and comes over to Arlene and the crib in which her doll is lying)) Arlene, remember, I'm the nurse, and the nurses getta do shots, remember?

10. Arlene: But I get to do some

11. Elaine: Just a couple, okay?

12. Arlene: I get to do some more things too. Now don't forget- now don't touch the baby until I get back, because it IS <u>MY</u> BABY! ((said to both of the other girls)) I'll check her ears, okay? ((puts down the syringe and picks up the ear scope))

13. Elaine: Now I'll- and I'll give her- I'll have to give her ((the same doll)) a shot ((picks up the syringe that Arlene has put down))

14. Arlene: There can only be <u>one</u> thing that you- <u>no</u>, she- she only needs one <u>shot</u>

15. Elaine: Well, let's pretend it's another day that we have to look in her ears together

16. Arlene: No, no, yeah but I do the ear looking. Now don't SHOT- ((lowering her voice but still insisting)) <u>don't shot her!</u> I'm the one who does all the shots, 'cause this is my baby!

17. Elaine:	((whispers)) Well- I'm the nurse and nurses get to do shots
18. Arlene:	((spoken very intensely)) An' me' – And men- well, men get to do the shots too even 'cause men can be nurses ((taunting, slightly sing-song)) But you can't shot her
19. Elaine:	I'll have to shot her after- after after- you listen- after you look in the ears
20. Erica:	She ((Arlene)) already shot her even
21. Elaine:	We have- she didn't do a shot on her finger
22. Arlene:	But she did- she did- I DID TOO! Now don't shot her at all!
23. Elaine:	We haftta do it- Well, I'm going to keep do it after it after she- this baby
24. Arlene:	((intense but lowered voice)) Now don't you dare!
25. Elaine:	((Voice lowered more than Arlene's but equally intense)) Stop saying that! ((pause)) Well, then you can't come to my birthday!
26. Arlene:	((voice still lowered)) I don't want to come to your birthday

You could go to Sheldon (1997) for a detailed examination of these data.

- Read Reading 3.3. Then read through the following sample of conversational storytelling and identify the participant roles using Ochs and Taylor's framework:

1. Bryan:	heh a (h) ctually when Sylvie said >>that about him
2.	having knocked down before sounded like that
3.	<<Jasper[Carrot thing about] the guy[('s .)]
4. Chris:	[hehehehheh]
5. Sylvie:	((taking wineglass)) [th(h)anks]
6. Bryan:	car insurance claim-
7. Mary:	[oh heh]
8. Chris:	[heheh]
9. Bryan:	(.) er oh the er (.) >man who was knocked
10.	down< said he'd been knocked down three
11.	times before
12.	((prolonged general laughter; approx 6 seconds))
13. Sylvie:	pretty frightening when a child walks into your
14.	car I can tell you
15. Bryan:	yeah yeah
16. Sylvie:	ouf
17. Bryan:	well I've (told you er) dr driving around these
18.	little estates and things quiet estates an' (.)
19.	>suddenly turn round a corner< and there's
20.	dozens [of kids] playing all over the road

```
21. Chris:              [ mm ]
22. Bryan:   y'know (.) urh (.) .hh heh
23. Sylvie:  we had a c- a dog walk into the car once and
24.          (.) .hh we'd stopped (.) and the dog had stopped
25.          (.) started again and as soon as we moved off
26.          this bloody dog just walked straight into the car
27.          there (was) nothing we could do (..)
28.          really upse (h)t at the time y'[know]
29. Bryan:                                   [yeah]
30.          [ >remember you tell]ing me<
31. Chris:  [yeah >but there wasn't<] (.)
32.          we hadn't actually stopped (.)
33.          it [almost had one one we]
34. Sylvie:    [just very slowed down]
35. Chris:  the one we hit on the Blackpool Road —
36. Sylvie:  yeah Blackpool Road on that (.)
37.          dual car[riageway]
38. Chris:          [yes (I was) doing a]bout sixty
39. Bryan:  mm
40. Chris:  and you could see this dog in the distance
41.          on the central reservation (..) and
42.          you could see it was halfway it was cross
43.          just half crossed the road=
44. Bryan:                            =yeah
45. Chris:  an' it was (.) y'know (.)
46.          oh shit >so slow down<
47.          so I slowed down to about thirty- (.)
48. Bryan:  [mm ]
49. Chris:  [made] eye contact with the dog n' was (.)
50.          y'know like you do with a person (.)
51.          an' it stopped an' it clocked me (.)
52. Bryan:  mm=
53. Chris:  =thought right he's okay y'know
54.          it's not (.) didn't look a stupid dog
55. Bryan:  yea (h)h
56. Chris:  yeah so I started to accelerate again (.)
57.          and bugger me suddenly he just (.) leaps
58.          in front of the car
59. Bryan:  heheh
60. Chris:  ((claps hands loudly))
61. Bryan:  mm
62. Chris:  and I saw it came out the back of the car
63.          in the mirror
64. Bryan:  hhhh shw
```

```
 65. Chris:   y'know 'nd er (.) he was sorta limping off
              n' (.) just y'know it just sorta lay down
 66.          on the [side of the road]
 67. Sylvie:  [and we could]n't even stop because
              there there were roadworks and [there were]
 68. Bryan:                                  [mm ]
 69. Sylvie:  cars behind as well
 70.          there was no way [ (we could stop)]
 71. Chris:                    [when it came out –]
 72. Bryan:   [( xxxxxxxxxxxx)]
 73. Sylvie:  [so we went to the] police station
 74. Chris:   when it reappeared from underneath the back of the car
 75. Sylvie:  oh
 76. Bryan:   mm
 77. Chris:   in the mirror (.) it was bounching y'know
 78. Bryan:   hhhhh yeah
 79. Chris:   and there's a heavy (xx) (.) you felt it go
 80.          underneath
 81. Bryan:   yeah yeah
 82. Sylvie:  mm
 83. Chris:   s'a crump at the front and (.)
 84.          bang under the driver's seat and bang again
 85.          by the back axle (.) then it sorta ro (.)
 86.          it sorta bounced down the road for about (.) sh
 87. Mary:    and it got up after that?=
 88. Bryan:   =it got up and limped off?
 89. Chris:   got up got got up and crawled off y'know
 90. Sylvie:  crawled oh[ god ]
 91. Chris:             [I felt] really sick (.)
 92.          and Silvie was crying ⎯
 93. Bryan:   mm
 94. Sylvie:  I was really quite upset
 95. Bryan:   well I was      [(I was) –]
 96. Chris:                   [I was] f I was sick for the dog
 97.          and I was also bloody annoyed because it'd
 98.          (.) bashed a big dent in the front of the car
 99.          [heh heh]
100. Bryan:   [heheheh]
101. Chris:   heheheh and Sylvie nev (h) er forgave me for that
102.          (she said said)
103.          [she > th(h) ought I was rea(h)lly callous< heh
104.          ((general laughter))]
105. Sylvie:  [( of course you were you )] stupid pillock
106.          [heheheheh]
```

107. Chris: [heheheheh]
108.   ((laughter subsiding: 2 to 3 seconds))
109. Bryan: yeah I was going t'Tuson once...

Other activities using the same data are:

Examine the way the couple structure the story between them, using this simplified version of a well-known six-part model of story structure (Labov and Waletzky 1967; Labov 1972b):

Abstract: What's it about? A thumbnail sketch of the story.
Orientation: Who, what, when, where? Establishing the characters and the scene.
Complicating action: What happened next? And then? And then...?
Evaluation: So what? How/why is all this interesting?
                       (nb. can occur at any stage)
Resolution: How did it end?
Coda: That's it, story over. Back to the conversation.

You can find an analysis of the data using this simplified model in Talbot (1998).

Can you find evidence in the data to back up the claims that neither power and solidarity nor competitiveness and co-operativeness are mutually exclusive?

- Read Reading 3.4. Then tape a television sitcom. Does it articulate a discourse of male natural entitlement? Can you find any of the rhetorical devices identified by Adams et al. being used? You may like to consider issues of irony, accommodation and resistance.

READINGS

Reading 3.1
'Pretend we wanted to get married, right?':
establishing the wedding scenario

Eva (4;9), Kelly (5;5), and Tulla (4;7) have been sitting in a semicircle, playing with large and small dinosaurs, ridable trucks, smaller dump trucks, and shovel trucks. Each one also has a miniature toy person. The sequence that follows starts with Eva suggesting a switch into a pretend frame and a new play theme. Eva's plan includes Kelly but not Tulla.

From: Amy Sheldon (1996), 'You can be the baby brother, but you aren't born yet: preschool girls' negotiation for power and access in pretend play', *Research on Language and Social Interaction*, 29: 1, 57–80.

1	Eva:	((*to no one in particular*)) Pretend you- we- we wanted
		to get married, right? Pretend we wanted to [get-
2	Kelly:	((*putting dinosaurs in her truck*)) [Who?
3	Tulla:	((*to Eva*)) Yeah, ((*to Kelly*)) us!
4	Eva:	Yeah.
5	Kelly:	((*to Eva*)) Me? My guy?
6	Eva:	((*to Kelly*)) Yeah, we both wanted to get married, [right?
7	Tulla:	((*to Eva*)) [Ho- how
8		'bout mine? ((*'mine' possibly refers to Tulla's toy person*))
9	Kelly:	((*responding to Eva in line 6*)) Right.

This strip of talk is constructed with a variety of double-voice discourse techniques that present the soon-to-be-controversial script in a self-serving but mitigated fashion (see Sheldon, 1992a, 1992b; Sheldon & Johnson, 1994). In line 1, Eva uses a joint directive with 'pretend' that is also a tag question which asks for agreement, 'Pretend you- we ... wanted to get married, right?' In lines 2–5, Kelly and Tulla try to clarify which one Eva meant to include, and Tulla thinks the suggestion includes her. In line 6, Eva repeats her joint directive with a tag question, clarifying that her proposal includes Kelly, but specifies no role for Tulla. She repeats her request for confirmation from Kelly, 'we both wanted to get married, right?' In line 9, Kelly agrees, whereas in lines 7–8, Tulla requests to be included but mitigates it by framing the request as a suggestion, framing the request indirectly, as a question, 'How 'bout mine?'

Negotiating inclusion in the marriage script

As the principal roles of wife and husband are now assigned, the next segment of discourse finds Eva and Tulla discussing how Tulla could – in principle – be included. Eva's alliance with Kelly is solidified by giving Tulla a secondary role. As it will turn out, it will be a rather nonexistent role but one that is consistent with the logic of the emerging domestic script. Meanwhile, Kelly, whose participation is assured, sits nearby taking toys in and out of a truck, but taking little if any part in the girls' discussion.

10	Tulla:	((*to Eva*)) How 'bout MINE? ((*i.e., her toy person*))
11	Eva:	Yeah. No, yours didn't- you have to be the brother,
12		remember?
13	Tulla:	Oh, yeah, I'll be the baby brother. ((*giggles*))
14	Kelly:	((*continues to play with dinosaurs and a truck*))
15	Eva:	((*to Tulla*)) Yeah, you have to be a baby brother.
16	Tulla:	Yeah, I was growing into your tummy.
17	Eva:	Yeah, but not yet.
18	Tulla:	Yeah, but not yet. You didn't eat enough yet, right?
19	Eva:	No. =
20	Kelly:	= No. Cuz pretend- =
21	Eva:	= Pretend we wanted to get married, right?

In line 10, Tulla repeats her wish to be part of the marriage scenario too. But Eva, acting as the stage manager directing their play, does not want her to participate, yet. In lines 11–12, Eva doesn't refuse Tulla outright but postpones her participation instead, consigning Tulla to the ordinarily desirable role of a sibling ('you have to be the brother, remember?').

Justifying one's actions and controlling other's reactions:
'you have to be the brother, remember?'

Throughout the entire episode, Eva and Tulla give plausible justifications to persuade each other to comply with their respective wishes. Their use of justifications in conflict talk is consistent with a gender-based pattern for preschoolers found by Kyratzis (1992, p. 327). She noticed that girls use more justifications than boys and try to 'justify the fit of their control move [e.g., directives, plans] to the overall theme or topic ... in terms of a group goal.' Kyratzis claimed that this reflects the relationship orientation in girls' groups. However, it also reveals their orientation to the workings of power and status in their group and how to get it.

The following is an analysis of Eva's statement in lines 11–12, 'you have to be the brother, remember?' Eva is reminding Tulla that she proposed to take the role of the brother 148 turns earlier, although they did not have a play script planned at that time.

Eva:	((to Tulla and Kelly)) Pretend this one ((a toy person)) was my husband, right?
Kelly:	Right.
Tulla:	And this ((another toy person)) is your brother, right? ((pause)) Some brothers are big.
Eva:	But he only knows how to drive those kinda ones, right? ((referring to a truck))
Tulla:	Yeah, and not real cars.

But with the subsequent emergence of the wedding scenario, Eva wants to play with Kelly, and it is not a good time for Tulla to enter their play. Reintroducing a pretend role that Tulla expressed interest in earlier provides a justification for postponing Tulla's participation now.

The tactic Eva is taking in lines 11–12 is a particularly subtle example of double-voicing. It is a sophisticated use of language to pursue her own agenda without disrupting the social fabric of the group. Eva reintroduces their previous discussion but reshapes it so it is relevant to what she is doing now.

Rather than *ask* Tulla, she presupposes that Tulla wants to, or will, continue in that same role now, when she says in lines 11–12, 'you have to be the brother, remember?' *Remember?* is a tag that requests agreement, like *right?* or *ok?* But *remember?* is different than these. It is a factive verb. It presupposes the *truth* of the claim that Tulla had agreed to play the role of brother. Eva also frames Tulla's obligation to the brother role by the way that she constructs the matrix sentence that precedes the tag. It places Tulla in a somewhat difficult position because Eva phrases it as an imperative for Tulla, 'you have to be the brother.' If Tulla were to contest Eva's demand, it would intensify their conflict. Note that Eva could have described Tulla's participation in a variety of other ways that would entail less obligation and would have made it easier for Tulla to refuse or negotiate than 'you have to be.' For example, Eva might have said: 'how 'bout you be the brother' or 'you're the brother' or 'you're supposed to be the brother' or even 'you said you would be the brother.'

Eva's use of the tag *remember?*, rather than *ok?* or *right?*, also makes the process of refusal more complicated for Tulla. For example, Tulla would have to deny or dispute what she said previously or would have to explain that just because she talked earlier about making her toy person be the brother does not obligate her to that role right now. However it might be done, countering Eva's *remember?* seems to involve a more complicated refusal than countering an *ok?* or *right?* would.

'Yes, but' as a strategy to preface refusal with token agreement

Eva's *'remember?'* is effective in getting Tulla to stay in the role of brother even though Tulla wants to be the husband. In line 13, Tulla agrees to be the baby brother. In line 15, Eva begins a 'yes, but' move, in which agreement prefaces disagreement, or token willingness prefaces actual refusal (see Pomerantz, 1984; Sacks, 1987; Sheldon, 1992a, 1992b, for other examples of this strategy and discussion of a preference for agreement in conversation). Eva tells Tulla that she can be the baby brother. After Tulla accommodates and adds the constraint that the baby is still growing in Eva's tummy, in line 16, Eva builds the 'but' component onto Tulla's turn and adds that the baby brother is not yet growing in her tummy. With these conditions imposed, and without directly refusing Tulla, Eva maneuvers Tulla out of her play. She has defined a potential role for Tulla, but one that is not actualized. Still, the promise is there. Tulla is symbolically included in the story plan, even if her participation is delayed. The result is an ambiguous inclusion of Tulla that is not exactly a refusal. The ambiguity is likely to temper opposition if Tulla were inclined to voice it. In short, Eva's tag question in lines 11–12, coupled with her 'yes, but' tactic in lines 15 and 17, captures much cognitive and interactional complexity.

Resisting ostracism: seeking to make oneself relevant, justifying a place for one's character in the script

In the following section, Eva directs her attention to Kelly, and although Tulla asks a number of questions and tries to invent ways to justify her entrance into their play, she is either ignored or admonished to 'be quiet.' This further postpones her entry into the play; she is kept off stage for quite a while.

22	Tulla:	Yeah. And then you were- after you got married you
23		wanted a re-
24	Kelly:	((*puts her toy person in Eva's dump truck*))

25	Eva:	((*to toy person Kelly put in her truck, spoken in a high-*
26		*pitched playful voice*) WHAT ARE YOU DOING HERE?
27	Tulla:	Yeah. =
28	Kelly:	((*high-pitched voice*)) ⌈MA::::!
29	Tulla:	⌊PRETEND ONE OF YOU
30		WANTED ⌈A REAL BABY BROTHER.
31	Eva:	((*to Tulla*) ⌊SH:::! BE QUIET! ((*Eva had put her toy person*
32		*on Tulla's truck, and talked to her impatiently, in the high-*
33		*pitched voice of the toy*))
34	Tulla:	((*brings her own toy person up to Eva's and uses a high-*
35		*pitched squeaky voice*)) OKAY, YOU WO- I WON'T BE YOUR
36		BROTHER ANY MORE! ((*Tulla moves her toy person away in a huff,*
37		*turns her back on Eva, and concentrates on playing with*
38		*her own truck and toys*))

Tulla tries to enter the play in line 22 and then again in line 27 with the justification that now that Eva is married, Tulla's role deserves to be played. Tulla wants the baby-in-the-tummy to materialize, to become 'real' so she can have something to do ('after you were married you wanted a re-'). But Eva and Kelly are unconvinced and continue to play, ignoring Tulla. In lines 29–30, Tulla tries again, loudly repeating an indirect directive to make herself heard over Kelly, 'PRETEND ONE OF YOU WANTED A REAL BABY BROTHER.' In line 31, Eva interrupts Tulla and admonishes her, in the falsetto of her character's voice, 'SH:::! BE QUIET'! Her words are direct, angry, and confrontational. Tulla counters angrily in lines 35–36 with a 'yes, but' reply, a threat that is further mitigated because it is still within the pretend frame and is spoken in the falsetto of her toy person, 'OKAY ... I WON'T BE YOUR BROTHER ANY MORE!'

Ventriloquating: animating one's character as a conflict management strategy

The girls mark the fact that they are speaking in the pretend frame by speaking as their toy characters. They speak in the first person, using a high-pitched falsetto voice. Animating the toy person as a speaker creates an intimacy with the invented character. It also blurs the distinction between oneself, the child, and one's character or role. This takes some of the responsibility away from the child for what she is saying, making it look as if the child is not the author of the words, and that someone outside of the child, the character, is saying the words as part of the story. Animating another's voice implicitly marks a shift in frame to 'pretend.' As I have discussed elsewhere (Sheldon, 1990), being in the pretend play frame helps to mitigate conflict.

Wolf, Rygh, and Altschuler (1984, p. 212) found gender differences in children's patterns of affiliation with the characters they create. Girls are more likely to 'speak through the [toy] figures to create a first person conversational narrative' than boys are. Animating another's voice also gives the girls more freedom to be direct and confrontational than they might feel they had if they were to speak in their 'own' words, or in Goffman's (1981) terms, as the 'principal.'

Angry words exchanged in quiet tones: a form of double-voice discourse

When the girls speak as a character in the story, animating a voice other than their own, it can also distance them from the effect of their utterances, which are now direct and confrontational. There is a lack of congruence between their angry words and the squeaky, constructed falsetto in which they are spoken. Sheldon (1992b, pp. 534–5) discussed a similar example of lack of congruence between form and content when girls exchange angry words, yet say them in a whispered, hushed fashion. Related to this, Linell and Bredmar's (1994, p. 14) study of talk between women noted that Swedish midwives changed their voice quality to indicate that they were discussing a delicate topic when talking with pregnant women.

Managing conflict by ignoring and withdrawing

After Tulla turns her back (lines 36–8), Eva and Kelly move closer to one another and continue playing the marriage script together. Tulla begins to narrate her own separate play theme and remains offstage with her back turned to Eva and Kelly. She periodically looks over her shoulder to watch their interaction. This continues until line 60, when Eva asks Tulla a question outside of the pretend frame, which brings her back into the group, if not their play, for a short time.

39	Kelly:	((*puts her miniature toy in Eva's dump truck*))
40	Eva:	((*brings her toy person up to the one Kelly put in*
41		*her truck and speaks irritatedly in the falsetto voice*
42		*of her toy person*)) NOW, WHAT DO YOU WANT?
43	Kelly:	((*moves her toy person closer to Eva's and uses a*
44		*falsetto voice*)) SHOULD WE GET MARRIED?
45	Tulla:	((*Turns from her own play and watches Eva and Kelly*))
46	Eva:	((*falsetto*) LET ME SEE ABOUT THIS. ((*She moves her*
47		*toy person to her side of the truck away from Kelly's*))
48	Kelly:	((*falsetto*)) ⌈ OKAY, YOU GO HOME- ((*takes her toy person*
49		*back to her truck and watches Eva*))
50	Eva:	((*falsetto*)) ⌊ FOR MY REAL HUSBAND- FOR MY REAL
51		HUSBAND ((*looking at her toy person*))
52	Eva:	((*to Kelly in her own voice*)) Pretend you were my real
53		husband.
54	Kelly:	Right.

55	Tulla:	((*playing by herself, adjacent to Eva and Kelly, gestures*
56		*toward Eva with her dinosaur, says something inaudible in*
57		*a high voice*))
58	Eva:	((*to Kelly, in a high voice*)) You're number B. ((*She*
59		*looks at the letter on her own vest*)) I'm number A. ((*To*
60		*Tulla*)) What number are you, C?

Resisting ostracism by bringing one's character to life

The three girls get diverted into a discussion about what the letters on their vests mean (omitted here) and then Eva ignores Tulla again and she and Kelly move closer to one another to resume playing with their toy people at Eva's truck. Tulla is sitting near Kelly's side and Kelly turns her back to her. Tulla continues as if standing by, offstage as the audience, ignored. She moves slightly away from them and plays with her own truck for a while. Then she attempts to persuade them again.

77	Tulla:	Sh::::! ((*in a falsetto pretend voice*)) ⌈I'M SLEEPING.
78	Kelly:	⌊((*laughs, not*
79		*clear why*))
80	Tulla:	((*excitedly*)) You know who's [sleeping? Your <u>brother's</u> =
81	Kelly:	((*looking up at ceiling*)) Bright lights.
82	Tulla:	= sleeping. ((*gleefully*)) Hee ee! Lookit, he's sleeping!
83		((*She brings her truck over to Eva and Kelly and points to*
84		*her toy person lying in the shovel of the truck*))
85	Eva:	((*To Tulla*)) He's still in the TUMMY. He's still in the
86		TUMMY.
87	Kelly:	((*She turns and takes the 'sleeping' toy person from Tulla's*
88		*truck, lifting it high in the air as if to drop it in her own*
89		*truck*)) ⌈Dum:ps:ter!
90	Tulla:	((*Quietly*)) ⌊Don't. ((*She reaches up and takes her toy back*))

Starting in line 77, Tulla tries to get the girls' attention in a variety of ways without moving out of the pretend frame. She indirectly asks them to stop their play by making a dramatic sound, 'Sh::::!' This signals that someone is sleeping. She starts to enact her role as the baby, first as the first person narrator, 'I'M SLEEPING,' and then (lines 80 and 82) as the observing narrator, 'Your *brother's* sleeping.' She directs Eva's and Kelly's attention to an actual, *embodied* baby brother, represented by a toy figure in her truck. She moves the figure closer to them, points at it, and says, 'Lookit, he's sleeping!' (line 82). In this way, she tries to get herself accepted in their play. She actualizes the character of the baby brother. She makes the baby relevant to the ongoing activity. She makes it appealing, but also unobtrusive.

She tries to get the others involved in her script in other ways. She challenges them to guess who the toy in her truck is supposed to be (line 80: 'You know who's sleeping?'), almost as a test of shared knowledge. She refers to the baby as a member of their family, someone they are connected to and, by implication, should be interested in or have something to do with ('Your brother's sleeping!'). She brings the baby closer, into their line of sight, and demands that they acknowledge it and, by association, acknowledge and accept her ('Lookit').

Managing conflict by postponement rather than direct refusal: a double-voice strategy

Yet in lines 85–6, Eva is not persuaded. She stays in control of the agenda and, in a double-voice refusal, counters, 'He's still in the TUMMY. He's still in the TUMMY.' Once again Eva postpones incorporating Tulla into her story, without entirely refusing her either, keeping the baby a possibility not yet realized. Eva continues to play with Kelly.

More double-voice discourse: angry words exchanged in a hushed voice

91	Eva:	((*to Kelly*)) Let's get- pretend we're getting married
92		now, 'kay?
93	Tulla:	And you- ((*Eva and Kelly are humming the Wedding March,*
94		*ignoring Tulla*)) one of you- Eva? Eva:? Eva! Eva! Eva!
95		Pretend- preten-
96	Eva:	((*to Tulla*)) Uh-uh! I'm talking to her. ((Eva and Kelly face
97		Tulla))
98	Tulla:	Can I tell you something after?
99	Eva:	Sure. ((*glares at Tulla and impatiently hisses*)) Just be quiet!
100	Tulla:	'Kay, I been trying to be.
101	Eva:	((*to Kelly as she enacts a wedding with their two toy people*))
102		Okay, 'kay, do you deserve to get married? Yes. Do you
103		deserve to love each other? Yes. ((*giggles*))
104	Tulla:	[I ge- I'm uh, really getting tired of waiting.
105	Eva:	Do you deserve- do you deserve to love each other?
106		Yes. You may kiss ((*makes two toys 'kiss'; she and*
107		*Kelly giggle, ignoring Tulla*))

In lines 91–2, after Eva suggests to Kelly 'Let's ... pretend we're getting married now' the two girls move toward one another and again turn their backs to Tulla. They stay this way as they hum the Wedding March. Tulla continually tries to get Eva's attention in line 94, at one point tapping her on the shoulder and speaking outside of the pretend frame. Eva finally acknowledges Tulla brusquely in line 96. But she admonishes her in line 99 in a 'yes, but' move in which token agreement, 'Sure,' prefaces a hissed, direct refusal, 'Just be quiet!' Even though the opposition escalates in line 99, verbally and nonverbally, Eva's speaking voice is muted. In line 100, Tulla replies that she's been trying to accommodate Eva. In lines 101–3, Eva returns to the wedding script, narrating the voices of all the participants, as Tulla and Kelly look on.

Resisting ostracism: complaining and being ignored

In line 104, Tulla interjects a complaint about waiting so long. The others ignore her. Then Tulla steps outside of the pretend frame and suggests a relevant new subtheme.

```
108 Tulla:   It's not funny. I need a question now. Pretend one of
109          you wanted a baby really much then- [that you had =
110 Kelly:   ((to Eva in the wedding, falsetto)) OKAY.
111 Tulla:   = to get [one
112          ((Eva and Kelly hum the Wedding March, as Eva
113          moves her and Kelly's toy people along the floor))
114 Tulla:   You got a baby in the 'doptive place.
115 Eva:     ((To Tulla)) Yeah, but I didn't go yet. =
116          ((To Kelly, referring to their toy people)) = Now,
117          we're dancing, right? [((hums dancing music))
118 Tulla:   Yeah, and then you wan[ted one.
119 Kelly:   ((To Eva, still humming)) I'll hold
120          this one.
```

Tulla's suggestion in lines 108–9 and 111 is ignored. Eva and Kelly continue their play Kelly interrupts Tulla in line 110, and in line 112, she and Eva break into Tulla's complaint, humming the Wedding March while walking their toy figures down an imaginary aisle and making them kiss. Tulla tries to develop the narrative again in line 114, 'You got a baby in the 'doptive place.' This gets another 'yes, but' refusal from Eva in line 115, 'Yeah, but I didn't go yet,' followed by a narration in lines 116–17 and 119–20 of Eva's and Kelly's continued activity in the pretend frame, 'Now we're dancing, right?' Tulla persists in line 118, still outside of the pretend frame, with a 'yes, but' tactic of her own that offers a justification framed in terms of Eva's interests – that after the marriage Eva will be ready for a baby. Tulla is still ignored though and remains a bystander while half-heartedly playing with her truck, offstage. There is then a diversion from the script as the three girls talk, animating their pretend characters' voices, about who has long or short hair and which length they prefer. Then play continues.

Success at last

```
128 Eva:     ((to Kelly, falsetto)) YOU GO GET YOUR TRUCK.
129 Kelly:   ((falsetto)) OKAY. WHERE SHOULD I MEET YOU?
130 Eva:     ((falsetto)) UM AT- AT MARKET- THE MARKET- THE
131          MARKETPLACE.
132 Tulla:   ((falsetto, distressed voice of baby brother)) OH NO!
```

133 Kelly: ((*falsetto, to Eva*))   ⌈WHICH MARKET?
134 Tulla: ⌊NOT AGAIN! I'VE WAITED SO LONG.
135   GOD!
136 Eva: ((*To Tulla*)) You're still in my tummy, <u>right</u>? =
137 Tulla: = <u>no</u>, no, at the d<u>o</u>ptive place.
138 Eva: Nobody adopt you yet, right? =
139 Kelly: ((*falsetto, to Eva*)) ⌈OKAY ((*playing with her truck*))
140 Tulla: ((*to Eva*))   ⌊= Yeah. ((*louder, talking over
141   *Kelly*)) Because there was only one, one baby, right? =
142 Eva: ((*to Tulla*)) = left, ⌈right? =
143 Kelly: ((*falsetto*))   ⌊OKAY ⌈LADIES ⌈OKAY .
144 Tulla: ⌊= Yeh. ((*louder*)) [And then
145   people were about ⌈to-
146 Eva: ((*falsetto*))   ⌊OH, I THINK WE SHOULD GO TO THE
147   DOCTOR'S AND GET OUR BABY. =
148 Kelly: ((*falsetto*)) = OKAY. ((*Kelly and Eva make vehicle noises
149   and push their trucks over to Tulla's truck*))
    ⋮
151 Tulla: ((*puts her toy person in the shovel of her truck, opens the
152   shovel and drops the toy person out, and says gleefully,
153   falsetto*)) THERE'S YOUR BABY!!

The wedding is completed prior to line 128 and in the subsequent lines new decisions are made about the script. In lines 132, 134–5, Tulla speaks in the falsetto voice of her toy figure once again to express her exasperation at still being put off. Animating her character's voice allows her to mitigate the impatience, disappointment, and confrontation she expresses directly and in the first person, 'OH <u>NO</u>! NOT <u>AGAIN</u>! <u>I'VE WAITED SO LONG</u>. GOD!' Eva finally takes notice and they collaborate on a script that includes Tulla. Moving seamlessly out of the pretend frame, in line 136 Eva asks Tulla for clarification of the story line, 'You're still in my tummy, right?' Tulla counters that she's at the ''doptive place.' Eva then gives a reason why 'the baby' is available for adoption, which Tulla elaborates on. In lines 146–7, Eva finally brings Tulla into the story when her character declares to Kelly in a mitigated joint directive, 'OH, I THINK WE SHOULD GO TO THE DOCTOR'S AND GET OUR BABY.' Kelly's character agrees, and in line 153 Tulla gleefully brings the baby onstage and incorporates it into the girls' play.

REFERENCES

Goffman, E. (1981). 'Footing' In *Forms of talk* (pp. 124–59). Philadelphia: University of Pennsylvania Press.
Kyratzis, A. (1992). 'Gender differences in the use of persuasive justifications in children's pretend play'. In K. Hall, M. Bucholtz, and B. Moonwomon (eds.), *Locating power. Proceedings of the Second Berkeley Women and Language Conference, 2* (pp. 326–37). Berkeley: University of California, Berkeley Linguistic Society.

Linell, P., and Bredmar, M. (1994, April). '*Reconstructing topical sensitivity: Aspects of face-work in midwife-pregnant woman talk*'. Paper read at the 1994 American Association for Applied Linguistics Conference, Baltimore.

Pomerantz, A. (1984). 'Agreeing and disagreeing with assessments: Some features of preferred/dispreferred turn shapes'. In J. M. Atkinson and J. Heritage (eds.), *Structures of social action: Studies in conversation analysis* (pp. 57–101). Cambridge, England: Cambridge University Press.

Sacks, H. (1987). 'On the preferences for agreement and contiguity in sequences in conversation'. In G. Button and J. R. E. Lee (eds.), *Talk and social organisation* (pp. 54–69). Clevedon, England: Multilingual Matters.

Sheldon, A. (1990). 'Pickle fights: Gendered talk in preschool disputes'. *Discourse Processes*, 13, 5–31.

Sheldon, A. (1992a). 'Conflict talk: Sociolinguistic challenges to self-assertion and how young girls meet them'. *Merrill-Palmer Quarterly*, 38, 95–117.

Sheldon, A. (1992b). 'Preschool girls' discourse competence: Managing conflict'. In K. Hall, M. Bucholtz, and B. Moonwomon (eds.), *Locating power. Proceedings of the Second Berkeley Women and Language Conference*, 2 (pp. 529–39). Berkeley: University of California, Berkeley Linguistic Society.

Sheldon, A., & Johnson, D. (1994). 'Preschool negotiators: Gender differences in double-voice discourse as a conflict talk style in early childhood'. In B. Sheppard, R. Lewicki, and R. Bies (eds.), *Research on negotiation in organizations, 4* (pp. 27–57). Greenwich, CT: JAI.

Wolf, D. P., Rygh, J., and Altschuler, J. (1984). 'Agency and experience: Actions and states in play narratives'. In I. Bretherton (ed.), *Symbolic play: The development of social understanding* (pp. 195–217). New York: Academic.

Reading 3.2
'Relativity' and misunderstanding

I begin by exploring what remains problematic in both 'dominance' and 'difference' approaches. A good starting point is the argument put forward in what I take to be the most fully elaborated account of Deborah Tannen's position, which is also her most extended critique of the position she attributes to the 'dominance' current: to wit, her article (1993, and reprinted in a slightly revised form in 1994) 'The Relativity of Linguistic Strategies: Rethinking Power and Solidarity in Gender and Dominance'.

In this article Tannen wants to clarify that she does not, as some critics charge, reject the political postulate of male dominance. Rather she objects to a particular way of relating this postulate to linguistic or discoursal phenomena. The evidence typically offered for men's dominance and women's subordination in conversation, such as frequency counts of features like interruption, silence, asking questions or performing speech acts indirectly, is equivocal or suspect, she argues, because it depends on identifying linguistic strategies as a prior either 'powerful' or 'powerless'. Tannen points out that strategies in discourse are 'relative', multifunctional: they have the potential to realize meanings that are diametrically opposed, along the familiar sociolinguistic poles of solidarity and

From: Deborah Cameron (1998), 'Is there any ketchup, Vera?': gender, power and pragmatics', *Discourse and Society*, 9: 4, 437–55.

status. Interruption, for instance, often treated as a marker of power or status (Zimmerman and West, 1975), may equally be used as a solidary strategy signalling 'high involvement'. Indirectness, often treated as a marker of power-lessness (Lakoff, 1975), can also be found where the indirect party is unequi-vocally dominant—as with the master who says 'it's cold in here' and knows that the servant will hasten to close the window. Tannen sums up (1993: 173):

> The potential ambiguity of linguistic strategies to mark both power and solidarity in face-to-face interaction has made mischief in language and gender research, wherein it is tempting to assume that whatever women do results from or creates their powerlessness and whatever men do results from or creates their dominance. But all the linguistic strategies that have been taken by analysts as evidence of dominance can in some circum-stances be instruments of affiliation.

The argument that linguistic strategies are multifunctional and potentially ambiguous has been well taken by feminist linguists for some time (Holmes, 1984; Cameron et al., 1988; Gal, 1991).[1] However, if we go no further than saying all strategies are 'relative', capable of realizing meanings of either power or affiliation, doubts must arise about the very possibility of *analysing* dis-course. It is one thing to say we cannot specify in advance and in general 'what interruptions mean' or 'what silence means'; it is another to suggest we cannot specify the function of some particular interruption/silence in some particular piece of data. So strong a version of 'relativity' would make discourse analysis impossible.

More importantly, it would leave unexplained how anyone is ever able to have a conversation. The relativity of linguistic strategies confronts ordinary conversationalists from moment to moment as a practical problem. The utterances they have to process are potentially ambiguous, but for the enterprise of conversation to proceed in the way we know it does, they must in practice narrow down the set of possible interpretations and come to some decision about what utterances actually mean. In most cases it seems they do this to their mutual satisfaction, i.e. they believe they have understood one another.

In Tannen's view, however, that belief is frequently mistaken, and this is a cause of conversational trouble between women and men. At this point I return to my earlier comment that her own analytic procedure is open to some of the same objections she makes to the 'dominance' approach. For while Tannen counsels against assuming that the meaning or function of a particular linguistic strategy is determined in advance of its use in conversation, in practice she seems to hold that it *is* determined in advance for any particular language-*user*, typically on the basis of that language-user's gender. A man confronted with an utterance whose underlying intention is ambiguous will tend to reach auto-matically for the status-oriented interpretation; a woman in the same position will reach equally readily for the affiliative reading. That is why the odds are good that the two will misunderstand one another.

Tannen gives the illustrative example of the co-workers, one male and one female, who are walking between two buildings on a cold day. She asks 'where's your coat?', and he replies 'thanks, mom'—an utterance which, as Tannen notes, frames the woman as bossy and interfering. Tannen's analysis is a reconstruction of the reasoning the man must have gone through to arrive at an interpretation of the woman's remark as maternal bossiness. She suggests that what he does is apply a (typically masculine) principle according to which the underlying aim of talk is to gain or maintain status. Within this framework he interprets the woman's remark as a put-down and responds by putting *her* down. She, however, is working within a (typically feminine) framework in which the underlying aim of talk is affiliative rather than status-oriented. Her comment is intended to express friendly concern, and she is hurt when she realizes that a less benign intention has been imputed to her.

Where is 'relativity' in this account? It is latent in the woman's initial comment, which is in principle liable to either a 'status' or an 'affiliation' reading; but it is not entertained in (Tannen's account of) the actual behaviour of either speaker. In practice, gender cancels out relativity: each party simply interprets the remark in a way that is consonant with their gendered worldview, and apparently makes no allowance for the possibility that it could be inter-preted differently. This gives rise to a 'misunderstanding', inasmuch as the intentions the man attributes to the woman do not match her 'real' intentions in issuing the remark.

It seems, then, that for the purposes of practical analysis Tannen has replaced the position she (rightly) criticizes: 'whatever women do results from or creates their powerlessness and whatever men do results from or creates their dom-inance', with an approach that is analogous, since it too depends on axioms about gender that are outside and prior to the data themselves: 'whatever women do results from their connection-oriented worldview and whatever men do results from their status-oriented world view'. Where else is Tannen's warrant for telling us (a) what the woman 'really' intended by her remark, and (b) what the man 'really' understood by it? All we have in the data is a record of what she said and then what he said.

There are a number of things I am *not* trying to argue here. I am not arguing that Tannen's account of what is going on in this exchange is necessarily *wrong* (though other interpretations are possible in the sense that the surface data would not rule them out; a point I expand on later). I am not arguing either that her way of proceeding—that is, by going beyond or 'underneath' the surface linguistic data in an attempt to reconstruct participants' interpretive pro-cesses—is misguided. And I am not arguing that there is no place in discourse analysis for assumptions which exist prior to the data. On the contrary, I take it such assumptions are a crucial part of what we have to bring to bear on interpreting utterances in conversation, whether as analysts or participants. My point is that you cannot criticize others (in this case, 'dominance' researchers) for making a priori assumptions when your own approach is equally dependent on them. Rather you have to engage in argument about why your particular a priori assumptions are 'better' than the alternatives.

If we accept Tannen's principle of 'relativity', then what the analyst has to explain in a case like the 'coat' exchange is how the 'relative' strategy used by one participant is taken up by the other and accorded a specific meaning. This is, indeed, a question about the assumptions the hearer brings to bear on the utterance and the inferences he draws as a result. Tannen has an answer, but she does not directly address the question of what makes her answer preferable to any other possible answer. Specifically, she does not explain why it would be illegitimate to entertain the possibility that among the participants' assumptions in this context are assumptions, precisely, about gender and about power. These are social realities, and while conversationalists are not obliged by some iron law to attend to them, nothing prevents them from doing so. Cultural understandings of social and power relations are part of the background to our interactions, and there is always the potential for them to be foregrounded in some way. Later I argue that looking at the network of assumptions participants in conversation are operating with may offer a more promising method for locating the workings of power in discourse than looking at the surface features where many dominance' analysts sought its workings in the past.

Another question is why we have to take it that the assumptions at issue in the interpretation of the 'coat' example are not shared, but in complementary distribution between women and men. Why count this as a 'misunderstanding', as opposed to a *conflict* about what was meant, and more generally about the relative positioning of the two interactants, who are equal/similar on one socially relevant axis (occupational status) but different/unequal on another (gender)?

Tannen provides no evidence that communication in this exchange actually breaks down, in the way it clearly does in many of the inter-ethnic examples discussed by Gumperz (1982). Whereas Gumperz's analysis of, for instance, an encounter between an Asian client and an Anglo-British worker assessing his training needs shows the parties at cross purposes throughout, with mutual frustration and bewilderment as the outcome, Tannen's account of the 'coat' incident notes that the woman's reaction to the man's 'thanks, mom' is to feel hurt by the implication that she was not just being friendly. This suggests that the woman, unlike the parties in the inter-ethnic encounter, has had no trouble reconstructing her interlocutor's interpretation of her remark. It may not be (only) because she did not intend this meaning that she finds his response (a sexist put-down) hurtful. Conversely, it may not be (only) because he failed to retrieve the woman's true intentions that the man responds to her original comment by positioning her as 'mom'. There is a cultural script or 'schema' in play here: it is likely to be *known* to both women and men, but it places them in different *positions*. By deploying it, the man foregrounds certain gender-stereotypical assumptions which could have remained in the background, given that the parties also have a gender-nonspecific relationship as co-workers. And he could have chosen to do this *strategically*, regardless of what intentions he 'really' attributed to the woman or whether these were 'really' her intentions. It seems reasonably clear from his response that the man took exception to the woman's remark; it does not necessarily follow that he must have misunderstood her intentions.

[...]

Assumptions about social roles, positions, rights and obligations are part of the (usually unstated) background knowledge that is routinely brought to bear on the interpretation of utterances in conversation. Information about who someone is and what position he or she speaks from is relevant to the assessment of probable intentions. Since gender is a highly salient social category, it is reasonable to assume that participants in conversation both can and sometimes (perhaps often) do make assumptions relating to it. Hence one source of potential divergence in interpretation between women and men in conversation is that assumptions about gender and gender relations are not always shared by the interacting parties. This reflects the fact that there is currently a degree of conflict, especially in modern western middle-class communities, about the respective roles, rights and obligations of women and men. Such conflict does not only (or always) position women and men on opposite sides. It can be just as marked, or more marked, between women of different generations and classes. Because of the conflict of *interest* it represents, however, it is likely to be felt as most salient when it arises in male-female interaction.

Feminists take it as axiomatic that in any patriarchal society there must be fundamental conflicts of interest between women and men, but we need not assume that these conflicts invariably manifest themselves in interactions between the sexes, only that they *may* do so.[2] I hope it is uncontroversial to point out that women and men do not always misunderstand one another, and a convincing account of cross-sex communication must be able to explain cases where there is no misunderstanding as well as cases where there (allegedly) is misunderstanding.

In this connection, a puzzling feature of Deborah Tannen's account of male-female misunderstanding is its failure to explain why there seems to be so much of it in what are, relatively speaking, gender-egalitarian sectors of society, and at the same time so little of it (at least as a matter for overt comment) in communities where both gender differentiation and male dominance are far more pronounced. If systematic misunderstanding arose, as most 'difference' analysts claim, from gender separation or segregation, then one would surely expect it to be most pervasive where those conditions are most extreme. Yet it seems to be less prevalent in communities that preserve complementary and hierarchical gender roles than in those where traditional role divisions have to some extent broken down.

Here it might be argued that I am confusing the existence of the problem with the conscious perception of it as a problem. Perhaps women in traditional working-class or peasant communities do not complain that their husbands 'just don't understand' because they have more pressing problems to worry about, or because their needs for intimacy and connection are met, in a way middle-class women's are not, by close-knit local networks of female friends and kin. Interestingly, however, Deborah Tannen herself has presented evidence that there may indeed be more male-female misunderstanding in some communities than in others. In a study of whether a potentially ambiguous conversational move was interpreted as direct or indirect by married couples of three different ethnicities (Greek, Greek-American and Anglo-American), Tannen (1982) found that Greek couples were more likely to converge on the same interpretation than were Anglo-American couples. Ethnic differences (roughly, the more 'Greek' the respondents, the more indirect their preferred interpretation) were complicated in the Anglo-American case by a polarization between women and men. These results imply significantly more potential for systematic miscommunication among Anglo-American husbands and wives than among Greek ones. But this can hardly be because Anglo-American couples observe a higher degree of gender role differentiation, or more hierarchical gender relations, than their Greek counterparts. As Tannen observes, the reverse is the case. So how is the finding to be explained?

My explanation would be that the root of what Tannen calls 'misunderstanding' is neither gender differentiation nor gender hierarchy per se. The key ingredient is *conflict*, not just in the abstract sense that two groups objectively have conflicting interests, but in the more concrete sense that subjective awareness of these conflicting interests has caused individuals within a society to diverge in their actual beliefs about gender relations.[3] Without this kind of 'subjective' conflict there will be no perceived problem of male-female misunderstanding, because assumptions about gender relations—however unfair or oppressive these may appear, and however differently they position men and women—will be largely shared by speakers of both sexes, who will therefore draw similar inferences from the same utterances. This is probably the commonest situation in most presentday communities. Both gender differentiation and male dominance are widespread, if not universal: but they can and do exist without giving rise to any explicit challenge, and therefore without giving rise to the kind of conversational trouble that has struck such a chord with the audience for popular texts like *You Just Don't Understand*.

If this argument is accepted, a further point follows. The conversational troubles that allegedly plague so many male-female interactions are often presented, especially in popular texts, as static and durable phenomena arising from a division that is socially and historically very 'deep'. That is why the response we are usually urged to make to them is tolerance: we should understand the differences and learn to live with them. If, however, one attributes male-female conversational troubles to the workings of conflict rather than difference *tout court* (or indeed, dominance *tout court*), this suggests that they are not an eternal fact of life, but rather the outcome of processes associated with social *change*.

One of the most important changes in this regard must be that in some societies and contexts, women and men are now in competition for the same kinds of power and status, as opposed to taking up complementary roles. This situation creates fertile terrain for 'strategic' misunderstanding, where the relativity of linguistic strategies is exploited as a weapon in conflicts between men and women. It is relevant to the analysis of two examples—one involving complementarity, the other competition—to which I now turn.

'Is there any ketchup, Vera?'

Although my argument is very much about where and how one locates power in the analysis of data, the focus of this paper is theoretical, and to make the argument clear it is desirable, ironically, to minimize the complexity of any data I use to illustrate it. I also want to emphasize the differences between my approach and Deborah Tannen's. With these points in mind I have chosen to discuss the same kind of limited material that Tannen does in both her popular work and the scholarly article referred to here (Tannen, 1993): to wit, anecdotal vignettes of male-female interaction which are made exemplary by their banal and even stereotypical quality. While I, like Tannen, may be criticized for this choice, examples of the kind used here are not without their virtues. As stereotypes, they condense a great deal of taken-for-granted cultural wisdom into a very small amount of surface discourse production. It is precisely the relationship of the surface utterance to the cultural assumptions 'underneath' that is at issue in the pragmatic approach I am proposing.

My first vignette comes from a magazine article advising women how to talk to men they work with if they wish to be understood. The (anonymous) feature advises: 'make requests directly to male subordinates. Women shy away from giving a blatant order, but men find the indirect approach manipulative and confusing'. One of the things women are advised *not* to do is frame what are really intended as orders in the form of questions, such as 'would you like to finish that report today?' This, it is suggested, will not convey unambiguously to a male colleague/subordinate that the report has to be finished; if he fails to make it a priority, and you then call him to account for that, the result may well be to compound the misunderstanding and damage your working relationship. *He* will say that if it was really urgent you should have made that clear, and *you* will suspect he is a chauvinist who secretly does not respect your authority and is trying to undermine you.

This vignette is from a 'popular' source, and there is no indication of whether the hypothetical exchange and subsequent misunderstanding have ever been attested in reality. But the vignette clearly draws on a 'real' research finding, namely that women tend to make more use than men of indirect requests and mitigated directives (see Goodwin, 1980; Holmes, 1995). It also shares with many of Deborah Tannen's own examples the quality of being recognizable— the writer feels able to count on readers not reacting with outright disbelief to the proposition that this misunderstanding might occur.

My second vignette, by contrast, concerns the use of indirectness by a man talking to a woman; and while it is anecdotal, I have no reason to think it is not a faithful report of a real incident—indeed, in this case, a repeated one. A friend described to me a dinner-table habit of her father's, glossing it as 'typically male behaviour'. Every night when her mother served dinner, my friend's father would look up from his plate and say to his wife: 'is there any ketchup, Vera?'[4] Needless to say, this was intended and understood by all family members to mean not 'I don't know if we have any ketchup in the house, please enlighten me', but 'I want ketchup on my food, please fetch it for me'.

These two vignettes are about the same linguistic strategy, that is, the performance of a speech act that is intended as a command or a request for action ('finish that report'; 'get me some ketchup') in the surface form of a yes/no question. Each vignette presents the strategy as typical of the gender to which the speaker belongs: of women in the first case and of men in the second. In the 'office' vignette it allegedly leads to a misunderstanding; in the 'ketchup' vignette it does not. How are these apparent contradictions to be explained? Is gender relevant to the explanation at all?

My answer would be that gender *is* potentially relevant to the extent that it affects the context-specific assumptions the man and the woman in each of the examples bring to bear on the work of interpreting one another's utterances. If there is a divergence of interpretation between the parties in one case but not the other, a satisfactory explanation must be sought not in gender-preferential responses to a particular linguistic strategy, but at the level of assumptions and inferences which are specific to the situations these conversationalists find themselves in.

How does Vera decide that her husband wants her to get him some ketchup? Up to a point she is following pragmatic principles that have nothing to do with gender. It is reasonable to suppose that a diner wouldn't enquire about the existence of a particular foodstuff out of idle curiosity: given what we know about the world, the most obvious inference that would explain why ketchup is interactionally relevant at this point is that the speaker wants some ketchup on the food he has just been served. Inferences are context-dependent, of course, and this one would not have been drawn so easily if the speaker had picked up his knife and fork and said 'are there any nine-inch nails?', or enquired about ketchup in the course of building a wall. In this case, however, the implication 'I want ketchup' is so strong, a speaker who, on being given the ketchup said, 'oh, sorry, I didn't actually want ketchup, I was just asking if we had any' would cause fellow-diners intense irritation.

But we still have to explain the other striking feature of the 'ketchup' example: that Vera understands it not merely as expressing a desire for ketchup but as a request that she, Vera, should get the ketchup. To understand this we have to look at context in a broader sense: at the social roles and relations that hold and are taken for granted within a given context. Vera and her husband apparently agree that if he wants ketchup, she should fetch it. None of this is specified in the form of the utterance, but it is part of the contextual information used to interpret the utterance. That is probably why my friend described it as 'stereotypically male' behaviour, even though in purely formal terms the strategy—indirectness—is stereotypically associated with women. The actors in this scene are playing recognizable roles which are gender as well as context-specific: the roles of a traditional husband and wife having dinner at home.

Once again, the interpretation I am proposing is context-dependent: the same form of words may be treated differently depending on who is speaking to whom in what situation. For example, Vera's obligation to her husband is not reciprocal. My friend found her father's behaviour irritating precisely because there was never any question of her mother making similar requests to him. Then again, Vera's obligation is *only* to her husband, not to everyone at the dinner table. If the daughter used the same 'is there any ketchup?' strategy to her mother, there was every chance it would meet with a different response, like 'yes, it's in the kitchen cupboard'—a challenge to the idea that a daughter is entitled to expect the same service as a husband. This underlines the point that speaker intention is not the final guarantor of interactionally produced meaning. Vera presumably attributes the same intention to her daughter as to her husband, but her response treats the utterance strategically as if it really were what it is framed as, a request for information. This is an example of someone *exploiting* the relativity of linguistic strategies to refuse what we might well think is the most obvious or conventional reading of a particular utterance; and at a 'deeper' level, therefore, to resist the way another speaker is attempting to position them.

We might speculate that it is specifically in situations and relationships where one person's role is centrally conceived of as a *service* role that the parties agree in treating 'is there any X, Vera?' as unambiguously a request for Vera to get X, in spite of the indirectness of the formulation. This is a good example of Tannen's principle of 'relativity'—indirectness does not always have this function—but it also illustrates how the relativity of a strategy in the abstract does not prevent its meaning being pinned down precisely by all parties (and by the analyst) in a concrete, specific instance. As long as the right contextual conditions apply, there will be no ambiguity about what the strategy means, because participants take for granted one person's entitlement to request an item and the other's responsibility to provide it.

Gender *is* relevant to this example, then, but not in the sense that the man has one way of making or interpreting requests, the woman has another, and the gulf between the two is fraught with the danger of misunderstanding. On the contrary, both parties understand his request in the same way, and both apparently agree that only he is fully entitled to make requests of this form at family meals. They are differently positioned in relation to the making of requests, but there is no misunderstanding between them.

It is also important to note that the gender-related phenomenon which is relevant in this situation is not simple male-female difference but a conventional

division of labour within traditional marriages, whereby wives provide
tic service to husbands. That it's a question of roles (rather than sin
gender) is underlined if we consider that the 'is there any X?' strategy is
universal among married couples nor confined to them. Qua strategy,
not have to be gendered: it could equally be used (by either sex to either
addressing other people performing service roles—such as a waiter in a restaurant, or the host when eating at someone else's house. If Vera were placed in a
situation of being a recipient rather than a provider of domestic services, there
would be nothing to prevent her from using the strategy herself. Here we may
recall Elinor Ochs's observation (1992: 340) that 'few features of language
directly and exclusively index gender': rather the use of strategies that conventionally index more specific roles (e.g. 'mother' or in this case 'domestic
service provider') may connote gender through a process of inference.

What if we apply a similar analysis to the 'would you like to finish that report
today?' example? Here, again, it would surely be perverse for any competent
speaker in this context to take the form of the utterance at face value, as a
straightforward question about the man's preferences. That would be analogous to treating 'is there any ketchup?' as an idle enquiry about the state of your
household supplies: not impossible, but unlikely to be your first guess. In a
business interaction, an employee's desires are conventionally assumed to be
less relevant than his or her obligations. Unless the man (a) has good reason to
believe this is not a business interaction but some kind of aside, or (b) has
absolutely no experience of workplace mores he ought to infer that 'would you
like to do X'—X being a part of his job—is probably not a request for
information or a tentative suggestion but an order, albeit a polite one.

Why would a man in this situation fail to understand the woman's message?
There are two possibilities. One is that he does *not* in fact fail to understand it,
he merely pretends later on that he did not understand it. Messages that are
inferred, as opposed to stated directly, are 'defeasible': it is open to the speaker
to deny that they were intended, and to the addressee to deny that they were
picked up. Such denials are a useful device for saving face. For instance, when
Vera's daughter says 'is there any ketchup?' and Vera replies 'it's in the kitchen
cupboard' this is a less overtly face-threatening exchange than 'get me some
ketchup'/'no' because neither the demand nor the refusal is made explicit; they
can minimize any suggestion of conflict by tacitly agreeing to pretend that the
daughter's utterance was issued, understood and responded to as a simple
request for information. Similarly, it is less face-threatening for someone who
hasn't finished a report to say 'I'm sorry, I misunderstood your instructions'
than to say 'I didn't want to do what you asked'. Once again, this is not to
overlook but rather to *exploit* the relativity of linguistic strategies.

The other possibility is that the man is operating with a different set of
assumptions from that of the woman—not about what meaning a particular
form of utterance conveys, but about his relationship to the woman in the
workplace context, their respective roles, entitlements and obligations. In short,

perhaps he disputes that the woman has a right to tell him when to finish the report. The woman's indirect strategy gives him just enough interpretive latitude to hear her not as 'telling' but as 'asking' or 'suggesting'—acts more compatible with his view of what it would be legitimate for her to do. In this scenario, the man may genuinely have misunderstood the woman; but not in a random or arbitrary way, and not because he has different rules for interpreting indirectness per se.

The woman who wants the report finished, like the husband who wants ketchup, positions her addressee in a subordinate role. If he accepted this positioning, he, like Vera, would find no ambiguity or difficulty with the request, because his responsibility to deduce and then accede to a superordinate's wishes would be part of the context for him as it is for her. But he may not accept it, and in consequence may entertain inferences which someone who saw himself as a subordinate would not consider.

Power, conflict and social change

I have suggested that the standard 'difference' account, which locates male-female misunderstanding in a clash of rules or conventions for interpreting utterances of a certain form, oversimplifies what is going on in (some) conversations between women and men. Such an account sees static (and arguably exaggerated) gender differences where it would be more enlightening to see differences of role, status or power (and, crucially, conflicts about these) as features of the contexts in which people use language, with the potential to affect the assumptions on which they base their inferences.

The approach I propose allows for the possibility that the same person can behave very differently depending on who she or he is talking to, from what position and for what purpose; that the utterance which is 'misunderstood' by an individual in one situation may be treated as perfectly transparent by the same individual in another (just as Vera in the 'ketchup' scenario responds differently to the same utterance depending whether it comes from her husband or her daughter); and that laying claim to a particular intention or interpretation can function as a strategic move in a game of power and resistance. What is commonly called 'misunderstanding' may often be better analysed as a kind of conflict; at bottom, conflict about the social positioning that is always implicitly presupposed when one person addresses another. Thus the crucial difference between Vera in the 'ketchup' scenario and the male addressee in the report scenario is not the difference between retrieving a speaker's true intentions and failing to retrieve them, it is the difference between accepting and resisting a form of subordinate positioning.

[...]

NOTES

1. I cite these sources to demonstrate that, in itself, the phenomenon Tannen calls 'relativity' has been recognized by language and gender researchers for more than a decade. It is probably fair to say that Tannen's point about 'relativity' has been

orthodox, even among researchers who disagree with her on other issues, throughout the 1990s. Recent surveys of the 'state of the art' in language and gender research (e.g. Wodak and Benke, 1997) point to the complex interplay between gender and other contextual phenomena as one of the most important current and future concerns of the field.

2. It is also a crucial part of what I am arguing that conflict, when it does arise, need not always manifest itself in *surface* features of discourse such as the unanswered questions, delayed minimal responses and silences pointed out by classic studies in the 'dominance' paradigm, such as Fishman (1983) and Zimmerman and West (1975). Researchers focusing on conflict in conversation (including 'dominance' feminists) have understandably tended to concentrate on conflicts which are marked as such on the surface of talk. But the analytically challenging thing about 'male-female understanding' is precisely that it need *not* announce itself overtly: it is realized in divergent interpretations rather than observable speech behaviour, and participants may not even realize anything has 'gone wrong'. That is one reason why 'misunderstanding' has not always been treated as a type of conventional conflict.

3. I say 'individuals' rather than 'groups' because interpreting utterances is ultimately something individuals do. One would obviously expect there to be a relationship between individuals' beliefs about gender and their membership of particular social categories, but one would not neccesarily expect perfect correlations: it is clear for instance that not all women hold feminist beliefs, nor do all men subscribe to male chauvinist ones. It should also be remembered that the individual's personal beliefs are not the only issue: people can—and in some circumstances must—deploy their knowledge of propositions to which they are *not* committed in order to interpret utterances. Sally-McConnell-Ginet (1998) gives the example of the feminist confronted with the statement 'you think like a woman', who takes this as an insult even though she herself does not accept that women think differently/in an inferior way to men. The point is that she knows that to be a belief held by other people.

4. The word 'ketchup' here stands for a larger set of condiment-terms: on different occasions the husband's actual utterance might contain the item *mustard*, or *pickle*, or *chutney*. I have edited out this variation because what interests me here is simply the 'is there any X?' formula.

REFERENCES

Cameron, D., McAlinden, F. and O'Leary, K. (1988) 'Lakoff in Context: The Social and Linguistic Functions of Tag Questions', in J. Coates and D. Cameron (eds) *Women in their Speech Communities*, pp. 31–53. London: Longman.

Gal, S. (1991) 'Between Speech and Silence: The Problematics of Research on Language and Gender', in M. diLeonardo (ed.) *Gender at the Crossroads of Knowledge*, pp. 175–203. Berkeley: University of California Press.

Goodwin, M. H. (1980) 'Directive-Response Sequences in Girls' and Boys' Task Activities', in S. McConnell-Ginet, R. Borker and N. Furman (eds) *Women and Language in Literature and Society*, pp. 157–73. New York: Praeger.

Gumperz, J. J. (1982) *Discourse Strategies*. Cambridge: Cambridge University Press.

Holmes, J. (1984) 'Women's Language: A Functional Approach', *General Linguistics* 24: 159–78.

Holmes, J. (1995) *Women, Men and Politeness*. London: Longman.

Lakoff, R. (1975) *Language and Woman's Place*. New York: Harper and Row.

Lakoff, R. (1975) *Language and Woman's Place*. New York: Harper and Row.

Ochs, E. (1992) 'Indexing Gender', in A. Duranti and C. Goodwin (eds) *Rethinking Context*, pp. 335–58. Cambridge: Cambridge University Press.

Tannen, D. (1982) 'Ethnic Style in Male-Female Conversation', in J. J. Gumperz (ed.) *Language and Social Identity*, pp. 217–31. Cambridge: Cambridge University Press.

nen, D. (1993) 'The Relativity of Linguistic Strategies: Rethinking Power and Solidarity in Gender and Dominance', in D. Tannen (ed.) *Gender and Conversational Interaction*, pp. 165–88. Oxford: Oxford University Press.

annen, D. (1994) *Gender and Discourse*. Oxford: Oxford University Press.

immerman, D. and West, C. (1975) 'Sex Roles, Interruptions and Silences in Conversation', in B. Thorne and N. Henley (eds) *Language and Sex: Difference and Dominance*, pp. 105–29. Rowley, MA: Newbury House.

Reading 3.3
Database

For several years, we have been analyzing discourse practices in twenty middle-class, European American families, focusing especially on dinnertime communication patterns in narrative activity. The present study isolates a subcorpus of these families: seven two-parent families who earned more than $40,000 a year during the 1987–1989 period in which the study was conducted. Each family had a five-year-old child who had at least one older sibling. Two fieldworkers video- and audiotaped each family on two evenings from an hour or so before dinner until the five-year-old went to bed. During the dinner activity, fieldworkers left the camera on a tripod and absented themselves.

The specific database for this study consists of the exactly one hundred past-time narratives (stories and reports) that the seven families told during thirteen dinners where both parents were present. As we elaborate in Ochs and Taylor (1992a, b) and Ochs, Taylor, Rudolph, and Smith (1992), we define a *story* as a problem-centered past-time narrative (e.g., the narrative activity eventually orients toward solving some aspect of the narrated events seen as problematic), whereas a *report* does not entail such a problem-centered or problem-solving orientation.

Narrative instantiation of gender roles in the family

The narrative roles that we address here as relevant to the construction of gender identities within families are those of *protagonist, introducer* (either elicitor or initial teller), *primary recipient, problematizer,* and *problematizee* (or *target*). Below we define each of these roles and discuss the extent to which that role was assumed by particular family members in our study.

Protagonist

A *protagonist* is here defined as a leading on principal character in a narrated event. Our examination is limited to those narratives where at least one protagonist in the narrative is present at the dinner table, such as in (1), where the chief protagonist is five-year-old Jodie:

From Elinor Ochs and Carolyn Taylor (1995), 'The "Father Knows Best" dynamic in dinnertime narratives', in Kira Hall and Mary Bucholtz (eds), *Gender Articulated: Language and the Socially Constructed Self*, New York: Routledge, pp. 100–17.

Protopnill (handwritten margin note)

(1) Jodie's TB Shots Report (Introductory excerpt)

Participants:

Mom
Dad
Jodie (female, 5 years)
Oren (male, 7 years, 5 months)

The following excerpt introduces the first past-time narrative told at this dinner, when the family has just begun eating.

introduc (handwritten margin note)

Mom: ((*to Jodie*)) = oh:: You know what? You wanna tell Daddy what happened to you today?=

primary recipient (handwritten margin note)

Dad: ((*looking up and off*)) = Tell me everything that happened from the moment you went in – until:

             [

Jodie: I got a sho:t?=

Dad: =EH ((*gasping*)) what? ((*frowning*))

Jodie: I got a sho::t

        [

Dad: <u>no</u>

Jodie: ((*nods yes, facing Dad*))

Dad: ((*shaking head no*)) – Couldn't be

Jodie: (mhm?) ((*with upward nod, toward Dad*))

        [

Oren: a TV test? ((*to Mom*))

        (0.4)

Oren: TV test? Mommy?

Mom: ((*nods yes*)) – mhm

Jodie: and a sho:t

Dad: ((*to Jodie*)) (what) Did you go to the uh:: – ((*to Mom*)) Did you go to the ?animal hospital?

Mom: mhh – no:?

Dad: (where)

Jodie: I just went to the doctor and I got a shot

Dad: ((*shaking head no*)) I don't believe it.

Jodie: ri:?lly:: . . .

Protagonist is an important role with respect to the 'Father knows best' dynamic in that the protagonist is presented as a topic for comment (e.g., in Jodie's case above, for belief or disbelief) by family members. While being a protagonist puts one's narrative actions, conditions, thoughts, and feelings on the table as a focus of attention, this attention is not always a plus, given that protagonists' actions, thoughts, and feelings are not only open to praise but also exposed to familial scrutiny, irony, challenge, and critique. Furthermore, if there is asymmetric distribution in the allocation of protagonist status, one family member may be more routinely exposed to such evaluation by others than the rest, impacting the degree to which some members' identities are constructed as protagonists more than others. In our corpus, such an asymmetry existed, whereby children were the preferred narrative protagonists, as exemplified in the report of Jodie's activities in (1). Children composed nearly 60 percent of all family-member protagonists; mothers figured as protagonists 23 percent of the time; fathers, 19 percent. Fathers' being least often in the role of protagonist meant that their past actions, thoughts, and feelings were least often exposed to the scrutiny of others and, in this sense, they were the least vulnerable family members.

Introducer

In light of the vulnerability of protagonists to familial scrutiny, an important factor to consider is the extent to which family members assumed this role through their own initiative as opposed to having this role imposed on them through the elicitations and initiations of other family members. To address this issue, we consider next how narratives about family members were introduced.

The narrative role of *introducer* is here defined as the co-narrator who makes the first move to open a narrative, either by elicitation or by direct initiation. We define these two introducer roles as follows. An *elicitor* is a co-narrator who asks for a narrative to be told. In (1) above, Jodie's mother assumes this role and, in so doing, introduces the narrative. An *initial teller* is a co-narrator who expresses the first declarative proposition about a narrative event. In (1), Jodie assumed this role but, because her mother had elicited her involvement, Jodie was not the narrative introducer per se. In unelicited narratives such as (2), the initial teller (in this case, the mother) is also the narrative introducer.

(2) Broken Chair Story
    Participants:
    Mom
    Dad
    Ronnie (male, 4 years, 11 months)
    Josh (male, 7 years, 10 months)
    During dinner preparation, as Mom brings Ronnie a spoon to open a can of Nestlé Quik, she scoots Ronnie's chair in to the table. Josh is at his place; Dad is in kitchen area to the right of the table, as shown above.

    Mom: Oh This chair? broke – today
                  [
                  ((*microwave? buzzer goes off*))
    Dad: I? know=
    ((*Mom heads back toward kitchen, stops by Josh's chair: Josh begins looking at Ronnie's chair and under table*))
    Mom: =I- no:: I mean it rea:?lly broke today
                  [
    Dad: I? know (0.2) I know?

Mom: Oh You knew that it was <u>split?</u>
Dad: yeah?,
Mom: the whole wood('s) split?
Dad: yeah,
Mom: Oh Did you do it?
        (0.4)
Dad: I don'?t know if I did? it but I saw that it wa:?s=
        [
Mom: (oh)
        ((*Josh goes under table to inspect chairs: Mom bends over to chair*))
Ron?:   (what? where?)
        =[
Mom: yeah I sat <u>down?</u> in it and the whole <u>thing</u> split so I – I tie:d
                                          [
Dad: ((*with a somewhat taunting intonation*))   (That's a)
        <u>rea:l si:gn?</u> that you need to go on a <u>di:?</u>et.
Ron?:   ((*going under table too*)) (where)
Mom: hh ((*grinning as she rises from stooped position next to Josh's chair*))
Ron?:   (where where where)=
Josh: =<u>Mi:ne?</u> broke?
Mom: I fixed it – I tied (it to the-)
        [
Josh: mi:ne? I'm not gonna sit on *that* chair (if it's broken)
        ((*Josh pushes his chair away and takes Mom's; Mom pushes Josh's chair over to her place, tells the boys to sit down; the subject of the broken chair is dropped*))

The role of introducer is one that we see as pivotal in controlling narrative activity. The introducer nominates narrative topics, thus proposing who is to be the focus of attention (i.e., the protagonist), what aspects of their lives are to be narrated, and when. In (1), Jodie's mother directs the family's attention to Jodie at a particular moment in the dinner, suggesting that there is a narrative to be told as well as the tone, focus, and implicit boundaries of that narrative. For that moment, the introducer proposes what is important (to know) about that family member, as a protagonist. In addition, the introducer controls who is to initiate the narrative account itself, either self-selecting, as in (2), or eliciting a co-narrator, as in (1). Finally, introducers also exert control in that they explicitly or implicitly select certain co-narrator(s) to be primary recipients of the narrative (see following section). In both examples above, mother as introducer selected father as primary recipient.

Although the majority of the protagonists in our corpus were the children, the majority of the narrative introducers were the parents (who introduced seventy-one of the one hundred stories and reports), mothers more often than fathers. (Mothers and fathers *elicited* narratives from others almost equally; their difference derives from mothers' greater tendency to introduce by *direct initiation* as well—and often about others rather than about themselves.) All family members were vulnerable to having narratives about themselves introduced by others. Moreover, for parents, there was relative parity in this regard: for mothers and fathers equally, fully half of all narratives in which they figured as protagonists were introduced by themselves—and almost half by someone else.

A striking asymmetry exists, however, between parents and children. Only one-third of the narratives about children were introduced by the child protagonists themselves (for five-year-olds and younger, the figure was only one-quarter). Children became protagonists chiefly because mothers introduced them as such and often by mothers' direct initiation of the narrative account. Thus, mothers were largely responsible for determining which children and which aspects of children's lives were subject to dinnertime narrative examination—and when and how. In light of this finding, we suggest that, for mothers, the role of introducer may be appropriated (at least in some family cultures and contexts within the United States) as a locus of narrative control over children—and, among family members, children may be particularly vulnerable in this sense.

Primary recipient

The narrative role of *primary recipient* is here defined as the co-narrator(s) to whom a narrative is predominantly oriented. This role is a powerful one in that it implicitly entitles the family member who assumes it to evaluate the narrative actions, thoughts, and feelings of family members as protagonists and/or as narrators. Anyone who recurrently occupies this position is instantiated as 'family judge.' As noted earlier, the introducer is critical to the assignment of primary recipient. In some cases, as in (1) and (2), the introducer designated another family member to be primary recipient, in other cases, as in (3), an introducer may select herself or himself.

> (3) Lucy's Swim Team Report (introductory excerpt)
> *Near the end of dinner, Lucy (9 years, 7 months) has been describing her swim class when Dad raises a new, related narrative.*
> Dad: (Your) mother said you were thinking of uh: – getting on the swim team?
> Lucy: ((*nods yes once emphatically*))
>   (1.0) ((*Mom, who has finished eating, takes plate to nearby counter and returns*))
> Dad: ((*nods yes*)) – (good) ...

Not surprising but nevertheless striking was the privileging of parents as primary recipients of dinnertime narratives: parents assumed that role 82 percent of the time. Within this privileging of parents as preferred audience, fathers were favored over mothers. Whereas fathers often positioned themselves as primary recipients through their own elicitation of narratives (as in example 3, above), in some families mothers regularly nominated fathers as primary recipients through their narrative introductions, such as in (1): *You wanna tell Daddy what happened to you today?* When we overlay this finding on those discussed above, the overall pattern suggests a fundamental asymmetry in family narrative activity, whereby children's lives were told to parents but, by and large, parents did not narrate their lives to their children.

This preference for fathers as primary recipients is partly accounted for by the fact that the father is often the person at the dinner table who knows least about children's daily lives. Typically, even the women who work outside the home arrived home earlier than their husbands and had more opportunity to hear about the events in their children's days prior to dinner. However, there are several reasons to see that being 'unknowing' is an inadequate account for fathers' prominence as primary recipients in these narratives. First, in two of the thirteen dinners studied here, mothers knew less about their children's day that day than did fathers, yet we did not observe fathers nominating mothers as primary recipients of narratives about children (i.e., in this corpus, we did not find fathers saying, 'Tell Mommy what you did today'). Second, child initiators oriented more narratives to mothers than to fathers in spite of the mothers' generally greater prior knowledge of children's lives. Third, mothers and children were typically as unknowing about fathers' reportable experiences as fathers were about theirs, yet fathers seldom addressed their lives to mothers or children as preferred recipients. (We also did not find mothers – or fathers – saying to each other the equivalent of 'Honey, tell the children what you did today.') These considerations suggest to us that it was not simply being unknowing (about family members' daily activities) that determined primary-recipient selection but, perhaps, a matter of *who* was unknowing.

By considering who the initial teller was for each narrative (i.e., the one who was typically the first to address the primary recipient directly), we determined that it was neither children nor fathers themselves who accounted for fathers' assuming the role of overall preferred recipient. Instead, it was mothers who—in addition to often directing children to orient to fathers through elicitations (e.g., *Tell Daddy about ...*)—also directly initiated many narratives to fathers as primary recipients. In fact, mothers' direct initiation to fathers was the single greatest factor in accounting for fathers' privileging as preferred recipient. Mothers initiated twice as many narratives oriented to fathers as fathers initiated toward mothers. In light of these findings, we suggest that a gender-socialization factor entered into the nonequation, prompting mothers' elevation of unknowing fathers into primary recipients—and judges—of other family members' lives, unmatched by fathers' similar elevation of unknowing mothers to such status.

We have noted above that narrative introducers exert control by designating primary recipients, but here we emphasize that, at the same time, such designation passes control to the co-narrator who is so designated: the primary recipient is in a position to evaluate, reframe, or otherwise pass judgment on both the tale and how it is told. In our view, the role of primary recipient affords a panopticon-like perspective and power (Bentham 1791, Foucault 1979). The term *panopticon* refers to an all-seeing eye or monitoring gaze that keeps subjects under its constant purview (e.g., a prison guard in a watchtower). Similarly, we suggest that narrative activity exposes protagonists to the surveillance of other co-narrators, especially to the scrutiny of the designated primary recipient (see Ochs and Taylor 1992b). Given that this role was played mainly by the fathers in our data, we further suggest that it is potentially critical to the narrative reconstruction of 'Father knows best' because it sets up the father to be the ultimate purveyor and judge of other family members' actions, conditions, thoughts, and feelings.

The family-role preferences we have found with regard to these first three narrative roles—protagonist, introducer, and primary recipient—already present an overall picture of the way in which narrative activity may serve to put women, men, and children into a politics of asymmetry. As noted earlier, in the family context, issues of gender and power cannot be looked at as simply dyadic, i.e., *men* versus *women* as *haves* versus *have-nots*. Rather, in two-parent families, women and men manifest asymmetries of power both dyadically as spouses and triadically as mothers and fathers with children. Although there *are* interesting dyadic observations here regarding women versus men (e.g., women tend to raise narrative topics, men tend to be positioned—often by women—to evaluate them), these apparently gender-based distinctions are part of a *triadic* interaction, or larger picture, wherein children are often the subjects of these narrative moves. Neither women's nor men's control is merely a control over each other but particularly encompasses and impacts children. Furthermore, a narrative role such as that of introducer (seen here to be more aligned with women, at least as initial teller) may have a complex relationship to power, both empowering the holder in terms of agenda-setting, choice of protagonist, and topic, but also disempowering to the degree that the introducer sets up someone else (here more often the man) to be ultimate judge of the narrated actions and protagonists.

Problematizer/problematizee

The narrative role of *problematizer* is here defined as the co-narrator who renders an action, condition, thought, or feeling of a protagonist or a co-narrator problematic, or possibly so. The role of *problematizee* (or *target*) is defined as the co-narrator whose action, condition, thought, or feeling is rendered problematic, or a possible problem. As such, in this study, we consider only problematizing that targeted co-present family members.

An action, condition, thought, or feeling may be problematized on several grounds.

[...]

When the husband indicted his wife for being overweight as the cause of the chair's breaking (*That's a rea:l si:gn that you need to go on a di:et.*), we suggest he was implicitly problematizing her for lack of self-control. In (4), the same father again problematizes his wife, this time as too lenient a boss and thus incompetent in her workplace as well.

(4) Mom's Job Story (excerpt)
> *Same family as in (2). At the end of dinner, Mom is at the sink doing dishes as Dad eats an ice cream sundae and seven-year-old Josh does homework at the table opposite Dad. This excerpt comes near the end of a story about Mom's hiring a new assistant at work, which Dad has elicited and already probed considerably.*

Dad: ((*eating dessert*)) Well – I certainly think that – you're a- you know you're a fair bo?ss – You've been working there how long?

Mom: fifteen years in June ((*as she scrapes dishes at kitchen sink*))

Dad: fifteen *years* – and you got a guy ((*turns to look directly at Mom as he continues*)) that's been workin there a few <u>weeks</u>? and you do (it what) the way <u>he</u> wants.

Mom: hh ((*laughs*))
(0.6) ((*Dad smiles slightly?, then turns back to eating his dessert*))

Mom: It's not a matter of my doin it the way he:wa:nt. It does help In that I'm getting more <u>work</u>? done It's just that I'm workin too <u>hard</u>? I don't wanta <u>work</u> so hard

Dad: ((*rolls chair around to face Mom halfway*)) Well – You're the <u>bo:ss</u> It's up to you to set the standards [...]

[...]

Men's preeminence as problematizers is further seen in the fact that they problematized their spouses over a much wider range of narrative topics than did women. Wives' conduct and stance concerning child care, recreation, meal preparation, and even their professional lives were open to husbands' critiques. Narratives about men's workdays, however, were exceedingly rare and were virtually never problematized. This asymmetry, wherein men had or were given 'problematizing rights' over a wider domain of their spouses' experiences than were women, further exemplifies how narrative activity at dinner may instantiate and socialize a 'Father knows best' worldview, i.e., it is men as fathers and husbands who scrutinize and problematize everything.

Given men's presumption to quantitative and qualitative dominance as problematizers par excellence in this corpus, an important issue to raise is the extent to which men's prominence as problematizers was related to their role as preferred primary recipients. There was clearly a strong link between the two roles for them: 86 of men's 116 problematizings occurred when they were primary recipients of the narrative. However, the status of primary recipient does not, in itself, completely account for who assumed the role of problematizer.

[...]

Rather, our corpus suggests conceptualizations of recipientship that differentiate women, men, and children, i.e., differing dispositions and perhaps entitlements to problematize, with men in privileged critical positions. The role of problematizer seems to be a particular prerogative of the family role of father/husband, manifesting the ideology that 'Father knows best,' socializing and (reconstituting paternal prerogative and point of view in and through narrative activity.

Because an important issue we are pursuing here is women's role in establishing a 'Father knows best' dynamic at the family dinner table and because we have seen that women's most notable narrative role was that of introducer, we examined the introducer-problematizer relationship to discover in particular the extent to which men's problematizings occurred in narratives introduced by women. Our finding is that women's introductions may indeed have triggered men's problematizations. First, when women introduced narratives, problematizing in general was more prevalent than when men or children did the introducing. In narratives introduced by women, family members were problematized, on average, 3.4 times per narrative, considerably more than for narratives introduced by men (2.0 times) or by children (1.1). Second, the majority of men's problematizings (72 out of 116) occurred in narratives introduced by women. Men problematized other family members 1.8 times per narrative in those introduced by women, i.e., an even higher rate than we noted above when the factor of men's status as primary recipients was considered. Furthermore, men problematized more often in narratives introduced by women than in narratives they introduced themselves. This higher number of problematizations in narratives introduced by one's spouse might seem expectable but it was not matched by women, who wound up (counter)-problematizing more often in the narratives they themselves introduced. We see in these data an asymmetrical pattern wherein women's raising a topic seems to have promoted men's problematizing but not the reverse.

Women's assumption of the role of introducer co-occurred not only with increased problematization by men but also with increased targeting of women themselves. Women were problematized most often in the very narratives they introduced: 75 percent of all targetings of women occurred in those narratives, an average of 1.6 times per narrative. These figures contrast markedly with those for men: only 33 percent of the problematizings of men occurred in narratives they themselves introduced, an average of only 0.7 times per narrative.

These findings suggest that women were especially vulnerable to exposing themselves to criticism, particularly from their husbands, and thus may have been 'shooting themselves in the foot' in bringing up narratives in the first place, as illustrated in (2), the Broken Chair Story, where a woman's designation (i.e., control) of narrative topic and primary recipient boomeranged in an explicit attack on her weight. In (1), Jodie's TB Shots Report, we see an example of how mother-introduced narratives also expose children to problematization by fathers. Reconsidering our earlier observation that women were problematized over a wider range of daily activities, including professional lives, than were men, we can posit that this may have resulted largely from women's introducing themselves as protagonists in a much wider range of contexts to begin with.

One final issue with regard to problematization concerns the extent to which family members self-problematized. In our corpus, women displayed the highest proportion of self-targetings and, in keeping with the findings just discussed, this was also associated with narratives that women themselves raised. Although such targettings account for a relatively small proportion (12 percent) of the targetings of women overall, and they came essentially from only two families, these female self-problematizings are noteworthy in their provoking of a 'dumping-on' response.

[...]

Our data also suggest that women's self-problematizing may have socializing effects. This was vividly illustrated in a lengthy story focusing on a mother and her son in a restaurant (the same family as in Jodie's TB Shots Report and Mom's Dress Story). In this narrative, the son, Oren, recalls eating a chili pepper his mother thought was a green bean. Although Oren initially frames the experience as funny, his mother tells him it wasn't funny, that his mouth was burning and hurting. While problematizing his stance as narrator, she also implicates herself as a culprit, thereby self-problematizing as protagonist. In the course of the story, Oren eventually takes on his mother's more serious framing of events, to the point of shouting, 'YOUR FAULT YOUR FAULT.' She agrees, nodding her head and saying, 'It was my fault.' While she is saying this, he leans over and pinches her cheeks hard. She gasps and pulls his hands away, saying, 'OW That really hurts honey?' As she holds a napkin to her mouth and cheeks, her son comments, 'Your fault – I get to do whatever I want to do once – (That was my fee?),' laughs, and adds, 'Just like it happened to me it happens to you.' Just as husbands piled on to wives' self-targeting, Oren thus follows up on his mother's self-problematizing, extending condemnation and executing punishment for her self-problematized actions. In so doing, he seems to be assuming a dramatic version of what, in this corpus, was a male narrator role.

This discussion calls attention to an appropriate ending caveat to our findings throughout this chapter. Namely, there is family variation even within this sample of seven families of similar socioeconomic status and racial-cultural background. There were men who took up the role of monitor and judge with what seemed almost a vengeance, there were others who displayed much less assertion of the prerogatives of power as primary recipient. Furthermore, we do not wish to fix particular men's (or women's) narrator personae based on two evenings in the lives of these families. Our aim is not to polarize the genders, but, rather, to shed potential new light on some underexplored aspects of gender construction and socialization in everyday narrative activity.

Conclusion

Synthesizing these findings—with the caveats noted above—we construe a commonplace scenario of narrative activity at family dinners characterized by a sequence of the following order. First, mothers introduce narratives (about themselves and their children) that set up fathers as primary recipients and implicitly sanction them as evaluators of others' actions, conditions, thoughts, and feelings. Second, fathers turn such opportunities into forums for problematizing, with mothers themselves as their chief targets, very often on grounds of incompetence. And third, mothers respond in defense of themselves and their children via the counterproblematizing of fathers' evaluative, judgmental comments.

[...]

REFERENCES

Bentham, Jeremy (1791). *Panopticon*. London: T. Payne.
Foucault, Michel (1979). *Discipline and punish: The birth of the prison*. Translated by Alan Sheridan. New York: Random House.
Ochs, Elinor, and Carolyn Taylor (1992a). 'Science at dinner'. In Claire Kramsch and Sally McConnell-Ginet (eds.), *Text and context: Cross-disciplinary perspectives on language study*. Lexington, MA: Heath. 29–45.
—— (1992b). 'Family narrative as political activity'. *Discourse & Society* 3(3): 301–40.
Ochs, Elinor, Carolyn Taylor, Dina Rudolph, and Ruth Smith (1992). 'Storytelling as a theory-building activity'. *Discourse Processes* 15(1): 37–72.

Reading 3.4
Introduction

Women who are abused by the men they live with find themselves progressively disenfranchised from their own beliefs, memories, values and emotions (Walker, 1979; Kurz, 1989; Douglas, 1994). In many cases the man endeavours to isolate his partner from any possible source of alternative reality; he may try to monitor or even restrict her access to family, friends, workmates and parents (Schechter and Gary, 1988; Dobash and Dobash, 1988). The way men talk about women and relationships can have the effect of justifying violence, concealing abuse and supporting entitlement to positions of power (Pagelow, 1981; Pence and Paymar, 1993).

From: Peter Adams, Alison Towns and Nicola Gavey (1995), 'Dominance and entitlement: the rhetoric men use to discuss their violence towards women', *Discourse and Society*, 6: 3, 387–406.

[...]

The current paper aims to illustrate how attention to the rhetorical features of men's accounts can assist in unpicking the various strands which reinforce male entitlement to positions of dominance.

We initially approached this research following fraught attempts to respond to knowledge about a perpetrator of violence from within our own profession. This experience alerted us to the power of dominant discourses to minimize and conceal violence in our midst. One of our responses was to undertake to study the language men themselves use to support abuse of their partners. Our choice to focus on this group was based on the assumption that it would present clear samples of the negative ways in which violence is talked about within our culture. We came to this project with a feminist/pro-feminist perspective which acknowledges the importance of gender and power in understanding violence towards women (Bograd, 1990). Each of us has also worked as clinical psychologists with either the perpetrators or survivors of violence against women.

Interviews were conducted with 14 men who had recently been violence to their partners and who were planning to attend or had recently begun attending 'stopping violence programmes' within the Auckland region. All men attended the programmes voluntarily but most had been encouraged to do so by their partners and/or the Family Courts. The interviews comprise the first stage of a larger study which we conducted during 1994. The study was approved by the University of Auckland Human Subjects Ethics Committee and all names and other identifiers have been changed to preserve confidentiality of interviewees and the people to whom they referred. The men attended the interviews voluntarily and were given a clear description of the nature and goals of the project. Each 90-minute interview invited the men to discuss their views on a range of topics associated with violence. The interviews were flexibly structured around five key question zones. These zones included their views on: (1) ideal relationships; (2) women's rights; (3) sexual practices; (4) causes of violence; and (5) wider social supports for violence. Eleven interviews were conducted by the first author (PA) and three by a therapist also experienced in working with perpetrators (Bruce Davis). The interviewer adopted a neutral and reflective interviewing style in order to encourage open disclosure. However, it was considered important by the end of each interview to question views which condone violence. All interviews were fully transcribed and these transcripts comprise the data for this paper. Analysis involved multiple readings of the transcripts by each researcher, combined with ongoing reflexive discussions among the research team on responses to the texts.

Of particular importance in unravelling the ways men use language to support violence is an understanding of the relevant discourses which operate in their use of language. In this paper the term 'discourse' is used in the sense of an evolving system of values, understandings or meanings specific to particular cultures, contexts and times. These in turn both construct and are constructed by the relationships of those they influence. In the following example, Gavin discusses his understanding of male authority and male superiority. Discourses of male dominance can be seen here as providing the cultural resources for his ways of making sense of his relationship to women. Gavin is a 31-year-old Pakeha (New Zealander of European descent) employed as a tradesman and currently in his second long-term relationship (2½ years) with a woman. The following extract occurred about half-way through a 90-minute interview:

PA: Can you explain what discipline means in your relationship?

Gavin: Well it's (.) well just respect and manners and that I s'pose y'now. A woman who's gonna put up when they shut up, so to speak

PA: For her to put up and shut up?

Gavin: Yeah. (PA: Okay.) Um, so for her not to undermine [laughing] my authority and ohh I don't know.

PA: Your authority?

Gavin: Saying, you know, meaning 'what I say goes', you know 'no we're not bloody going out tonight. We're staying at home.' 'Ohh I wanna go out.' ((laughing)) 'No, we're not. I don't wanna go.' Y'know. Or like Friday night she said, 'Ohh I don't really want you to go out'. 'Well fuck, tough, I'm going.' Y'know. And I went out. That's my authority, my—

PA: When, when a court has authority, or a judge has authority, or, it's given to them from someone, somewhere. Authority comes from somewhere, or it's based on something. I mean what, what is your authority based on, do you think?

Gavin: ((sigh)) Being the (.) protector. Um, the breadearner, y'know the provider, that's my authority. Like okay we're not physically married, as in we've signed a piece of paper, but we're living as if we are physically married. And y'know. I'm the ((laughing)) breadearner, (PA: Yeah.) um, I'm the protector of this household. Um, when it comes down to it what I say goes.

PA: So, so your authority's based on being the protector and—

Gavin: Yeah, well um—

PA: Women are at the moment moving out of the home and doing lots of different things. (Gavin: Oh yeah.) becoming bread-winners and things like that. As well um they're shifting, feminism is trying to seek more power for women and all that sort of thing. How do you see that?

Gavin: Well, my missus at the moment, she's a draughtswoman and she works five hours a day y'know. Um, she actually brings in good ((sniff)) money and that for us, so I, I got no quells about that. Um, I dunno, but I still think a man's home is his castle, y'know. King of the, gotta have a king of the castle, don't ya?

	That's why I reckon if some prick comes on to your property you got full rights to do whatever you like to him. It's your property. He shouldn't even be on there unless he's invited. (PA: Yeah, yeah.) A man's home is his castle. That's it. Pure and simple.
PA:	What's that mean, a man's home is his castle?
Gavin:	(.) Where else can you escape and be private, y'know it's, that's your little piece of privacy. That's where you can lock yourself away from the world if you want to. (PA: Yeah, yeah.) And it's your home.
PA:	So with women trying to seek equal rights, they would probably be seeking equal rights in the home too, wouldn't they? How would you see that? I mean they're challenging that view, I think.
Gavin:	Well definitely.
PA:	What happens to you when you hear that, being said?
Gavin:	Well it, it takes away the whole thing of what I think, well what I think it, the whole purpose of life was.
PA:	Yeah. Can you, can you explain that?
Gavin:	Well you got the male and you got the [laughing] female. And the male earns the bread and the woman brings up the family and that. And that's what we need to get back to, is more family morals I think. I think woman have gotta stop worrying about making out y'know. I think they got to put more emphasis on being a mother. And it's a fact of life that only women can be a mother. There's no, there's no other way around it. And the man's still gotta go and earn the bread and the woman's still gotta have the children. (PA: Yeah.) I mean it's just what, is part and parcel.
PA:	They go together?
Gavin:	Well they do.
PA:	Yeah, yeah. Okay. Um, in, in your relationships, um—
Gavin:	Do I sound like a male chauvinist or what? ((laughter))
PA:	No, no. It's, what's important is just what you're thinking. Y'know what your views are and I'm, I'm not in judge, sitting in judgement, really it's just—
Gavin:	Yeah. Like I don't actually, I don't actually try, I don't actually think I am a chauvinist, but I think that it's just (pause) what life is about, y'know. It's a fact that only women can have children. Sure if they wanna, if they wanna have a career, have a career. Don't, but it, you get these women that wanna have children and have a career. I don't think they can balance the two. It's not right. It's not right on the husband, it's not right on the children and it's not fair on her. Because then they

start moaning about how stressed out they are, about how much work they're doing and they gotta do the kids and that. Well they don't have to.

Gavin's speech here presents multiple and overlaying messages of male authority. We have chosen this extract as a reference point because of the dense variety of ways in which Gavin implicitly supports his position of dominance. At first glance the discourse of dominance can be seen in claims like 'what I say goes' and 'that's my authority'. But the effect of his account extends beyond these simple assertions. This paper explores how some of the more subtle and less visible features of his language, and that of other men we have interviewed, reinforce the conveyed sense of entitlement.

Rhetoric
The formal aspects of language provide the required meanings and structure, but it is the use of available rhetorical devices that increases the likelihood that the communication will have impact and persuasiveness. For example, a woman describing an episode of abuse could portray in accurate detail what happened, but it will be the extra features of the communication, the emphasis placed on certain words, the timing, the hints and the use of analogies which will convey the full terror of the experience. These 'extra' features are what is understood as rhetoric, and as in this example, they can have more than a peripheral, and sometimes have a central function in the effectiveness of a communication.

[...]

Reference ambiguity
Ambiguity in our speech is often either incidental or a product of poor conceptual clarity. But we also use ambiguity for strategic effects. Bavelas et al. (1990) concluded a review of studies into how children respond to ambiguous language by claiming they sometimes use it for interpersonal reasons such as politeness or avoidance of confrontation. Some men employ ambiguity with strategic effects in what they do and say towards women. Consider a case example reported by Busch et al. (1993: 29). A woman who had separated from an abusive partner and was subject to frequent breaches of a protection order found on her doorstep one morning a bouquet of flowers for Mother's Day from her ex-partner. From outside the relationship, this act could be seen as a loving gesture, an attempt to indicate the man's willingness to reconcile; within the context of a history of abuse and intimidation, this act could be interpreted as stating that whatever steps she takes to prevent him having contact, he will always find a way of reaching her. One interpretation evokes warmth, the other terror. The ambiguity serves both to increase the woman's sense of isolation and to limit her ability to respond by camouflaging to outside observers the threatening message.

The extract from Gavin's interview illustrates how pronouns can be used with ambiguous effect. For instance, at one point he stated:

> And that's what *we* need to get back to, more family morals . . . (emphasis added)

The received meaning of his 'we' is likely to be 'we'—*our society*. But it could be received with other senses. It could be taken to mean '*we*'—*me and you*. It could also be taken to mean 'we'—*us men*. Had his partner been present, her received meaning could have been 'me and you' or 'us men'. Either way, she could interpret it as saying 'we men have the authority and know what is required . . .' But since his use of 'we' is ambiguous. in the face of any challenge to his assumed authority, his meaning could be taken in the former sense thereby covering up any suggestion of superiority.

Ambiguous use of the speaker's first-person plural occurred relatively frequently in the men's texts. Consider its use in another extract:

> Um—the fact that, I think in *our* relationship, I think both of us are very dominant pe—, um, when I say, ah, not dominant, that's not the right word. *We* are both very determined people. Very determined. I mean Doreen's no sloth; she's pretty clever. She's, er, she's been a social worker and, um, you know, maybe that's one area that I've um—although my first wife was a social worker, but I don't think it's had the same—how would I say? Um, my first wife wasn't as, as what I feel, as dominant as Doreen is. (emphasis added)

From outside the relationship, Doug's 'we are both very determined people' could give the impression of consensual agreement. But in the context of violence and other oppressive acts, the effect of the statement for Doreen could be to parcel up any interpretation she may have and replace it with Doug's own construction. When challenged about assumptions of authority, Doug could use the ambiguity of this reference to retreat to a position of neutrality. He could, for example, argue that the 'we' actually does refer to a consensual position agreed on following extended discussion with Doreen. A similar use of reference ambiguity occurs in the following extract by Jay:

> So I say that she talks negative. I say, 'why don't you talk positive?' Say 'you can do it' and oh, I sort of try and be a real positive person and say— but she sort of—Oh I think any way she talks from a negative point of view. She'll always bring up the negative, you know, instead of saying, you know, 'well we can try and do it', or, 'we can, oh, we'll give it a go and see what happens' type of thing.

From one angle, the encouragement Jay gives his partner to 'be positive' could be interpreted as a caring and supportive act; but from another angle, this encouragement could be seen as a way of dismissing her genuine concerns and overriding them with a statement on what attitudes he would prefer her to take.

Furthermore, Jay specified his preferred expression of these attitudes with the construction, 'we can'; as with Doug's use of 'we', it could be read as assuming, without consultation, objectives that apply to both parties.

A variety of types of ambiguous reference occurs in the language that partner abusers use in psycho-educational group programmes. The first author has taken the following examples from statements made by men participating in these programmes:

(i) *First-person plural*
- We allow our women more choice.
- We're both very stubborn people.
- We shouldn't be arguing.

(ii) *Generalized pronouns*
- It takes two to tango.
- There is no middle ground.
- It would be better to go now.

(iii) *Generalized reference*
- A man has a right to some peace.
- Women are over-emotional.
- People take me the wrong way.

In each of these examples the man's personal position and perspective is buried in authoritative statements about either the relationship or the world as a whole. The woman's personal position is overshadowed by the general assertions; she may disagree with them applying to her, but because of the ambiguity she may have difficulty specifying her disagreement.

Axiom markers
Gavin made repeated use of statements which refer to the nature of reality as a whole. At one point he declared:

A man's home is his castle. *That's it. Pure and simple.*

Further on in the extract he claimed:

> ...I think women have gotta stop worrying about making out y'know. I think they got ... to put more emphasis on being a mother. And *it's a fact of life* that only women can be a mother. There's no, *there's no other way around it.* And the man's still gotta go and earn the bread and the woman's still gotta have the children ... I mean *it's just what, is part and parcel.*

We noticed that these global assertions about the nature of reality as a whole or life in general were a common characteristic of the men's talk. We labelled them 'axiom markers' because they appear to function as a means of qualifying adjacent statements. In the last example, Gavin's 'it's a fact of life' serves to mark in some way the statement which follows, 'only women can be a mother'. Within our research team, we initially had quite different interpretations of the possible rhetorical effects of these axiom markers. The male member of our team viewed their function as adding emphasis or conveying a strength of belief in what was being said. Consider their effect in the following extracts:

> My advice has always been to, not just to partners but to all females, that um if you have [phrase indistinct], then you've got to expect it back ... It's a physical thing coming again, but *the bottom line is* y'know, whether it's male or female, if you're gonna go and hit someone you've gotta expect it back ... I'm not saying it's okay, but ... *that's how in most cases a lot of it happens.*

> You know, guys should pay. 'Cos I like to give, you see, *that's what it comes down to*. I like to take her out and say 'here you go, my shout' you know, 'order what you want off the menu and I'll eat what I want' you know. And 'it's my treat' ... Whereas the other way I felt like, she's giving, but she doesn't really want to, she knows it should really be me that's doing it. *Really it should be* shouldn't it?

Tom's use of 'the bottom line is' and Bill's 'that's what it comes down to' give the impression that what the speaker is about to say is held with some conviction. However, the female members of our team were able to draw on past experience with men who were controlling and/or violent. The effect of these statements on them was considerably more powerful. Both women interpreted these axiom markers as forms of speech which, in the context of an unequal relationship, forcefully communicate the speaker's authority and power. They are statements which proclaim omniscience. When used by a man in conversation with a woman he is violent towards, possible rhetorical effects would be to terminate discussion, silence the woman and signal danger. Interestingly, we found that the personal experience of the listeners may determine whether or not they are responsive to such effects.

Metaphor
Gavin uses a familiar metaphor to explain male authority in the home:

> ... but I still think a man's home is his castle ... gotta have a king of the castle, don't ya?

Here he explores the interlinked concepts of 'king' and 'castle' to cast himself in a position of authority and by implication casting others who live in the home as subject to this authority.

Metaphor is the most familiar and most frequently discussed of rhetorical devices (Ricoeur, 1978; Ortony, 1979; Paprotte and Dirven, 1985; Kittay, 1987). Familiar instances of metaphor abound in everyday speech (Lakoff and

Johnson, 1979; Lakoff, 1987) and in the following extracts the men have referenced some common examples (metaphors in italics):

- Anger-is-heat
  How come I behave violently? ((sigh)) Most of the time it was mainly because I couldn't get my point through ... And um, used to just get frustrated ... and then, then the *temperature's just, just rises*, and just over the edge, and then just lose it.
- People-snap
  ...I pushed her on the bed and I got—went to the kitchen and got a carving knife and said 'I'm going to kill you, you're gonna get out, pack your bags, get out or I'm going to kill you.' Um, no, I've never ever done that before in my life. I've never ever, never hit anybody before in my life. But something there just *snapped* for some reason.
- Emotions-build-up-pressure
  I think Dad used to let things *build up and build up and build up* without expressing them prior. So that it eventually *exploded*. Um, I'm only assuming that because that's more or less what happens to me ... Y'know I *keep it inside* until it *builds up and builds up and builds up*, then I *explode*.

The imaginative response of listeners here could include a sense of men getting hotter, snapping and exploding. But further to this, metaphor exploits imaginative connections which are shared within a culture and which link the familiar with the unfamiliar: 'frustration' implies anger, 'snapping' implies a source of stress and 'building up' implies a source of pressure. Each of these common examples suggests a limit to which a man can reasonably be expected to handle pressure and thereby soften the responsibility for violent behaviour.

Gavin's use of 'man as king of his castle' involves a more complex metaphorical structure than the examples cited above. By using a metaphor involving social hierarchies he also brings in the relationships which are typically associated with such social organizations. For instance, the term 'king' implies authority has been sanctioned somehow; it could be sanctioned by God, by the people, by force, Gavin did not specify the source of the sanctioning—which leaves it to listeners to draw their own conclusions. A further consequence of casting men and hence himself as king means he is positioning his partner as subject to his authority. In order to represent this double positioning, we will label this type of metaphor using the following format: *man-as-king: woman-as-subject*.

A range of metaphors based on social hierarchies is evident in the transcripts. A common example involves speaking about the relationships at home as though they reconfigure the relationships at work. This *man-as-boss: woman-as-employee* is explicitly referenced in the following:

Probably before—I would have thought, or I would have said, ah, you know, 'there's one boss and that's me and end of story'.

Another common example involves speaking about a woman as though she is an object which can be possessed or owned:

PA: So you punched her and then you put her pillow over her. Were you trying to hurt—to, to suffocate her?

Chris: No, I just wanted her to, to stop screaming ... You know, because I, I'd suddenly went into a shock of my own, a miniature type of shock as to what the hell have I just done? [pause] 'Cos, um, I never thought that I would do that with her.

PA: What went through your head?

Chris: I was just a bit terrified, and just thought [pause] you know, as I will probably reveal in the later half of this interview, with other girl-friends, um I just couldn't believe what I'd just done. I thought that I was on the pa—, on the path of get—, to getting better, because I mean this relationship was something that I really, really wanted. You know, I hadn't had one for two years and finally she came along and she was just about *everything in the package* that I could want.

Later in the interview Chris stated, 'I'm very fussy about the way my ladies look'. His use of *man-as-owner: woman-as-commodity* metaphor has the effect of positioning his partner as an object which can be possessed, judged and commented on.

As with reference ambiguity and axiom marking, the use of metaphor promotes a multilevelled response from listeners which can serve both to camouflage and signal messages of superiority. In the following example, Alan reflected on his own past use of the *man-as-parent: woman-as-child* metaphor:

I probably started looking at Sandra as, 'oh this is the person I've got to look after, I gotta protect her from the world.' I started probably treating her as a daughter as opposed to a wife, or as a fiancée.

From one perspective, Alan's wish to 'look after' and 'protect' his partner portrays a stance of love and caring. But from another perspective, to speak of a partner as though she is a child immediately casts the speaker in the role of a parent; it prepares the way and adds strength to the view that men are naturally dominant to women. As with the earlier devices, the use of metaphor allows different listeners to hear the same passage of speech in radically different ways.

Synecdoche
Synecdoche is generally understood as a reference which substitutes either a species for a genus—a part for a whole—or a genus for a species—a whole for a

part (Gray, 1977; Soskice, 1985). For example, a builder comments to his friend during their coffee break 'Did you see those tits walking by?' meaning perhaps less offensively, 'Did you see that woman walking by?' Breasts are a part of the body—a member of the category of parts of the body—and in making the synecdochal reference the speaker need only refer to the part in order for the listener to understand that the whole is being referenced. Other examples include the following:

- Here comes that *prick* again (= man, person).
- I'm going home to *women's liberation* (= my partner).
- Hi *blondie*! Hi *muscles*! (= person, friend).
- A little *pushing* never did much harm (= physical violence).

Notice how with synecdoche the link assumes the reader or listener is familiar with the relevant category and the conditions of membership for that category. To comprehend the message the listener needs to know that 'pushing' belongs to the larger category of 'physical violence' and that 'his partner' belongs to the group of people who advocate 'women's liberation'. In this way synecdoche functions in linking parts to whole and vice versa, thereby exploiting categorical links between terms.

The use of synecdoche can result in various effects. It can be used as a form of humour, it can reinforce language which objectifies and depersonifies women and it can signal interpretations of intent.

In Gavin's extract cited earlier he was asked what he meant by discipline in his relationship; he responded:

Well it's [pause] well just respect and manners ...

Both 'respect' and 'manners' are global terms with a variety of meanings. For instance, 'respect' can refer to 'respecting authority', 'respecting humanity', 'respecting risk'. Gavin's next sentence was more specific:

A woman who's gonna put up when they shut up, so to speak.

The global term 'respect' is linked here to the more specific sense of 'submitting to male authority'. He clarifies this further in his next statement:

Um, so for her not to undermine [laughing] authority ...

This sequence of statements references and reinforces the link between the general term 'respect' and its more specific sense 'submitting to male authority'. For subsequent uses this linking of general and specific meanings allows the speaker to begin to use the term 'respect' as a synecdoche for 'submitting to male authority'.

As with reference ambiguity, synecdoche can serve to camouflage the colonizing effects of the language. For listeners less familiar with the speaker, global statements about 'respect' and 'manners' sound understandable and reasonable. But for a partner who has been repeatedly reminded through word and action that 'respect' means 'submitting to male authority', the global statements function synecdochally to convey the potential for abuse.

A similar forging and exploiting of general vs specific meanings occurred in our texts for use of the term 'strong'. In common parlance the concept of *strength* spreads its meanings in several directions. There is strength in terms of muscular force, strength in terms of perseverance, strength in terms of resilience, strength in terms of courage and so on. We found in our texts that the general term 'strong' was used in contexts which tended to convey the more specific sense of 'muscular force', particularly when discussing the men's views of equality for women:

> I'm not a chauvinist male ... There is a limit to what you really can do They've had this argument at the fire station. Women trying to be firemen ... You got a high pressure hose that takes two full grown *strong* men to hold, it's gonna take four or five females. Y'know. I'm not saying they can't be in the fire brigade or anything because there are other things they can do; driving the engine, whatever, you know. But there is a limit to what a person is, all persons are capable of.

The global term 'strong' appears to refer here to the more specific sense of 'muscular force'. The whole is referenced but only a part of the meaning is conveyed. This synecdochal referencing has the effect of dismissing the other senses of 'strength' and thereby increasing the justification for male dominance in other realms than muscular force.

In a similar example, Doug used the images of lifting and struggling with heavy objects to refer to differences in strength:

> But as the guys say, 'equal pay for equal work,' and um, you know when a van backs into the, into the dispatch part of the um spare parts department and there's an engine to move, who moves the engine? (PA: Yeah). It's not, it's not the women who do it, it's the guys who get out there and *lift the heavy* motor and, so I think if you're expecting equal pay for the same type of work then I guess you, you've got to be prepared to do that sort of work as well. I, I, I don't agree with that. There's no way I'd stand by and watch a, watch a woman *struggle with a heavy* engine or something like that, I, I would get in there and do it myself.

The synecdoche here references 'muscular force' via attributes or parts of the concept such as 'lifting' and 'struggling' with something 'heavy'. Furthermore, Doug uses this sense of strength to justify inequality through male roles in protecting women.

In a further example, Chris specifies clearly that 'being strong' means 'being physically strong':

PA: You mean there's a lot of similarity between men and women? ...

Chris: Yep. As long as they're prepared to do, yeah, the same amount of work ...

PA: Yeah? How do you, how do you see that?

Chris: As in, like, they want equal wages and stuff, but if it's a physical job and they can't do half the stuff.

PA: Yeah ...

Chris: I don't mind helping them and stuff and um, you know, 'cos they're *physically* not as *strong* as men. You know, I don't mind that, but like other jobs, you know, if they're, if they're not up to really putting in the hard physical stuff, you know, maybe they should get paid a little bit less.

In considering the issue of similarity between men and women, Chris conveys a sense that while men and women are equally human, men have qualities which set them apart. In particular, it is a man's superior physical strength which provides tangible proof of these qualities. By saying, 'I don't mind helping them', he casts himself in a position of reasonable and benevolent physical superiority which could be built on elsewhere into a more general sense of superiority.

[...]

The discourse of natural entitlement

The discourse of natural entitlement presents one example of the way rhetorical devices and discourse combine to resource assumptions of male dominance. In its simplest form it advocates that men are entitled to dominate women because they are designed to be that way. In the following extract, Rob provides an interesting discussion about dominance and its relationship to equality:

PA: So what do you think of women's rights and feminists?

Rob: Aw **fuck** them. No they they shouldn't be allowed. Well I believe in ... they only want equality when it comes down to the workplace or earning money but they don't wanna be equal when it comes to fuckin digging ditches or or or you know, or giving up their seats. I've never seen a woman get up and give up her seat for a man in a bus or anything like that ... they want their cake and eat it too ... I dunno, it's evolved over years and years and now they're getting too cocky and all these business women. I believe a woman's place (pause) is is like is equal. It should be more of a lesser scale than a man really. That's what I think. I think they shouldn't be too dominant. They should be equal. I don't think they should dominate a man. It's not right. It's not nature. (pp. 9:7–8)

The listener might be left pondering just what Rob means by 'equality'. At one level he seems to view equality as 'women not being dominant'; but at another level he views it as 'women being equal on a lesser scale'. He backs up these positions by claiming it is neither 'right' nor 'nature' for women to occupy positions of superiority. The implication is that men are naturally superior and that this superiority extends beyond mere physical superiority.

When these men were pressed to explain the dominance of their partners, they repeatedly referenced the discourse of natural entitlement to support their position. But, aside from Rob's example above, the discourse was seldom delivered in an explicit and literal fashion. A combination of rhetorical devices tended to be interspliced with the presentation of the discourse. Operating by themselves, the individual devices examined here (reference ambiguity, axiom marking, synecdoche, metonymy and metaphor) add colour and interest to a text. But, as the extract from Gavin's interview illustrates, when multiple devices work together, the expressive function of these devices extends beyond mere decoration. They can be seen to work cooperatively throughout a passage of text; a metaphoric reference in one sentence will be reinforced by metonymic links in the next sentence and synecdochal links in the next. The text slowly develops a system of links that promote particular ways of looking at familiar objects. The devices work together with discourses in building up the credibility of a particular position for the speaker.

Gavin called on the discourse of natural entitlement when he stated:

> It's a fact that only women can have children. Sure if they wanna, if they wanna have a career, have a career. Don't, but it, you get these women that wanna have children and have a career. I don't think they can balance the two. It's not right. It's not right on the husband, it's not right on the children and it's not fair on her.

Women are natural child-bearers and by association they are natural child-carers. The metonymic link between 'child-bearer' and 'child-carer' passes without apparently requiring further explication. The use of ambiguous references—'you get', 'these women', 'it's not'—and the use of axiom markers—'it's a fact', 'it's not right'—enhance the impression of authority. The rhetorical devices function in conjunction with the discourse in promoting a sense that it is reasonable and correct that men are naturally superior to women and are consequently worthy of positions of dominance.

The combined impact of discourse and rhetorical device may not always be persuasive. In response to the interviewer explaining the main goals of feminism. Bill stated:

> Bill: Yeah, those are all good points, yeah. But I think the male should have a final decision, in a relationship.
> PA: How's that—
> Bill: Because he's dominant.
> PA: The male's dominant—
> Bill: Yeah, in a relationship.

PA: Why is the male dominant? I mean—

Bill: Because he's bigger and he's stronger.

PA: OK, so the final decisions, some of the final decisions need to be made by men (Bill: Yeah) 'cos they're bigger and stronger?

Bill: No, that's where dominance comes in, the root of dominance, but, because someone's gotta make the decision, you know, and two people can't always make a decision, so the final decision [phone rings] the one person, and there should be, that boundary should be set at the beginning of a marriage.

In this extract Bill attempted to explain why men are justified in occupying positions of dominance. His central line of reasoning, *men-should-be-dominant-because-they-are-bigger-and-stronger*. calls on the synecdochal link discussed earlier between the specific sense of strength as 'muscular force' and wider notions of strength. He also incorporated other rhetorical devices to enhance the delivery of his central message: he referred metaphorically to 'roots' and 'boundaries', and he anchored his position with an axiomatic declaration 'someone's gotta make the decision'. As it stands on the page, Bill's use here of the rhetorical devices appears to lack impact and persuasiveness. However, it is possible that when received in the context of vulnerability and a history of abuse, and when the listener faces someone who is stronger and clearly willing to hurt, the rhetoric would take on considerably more persuasiveness.

[. . .]

REFERENCES

Bavelas, J., Black, A., Chovil, N. and Mullett, J. (1990) *Equivocal Communication*. Newbury Park, CA: Sage.

Bograd, M. (1990) 'Why We Need Gender to Understand Human Violence', *Journal of Interpersonal Violence* 5: 132–5.

Busch, R., Robertson, J. and Lapsley, H. (1993) 'Domestic Violence and the Justice System: A Study of Breaches of Protection Orders', *Community Mental Health in New Zealand* 7: 26–44.

Dobash, R. and Dobash, R. (1988) 'Research as Social Action: The Struggle for Battered Women', in K. Yllo and M. Bograd (eds), *Feminist Perspectives on Wife Abuse*, pp. 51–74. Newbury Park, CA: Sage.

Douglas, K. (1994) *Invisible Wounds*. Auckland: Penguin.

Gray, B. (1977) *The Grammatical Foundations of Rhetorics: Discourse Analysis*. The Hague: Mouton.

Kittay, E. (1987) *Metaphor: Its Cognitive Force and Linguistic Structure*. Oxford: Clarendon.

Kurz, D. (1989) 'Social Science Perspectives on Wife Abuse: Current Debates and Future Directions', *Gender and Society* 3: 489–505.

Lakoff, G. (1987) *Women, Fire, and Dangerous Things: What Categories Reveal about the Mind*. Chicago, IL.: University of Chicago Press.

Lakoff, G. and Johnson, M. (1979) *Metaphors We Live By*. Chicago, IL.: University of Chicago Press.

Ortony, A. (1979) 'Metaphor: A Multidimensional Problem', in A. Ortony (ed.) *Metaphor and Thought*. London: Cambridge University Press.

Pagelow, M. D. (1981) *Woman-battering: Victims and Their Experiences*. Newbury Park, CA: Sage.

Paprotte, W. and Dirven, W., eds (1985) *The Ubiquity of Metaphor: Metaphor in Language and Thought*. Amsterdam: John Benjamins.

Pence, E. and Paymar, M. (1993) *Education Groups for Men Who Batter: The Duluth Model*. New York: Springer.

Ricoeur, P. (1978) *The Rule of Metaphor: Multi-disciplinary Studies in the Creation of Meaning in Language*. London: Routledge and Kegan Paul.

Schechter, S. and Gary, L. T. (1988) 'A Framework for Understanding and Empowering Battered Women', in M. Straus (ed.) *Abuse and Victimisation across the Lifespan*, pp. 240–53. Baltimore, MD: Johns Hopkins University Press.

Soskice, J. M. (1985) *Metaphor and Religious Language*. Oxford: Clarendon.

Walker, L. E. (1979) *The Battered Woman*. New York: Harper and Row.

4

LANGUAGE AND YOUTH

In advocating a change of direction for research on youth, Angela McRobbie (1994: 186) asks 'what are the discourses within which "different, youthful, subjectivities" are constructed? How are they expressed?' In exploring language, power and young people, this chapter maps some of the discursive constructions of self that articulate youth identities in everyday modern life. It examines the ways in which language is taken up and used as resistance to mainstream norms and values. It looks at the sorts of discourse practices drawn upon to constitute, shape and signal membership of particular youth cultures. And, as contemporary social change demands that greater attention be given to cultural plurality, ethnic mixing and **hybridisation**, it tracks the way in which young people negotiate status locally within their own multiracial social worlds.

After considering questions of definition regarding 'youth culture' and 'power', there follows a brief synopsis of some sociolinguistic research conducted in the past on the language of young people. Work by Montgomery (1995), Cheshire (1982) and Labov (1972c) documents how vocabulary (lexis), grammar and discourse have been used to exclude outsiders, challenge authority and signal hierarchy within a peer group. From here, we look at other discursive spaces as sites of negotiated identity, from the 'tags' (names of graffiti writers), threats and 'disses' (disrespectful comments) written on walls to the talk of young Pakistani Scottish women on radio. New technologies too offer multiple terrains for young people to define self, forge social relationships and innovate as the discourses of e-zines and texting reveal.

Recently, academic research has focused on the multiracial nature of youth culture in modern society and issues of 'race' and 'ethnicity' loosely tie together much of the later discussion and all five readings for this chapter. The selected extracts have been chosen because they reflect contemporary themes and perspectives. The first two readings examine the recent **ebonics** (African American Vernacular English) controversy in the US and its importance to youth identity. The first of these gives an overview of what happened, and considers future pedagogic directions. The second focuses on a particular instance of black students employing language as a form of 'rhetorical resistance' against mainstream practices that devalue black youth culture. Their use of ebonics challenges the assimilationist and discriminatory tendencies of the educational system, yet, recognising that high academic achievement is associated with speaking standard American English, these young people have also learned to 'act white' and 'rent' the discourse of institutional power during class. From here, the focus shifts to the UK to consider how young black speakers also subvert racist discourses through their adoption of what they see as a 'white' style of language. In contrast, we explore white youths 'acting black' as they talk in Creole, urban black American vernacular and black London speech. Young people's switches to 'Indian English' are also discussed.

These transgressions of cultural identity play their part in the reconstruction of 'new ethnicities' (Hall 1992; Rampton 1999). As these emerge, issues of power, 'race', 'ethnicity' and language are foregrounded, and in turn what it means to 'be white' is interrogated. In its account of a group of young white people rejecting black linguistic forms and the 'coolness' they bring, the final reading develops further our discussion on 'whiteness' and youth discourses. Their dissociation from 'trendiness' is articulated through using 'superstandard English' – a divergent style of language characterised by increased formality, prescriptively standard grammar and carefully articulated standard pronunciation. In speaking like this, these young people set themselves apart and culturally mark themselves as 'hyperwhite'.

'YOUTH CULTURE' AND 'POWER': SOME QUESTIONS OF DEFINITION

Defining 'youth culture' is no easy task, not least because rather than being unitary, singular or static, there exist many different, diverse and dynamic 'youth cultures'. What's more, defining 'youth' itself is problematic. For example, seeing it as a specific chronological age range (say, twelve to twenty-five years old) is limiting. Some 'middle-aged' people appear 'youthful' and some young people seem 'older than their years'. Viewing 'adolescence' as a transitory stepping-stone to 'adulthood' – as early academic research on 'youth' did – also throws up problems. Young people are seen as 'not quite finished human beings' (Bucholtz 2002) and, accordingly, not worthy of study in their own right. To an extent, work undertaken in the 1970s by the Birmingham Centre for Contemporary Cultural Studies remedied this by focusing on working-class youth and their resistance to forms of social control (Hall and Jefferson 1976; Willis 1977; Hebdige 1979). Such studies positioned as central the everyday practices of youth culture, though they were later critiqued for neglecting issues of gender (McRobbie 1991; 1994) and ethnicity (Hemmings et al. 2002).

Today, research on 'youth' – and accompanying definitions of what it means to be 'young' – has moved on. Earlier, inflexible, definitions have been replaced largely by approaches that take into account the new formations of youth culture as they are actively constituted in late modern society. There is an appreciation that young people draw on a range of heterogeneous and fluid cultural practices to articulate their multiple identities. Moreover, understanding the dynamics of this rests upon being sensitive to how discourse, definitions of self and local contexts interrelate. In deconstructing the meaning of 'youth', Bucholtz, following Durham (2000), suggests:

> applying the linguistic concept of a 'shifter' . . . to the category of youth. A shifter is a word that is tied directly to the context of speaking and hence takes much of its meaning from situated use . . . the referential function of 'youth' cannot be determined in advance of its use in a particular cultural context, and its use indexes the nature of the context in which it is invoked. As a shifter, then, youth is a context-renewing and a context-creating sign whereby social relations are both (and often simultaneously) reproduced and contested. (Bucholtz 2002: 527–8)

Along with this more insightful view of what 'youth' may mean has come a more sophisticated understanding of power, as young people, with their many cultural practices and identities, are no longer simply defined as defiant of conventional life and social institutions. There has been a shift to examining the microstructures of power, as they are discursively constituted within and across social groups of 'youth'. For instance, McDonald explores young males' graffiti on an Australian train line and analyses it as 'not constructed against parents, teachers or employers. What is happening here is not conflict' with authority (1999: 149). Their 'tags' are more to do with articulating an identity that only has meaning as long as other graffiti writers see it. If crossed out and replaced by someone else's name, the writer loses face and their identity. In being very much defined within the graffiti world itself, power and status in this context have less to do with challenging conventional culture than with the interactional dynamics and social relationships between taggers.

Accompanying this deconstruction of 'power' is an unpicking of what constitutes 'resistance' (also discussed in the chapter on language and organisations). However, while clearly young people should not be singularly characterised as 'resistant' to mainstream culture, as some of the examples in this chapter evidence, oppositional discourses *are* drawn upon at times in their constructions of self. Moreover, such linguistic practices can be direct and explicit as they are used in the fight to define identity. At other times, 'resistance' takes the form of apparent accommodation (see for example, black students' use of standard American English in Reading 4.2). 'Resistance', it appears, is a complex practice and what constitutes it is locally determined. In conducting research on club cultures, Thornton (1995) questions the rather simplistic assumptions that theorists in the past have sometimes made about what 'resistance' means. She explains how, for example, many youth cultures have been seen as separate and distinct from the media discourses which pejoratise them as resistant and disruptive to mainstream values and culture. As such, academic study has tended to see young people as the innocent victims of journalistic sensationalism. However, in her work on the connection between club cultures and the media, she uncovers a more complex relationship at play. Thornton describes how the dance industry actually basked in the mass media's condemnation of it as 'drug-crazed', and notes how 'disapproving "moral panic" stories in mass circulation tabloid newspapers often have the effect of certifying transgression and legitimising youth cultures' (1995: 6). In wanting to be positioned as subversive and defiant, she argues, clubbers enjoyed the derogatory media coverage that proved to be 'not the verdict but the essence of their resistance' (1995: 137).

SECRECY, CHALLENGE AND STATUS

In the past, particular sociolinguistic studies on language and youth have chosen to focus on 'exclusion'. For instance, it's been documented how some young people have employed a 'secret' language specifically in order to circumscribe boundaries between their own and mainstream culture. Montgomery (1995) reports on adolescent males in Glasgow who engaged in **over-lexicalisation** when talking about their drinking and other drug-taking practices. 'Being drunk' would be expressed as 'steaming', 'blootered', 'swallied', 'rockered', 'slappered', 'pished'. 'Cannabis' was termed 'doobie', 'shit', 'soap bar', 'black rock', 'blaw'. Some of these terms, at least, were likely to be unfamiliar to older authority figures in positions of power (teachers, parents, police) and used in part because drug use and underage drinking are illegal activities. Clarke (1996) found similar linguistic practices in the talk of teenage girls involved in the rave scene in the late 1990s. A 'rave' was relexicalised as 'party', and 'drugs' became 'chemicals'. Amphetamines were overlexicalised as 'speed', 'billy' or 'whizz', and a bad experience on drugs was referred to as being 'mashed up' or 'trashed', or having 'lost it'. Drawing on discourses of resistance, one of Clarke's seventeen-year-old interviewees, Jessica, explained how this language functioned as oppositional to parental culture and authority:

> everybody that's into it knows what a pill is and what billy is and all the rest of it but the people that aren't . . . it might confuse them a bit . . . which I suppose in a way we quite like the thought . . . I quite like the thought my dad obviously wouldn't understand it all . . . I guess in a way it's like a way of rebelling like . . . you won't accept us . . . you're against us . . . I guess in a way it's developing our own culture when we've got a different language. (Clark 1996)

The exclusionary nature of such terms, however, only works insofar as their meanings remain unknown to the wider community. In her work on club cultures, Thornton (1995: 6) found that as soon as the term 'acid house' became familiar to readers of national newspapers, the word 'acid' was dropped from club names and music genre classifications.

In addition to vocabulary, attachment to peer culture can be signalled through grammar and pronunciation. Cheshire (1982) looked at the talk of white adolescents in two contexts: at school with the teacher present and then among themselves away from the classroom environment. In their peer group, her male participants typically adopted an informal style of speech, with swearing, vernacular grammar and pronunciation. In the more formal school context with the teacher present as an authority figure, most of the adolescents **upwardly converged** to standard English. Interestingly, however, one informant opted to challenge school philosophy and practice by increasing his use of non-standard linguistic forms. Cheshire's research is not alone in identifying young people using language antagonistically in this way. In a study that examined black adolescents employing 'Patois' in UK schools, Edwards concludes that, in a context where black identity and discourse was typically discredited, it served 'as a means of expressing defiance of teachers' (1997: 413).

What is additionally interesting about Cheshire's work, however, is the part that language apparently played in the complex power negotiations *between* male friends (girls organised themselves differently). Close examination of their talk enabled her to relate status in the gang with use of certain linguistic features. Non-standard verb forms (for example, 'they *calls* me all the names under the sun') and negative concord (for example, 'it *ain't* got *no* pedigree or nothing') marked how integrated a male participant was in the behaviours, norms and values of the group. Through their use of the vernacular, members signalled how they positioned themselves hierarchically to one another.

The link between adolescents' language and their status was also an issue that Labov (1972b) explored in work focusing on black male teenagers using African American Vernacular English (AAVE) in New York. Here, youths engaged in an exchange of formalised ritual 'insults' called 'sounding', 'signifying' or 'playing the dozens'. Taking part meant having:

> to match or top your opponent with an appropriately selected 'sound' or insult which denigrates your opponent's origins (mother, occasionally father) or current circumstances (house, living conditions). This leads to rounds of insults between players, each successful sound being greeted with laughter or approving comment. (Montgomery 1995: 212)

The language games performed between these young people were clearly competitive: status in the group was achieved by producing a cleverer, more skilful retort to the previous utterance.

CREATING DISCURSIVE SPACE

In a contemporary post-industrial society of social change, young people have also found other ways in which to negotiate social relationships, identities and power. New discursive terrains are created in which struggles for subjectivity are acted out according to the 'rules' of particular youth cultures they inhabit. Adams and Winter (1997) track how young gang members in Phoenix, US, reappropriated and redefined everyday physical space by writing graffiti on walls. Like McDonald (1999) above, they found that this was intended to be not so much a challenge to mainstream society but more an expression of identity within and across gang communities. In claiming it as interactional in nature, they note how such graffitti follows Grice's (1975) **co-operative principle**. Adams and Winter (1997: 341–2) describe it functioning as 'a conversation . . . the writing contains examples of direct address to other groups and garners responses from these and others . . . but for dialogue to occur the act must be truthful, relevant and comprehensible to potential responders'. Interestingly, a detailed linguistic analysis of this graffiti revealed elements of community dialects and several languages. For instance, phonological features of African American Vernacular speech led to the writing of 'gangsta', not 'gangster', while Hispanic graffiti writers switched between Spanish and English to varying degrees. Threats and 'disses' between gangs took a variety of forms, from a simple crossing out of the words written by rival groups to 'inversions' where the graffiti would actually be changed so as to turn the writers' words against them. Not all graffiti was primarily antagonistic, however. Additional types of writing signalled solidarity with other gangs, while an absence of 'crossing-outs' marked a visible sign of their allegiance with each other. Graffiti also constructed status within this youth culture. Echoing McDonald (1999), Adams and Winter found that one of its most important functions was to rank writers hierarchically within their own social network:

> Writers tend to be younger gang members who are trying to get their name out for more respect and status in a gang . . . Not only are they writing their names in the neighbourhood but crossing out another gang's in an area where many gangs advertise. The battle is not for territory but to let other gangs know of their existence and willingness to demonstrate their commitment through action. This also sends a message to their own gang that they want to establish themselves as important members. (Adams and Winter 1997: 356)

Evidently, contestations of power here revolve around a struggle for an identity that is afforded peer esteem. Relations within the gang are obviously of paramount concern as writers seek, challenge and defend positions that command deference from the others.

The development of new technologies has thrown up other sorts of discursive terrains where young people construct identity and socially connect with others but without having to be physically co-present. For instance, mobile phone texting has been appropriated by younger teenagers to enhance friendship ties, and cultivate a sense of self away from parental authority. Like the adolescents in Montgomery's work discussed earlier, Kasesniemi and Rautiainen found that the telephone talk of Finnish young people aged from thirteen to fifteen years old frequently contained references to sex, alcohol or cigarettes, with 'daring chain messages and logos [being] a hidden aspect of teen text messaging culture. They are not meant for adults to see' (2002: 180). The internet too has offered young people a way of linking up with each other while being geographically distant. Youth Speaks, an organisation with its own website, is promoted as being 'committed to creating spaces that celebrate the youth voice' across boundaries of 'age, race, class, gender and sexual orientation' (www.youthspeaks.org, 5/7/2002). In advocating feminism, the (largely white) movement of Riot Grrrls, whose original concern was to counter sexism in the underground rock music scene, has turned its attention to creating opportunities for young women to engage actively with new technology on their own terms. They are encouraged to express their views and contribute to an 'e-zine' (an electronically published, alternative magazine). Unlike Youth Speaks, Riot Grrrls resist defining themselves as a unified culture, preferring instead to highlight their diversity and multiple identities. However, there exists a common theme to their messages. One contributor to a 'grrrlzine' site wrote, 'with "grrrl" and "ladies" I think of rebellious, resistant "girls"' (http://grrrlzines.net, 10/7/ 02) while Leonard quotes another Riot Grrrl saying 'we're tired of being written out – out of history, out of the "scene", out of our bodies ... for this reason we have created our zine and scene' (1998: 105). She describes how the 'Friendly Grrrls Guide to the Internet' explains 'Girls are not girls, but grrrls, super kewl (cool) young women who have the tenacity and drive to surf the net [and] network with other young women on-line' (ibid.: 111). As Leonard points out, their texts 'can be understood as creating "rhetorical spaces" ... where individual voices and particular feminist ideas can be articulated' (ibid.: 107).

'Telling their own stories'

In looking at how young British Muslim women were 'actively engaged in challenging dominant representations [of themselves] and producing new meanings', Dwyer (1998) too was concerned with the contestation and reconstruction of identity. Racialised discourses about Asian women typically define them as passive victims of oppressive cultures, neglecting their active reworkings of subjectivity, multiple subject positions and contributions to the 'reinvention of ethnicity' (Gilroy 1993a). In an interview quote that highlights how these young people had to deal with 'the burden of representation', one young woman noted how 'every time they put something on TV about black and Asian people, it's always negative'. Gilroy (1993b) claims that, in offering new spaces of representation, youth cultures function partially to counter racism. Dwyer documents this happening in practice as she describes how her sixteen to nineteen-year-old London school students challenged, unhinged and rearticulated the 'fixed' meanings of 'Asian' and 'Western', innovatively fusing the two together in a way that made sense for them.

Discourses of representation were also a focus of concern in Qureshi's (2000) work on some young Scottish Pakistani women who produced a weekly magazine-style programme on an 'Asian' radio station set up on a temporary and restricted licence in Edinburgh. Conceived as an attempt to 'construct a public space for themselves where they [could] make their voices heard', these women were concerned to negotiate an acceptable definition of what it means to be Scottish-Pakistani, Muslim and female. Like the young women in Dwyer's study, Qureshi's participants were looking to counter the negative and sexist dominant discourses to which they were typically subject. The programmes, in part, focused on various issues that were deemed relevant to young people like themselves – women's safety, 'back to work after childbirth', as well as regular items on beauty, health and the role of Asian women in modern society. Such content, along with the women's presence on radio, certainly questioned some of the stereotypical assumptions made about Muslim females. However, broadcasting in such a local context also meant that their programme ran counter to patriarchal community discourses that prescribed how these young women were supposed to behave. This clearly mediated their public representations of self. Out of a fear that their opinions on 'sensitive' issues might harm their family's 'izzat' (honour and respect), the women self-censored, limiting their 'on-air' discussions and issuing disclaimers whenever a potentially controversial matter arose. Following a call from a female family therapist who saw 'Asian parental pressure' to be the cause of their daughter's emotional breakdown, one of the group felt it important to add, 'I'll just reiterate that was Margaret Robertson's point of view and not anybody in the ... group' (ibid.: 185). Talk control was also exercised by the station's management who were keen to pursue the adoption of a more permanent licence and did not want to jeopardise this by offending a broader Asian audience or advertising sponsors. The young women were censured for discussing 'bikini lines' in the health and beauty feature, and told that 'postnatal depression' was an inappropriate topic to discuss 'on air' in their allocated programme slot. Under pressure, the group were forced to restrict their broadcast to music and 'lightweight' talk, but in doing so felt stifled and frustrated. Eventually, they withdrew their programme.

LANGUAGE, EDUCATION AND AFRICAN AMERICAN YOUTH

The ebonics controversy

As we've seen, contestations of identity can be acted out through language in different ways – at the level of content (what is said), or style (how it is said). We have discussed how 'non-standard' varieties of English can hold great significance for their young users. In constituting allegiance to a particular youth culture, they score highly in solidarity terms. Yet, the power of non-mainstream language to articulate much more than this can be seen by the storm that greeted a US School Board when it proposed in the mid-1990s to implement teaching standard English through the medium of AAVE (African American Vernacular English) or what is commonly termed 'ebonics'.

The part language plays in young people's academic success – an issue to which Reading 4.1 attends – has been well-researched in sociolinguistics to date. It's long been known that negative attitudes towards 'non-standard' varieties of English often serve to stigmatise and discriminate against their users (Giles and Coupland 1991). What's more, teachers' prejudicial views towards students' vernacular speech can lead to damaging judgements about their personalities, social backgrounds and academic potential, and ultimately affect school performance. In the Oakland School district in California, African American students were found to be continuously underachieving and, consequently, over-represented in special education classes. It was determined that the cause of this, in part, was due to a culturally-insensitive academic system and teachers' ignorance of the nature and history of AAVE – the language that young black students typically used in their everyday informal interaction (see Smitherman 2000 for a detailed description of this variety). Like the decision passed in Ann Arbor over a decade earlier (Mesthrie et al. 2000: 376–8), it was thus recommended that educators undergo training in AAVE in order that social and linguistic prejudice be addressed. In December 1996, the School Board passed a resolution that declared ebonics to be the primary language of black students in Oakland's schools. It claimed it to be a legitimate, rule-governed and systematic language in its own right; recommended that it be maintained as such, and used in classrooms to help students acquire standard American English (SAE).

The timing of the resolution was unfortunate. In the holiday period between just before Christmas and New Year, news was relatively quiet, and as the story fell into the lap of the mainstream media it made headline copy. Almost without exception, the Oakland School Board decision was misreported as a policy designed to abandon the teaching of standard English and replace it with AAVE. Despite official statements to the contrary, press and television journalists seemed intent on propagating the view that majority standard language teaching in Oakland was to be completely discarded. Widespread public controversy ensued. Radio and TV talk shows took up the issue, more often than not erroneously equating AAVE with 'slang' or 'bad grammar' (Lakoff 2000). Newspaper editorials and letters expressed outrage that AAVE was to be legitimised as a form of communication in schools. The *New York Times* (24 December 1996) labelled the decision a 'blunder', while the *San Francisco Chronicle* (20 December 1996) attacked the School Board for 'doing its students a disservice' (Baron 2000: 7). In the wake of so much furore and criticism, the Oakland School Board amended its resolution, revising its position on the teaching of English through AAVE to a statement that, alternatively, called for 'a general recognition of language differences among Black students in order to improve their proficiency in English' (quoted in Mesthrie et al. 2000: 380).

Although critics were somewhat appeased by the amendment, what the backlash against ebonics revealed was the extent of racial hostility and prejudice against its speakers. At the time, a proliferation of tasteless and malicious internet web sites sprang up parodying AAVE ('mock ebonics') and drawing on negative speech attitudes and stereotypes. Baugh (2000) describes how one of the earliest of these included 'The Ebonics Translator' which used a 'search-and-replace' function to change submitted SAE sentences into (mock) African American Vernacular English. Prayers, classics of literature and nursery rhymes were also rewritten in the name of humour. By oversimplifying AAVE's linguistic grammar for supposedly 'comic' effect, it reduced its users to caricature. For example, a typical feature of ebonics is the use of the verb particle 'be' to indicate a moment that is recurring (habitual aspect). 'He be looking good' (as opposed to 'he looking good') refers to a man's style, not just at any one moment (present aspect), but in the past and the future too. Yet a 'search-and-replace' key fails to appreciate grammatical complexity. In the mock ebonics translation of the nursery rhyme, 'Baa Baa Black Sheep', 'be' is inserted gratuitously ('One be fo da masta', And one be fo yo mama, An one be fo da little homey dat libs down da screet') where ellipsis occurs in the standard English version ('One . . . for the master, one . . . for the dame, one . . . for the little boy who lives down the lane') (Rankin and Karn 1999: 366–7). The crude misappropriation of AAVE's linguistic rules also meant that its regional, social and stylistic variation was ignored. Lippi-Green (1997: 176), in fact, notes how 'African American youth integrated into urban Hip Hop culture must choose among grammatical, lexical and phonological variables which identify them as aligned with either the west or east coast'. Perniciously racist jokes proliferated enormously and reached such a peak at one stage that, in July 1997, the Equal Employment Opportunity Commission ruled them as work-place harassment, stating that 'disseminating derogatory electronic messages regarding "ebonics" to your co-workers is against the law' (quoted in Baron 2000: 8).

In commenting on the uproar over the Oakland resolution, Perry and Delpitt (1998: xiv) note how it went beyond linguistics and became 'a debate about culture, power, identity and control'. Lippi Green points out that 'there has never been an outcry about Chicagoans' inability to distinguish between "merry", "Mary", and "marry" . . . But people do lose jobs and schoolchildren are belittled because . . . they say . . . "aks" rather than "ask"' (1997: 240). She goes on to argue that, for mainstream society, 'the real trouble with Black English . . . is simply this: AAVE is tangible and irrefutable evidence that there is a distinct, healthy, functioning African American culture which is not white, and which does not want to be white' (ibid: 178). Such a view has a certain legitimacy – we saw in Chapter 1 how mainstream media never problematise 'being white', while 'being black' is typically associated with crime, deviance and subversion. Moreover, the powerful 'English-Only' lobby in the US (see Chapter 5) works to undermine any language variety other than mainstream American English used by white middle-class speakers.

However, seeing the division of opinion over the Oakland decision along purely 'ethnic' lines is too simplistic. As the first reading discusses, objections to the resolution did not come solely from white critics, but from some older, professional, African Americans too, including well-known figures like the preacher Jesse Jackson and the writer Maya Angelou, both of whom, ironically, have drawn on AAVE in their own work. In accounting for such opposition, Smitherman and Cunningham in the first reading of this chapter, point to a prejudice against youth itself, quoting one young AAVE speaker as saying: 'Most of the people who have been opponents of Ebonics are the same ones who have been dismissive of Hip-Hop. There is a segment of the older Black generation, the middle class, civil rights leadership, that is anti-youth'.

Elsewhere, Smitherman argues that an 'assault on the language of African America is a way of reinscribing the subordination and powerlessness of Black youth' (2000: 157). She contends that opposition to AAVE from the 'Talented Tenth' (leading members of the black community who have succeeded in mainstream American life) signals just how far removed they are from young people whose very culture is constituted through such language. In Reading 4.1, Smitherman and Cunningham propose three solutions to resolve what they see to be an impending crisis that threatens 'to tear the Black community apart'. Centred around the acquisition of Critical Language Awareness (CLA) (Fairclough 1992b), they seek to make visible how power and discourse interrelate. First, there must develop an appreciation that language is integral to the constitution of self. Next, African American youths should be encouraged to use and understand ebonics as it relates to their identity, culture and background. Thirdly, the authors advocate that a close and critical examination of both AAVE and standard American English be undertaken, including 'their history, their socio-political constructions, and their sociolinguistic uses'. In asking 'what is standard and exactly who chose to make it the representative of *all* people', issues of race, power and language policy would, accordingly, be interrogated and challenged.

Dissin' the standard: language as 'rhetorical resistance'

While the formal inclusion of critical language awareness in educational programmes is to be supported, for most young AAVE speakers, this has yet to happen. In being told to drop their community variety in favour of SAE, they confront linguistic prejudice and discrimination on a daily basis. In documenting how language practices function as 'guerilla warfare' at 'Capital High School' in Washington, DC, Reading 4.2 describes how black students manage to reconcile black identity with the institutionally prescribed discourse that discredits African American Vernacular culture. The author,

Fordham, notes how, despite black students 'valuing forms of interaction that emphasise visibility, possession of voice, and a semantic code outside the mainstream culture', school language practices oblige them to 'appropriate not only standard English grammar but also the entire power discourse of the dominant White community'. Failing to do so means failing academically. Despite this, many students opt to maintain their use of ebonics as a sign of linguistic and cultural contestation. Moreover, those who seek school achievement risk being judged negatively by their black peers for taking up a 'white identity'. In exploring the ways in which educationally successful students manage this dilemma, the reading describes how language users can astutely adopt and rearticulate dominant discourses to their own advantage.

Academic achievers at Capital High, claims Fordham, engaged in a form of 'rhetorical resistance' by strategically 'renting' the dominant 'white' English in class, and returning to speaking ebonics when with their friends. At some level then, it appears that students had clearly developed their own brand of critical language awareness. In a way, 'black street speech' had become their 'standard' in that it constituted the high prestige variety that they used much more frequently. As the author points out, black students using 'white' forms of talk in informal peer contexts risked heavy censure and marginalisation, not only as 'power seekers but as people who might use power just as the larger society has historically done, to exploit and dehumanise African Americans'. Representing themselves as merely 'leasing' the classroom variety – as opposed to seeking its ownership – meant that they could academically progress while simultaneously articulate their commitment to their community culture. In describing such a strategy as 'inversion', Fordham notes how it functioned as a sort of pretence in that black students 'appear[ed] to but not to' be SAE speakers. The practice of 'accommodation-as-opposition' has already been discussed in the chapter on language and organisations, and we see a similar process at play in what the author calls this 'dissin' (disrespecting) of standard American English. In a different article describing the linguistic choices made here by young AAVE speakers, she states: 'Resistance-as-conformity is the academically successful students' weapon of choice in their efforts to maintain a Black identity and in fighting the ongoing linguistic war' (Fordham 1999: 286).

Echoing the authors of the first reading, she notes a clear generational divide in recognising what AAVE means to its young speakers. Resistance to mainstream English is not understood by school officials, or by the larger community. Rather, it is framed as student inability to acquire 'appropriate' communication skills. To neglect the issues of culture and identity that surround the speaking of African American Vernacular English and SAE, however, is to disregard these forms functioning as 'rhetorical resistance'. Fordham concludes by arguing that attention needs to be redirected away from perspectives of 'linguistic deficit', and towards an appreciation of how language, power and identity work in relation to each other.

NARRATING THE OTHER
Parodying racism and subverting racial meanings

In exploring how some young black speakers in the UK challenge and subvert discourses of racial prejudice and discrimination, Reading 4.3 also focuses on resistance. The author was interested in detailing how they 'articulated their notions of identity and ethnicity ... within the context of adolescent interactions' (Back 1996: 1). He was particularly interested in how such negotiations of self were mediated by discourses of racism. A white male ethnographer who took a job as a youth club worker, Back was conscious of 'the need to remain vigilantly cautious about projecting romantic and utopian desires on to the accounts and interpretations of the culture of young people' (ibid.: 22). Moreover, he was sensitive to how his own age, ethnicity, status and gender mediated, not only his relationship with the black and white participants of the study but also his understanding of how racist discourses worked in their everyday lives.

During the research period, Back became the only white member of a youth basketball team in Southgate (one of the two areas in London he investigated) that travelled in and around London to play matches. The reading focuses on a monologue produced by a young black male, Winston, during a bus ride to one such event, and Back records it as illustrative in detailing 'the sophisticated way in which these young men acknowledged racism and inverted racial meanings' (ibid.: 173). The performance takes the form of a parody as Winston slips in and out of different roles. The chief figure of fun is the stereotypical white 'upper class twit', who comes from a wealthy, land-owning family and who finds West Indian culture in Britain to be rather bemusing and 'exotic'. Particular elements of black youth culture are seen as perplexing, while black youths themselves are described as 'lazy'. The grammar and vocabulary associated with such a character are also reproduced for comic effect. In performing this caricature, Winston employs the strategy of 'double-voicing' (discussed also in Chapters 2 and 5) where a speaker adopts someone else's discourse for their own ends, so that what's introduced is 'a semantic intention directly opposed to the original one' (quoted in Rampton 1995: 233). The relationship between class, 'race', language and power is wittily addressed and deconstructed as other 'voices' are brought into play – a Creole-speaking Ragamuffin and a black London Cockney. The humour works, argues the author, because both performer and audience have the 'same semantic points of reference'.

Critical engagement with white discourses of racism is also evident in the discussion by two young black women about an absence from work because of illness. Back notes how they too engage with racist terms by exposing white stereotypes and holding them up to ridicule. Once more, we see the use of 'double-voicing' ('you niggers are all the same, you just don't want to work' [starts to laugh]) to subvert prevailing pejorative discourses of black employees as 'lazy'. Back points out that both these examples of linguistic play are 'instances where ideological struggles over meaning are taking place', arguing that, rather than passively experiencing racism, young black people locally challenge and rework the discourses that discriminate against them.

In his ethnographic work on multiracial groups of young people in the South Midlands of England, Rampton also offers an example of racist discourses being subverted. He describes how Asian youths are empowered by their strategic switches into **Stylised Asian English** (SAE):

> Sometimes Asian kids may put on an Indian accent and pretend that they don't understand what is happening, or act as though they think everything is good: they may pretend that they're not in control. In fact they are taking an idea which says Asian people are powerless and turning it inside out: they are putting on this act and using it as a kind of power for themselves. (Rampton 1992: 63)

An example of this happening in practice is analysed in his report of one particular fieldwork incident where he was trying to persuade the boys he was audio-recording to take the event seriously. The task involved them listening to extracts of their previous interactions and explaining why they spoke as they did. The transcribed recording below features Rampton ('BR') and three young males – Asif and Kazim (both fifteen years old and of Pakistani descent) and Alan (also fifteen, of Anglo descent):

1.	BR:	right shall I – shall I shall we stop there
2.	Kazim:	no
3.	Alan:	no come ⌜on carry on
4.	Asif:	⌞do another extract
5.	BR:	le – lets have (.) ⌜then you have to give me more=
6.	Alan:	⌞carry on
7.	BR:	=attention gents
8.	Asif:	((quietly)) yeh alright
9.	Alan:	((quietly)) alright
10.	Asif:	((quietly)) yeh
11.	Kazim	((in SAE)): I AM VERY SORRY BEN JAAD
		[aɪ æm veri sƀri ben dʒaːd]
12.	Asif	((in SAE)): ATTENTION BENJAMIN
		[athenʃaːn bendʒəmɪn]
13.	Asif:	⌜((laughter))
14.	BR:	⎸right well you can – we -cn
15.	Alan:	⌞BENJAADEMIN
16.	BR:	we can continue but we er must concentrate a bit
17.		⌜more
18.	Asif:	⌞yeh =
19.	Alan:	=alright ⌜then
20.	Asif	((in SAE)): ⌞concentrating very hard
		[kõnsəstretiŋ veri aɾ]

21. BR: okay right
22.   ((giggles dying down))
23. Kazim   ((in SAE)): what a stupid (boy)
               [vʌd ə stupɪd]
24. BR: ((returning the microphone to what he considers to be a
               better position to catch all the speakers)): concentrate a
               little bit
25. Alan: alright then
26. Kazim   ((in Creole)): stop movin dat ting aroun
               [dæl tɪŋ əɹaʊn]
27. BR: WELL YOU stop moving it around and then I'll-
28.   won't need to
29. Kazim   ((in Creole)): stop moving dat ting around
               [dæl tɪŋ əɹaʊn]
30. BR: right okay [...]

(adapted from Rampton 1995: 115–16)

Rampton explains how the boys' switching into other varieties of language here functioned as a rejection of what was being asked of them at a local level. What's more, in their mimic of stereotypical Indian deference, they significantly brought into play broader, colonial white discourses of racism that prevailed in the past. Their use of Creole a bit later underscored this:

> By switching to Asian English in a sequence where they were bowing to my calls to order, the boys conjured a stereotype of Asian 'babu' deference which is historically ensconced in white British racism and which can be depended on to embarrass a white liberal conscience. The effect here was to index race stratification as a potentially relevant issue in our encounter, and this strategic racialisation was carried further in the switch to Creole, a code associated with the rejection of illegitimate white power. (Rampton 1999: 365)

'Nicing up': white appropriation of black codes

> In no small measure, black culture simply *is* youth culture in London today. Bizarre as it first seems, speaking with a Jamaican inflection has become hip among working-class white kids. (Gates, jr, 2000: 174)

In the last decade or so, studies of identity in late modernity have turned their attention to the emergence of 'new ethnicities'. Recent attention to ethnic mixing and cultural blending has demanded a reconceptualisation of 'full subjectivity' to take into account the fact that people's identities are unfixed, fluid and open to change. What's needed, argues McRobbie, is a definition that more closely reflects these as 'fragile, "shaggy" [and] hybridic', capable of 'endless diversity and intensive cultural crossover' (1994: 192). This is especially so when accounting for how youth construct their many different selves since 'it is young people who seem to be at the forefront of exploring and inventing these categories'. She goes on to point out that 'the whole question of identity which is posed by the new ethnicities work has a special resonance for youth' (ibid: 182). Rampton, too, notes how:

> [E]xclusive and hierarchic discourses of nation now no longer seem to be taken for granted among youth; ethnicity has been denaturalised/destabilished; and consumption and cultural bricolage have become primary means for identity construction. (Rampton 1999: 357)

As evidenced in the transcript discussed earlier, one way in which this manifests itself is through 'crossing' which is 'the use of language varieties associated with social or ethnic groups that the speaker does not normally "belong" to' (Rampton 1995: 14). In exploring how young people work, locally, to redefine dominant orders and boundaries, the connections between 'race', 'ethnicity', language and power are opened up to scrutiny.

Reading 4.4 (also by Back) addresses these links as it describes young white speakers' appropriation of black talk in multiracial friendship groups in London. In the accounts given to Back, adolescents initially denied the salience of 'race' in their everyday lives ('Colour don't come into it!', 'I don't believe in racial things'). For some, the rejection of 'race' (and, by extension, 'Englishness') meant a rejection of 'racism'. The author argues that the refusal to accept 'race' as significant enabled white adolescents to draw on a cross-section of black forms of talk ranging from Jamaican Creole and African American Vernacular English to black London speech. Termed by one young woman as 'nicing up' her language, the extent of appropriation could vary from using just a few words to the extensive adoption of phonological and grammatical features. Switching between the different black codes was not uncommon. For instance, one white fifteen year old, Mark, used both African American 'inversions' ('baddest' to mean 'best') and Creole ('pure murderation them jus nice-up deh dance and dem bass jus lick off your head') in the same utterance.

However, white adoption of black linguistic forms among young people in multiracial settings is subject to approval from their black and white peers. In an earlier London study, Hewitt found that, although it was sometimes accepted as a gesture of solidarity within close friendship groups, outside this context young black speakers were often antagonistic to white use of Creole which they interpreted as linguistic theft and an 'assertion of white superiority' (1986: 162). He quotes one black fifteen year old who commented, 'It seems they are stealing our language' (ibid.: 161). Generally, states Hewitt, when young whites attempted to identify with black codes, they 'failed to perceive the social and political aspects of the culture or failed to be sensitive to the issue of group boundaries' (ibid.: 48). As one white male adolescent reported:

> I had a real argument with a girl at college, Carol, a white girl. She was talking to Glenford [a black boy] the other day. They were talkin' and she was saying 'did you go this blues. Did you go to that blues' and they were talking about trouble. Then she says this one thing. She went 'our people are getting a lot of trouble down that way', I went, 'what did you say?' she went all red. She said 'they get a lot of trouble down there'. 'But you said our people didn't you?' She goes all red. I said, 'Carol, what are you? You're white for God's sake!' (Ibid.: 49)

In also describing the limits placed on white appropriation of black culture, the reading describes an incident involving a seventeen-year-old white speaker, Tony, and his two Afro-Caribbean friends, both of whom usually sanctioned his identification with black language, music and styles. In this episode, Tony's use of Creole is accepted, but his comment about wishing to be black is negatively received. For Tony's friends, this overstepped acceptable boundaries of cultural alignment. Back argues, however, that their disapproval obliges Tony to confront wider discourses of prejudice. In doing so, he is led to question what it means to be 'white'. As Back explains in Reading 4.4:

> Through these engagements with blackness, young whites are forced to interrogate the meanings of their whiteness. They move from a youthful assertion of 'it doesn't matter what colour you are' to a more profound and lived knowledge of how racism structures their lives and relationships.

But to what extent can we assume that young white people's engagements with black language and culture inevitably lead them to problematise issues of 'race', 'ethnicity' and power, or to go as far as deconstructing the naturalised relationship between 'whiteness' and nationalism? In particular local contexts, this might happen, but not all 'language crossings' necessarily result in a more sensitive appreciation of the discourses of discrimination. As Gates, jr, warns, 'it would be a mistake . . . to come to any hasty conclusions. Imitation and enmity have an uncanny ability to coexist' (2000: 174).

In her work on white teenagers involved in the US hip-hop scene, Cutler provides evidence of how appropriation of African American Vernacular English rests on an 'essentialized version of urban black male youth culture' (1999: 439). She focuses on Mike, an upper middle-class speaker from a wealthy district of New York, who she observed over a period of six years. At around age thirteen, he became increasingly interested in hip-hop culture and began 'crossing' into AAVE. Mike's knowledge of black vernacular came from a variety of sources. Not only did he come into contact with this way of speaking from hanging out around the streets, subways and night clubs, but also he picked up AAVE by way of his involvement in hip-hop culture. For white urban youth, rap music videos and the lyrics sheets in CD cases provided quick and easy access to hip-hop terms and expressions. The internet too afforded opportunities to widen vocabulary by way of instant access to on-line rap dictionaries and chat lines. Moreover, as Cutler notes, films depicting black inner-city life (for example, *Do the Right Thing*, *Boyz'n the Hood*) – many of which Mike claimed to have seen – 'played a role in the transmission of AAVE to whites' (Ibid.: 434). Yet in doing so, they offered a somewhat glamourised, stereotypical picture of African American culture which white teenagers drew upon to construct their own identities.

Although Mike's competence in AAVE grammar was limited, his use of phonological variables showed him to be closer in language style to AAVE speakers than to his own socio-economic group. For instance, instead of standard American English pronunciation of 'the' /ði/ in front of words beginning with a vowel, he frequently used the variant /də/ typical of African American Vernacular English. The vowel lengthening, stress and rhythm of AAVE also became a feature of his speech, and he peppered his talk with lexical expressions from mid-1990s hip-hop culture such as 'chill' (calm down), 'mad' (very), 'phat' (good, great) and tags such as 'know what I'm sayin' and 'yo'.

Around age sixteen, Mike began distancing himself from the black community, although still maintaining a significant involvement in hip-hop culture. He continued to draw on AAVE as part of his linguistic style, yet what it signalled for him and his white friends had now changed. Cutler accounts for this redefinition of African American Vernacular English:

> Hip-hop is increasingly claimed to be a multi-cultural lifestyle rather than a symbol of ethnic group identity, particularly by white adolescents but also by others. As such, it seems to allow whites access to a commodified, ephemeral black experience at various moments or phases of their lives without requiring overt claims of black ethnicity, and the sociolinguistic meaning of AAVE appears to be adjusted in the process. (Cutler 1999: 435)

The reframing of AAVE itself raises important issues to do with language and power. Yet, like the young white people in Hewitt's study, Mike and his peers remained largely insensitive to these. On the contrary, as Cutler notes, 'he and his friends seemed at times to demand the erasure of differences in race and class history and position' (Ibid.: 436). She describes one interview where, alongside their own 'unperformed' phonological and lexical crossings into AAVE, they unreflexively caricatured its use by black speakers:

Mike: ... they [black men] go up there and they have a 'Black as Hell' white shirt, white sweat shirt and they're up there, 'yo, man, you know I was walkin' down the street the other day and I was wit my girl Juanita ... you know! An' wit Juanita, you know, I was jus' chillin' you know, my BLACK girl, my BLACK princess, my BLACK' ... and I emphasize twenty more times that she's black ((laughter)) to make sure everybody knows that she's black ((laughter)) because I don't want anyone to think I had to do with white! (adapted from Cutler 1999: 436)

Crossing: playful transgression or power discourse?

What, then, are we to make of young white speakers' appropriation of black varieties of talk? At first glance, it might appear that it signals a new cultural rapport, even 'the creation of a new multi-ethnic youth culture' (Cutler 1999: 439). Without a doubt, some kinds of linguistic 'crossing' appear to be regarded positively by many young people. Rampton's (1999: 366) study evidences how 'Creole stood for an excitement and excellence in vernacular youth culture which many youngsters aspired to, and it was even described as a 'future language' ... Its use lent power to the speaker'. But do these local, often playful transgressions (Hill 1999) signal less racism for society generally? Are we to believe that racial prejudice and discrimination are 'on the wane' because some young speakers find it 'cool' to 'cross' into Creole? Time will tell, although for now critical examination of 'crossing' in the sorts of micro context we've seen here can reveal much of its complex multifunctionality. As Rampton additionally notes, switches to another variety, that of Stylised Asian English were not necessarily as positively valenced:

> On some occasions, stylised Asian English seemed probing or subversive, particularly when directed at white adults (who in turn could take it as threatening, embarrassing or simply inconsequential). But, on others, it constituted a crude form of racism itself, particularly when directed towards Bangladeshi peers. (Rampton 1999: 367–8)

Other critiques of 'crossing' are circumspect too. According to Hill, African-American 'crossovers' inevitably constitute a 'covert racist discourse' (1999: 553–4) that reinforces stereotypes. She argues that even if individual utterances are solidary and well meaning, 'the larger impact of such usages is to continually, covertly, reproduce the racialization of ... Black populations'. In conclusion, she echoes some of Hewitt's (1986) young black speakers who regarded white 'crossing' as an abuse of their linguistic resource, linking this to wider process of social and material discrimination:

> At the very least, crossings and stylings can be seen as attempts to delimit and control what the resource shall mean. These implicatures, of denigration and control, may be the inevitable pragmatic effect of speaking in a world that contains such gross differentials of power, a world where the populations who are being 'styled' are only a few years out from a history of slavery or genocide, and are even today isolated in poverty by a thousand kinds of fully material discrimination. In such a world it is very hard for a member of a dominant group to simultaneously 'use' and yet signal 'this is not mine, it is truly yours, and I honor you by adopting it'. (Hill 1999: 553–4)

'NERDY HYPERWHITENESS': SUPERSTANDARD ENGLISH AND RACIAL MARKING

Evidently, in their deracialisation of black talk, increasing numbers of white youth involved in rap and hip-hop culture view linguistic appropriation of AAVE as unproblematic. Reading 4.5 however, presents a rather different perspective in its account of other white young people rejecting outright the use of African American Vernacular English, and its associations with 'coolness'. Known as 'nerds', these constituted a group who resisted the fashions and practices of more wide-spread popular youth cultures, preferring instead to embrace high standards of academic attainment. The desire to dissociate themselves from those who crossed racial boundaries in an effort to be 'trendy' led to them being seen as 'hyperwhite'. Linguistically, they used 'superstandard English' to construct what they perceived to be 'an intelligent and nonconformist identity'.

'Superstandard English' is described as contrasting with standard English in a number of ways. For instance, nerds tended to avoid slang terms. For 'trendy' speakers, particular expressions underwent a process of 'iconisation' – where the characteristics of a variety are seen as a reflection of the 'essential' characteristics of its speakers. So, as slang was 'cool', so too were its users – and nerds were concerned to distance themselves from such an attribute. Instead, the grammar and lexis usually associated with intellectual ability and used in areas of science and in academic textbooks were recurrent features of their language style. For instance, the author comments on one student's use of the Latinate intensifier ('extremely'), nominalisation ('my observation') and formal expression ('all the outward signs') as indicative of the scholarly, detached tone typically employed by white nerds. They also resisted the usual pronunciation processes associated with colloquial speech. For example, rather than employ the common practice of phonological reduction of unstressed vowels (as in 'gonna'), nerds would carefully articulate each sound ('going to'). Sometimes their spoken language style appeared to rely on how words were written. Their pronunciations closely followed the orthographic form of words, almost, it seemed, to further underscore their literacy and academic knowledge.

In exploring how nerds discursively built their social identity to be distinct from other white young people, the reading deconstructs assumptions regarding the monolithic nature of 'whiteness' itself. Ultimately, the question Bucholtz asks is what does it mean to 'be white' in the contemporary world? Moreover, in the everyday life of youth culture, how does 'whiteness' relate to broader issues of power and prejudice? We've seen earlier how young white speakers' appropriation of an African American language style can run alongside and even articulate their discourses of racism. In this final reading Bucholtz points out that those who drew heavily on AAVE to be 'cool' did not participate in organised anti-racist protests. Conversely, nerds – whose cultural identity was 'hyperwhite' and who refused to use African American Vernacular English – appeared more willing to challenge discriminatory practices. Indeed, in their rendering visible the racial category of 'whiteness', these young people under-mined the privileged position of 'white' as 'natural'.

Yet simultaneously, nerds' construction of themselves rearticulated racial division and hierarchy. In opposing their 'cool' white peers, they marked their 'white' difference and distance from black culture and language. In choosing to voice their identities through Superstandard English, they reinforced the view that Standard American English was the norm against which other forms of language should be measured. Moreover, their use of this reiterated ideologies that equate Standard English varieties with 'intelligence'. Even their perfor-mance of 'nerdiness' rested upon an easy access to white cultural forms that were relatively unavailable to black students. Located within broader structures of discrimination, the linguistic practices of nerds were powerful constructions of their privileged position. In its analysis of racial marking through language, the final reading of this chapter documents clearly the complex contradictions in the discursive production of youth identity.

ACTIVITIES

- Do you or anyone you know 'cross' linguistically? Does 'crossing' take place regularly in your community? If so, in what ways and for what purposes?
- In the past, how have you discursively constructed your own 'youthful subjectivities'? In what ways has the language you have used contributed to your membership of particular youth cultures?

READINGS

Reading 4.1

[...]

As in the past, today's negative pronouncements on Ebonics reveal a serious lack of knowledge about the scientific approach to language analysis and a galling ignorance about what Ebonics is (more than slang) and who speaks it (at some point in their lives, 30% to 90% of African Americans; see Dillard, 1972).

[...]

Koch and Gross (1997) set out to examine attitudes toward Black and Standard English speakers, focusing their study on Black youths' perceptions of such

From: G. Smitherman and S. Cunningham (1997) 'Moving beyond resistance: ebonics and African-American youth', *Journal of Black Psychology*, 23: 3, 227–32.

speakers. Using the classic sociolinguistic matched-guise technique (i.e., subjects unknowingly rate the same speaker who uses two different languages), they measured the youths' reactions to the likeability and competence of the speaker when speaking Black versus Standard English. The researchers concluded that unlike previous studies, where African American adults were negative toward Black English, Black youths perceived Black English as more positive than Standard English in fact, when the speaker was using Black English, he was rated as more likable and honest.

In our research as language arts educators, we witnessed the first sign of this generational struggle in Smitherman's 1989 study, conducted in five cities, of changing racial semantics and the shift in use of Black to African American (Smitherman, 1993; see also Baugh, 1991). In that study, it was Black youths, more so than older Blacks, who preferred the new racial designation; similar results were found in a poll of Black youths attending historically Black colleges ('Black College Students,' 1989).

Linguist Arthur Spears (1996) notes similar generational differences toward the frequent and widespread perception and public use of what he labelled 'uncensored mode' language, that is, words and idioms once considered offensive, including the oft-used n—. In spite of older and middle-class Blacks' disdain for and compaigns against the public widespread use of n—,sociolinguistic research analysis demonstrates that the term actually has at least six different meanings, only one of them derogatory (Smitherman, 1994; see also Major, 1994; Spears, 1996).

The current Ebonics controversy showcased for the entire nation the severe crises affecting Black youths, particularly in the schools. At a historical moment when vision and the wisdom of experience are needed to address these crises, older, middle-class, and established Blacks – including some of those who are perceived as leaders such as the Reverend Jesse Jackson—came up short. Jackson, the Reverend Al Sharpton, and Maya Angelou condemned the Oakland school board decision, arguing that this would 'build barriers between the races' and 'insult the Black community' (see Boyd, 1996). On the national television program, *Meet the Press*, Jackson went so far as to call the use of Ebonics as a teaching tool 'unacceptable surrender borderlining on disgrace.' On the other hand, younger Blacks – writers, intellectuals, students, rap artists, and so on – embrace Ebonics. Bill Stephney, of Stepsun Records, captured the thinking of his peers eloquently:

> Most of the people who have been opponents of Ebonics are the same ones who have been dismissive of Hip-Hop. There is a segment of the older Black generation, the middle class, civil rights leadership, that is anti-youth. Most of them have no idea if Ebonics works as a method of reaching Black students. But because they are so busy being reactive to anything that mainstream White politicians are against, once again they are not speaking out. And they haven't scratched the surface in

understanding how the Hip-Hop Generation views the issue. (quoted in Kelly, 1997, p. 26)

The communicative practices of African American youth are not some bizarre, unknown linguistic creation. Rather, theirs is a language rooted in the Black linguistic cultural tradition, which has simply now come out of the closet of the 'hood.' Indeed, this language and its accompanying cultural practices now has crossed over into the public culture to such an extent that [...] this phenomenon has been termed the 'Afro Americanization of youth.' The Black 'Talented Tenth,' above all, needs knowledge and understanding of Ebonics and its communicative practices, for they have the power, authority, resources, the necessary critical mass formation—and the responsibility—for addressing the crisis of Black youth. To do so, however, they need credibility with Black youth.

The challenge to Black adults in the middle and upper classes is heightened by the cultural and geographical separation between lower- and higher-income African Americans, due to the creation of Black suburbs and other economically segregated residential enclaves and the occupational shifts that thrust Blacks into higher paying and higher status jobs resulting from the Black Movement of the 1960s and 1970s. In line with this analysis, Spears (1996) provides a lucidly constructive, if brutally frank, analysis of the sociolinguistic cultural clash between the Talented Tenth and Black youth:

> The problem is that critics and social commentators ... *typically* lack the communicative competence necessary ... With Blacks, this is because they may indeed be competent in some Black groups ... and take for granted that they are competent in all Black cultural spheres.
>
> In some ways, such Blacks are victims of not realizing how fast cultural change has occurred in Black America since the 1960s, whose events and movements unleashed the significant cultural divergence within the African American world that we see today. Under segregation, upper-status Blacks did have a clearer picture of the range of behaviors throughout the social continuum. Those who have reached the age and position to see their writing published in major outlets of hegemonic discourse such as the largest-circulation newsweeklies and *The New York Times* are too old and too removed by class and cultural change to retain any authority they may once have had. (p. 12)

It is obvious that the current controversy over Ebonics is a symbolic issue that goes beyond some narrow conception of teaching correct English. The question is how Black leadership and the Black Talented Tenth can seize this historical moment to begin the complex and difficult task of addressing the educational and social crises of Black youths—crises that threaten to tear the Black community apart.

As language art educators, we offer the following solutions toward answering this question. First, we need to recognize that language is the foundation of individual and group identity construction. Second, in teaching that fundamental principle to Black youths, we also need to teach acceptance of our language as it relates to who we are and where we come from. Third, not only should we critically study the history of Black English, we should also teach a critical examination of the history of Standard English. A close examination of the two languages, their history, their sociopolitical constructions, and their sociolinguistic uses, would serve as a basis for looking at what is standard and exactly who chose to make it the representative of *all* people.

Once students begin to interrogate the social and cultural history behind their words, the next step is to move them beyond negative associations into more positive perceptions of both Black and Standard English. Consciously relating to one's own cultural heritage and refusing to learn the ways of another culture is what Herb Kohl (1994) calls 'not-learning.'

> Learning how to not-learn is an intellectual and social challenge; sometimes you have to work very hard at it. It consists of an active, often ingenious, wilful rejection of even the most compassionate and well-designed teaching. It subverts attempts at remediation as much as it rejects learning in the first place. It was through insight into my own not-learning that I began to understand the inner world of students who chose to not-learn what I wanted to teach. Over the years I've come to side with them in their refusal to be molded by a hostile society and have come to look upon not-learning as positive and healthy in many situations (p. 2).

Many of our students resort to not-learning as a means of resistance; a way to hold on to the one part of themselves that they feel cannot be taken away. Although we should encourage this stance, at the same time, we need to help them move beyond the resistance that keeps them stifled and saddled in the same place. To help in accomplishing this task, we look to the work of Cross and other researchers on Black identity formation. Gay (quoted in Frisby and Tucker, 1993), for example, describes the final stage of ethnic development as follows:

> For Afro Americans, that shift is from concern about how others see them to confidence in their own personal standards of Blackness; from uncontrolled rage against individuals of other ethnic groups to conscious, directed anger against oppressive, racist institutional and group actions; from symbolic pontification rhetoric to quiet introspection and commitment; from anxious feelings of inferiority to pride, self-love, and a deep sense of Black communalism. Once their transformed ethnic identity is internalized, individuals have the psychological disposition and ethnic receptivity to be biethnic, multiethnic, and/or globalistic in their relations if they so choose (p. 148).

In sum then, we are advocating that educators provide Black youths with the history of Black and Standard English and encourage them to critically examine these two linguistic forms and the social and political situations that created them. Merging this knowledge with the pride and confidence that comes from a healthy sense of self and peoplehood, Black youths can move forward knowing the differences between languages and the value of language and culture, never having to surrender one language (Black English) for another (Standard English).

REFERENCES

Baugh, J. (1991). 'The politicization of changing terms of self-references among African American slave descendent'. *American Speech*, 66, 133–46.

'Black college students—Black or African American?' (1989, June 17). *Michigan Chronicle*, p. 3A.

Boyd, H. (1996, December 27–29). 'Karenga on Jackson criticism: "Jesse is versed in Ebonics."' *Daily Challenge*, 25, 2.

Dillard, J. L. (1972). *Black English*. New York: Random House.

Frisby, C. L. and Tucker, C. M. (1993). 'Black children's perceptions of self: Implications for education'. *Educational Forum*, 57, 146–55.

Kelly, D. (1997, April). 'Native tongues'. *The Source*, pp. 26–7.

Koch, L. M. and Gross, A. (1997). 'Children's perceptions of Black English as a variable in intraracial perception'. *Journal of Black Psychology*, 23, 215–26.

Kohl, H. (1994) *'I won't learn from you:' And other thoughts on creative maladjustment*. New York: New Press.

Major, C. (1994). *From juba to live*. New York: Penguin.

Smitherman, G. (1986). *Talkin and testifyin: The language of Black America*. Detroit, MI: Wayne State University Press. (Originally published in 1977)

Smitherman, G. (1993). '"What is Africa to me?": Language, ideology, and African American'. *Word*, 2, 1–28.

Smitherman, G. (1994). *Black talk: Words and phrases from the hood to the amen corner*. Boston: Houghton Mifflin.

Spears, A. (1996). 'African American language use: Ideology and uncensored mode'. Unpublished manuscript. (Forthcoming in S. Mufwene, J. Rickford, J. Baugh, & G. Baily [Eds.], *The structure of African American English*. Boston, Routledge)

Wilkins, R. (1971, April/May). 'Black nonsense'. *Crisis*, p. 78.

Reading 4.2

Black ... [Americans] gradually developed their own ways of conveying resistance using The Man's language against him as a defense against sub-human categorization. ... The function of white verbal behavior toward Blacks was to define, force acceptance of, and control the existing level of restraints. Blacks clearly recognized that *to master the language of whites was in effect to consent to be mastered by it through the white definitions*

From: Signithia Fordham (1998), '"Speaking Standard English from nine to three: language as guerrilla warfare at Capital High', in Susan Hoyle and Carolyn Temple Adger (eds), *KidsTalk: Strategic Language Use in Later Childhood*, Oxford: Oxford University Press, pp. 205–16.

of caste built into the semantic/social system. (Holt 1972: 153–4, emphasis added)

Students at Capital High, most of them Black, rent the discourse of power—'standard English'—from nine to three, five days a week. As I use the term here, standard English is more than a structured variety of the language, more than its phonology, syntax, and lexicon. It includes Gee's (1990: xix) notion of Discourses (with a capital D) as

> ways of behaving, interacting, valuing, thinking, believing, speaking, and often reading and writing that are accepted as instantiations of particular roles by specific *groups of people*, whether families of a certain sort, lawyers of a certain sort, business people of a certain sort, churches of a certain sort, and so on through a long list. [Discourses] are always and everywhere *social*. Language, as well as literacy, is always and everywhere integrated with and relative to *social practices* constituting particular Discourses. (emphasis in original)

In this expanded sense, standard English incorporates attitudes and styles of speaking and behaving. Of specific interest here, it includes attitudes of hostility and opposition to African American Vernacular English (AAVE) and styles associated with it. Thus, it comes as no surprise that standard English, understood in this broad sense, might be resisted by African Americans, for its 'definitions of caste,' which stigmatize Black speech, extend easily to Black people as well.

At Capital High, students sense antipathy to Black discourse traditions emanating from the demands of the formal curriculum and from teachers and staff who constantly admonish them to temper their voices, speak in modulated tones, act like 'ladies and gentlemen,' and generally appropriate not only standard English grammar but also the entire power discourse of the White community. Most Capital students—valuing forms of interaction that emphasize visibility, possession of voice, and a semantic code outside the mainstream culture—reject these adult admonishments, and those who do not are accused by their peers of 'acting white.' Students at Capital High do use standard English—some more than others—but to most of them it is a socially stigmatized dialect (just as in the wider society AAVE is stigmatized).

I propose a metaphor for the linguistic practices of Capital High students that reflects both their reluctance to be 'mastered by . . . the white definitions of caste built into the semantic/social system' (Holt 1972: 154) and the strategies they use to appropriate the power discourse that I refer to as standard English. That metaphor is *renting*. Students rent standard English, return it, and rent it again during the next class session. They do not seek to own it. By using it only between nine and three, they display their awareness that it is deemed crucial to academic success, but at the same time they demonstrate their commitment to the Black community, its cultural traditions and practices, and Black 'Self production' (Friedman 1992). For some students, renting the discourse of power is a successful, albeit tension-producing, strategy: they manage to retain affective ownership of (a less powerful) Black discourse even while temporarily using the dominant school discourse. Sadly, though, for others, refusal to rent discourse practices that they view as foreign and hostile to their own identity is influential in marking them as academic failures.

[...]

Discourse style and rhetorical resistance

Renting the discourse of power at school is not a simple, dichotomous, full-scale switching between one dialect and another, because standard English and AAVE are distinguished not only by relatively minor grammatical differences but by an overarching rhetorical and stylistic divergence as well. Capital students who choose to pursue academic excellence have to maintain a fine balance between the discourse traditions promulgated by the school and those growing out of their own sociocultural history, which embody the reluctance of African American people to become, symbolically, the Other.

Holt (1972: 154) asserts that once African Americans were freed from official enslavement, 'language [became] the major vehicle for perpetuating the legitimation of the subsequent stages of oppression.' Those who were unwilling or unable to accept and embrace the discourse practices of the larger society were tracked for failure, academic and otherwise. But, in Lorde's (1990: 287) words, 'the master's [language] will never dismantle the master's house' (cf. Gates 1994); the dominant discourse is ineffective in fighting oppressive social conditions because language propels us to interpret the world through a specific culture and its texts. African Americans resorted to a number of strategies to avoid becoming mited in the larger society's oppressive social structure, including 'inversion,' whereby '[w]ords and phrases were given reverse meanings and functions changed . . . enabling blacks to deceive and manipulate whites without penalty . . . The purpose of the game was *to appear to but not to*' (Holt 1972: 154, emphasis added). Engaging in inversion is just what Capital students do when they rent the standard discourse—when they adopt temporarily, but refuse to claim as their own, the discourse sanctioned by the academy. 'Appearing to but not to' be standard English speakers is one way adolescents can negotiate contradictory values centering around academic success and failure.

Inversion, often used for 'rhetorical resistance', draws on common African American rhetorical practices that 'use speech and performance' (Dyson 1995: 16). (Such fusion is evident in Martin Luther King, Jr.'s 'I Have a Dream' speech: he did not simply say the words; he performed them.) In this regard, Andrews (n.d.: 24–5) chronicles the power of 'improvisational expression' that embellishes the basic action with decorative flourish. In the predominantly Black high school that he attended in Oakland, California, both talk and athletic events were judged as performance. On the playing field, merely winning was insufficient. How one played (analogous to how one spoke) was even more important. Getting a touchdown, for example, was the easy part; how the player scored was more remarkable—it should be done with the appropriate 'attitude' or expressiveness. Here Andrews speaks of running track:

> Valrey started out about two lengths behind. He paced himself, was cool, and didn't panic. His head was level and he looked confident. As he neared the finish line he was breathing down the neck of the [other] trackstar. Valrey passed the grandstand and quickly rocketed ahead of the [other trackstar] toward victory. But this wasn't enough. This wasn't a *signature*. This was merely winning, and sports in East Oakland was not about winning or losing, but how you played the game. Valrey ... knew what [both schools'] fans wanted: they wanted him to cross the 't' and dot the 'i's' of individuality. So in the spirit of customer satisfaction ... be flipped his body around and trotted backwards toward the finish line ... gazed at the [other trackstar] long enough to tip his shades up to his forehead to politely show his eyes, and then waved goodbye to his opponent...—task accomplished—and dashed to the winning 440 finish, arms raised in forever recaptured East Oakland glory (emphasis added).

Sports, then, as well as other forms of entertainment, provide very vivid examples of individuals merging accomplishment and performance to resist some expectations of the dominant culture. Young Black males do not believe they have to become an Other to succeed at sports. Many boys at Capital, viewing the sports world as one in which Black performance style is valued, dreamed of succeeding there, and such dreams—which are only remote possibilities—far outweighed their effort to succeed academically. Many such young men refused to rent standard English in the classroom, and many of them were failing academically.

Acting white

Outside of sports and entertainment and especially at school, it is a continual challenge, Capital students believe, to avoid 'acting white'. Black people who act white are thought to be (perhaps inadvertently) delegitimizing, evading, or repressing the knowledge attendant to an African American cultural system. They are seen as dissolving and reconstructing their identities in order to be perceived as powerful individuals. The danger in acting white is captured in Gramsci's (1971) notion of hegemony, the tendency of all members of a system to unwittingly uphold its implicit power relations by engaging in those practices sanctioned by the powerful. As Paul, a high-achieving student, commented, 'Black judge other Blacks according to White standards' (interview, February 17, 1983). But Black people who choose discourses that mimic those of Whites *while in predominantly Black contexts* may well be marginalized by their community, not just as power seekers but as people who might use power just as the larger society has historically done, to exploit and dehumanize African Americans.

The adolescents at Capital have a long list of ways in which it is possible to act white, including playing golf, going to the country club, going to the Smithsonian, hiking, dancing to lyrics rather than music, and speaking standard English. An important issue, though, is appropriateness. For example, if one chooses to respond to a teacher in the discourse of the academy, one is applauded and respected for being able to display that facility. What many Capital community residents find problematic is the uncritical adoption of the discourse of power when interacting with (or when inappropriate in the presence of) other Black people.

At Capital, acting white extends to the pursuit of academic excellence: many students are enormously conflicted by the prevalent assumption that to get good grades is to act white. On the one hand, acting white may be perceived as unavoidable in order to achieve success as defined by the larger society, both in school and later in the workforce. On the other hand, embracing the cultural principles promulgated by the larger society (including its definition of success) is believed to constitute uncritical acceptance of the dominant aesthetic and moral system that oppresses the Black Self. Wendell, one of the high-achieving students, asserted unequivocally that the most important step for school success is to rid oneself of Blackness: 'Don't be looked upon as Black [i.e., not being seen as Black] seem like it change a lot of things sometimes' (interview, May 20, 1983). He explained: '[White folks] look down on Blacks ... They think we ignorant or something. Something like that. They think we ignorant ... animals or ... I don't think nobody really ignorant—unless their mind gone or something' (interview, March 2, 1983). High-achieving students accused of acting white may be labeled 'brainiacs.' Alice defined the term: ' "Brainiac" means like, a computer mind—know all the answers. Call me "computer," "computer-head" and "brainiac." I think it's a ... you know, I don't—I used to say, "No, I'm not," and now I say, "Sure, I am. Don't you want to be one" ' (interviews, March 14, May 23, 1983).

On the list of discourse practices that must be shed if one is to be successful in White society are most forms of improvisational expressiveness. As Kochman (1972) suggests, the 'kinetic element' in Black speech—discourse practices that embrace movement and energy—stigmatizes speakers in the larger society as being devoid of rationality, dispassion, and other logocentric values. Another characteristic that conveys Blackness, and that students like Wendell believe must therefore be jettisoned, is what Williams (1988: 47) calls *texture*: 'dense, vivid, woven, detailed narratives, relationships, and experiences' with a primary focus on the local and the familiar. Here, too, there is disjuncture between what is valued in the community and what is honored in academic talk. Depersonalization, attention to the universal, argumentation that is sparse and sequential—these attributes typically valued in school speech are at odds with the richly textured discourse of the African American community.

Language in power relationships

The accusation of acting white is not the only problem faced by students who seek academic success; another aspect of the web of contestation in which they are tangled comes from experiencing differences in the construction of hierarchical relationships at home and at school. This discontinuity adds to the ways in which the school, as an institution essentially part of the dominant society, tends to define these young people as Other. The discourse practices that are valued by the adolescents, their families, and their community derive from an understanding that, in order to wrest power, a speaker must voice authority. The language of home is direct and powerful, glazed with an icing of bantering, repartée, and deliciously decorated one-liners. Most segments of the African American community assume that power must be conveyed and deference earned through an authoritative use of language; as Delpit (1988, 1995) notes, merely occupying a position of authority (e.g., that of a teacher) does not in and of itself grant power. This assumption is at odds with that of the dominant culture, which practices and values the veiling of power (Delpit 1988, 1995). Many students at Capital complained bitterly that the White (and some of the Black) teachers had no authority in the classroom. Alice, a high-achieving student, said that White teachers were unable to get students' attention. In fact, they did not demand it in ways familiar to the students.

[...]

Renting a dialect: managing standard English

School presents students caught between colliding cultural systems with inescapable contradictions. Academic success demands that they adopt the very discourse practices that they perceive as ineffectual and oppressive. In their passage into adult status, though, they realize the political reality in which they participate. Some students refuse to display a critical symbol of the pursuit of power in the school context—speaking standard English—and therefore experience the implications of marginal to low academic performance. Many others settle for renting standard English from nine to three while retaining ownership of the discourse practices generally used in the African American community. They do not do so easily, but those who manage it participate in a type of inversion that resonates with the discourse practices of their ancestors, who had various ways of 'appearing to but not to.' It is both a resistance that preserves the essential Black Self and a means of social mobility. Here I present two typical approaches to the contradictions imposed on Capital students.

Maggie, a high achiever, was well aware of the dialect contrasts in her speech community. In discussing her mother's speech practices, Maggie suggests that she herself rejects bidialectalism, refusing to be seen as both 'Us' and 'Them,' primarily because, as she sees it, such 'passing' behaviors are disingenuous at best. She asserts that her mother 'talks white' on the phone or in contexts outside their home:

> She just talks like that on the telephone, I'll put it like that. When she talks, she puts on airs, you know, sounds White, so you can't tell whether she's White or Black. But when she's around the house, she talks, you know, regular, but when she's out around other people, anywhere out besides the house, she talks in a proper manner. ... When my mother [speaks standard English], it appears that she's trying to be someone she's not. (interview, February 25, 1983)

Maggie views her mother's speech practices as fraudulent—'She's trying to be someone she's not'—and deceptive—'You can't tell whether she's White or Black.' Rather than viewing her mother's linguistic practices as evidence of appropriate code-switching within a bidialectal society, she sees them as acting white and therefore inappropriate. In contrast, Maggie declares that she rarely participates in such linguistic fraud. Indeed, she insists that 'I talk the same way all the time' (interview, February 25, 1983), in all contexts. More important, she categorizes her consistent linguistic behavior as a more appropriate, more correct—or more standard—way to structure a Black identity. To a large extent, Maggie's characterization of her own linguistic practices was accurate. In some instances, however, she was forced to rent the school-sanctioned standard English dialect in interactions with teachers and other school officials, and she could be heard switching just as her mother did.

Norris, a brilliant student, had learned to camouflage his academic achievement by renting standard English from nine to three so that his peers did not feel threatened by him. He used Black 'street speech' (Baugh 1983) as a standard and standard English as a vernacular, and neither his cohorts who were underachieving nor those who were performing as well as he obstructed his academic efforts. He was therefore able to pursue his goals virtually unmolested by his peers.

At Berkeley Elementary, which was, in Norris's terms, filled with 'hoodlums, thugs, and the dregs of society,' he had been academically ahead of most of the students in his class and in the school. At the same time, however, realizing that he had to live with those students, he planned a course of action that would minimize any obstacles to his academic future. Norris deliberately chose for friends those individuals whose resistance to standard English discourse practices was greater than his. These peers, he reasoned, would act as camouflage, in exchange for his help on homework assignments and tests. He was not picky about who they were. He simply wanted them to keep the other kids from beating him up or verbally harassing him so that he would be free to pursue his dream of academic excellence:

> I didn't want to—you know—be with anybody that was like me [academically] 'cause I didn't want to get beat up. The school I went to, Berkeley, was really rough, see? It was really rough. So I had to hang with people that were tough, you know? Lived in the projects and everything, and known tough and everything. So I used to hang with them. If anybody ever

came in my face and wanted to pick on me, they'd always be there to help me. So I always made sure I had at least two or three bullies to be my friends. Even though if it does mean I have to give up answers in class . . . . I was willing to give up a little to get a lot. So I did that for elementary school. (interview, January 11, 1983)

Norris's alliance with the bullies and hoodlums in elementary school was a successful strategy. His close association with peers whose behavior clearly indicated they were not committed to the school-sanctioned discourse empowered him by removing any question about his loyalty to the Black community.

In junior high school he chose to embellish this strategy. Besides making alliances with bullies, he adopted a clown or comedic person (one component of which was the use of Black street speech), which suggested that he was not very skilled academically. Wearing this mask protected him from the scorn of those who held academic prowess in contempt. The merging of these strategies was still a part of his school persona:

I had to act crazy then . . . you know, nutty, kind of loony. They say . . . 'He's crazy'—not a *class* clown to get on the teachers' nerves, I never did that to the . . . around *them*. I'd be crazy. But as soon as I hit the classroom door, it was serious business . . . Only the people who knew me knew my crazy side; when they found out I was smart, they wouldn't believe it. And the people that knew that I was smart, they wouldn't believe it if they were told that I was crazy. So I went through [school] like that. I'm still like that *now*; though. (interview, January 11, 1983)

In acting a role, Norris became a discourse chameleon merging with the surrounding context. Among friends, he behaved as if school meant nothing to him; among classmates who were not close friends but who were seeking the same academic goals as he, he conveyed an image of a standard English speaker and an academic competitor. He moved from one discourse style to another in order to alternately mask and display his academic abilities. He realized that he must 'fake it in order to make it' (Granfield 1991), and he recognized the drastic differences between the speech practices of Black Americans and those of the dominant population:

Black people [talk to] each other like—as if they were enemies. And you know, you can be good friends [with another Black person], but you [talk to] them like an enemy. Well, another person [a non-Black person] would consider it as treating them as an enemy, but we call it friendship. Like we tease each other and hit on each other and talk about each other all the time, that's considered friendship. And that's what [the dominant society] call[s] abnormal. But that's the way most Black people I know who are friends *are*. They say, if you can talk about their mother and get away with it, you must be their friend. (interview, February 18, 1983: 61)

At seventeen, then, Norris made a profound observation about contrasting cultural norms—an observation that, if emphasized by teachers and school officials, could allow them to be more successful at helping their students achieve academically.

Like most other students at the school, both Norris and Maggie spoke standard English at least intermittently between nine and three. Both recognized the discontinuity between the two discourses. Maggie strongly criticized her mother's shifting speech practices and declared that she, unlike her mother, was a greater warrior in the linguistic guerrilla war because she 'talks the same way all the time.' Norris fully acknowledged his efforts to rent the standard discourse for school purposes. This is extremely telling. Unlike many of his peers, Norris's future was fairly well charted. He was performing well in school, and he realized that he had to continue to do so in order to go to college, especially since his mother was not financially able to send him to school. Even though Maggie's and Norris's perceptions differ, they share the common element of renting the standard discourse style—Norris more willingly than Maggie—and using it almost exclusively for instrumental purposes.

Maggie's and Norris's strategies for renting standard English minimize the appearance of social distance between them and other academic strivers and also demonstrate their continuous allegiance to the Black community in spite of their school success. Their use of Black street speech as a standard allows them to avoid the predictable cacophony—or worse, silence—that accrues to Black adolescents who opt to use the standard English vernacular in inappropriate contexts.

Conclusion

Capital High students who desire to achieve academic success must find ways to confront the fact that a people's '[l]iberation begins with language' (Holt 1972: 156). They do so, largely, by inverting the language norms of the wider society: by treating as a vernacular the Discourse that is elsewhere considered standard. Stigmatized as one way of acting white, this Discourse cannot be owned; it can only be rented for specific instrumental purposes.

The fact that these African American adolescents are engaged in an ongoing war through language does not mean that they are conscious of it—or, if they are aware of it, that they feel free to discuss it publicly. On the contrary, at Capital High, the students' language use fits Scott's (1985) description of a 'weapon of the weak' Their resistance to adopting the standard version of English discourse as their standard is not generally understood either by school officials—most of whom, ironically, are Black—or by the larger Black and White populations in Washington. Neither of these populations appears to see African American adolescents' use of the Black discourse style as a deliberate, self-conscious linguistic practice. Rather, the students' failure to embrace the standard is generally understood as group in competence, an inability to perform a culturally sanctioned task [...] In contrast to this prevalent view, Lee (1994) has suggested that Black discourse style increases rather than diminishes the longer Black students are in school. Paradoxically, African American adults—parents, teachers, and other school officials—contribute to the continuation of this below-the-surface warfare. These adults seek to teach their children to make the power discourse their standard. A more viable approach, however, might be to recognize and actively promote a strategy that some students already have adopted: to use standard English for purely instrumental purposes. This limited utilitarian use would validate its vernacular status.

What can we do to end the larger guerrilla warfare encoded in these discourse practices? How might we alter social policies and practices in such a way that African American adolescents' daily stigmatization of the standardized version of English is discontinued? What can we do to maximize African American adolescents' academic effort, thereby diminishing academic failure? I do not have complete answers. Nevertheless, it seems to me that we must first understand the *meaning* of the linguistic practices of African American adolescents. I have offered a first step here. While understanding this meaning does not necessarily mean acceptance, it does suggest, at the very least, a questioning of the conventional explanation, linguistic deficiencies of AAVE speakers. What I have suggested here is that conventional explanations miss the mark because they minimize the functioning of Black people's discourse practices as instruments of rhetorical resistance, which nurtures the liberation of a people and reinforces their identity. Given the centrality of Black resistance in the situation presented here, successful policymakers must discontinue the ineffective practice of disregarding cultural and identity issues. Indeed, instead of trying to repair the linguistic practices of African American adolescents, successful policymakers will redirect their energies toward minimizing the linguistic warfare inherent in the ongoing convention of marginalizing and stigmatizing the Black Self.

REFERENCES

Andrews, Vernon Lee. n.d. 'Black bodies—white control: The Black male athlete, media discourse and the contested terrain of white sportsmanship'. Unpublished paper, Department of Sociology, University of Wisconsin-Madison.

Baugh, John. 1983. *Black street speech: Its history, structure, and survival.* Austin: University of Texas Press.

Delpit, Lisa. 1988. 'The silenced dialogue: Power and pedagogy in educating other people's children'. *Harvard Educational Review* 54: 280–98.

———. 1995. *Other people's children: Cultural conflict in the classroom.* New York: New Press.

Dyson, Michael Eric. 1995. *Making Malcolm: The myth and meaning of Malcolm X.* New York: Oxford University Press.

Friedman, Jonathan. 1992. 'The past in the future: History and the politics of identity'. *American Anthropologist* 94: 837–59.

Gates, Henry Louis, Jr. 1994. *Colored people: A memoir.* New York: Alfred A. Knopf.

Gee, James Paul. 1990. *Social linguistics and literacies.* New York: Falmer Press.

Gramsci, Antonio. 1971. *On intellectuals: Selections from the prison notebooks*, ed. Quintin Hoare and Geoffrey N. Smith. New York: International.

Granfield, Robert, 1991. 'Making it by faking it: Working-class students in an elite academic environment'. *Journal of Contemporary Ethnography*. 20: 331–51.

Holt, Grace Sims. 1972. ' "Inversion" in black communication'. In *Rappin' and stylin' out: Communication in urban black America*, ed. Thomas Kochman, 152–9. Urbana: University of Illinois Press.

Kochman, Thomas, ed. 1972. *Rappin' and stylin' out: Communication in urban black America*. Urbana: University of Illinois Press.

Lee, Felicia R. 1994. 'Lingering conflict in the schools: black dialect vs. standard speech: Grappling with ways to teach young speakers of black dialect'. *The New York Times*, January 5: A1, D22.

Lorde, Audrey. 1990. 'Age, race, class, and sex: Women redefining difference' In *Out there: Marginalization and contemporary cultures*, ed. Russell Ferguson, Martha Gever, Trinh T. Minh-Ha, and Cornel West, 281–88. Cambridge, MA: MIT Press.

Scott, James C. 1985. *Weapons of the weak: Everyday forms of peasant resistance*. New Haven, CT: Yale University Press.

Williams, Brett. 1988. *Upscaling downtown: Stalled gentrification in Washington, D.C.* Ithaca, NY: Cornell University Press.

Reading 4.3
Parodying racism and subverting racial meanings

[...] The following exchange took place during a bus ride with the basketball team when we were travelling to West London. In doing so we passed through some of the affluent areas of the city. During the bus ride Winston performed a monologue for the entertainment of the team, and throughout the performance 'race' ideologies were subverted and 'commonsense' racism publicly ridiculed. Winston adopted the guise of a series of characters in order to make the performance work. The principal character was the crassly affected 'Upper Class Twit'.

The monologue

Oh, you see these buildings. My uncle owns them. I can't remember what it's called. I think it's Buckingham Palace. We rent them out to a rather nice family. In fact we own quite a lot of land in this area – um, I think it's called London. Yes, it's rather nice round here. We don't have any of you strange coloured people, except the Arabs. Nice people those Arabs. I sold one of these buildings to an Arab. Do you know the Hilton?

We don't have any of you West Indian people around here. Of course you know you West Indian people eat rather peculiar food. Oh yes, what is it called now. Is it the yellow stuff – acke and salt fish? That's it. And there is another yellow dish, um plantain – that's it. Rather strange but it's very nice. Of course, it is not like roast beef and Yorkshire pudding but it is quite nice. And you listen to that music, what is it called – regg? reggi?

From: Les Back (1996), 'Parodying racism and subverting racial meanings', *New Ethnicities and Urban Culture: Racisms and Multiculture in Young Lives*, London: UCL Press.

reggae? Yes, yes that's it. Frightfully good, lots of rhythm, good to move about to. And you have those fellows – ragga? ragamuffins? Yes, that's right. Mind you I don't know what kind of fellows they are. And what is that other kind of music you listen to – acid? The only kind of acid I've seen is in a chemistry lab ((laughter)). But you people have got no class. I mean you don't even speak the Queen's English, do you? I mean you West Indian people speak what is it...

Switches character to the street-wise Ragamuffin, speaking out of the corner of his mouth in Creole:

Whappen now star!!! Seckle, seckle now people. Cool, cool na baass! ((translation: What is happening friends, settle down))

Switches back to the Upper Class Twit:

You see what I mean? I mean you West Indian people can't speak the Queen's English, I can't even understand what he's saying.

Switches characters to a Black Cockney:

I mean that's the way we talk like, na what I mean, innit?

Switches back to the Upper Class Twit:

That's better, I can understand what he's saying, but still no class, no class at all. You see the way I speak, it has a certain manner – class. Of course, it comes with education. I mean where was you educated ((looks at Les)). What did you say? Southgate High? Not bad but not very much class. I went to Cambridge then Harvard and that's why I can talk like this. You see it's all down to class. I'm travelling with you boys – incognito. incognito! ((Looks at Clive)) Do you know what that means? I thought not – no class. I mean you have to watch these dark-skinned fellows. Of course, I've been all around the world – you know – with the army. In fact I went to a rather large place where they have a lot of these different colour[ed] people – it's called Africa. ((Les, Alton and Phil laugh hysterically)) In fact, I spent a lot of time in the Gambia. Yes, yes in the Gambia. Of course those Africans speak very strangely–

Switches to an African and says in affected 'African speech':

I thank you very much. ((Whole group laughs))

Switches back to the Upper Class Twit:

I know you fellows find it hard to get work over here and we all know that you're lazy, I might be able to get some jobs for you. In fact, I have a perfect job for you Beefy, wrestling lions. Yes, there are a lot of lions in the jungle and they need big boys like you to deal with the lions. And Phil, you can be Beefy's assistant. Clive, we have a special job for you – we'll put you in charge of the monkeys. You can be our monkey expert. ((Looks at Alton)) Of course, you know the jungle is a very dangerous place. ((Whole bus laughs)) And I've got a very special job for you Les. Yes, we'll make you a diplomat because you know you've got those white skins. You have a little more class.

The 'Upper Class Twit' is the principal voice used in the narrative. He is presented as a product of his education and as 'having class', a member of a wealthy, land-owning family travelling 'incognito' with the group. He has a tourist-like curiosity about West Indian people and black British culture. He is fascinated by West Indian food, which is 'rather strange but nice', likes reggae because 'it's frightfully good, lots of rhythm, good to move to', but is perplexed about more recent cultural phenomena (i.e. ragamuffin/reggae style and acid house music). The image parodied is a mixture of middle-class racism and colonial curiosity. Here the racist stereotyping is refined and subtle: 'You people are interesting ... but you've got no class.'

Significantly, this monologue works because all the actors share the same semantic points of reference. The caricatures are drawn from the performer's constituency of meaning, which is shared with his audience. By utilizing various characters with contrasting 'social voices' Winston addresses a wide range of issues including: a concept of class rooted in material and educational inequalities, the relationship between class, language and power, the 'skin-sensitive' nature of the job market and the characterization of young black people as 'lazy' victims of problems that are of their own making. The 'culturally impoverished' (in this case black people) can't even speak the 'Queen's English', a result of their lack of education. This version of reality is then challenged in the structure of the narrative by incorporating two black voices: a Creole-speaking Ragamuffin and a Black Cockney. The Creole voice is offered both as an example of 'the way West Indian people speak' and as a linguistic adversary, both of which are incomprehensible to the Upper Class Twit. The Black Cockney appears as a partisan intermediary translating and defending black language against the claims made by the Upper Class Twit.

For the Upper Class Twit, the relationship between educational inequality and social class is clearly stated and the reference to the army points to a British nationalism that is ideally white – not like 'foreign places' that have a lot of 'different coloured people'. Those with class are educated, patriotic and white. Lastly, the skin-sensitive nature of the British job market is parodied in the section that documents employment possibilities in the Gambia. Here white skins are shown to have a 'little more class than different colour people – not much more but a little bit more'. Again my 'whiteness' and the public meanings attached to it are being referred to and ridiculed at the same time. The constructs being applied to people in the group are not being attributed to individuals. Rather, the 'race' of individuals is used to ridicule the way racist discourses confer attributes according to skin colour and origin. In this way my 'race' provides a vehicle for criticizing the process that imbues 'whiteness' with a superior status.

Young black people engage with racist terms. In play settings they use abusive words such as 'nigger' against one another. The meanings of these exchanges are not simple. It is not merely a matter of black young people using racist materials to hurt other black young people. In the following extract the significance of these terms is explored. The exchange took place between two black young women, Donna (19 years old) and Jennifer (18 years old). Both women are from Southgate and they both work as secretaries in central London. Jennifer had been off work for two weeks with a viral infection. I was standing talking to Jennifer at a bus stop in Southgate when Donna approached us. The following exchange took place:

> Donna: Are you still off work then?
> Jennifer: Yeah, the doctor has signed me off 'til the end of the week you know.
> Les: How long have you had this bug for then?
> Jennifer: Two weeks.
> Donna: Is it?
> Les: You don't want to go back too soon or . . .
> Donna: You niggers are all the same, you just don't want to work ((starts to laugh)).
> Jennifer: ((sucks her teeth)) That's charming. ((Laughing)) I'll have you up for racism, you know. ((All three laugh))

In this extract Donna is not applying an internalized racist stereotype [. . .] to a peer in an unaltered way. Rather she is exposing the content of this stereotype and ridiculing its meaning. My whiteness in this situation may have played a part in this interaction but I think that this did not necessarily alter or influence the outcome. Here a racist formula is simultaneously possessed and subverted. [. . .]

The question of the degree to which this process results in the mere reproduction of racist ideas has to be posed. However, I did not record instances where this was the case. I am not suggesting that critical encounters with racism always result from exchanges of this kind. The boundaries of significance and the semiotics of these interactions are ambiguous. But clearly they exemplify instances where ideological struggles over meaning are taking place. In this case it is perhaps more accurate to speak about the *extent* to which racist ideas are subverted. In a sense there is a tension between, on the one hand, the reproduction of racist images within this process and, on the other, the potential to subvert the content of racist ideas through parody.

Conclusion

[...]

Black young people do not passively experience racist discourse. There exists a level of experience in which racist ideas and meanings are worked on, subverted and partially transformed. I have shown evidence of this process in action. However, the meaning of these practices is ambiguous and the outcome of the engagements with racist ideology does not always lead to the dismembering of racism. However, I maintain that the play exchanges I have described in this chapter are examples of how black young people develop a micro critique of racial inequality.

Reading 4.4
'White identities' and refusing dominant definitions

I think for black people who live in Britain this question of finding some way in which the white British can learn to live with us and the rest of the world is almost as important as discovering our own identity. I think they are in more trouble than we are. So we, in a curious way, have to rescue them from themselves – from their own past. We have to allow them to see that England is a quite interesting place with quite an interesting history that has bossed us around for 300 years [but] that is finished. Who are they now? (Stuart Hall, taken from '*After dread and anger*', BBC Radio 4, 1989)

This provocative quote from Stuart Hall sums up the position that I have adopted throughout this study. In this section I want to examine how young whites identify with their black friends in an attempt to resolve their position.

'Colour don't come into it!': youth egalitarianism and white use of black cultural codes
Evident in many accounts recorded with young white people in this area is a constant denial that 'racial' differentiation is relevant or meaningful to them. [...] Yet 'race' vernaculars abound in Southgate. Although white youths recognize the existence of categorizations of 'race', they almost unanimously deny their salience. Comments such as 'It does not matter what colour you are', 'It doesn't make any difference', 'I don't believe in racial things' are common. Encoded in these statements is the desire to banish 'racial things' because of their

From: Les Back (1996), ' "White identities" and dominant definitions', *New Ethnicities and Urban Culture: Racisms and Multiculture in Young Lives*, London: UCL Press.

potentially divisive nature. [. . .] In Southgate the denial of racial difference leads young whites to adopt black cultural practices in a more spectacular and profound way.

The degree to which 'black' cultural forms are adopted by white peers can vary and depends on numerous factors, including whether black friends censure or challenge these appropriations. Where young people distance themselves and avoid 'race' and Englishness as salient identities, a cultural vacuum results. This process is most prevalent in early to mid adolescence. It is during this time that white young people are most free to adopt cultural and linguistic materials outside of the ideological inheritance of the adult world. This is what Gerald Suttles (1968: 26) has referred to as the development of a cultural space that is based on 'private understanding rather than public rulings'. Young whites are able to fill this cultural space with black symbols precisely because the significance of colour is denied. English racism that characterizes black and white cultures as mutually impermeable phenomena is ridiculed by the development of a style, language and culture that cannot be defined as being black or white but is somehow a synthesis of both. This hybrid culture is composed of items that are equally valued, relating to one another in what Bastide (1978: 283) refers to as a 'system of equivalences'.

One of the results of this process is linguistic sharing and the incorporation of black linguistic items into white speech. This operates at three levels, ranging from Creole language of Caribbean origin, to urban black American vernacular and lastly to black London speech. I refer to these linguistic forms as black codes. Code is defined as grammatical rules, pronunciation and lexical items that are associated with a socially defined group of speakers. Thus I am examining the way that codes that are associated with black speech are appropriated by white speakers.

The most spectacular manifestation of this process is white Creole use, which varies from just a few words to ethnically marked pronunciation and a high degree of proficiency in Creole (Hewitt 1986: 128–33). For example, within Jamaican speech, adverbial tags or particles are often connected to verbs, the most common of which are 'off' and 'up'. In the following extract, Mark, a white boy aged 15, uses this form. He is talking about a local reggae sound system called Saxon Studio:

> Saxon is the baddest [best] sound, [switches to Creole] *pure murderation them jus nice-up deb dance and dem bass jus lick off your head*, [switch back] you know what I mean.

Mark also uses inversion (i.e. 'bad' meaning 'good'), which has its origins in black American speech (Sims Holt 1972). Black American forms are particularly important because their presence runs parallel with the emergence of black American youth culture. However, the influence of Caribbean Creoles persists. The use of Creole by whites may be checked, particularly in the presence of black strangers. In this sense, white Creole use is dependent on peer consent.

The third level at which black speech enters into white usage is from black South London vernacular. This black code is completely accessible to whites. It is created by incorporating standard English words that, when used by black young people, take on an altered meaning. This dominant forms of communication are appropriated and subverted. Some linguists have referred to this as 'Black London English' (Sebba 1983). For example, a word such as 'safe' (meaning free from danger) is appropriated as a prestigious term to mean excellent, sound and certain (this word has been re-translated into Creole and pronounced 'seafe'). These altered meanings were then re-circulated to white Londoners, who operated these words, complete with their black inflections and connotations. These codes take their place alongside words of various origins, including Yiddish e.g. *nosh* (verb: to cat), *schlepp* (verb: to drag or travel), *schtum* (noun: secret) – and Irish lexis – e.g. *crack* (noun: a happening or atmosphere), *ninety* (adjective: brilliant), *poladic* (adjective: intoxicated) – which all contribute to South London speech. This form has been referred to as a de-ethnicized, racially mixed 'Community English' that is open to all young people regardless of origin (Hewitt 1988).

Thus the language of white young people in this area has a rich syncretic quality. Where there are strong relationships of trust, whites can gain access to all three black codes. Greetings such as *'whaapen'* and other ethnically marked forms of speech are important because they mark both the boundaries of adolescent peer networks and the cultural frames of reference in which multi-racial friendship exists. Being around young people in this area, one can see that ritual greetings mark the boundaries of an alternative public sphere (Gilroy 1987). Within these spaces whites can take on black codes as their own. These appropriations are recognized as legitimate in this context, resulting in what one white young woman called 'nicing up' her language.

Cultural exchanges are not just confined to language. Black youth cultural styles are also viewed positively by whites (Gilroy 1987: 231). In the following extract, an 11-year-old white girl discusses her affiliation to black music and style. She shows how the rejection of 'race' and racism facilitates her use of black symbols.

> All sorts of people like reggae, black, white, um Chinese … Yes, because I don't think people should be racist, just because, like say I was black right and I was singing it, white people might not like that, but I've been brought up not to be racist.

When asked how she would define herself, Corina replied that she is a 'ragamuffin'. This is a style associated with dance-hall reggae and sound system culture [...]. Corina speaks Creole with a high degree of proficiency and has a network of black peers. Her friends refer to her as 'Ragga'. These nicknames are the most positive classifications that black young people apply to white peers. Whites are placed on a continuum ranging from racists (common names were 'satan' or 'devil', 'porkhead') to white insiders who are given black style names or personalized Creole names.

When asked about her friends Corina launched into a tirade denouncing racism:

Corina: They [my friends] are nice people, not racist, because our mums have brought us up not to be racist. The people that are racist are stupid.

Les: What kind of people are racist then?

Corina: People just say like 'white honky', and to black people say – this is a bit racist – 'black niggers', but if my mum heard me say that, I wouldn't live to say that again. My mum says that I'm not to be racist to other people.

Les: Do you know any racist people?

Corina: Yes. My mate. She was racialist and she called my mate a black bitch. So I said if you want to cuss someone's colour, or any religion you can just go away from me and I won't play with you any more. And she goes, 'I can cuss them if I want.' And I goes, 'If you want to cuss them you can cuss them, but if you are walking around with me then I will hit you.' Which I would because I don't like people who are racist. I've never been brought up to be racist.

Corina does not accept that 'whiteness' is an appropriate social classification. Her rejection of 'race' is closely bound up with a rejection of racism. This is astonishing given that she is just 11 years old and it indicates how threatening racism is to young whites in this area. Corina explains her anti-racism in terms of her mother, who condemns racism, and her friendships with black peers. [. . .]

The rejection of racism and the denial of the importance of race opens black cultural symbols to white appropriation. What results is an identification with black people and black symbols.

[. . .]

Limits on the white appropriation of black forms

When I met Tony he was 17 years old. He was intimately involved with black cultural practices and in friendships with black peers. He maintained that his use of black talk was legitimate because he shares the same social locations as his black friends:

I mean people often say I sound like a black man – that is to say I sound black. But you see when I learned to speak English, I suppose it ain't really English, I learned to speak it the way people around me spoke – na mean? I mean when Michael [a black friend] comes up to me and says to me ((switches to Creole)) 'Whappen Tony cool', I don't answer him with ((fakes a public school accent)) 'Oh yes Michael, I am quite cool thank you'. I say 'Yeah man – safe!' I might not use the talk as hard or exaggerated as him, but I'm talking the language I learned to speak, it's – it's my natural language.

Tony is talking here about a social and linguistic space where emergent identities between young people, regardless of background, are formed. However, the boundaries of this process are subject to close scrutiny, as we see in the following extract. It involves Tony and Michael (the boys mentioned above) and Brian. All three boys were 17 at the time of this incident. Michael and Brian are of Afro-Caribbean origin and Tony is white. The incident took place outside a kebab shop in Southgate. The three boys had just walked out of the shop with some food. There had been some banter between the person serving and Tony, and all three boys were laughing.

Michael: What did he say to you? Something about...
Brian: He said next time he is going to run you out of the shop if you don't give him the money straight away ((laugh)).
Tony: You know what I mean, ((switches to Creole)) the man chat nuff lyric.
Michael: [in Creole] The man was bad rasta.
Brian: I tell you, I think Tony gets blacker everyday ((laugh))!
Tony: Yeah sometimes I wish I was black you know ((laugh)).
Brian: ((turns and his mood changes)) No you don't!

((All three boys stop talking, an air of seriousness descends on the group))

Tony: Anyway I ain't going back in there again in a hurry.

((All three boys start laughing))

Tony uses black forms of language in this situation. His use of these symbols is legitimized by his two black peers, who both allow him access to these cultural forms but also encourage him to be involved in black music and black styles. However, this incident marks the limits of Tony's participation. Simply, Tony's claim to 'want to be black' is too much for Brian, who checks Tony's over-zealous claim. Being close to this interaction, I felt that the boundaries of Tony's relationship to blackness were being defined. In the private context, the presence of racism can be exorcised. But Tony's lack of appreciation of the public prevalence of racism is not reckoned with in his playful desire to be black. This is what offended Brian. When I asked Tony about this incident he said:

Well, I realized that I had gone too far – you know what I mean. I know I can't ever be black or nothing and I realized that what he was coming off with was right. I mean they go through a harder time and all that – that is to say there are things I don't have to deal with when I am on my own because I am white, but because I am with them, I see what goes on and how people act the same towards me when I'm with them.

Tony's account is interesting because he realizes that he overstretched his relationship with his black peers. Clearly, he understood that there is more to being black than ebullient street styles and prestigious linguistic codes. By adopting and articulating black forms of style and speech Tony was encoding his identification with blackness. However, the contradictory nature of this identification becomes impossible to sustain when it is made explicit. Tony identifies with 'black' symbols but knows he can never feel the consequences of racism and the experiential foundations of blackness.

Accounts of young white people wanting to be black during the period of mid-adolescence are not uncommon in Southgate. In a sense, these constitute extreme moments of identification but they are continuous with the operation of black cultural forms by white young people. [. . .] Through these engagements with blackness, young whites are forced to interrogate the meanings of their whiteness. They move from the youthful assertion of 'it doesn't matter what colour you are' to a more profound and lived knowledge of how racism structures their lives and relationships.

These identifications with blackness often go hand in hand with the rejection of Englishness. Although many of the young people locate themselves within this notion of national identity, others either distance themselves from the concept or qualify its meaning. In the following quotation, Paul (17 years old) accepts the descriptive notion of English but then unpacks and disposes of some of the ideological baggage associated with the concept:

> Yeah, I am English. I was born in England but there are things about it that I don't agree with – like when I was younger I remember seeing the Union Jack on NF [National Front] stickers. If that is being English, I am not English. Like skinhead and all that. They were proud to be English, like I'm English and I'm going to kick your head in. They are things that I don't want to be associated with – I mean I've grown up with black people.

Accounts such as this associate 'Englishness', 'whiteness' and racism in an interrelated ideological triangle. In this sense, racism is coupled with a particular construction of nationhood that is unattractive to many white young people who have close black friends (Hewitt 1986: 93). To accept this identity would in turn make close relationships with black friends untenable or less feasible. Paul has had close 'black' friends all of his life. At school he was best friends with a black young man. Thus the lived experience of whites and their social knowledge of black youngsters is directly at odds with new racism and its attendant definition of English nationalism. In this sense the aesthetic of Englishness is totally unattractive to young whites in Southgate. For them the Union Flag is not associated with national unity and pride; rather it connotes neo-fascist politics and an image of skinhead youth who champion the bigotries of racism and national chauvinism. In this way young whites vacate whiteness and Englishness as appropriate identities in favour of an encoded identification with blackness and black people.

[. . .]

REFERENCES

Bastide, R. 1978. *The African religious of Brazil: towards a sociology of the interpretation of civilisations*. Baltimore and London: Johns Hopkins University Press.

Gilroy, P. 1987. *There ain't no black in the Union Jack: the cultural politics of race and nation*. London: Hutchinson.

Hewitt, R. 1986. *White talk, black talk: inter-racial friendship and communication amongst adolescents*. London: Cambridge University Press.

—1988. 'Youth, race and language: deconstructing ethnicity?' Paper presented at the Conference on the Sociology of Youth and Childhood, Philipps University, Marburg, West Germany, 14–15 November.

Sebba, M. 1983. 'Code-switching as a conversational strategy'. Paper presented at the York Creole Conference, University of York.

Sims Holt, G. 1972. ' "Inversion" in black communication'. In *Rappin' and stylin' out: communication in black America*, T. Kochman (ed.), Chicago and London: University of Illinois Press.

Suttles, G. 1968. *The social order of the slum: ethnicity and territory in the inner city*. Chicago: University of Chicago.

Reading 4.5

[. . .]

Nerds are members of a stigmatized social category who are stereotypically cast as intellectual overachievers and social underachievers. From the Columbine High School killers to Microsoft monopolist Bill Gates, the label *nerd* clearly has negative associations in American culture (especially when, as in these cases, it is used to explain highly antisocial behaviors). It is also, as such examples suggest, a cultural category that is both ideologically gendered (male) and racialized (white), although these dimensions are not always contextually foregrounded. Despite such cultural images, to be a nerd is not an inevitable social death sentence but instead is often a purposeful choice that allows those who embrace this identity to reject locally dominant social norms. In U.S. high schools, where such norms usually center on participation in youth culture, nerds stand out for their resistance to current trends, and more generally for their rejection of coolness as a desirable social goal. As the basic value of youth culture, coolness may be defined as engagement with and participation in the trends and practices of youth culture; it frequently involves a stance of affectlessness as well. In rejecting coolness, students who consider themselves nerds signal their distance from both the practices and the stances of trendier youth. Instead, they embrace the values of nerdiness, primarily intelligence. But in so doing, especially in contexts of racial diversity, the oppositional identity of the nerd becomes as salient for its racialized position as for its subcultural orientation.

From: Mary Bucholtz (2001), 'The whiteness of nerds: superstandard English and racial markedness', *Journal of Linguistic Anthropology*, 11: 1, 84–100.

Youth culture and racial appropriation

One such context is Bay City High School, a large urban high school in the San Francisco Bay Area where I conducted a year of fieldwork in 1995–96. In spite of the school's tremendous racial and ethnic diversity, resulting in the visibility of whiteness as a racial category, white students at Bay City High frequently operated according to an ideological dichotomy between African Americans and European Americans, the two largest racialized groups at the school. This binary put many European American students into a double bind: on the one hand, they were often monitored by their white peers for incursions of blackness into their cultural styles, but on the other hand, many of the practices of European American youth cultures, including linguistic practices, are borrowed from African American teenagers. To remain both culturally and racially acceptable, white students had to maintain a delicate balance between embracing coolness and avoiding cultural practices that were racialized as black by their European American peers.

The black origins of many elements of youth culture in the United States have been well documented; trends in music, dance, fashion, sports, and language in a variety of youth subcultures are often traceable to an African American source [. . .]. This connection is often obscured, however, for as increasing numbers of European American teenagers embrace particular black cultural practices, these practices become detached from blackness—they become *deracialized*, or racially unmarked, at least in the eyes of the white youths who participate in them. At the same time, such practices often lose their urban associations and become normalized in suburban and rural settings as well (witness the expansion of rap in the past decades). Even the concept of coolness itself stems from African American traditions (Morgan 1998).

As a result of their status as cultural innovators and trendsetters, black students at Bay City High, as elsewhere around the country (Solomon 1988), were often viewed by their white counterparts as cool almost by definition. Yet for European American teenagers to adopt elements of African American youth culture before the deracializing process was well under way was to risk being marked by their peers as racially problematic; this was the situation for many white hip-hop fans at the school. Conversely, for white teenagers to refuse to participate in youth culture in any form was likewise problematic, not only culturally but racially. It may be said that appropriate whiteness requires the appropriation of blackness, but only via those black styles that are becoming deracialized and hence no longer inevitably confer racial markedness on those who take them up.

White nerds disrupted this ideological arrangement by refusing to strive for coolness. The linguistic and other social practices that they engaged in indexed an uncool stance that was both culturally and racially marked: to be uncool in the context of the white racial visibility at Bay City High was to be racialized as hyperwhite, 'too white.' Consequently, the production of nerdiness via the rejection of coolness and the overt display of intelligence was often simultaneously (though not necessarily intentionally) the production of an extreme version of whiteness. Unlike the styles of cool European American students, in nerdiness African American culture and language did not play even a covert role.

[...]

In general, then, white nerds were identifying not against blackness but against trendy whiteness, yet any dissociation from white youth trends entailed a dissociation from the black cultural forms from which those trends largely derive.

Membership in the nerd category, for purposes of this study, was not assigned by me but reported by students themselves, both nerds and non-nerds. Nerdiness is not an essence, of course, but a set of practices, engagements, and stances, and individuals oriented to nerdiness to a greater or lesser degree in their actions. Central to nerdy practice, as I have argued elsewhere (Bucholtz, 1998, 1999), is a particular emphasis on language as a resource for the production of an intelligent and nonconformist identity. I focus on a linguistic practice that simultaneously indexed such identities and marked speakers as non-normatively white: the use of superstandard English.)

Language ideology and superstandard english

[...] ideologies of race are also ideologies of language. [...] The ideology of racial markedness therefore has as a corollary an ideology of linguistic markedness. In particular, the difficulty (which afflicts only white people) in seeing whites as racialized is matched by the difficulty (again, only for whites) in hearing white speakers' language as racialized: as specifically white rather than neutral or normative—or standard. In such an arrangement, unmarked status confers power by allowing whiteness to move through the social world ghostlike, unseen and unheard, evident only in its effects. Likewise, the notion of a linguistic 'standard,' which in the U.S. context is closely bound up with whiteness (Lippi-Green 1997), implies both unmarkedness (standard as ordinary) and power (standard as regulative).

[...]

Superstandard English contrasts linguistically with Standard English in its greater use of 'supercorrect' linguistic variables: lexical formality, carefully articulated phonological forms, and prescriptively standard grammar. It may also go beyond traditional norms of prescriptive correctness, to the point of occasionally over-applying prescriptive rules and producing hypercorrect forms. But the recognition of such difference is at least as ideologically as linguistically motivated. It is precisely because of the robustness of the ideology of Standard English in the United States that those linguistic varieties generally classified as nonstandard—African American Vernacular English foremost among them – are regularly held up as divergent from the standard despite considerable overlap in grammar, phonology, and the lexicon. By the same token, the superstandard need not deviate substantively from the colloquial standard in order to be considered distinctive; because it is marked with respect to Standard English forms, even relatively slight use of supercorrection and hypercorrection can call attention to itself. Superstandard English is therefore a marked variety that may contrast ideologically both with the unmarked colloquial standard and with marked non-standard English. However, because it draws on the prescriptive standard, it also contributes to the linguistic ideologies that elevate one linguistic variety over others. How these varieties come to be associated with particular racial positions—that is, how they become racialized styles—is likewise the work of ideology.

[...]

Nerds and Slang
[...]

One characteristic of superstandard English is its lack of current slang. By avoiding particular linguistic forms, speakers can separate themselves from the social category indexically associated with such forms; thus the absence of slang in nerds' speech symbolically distanced them from their cooler peers. When I asked nerdy students to discuss current slang, which other students usually found the most enjoyable part of the interviews I conducted, most expressed dismay at the task and professed unfamiliarity with the terms (one of the rare instances when the nerdy teenagers I spoke to were willing to admit to ignorance). They also removed themselves from the slang terms they did know in various ways, such as providing literal, nonslang definitions for the slang terms I presented to them on slips of paper (Example 1) or offering nonslang terms that convey the same meaning (Example 2).

In Example 1, Bob, Conqueror of the Universe, announces to her friends the slang word (*blood*), an affiliative address term, which is printed on the slip of paper she has selected:

1. Bob: [bl:ɐd]. B-L. O-O.D. The word is [blʌd] ... That's the stuff which is inside of your veins. That's the stuff that—I don't know. I haven't gotten to that chapter yet.

Bob turns the task of defining slang terms into a quasi-academic activity by humorously invoking the format of a spelling bee (state the word, spell it, restate it). This academic orientation continues in her formal, literal definition of the term and her allusion to one of her textbooks where the answer can be found. Through such strategies Bob repeatedly distances herself from the use of slang while simultaneously involving discourse genres and topics associated with intelligence.

Where Bob emphasizes her unfamiliarity with this slang term (even as she reveals her awareness of it through a marked, 'black,' pronunciation, as discussed below), Erich asserts that the absence of slang in his lexicon is a matter of preference. As with other people, I asked Erich to comment on which of the printed slang terms he uses. In response, Erich rejects slang as a whole while making clear that some of the activities that the words refer to are relevant to his life:

> 2. Erich: The idea behind the term fits but the term itself doesn't – isn't the way I prefer it to be. Like 'kick back.' I just prefer something-some normal term . . . Like 'to relax.' . . . Something like that.

Erich's view of slang involves a process of iconization that brings youthful trendiness into the pragmatic orbit of such lexical items. Just as slang is trendy (not 'normal'), so too are its speakers. Erich avoids slang not because of its referential meaning but because of the semiotic meaning that iconization assigns to it.

Of course, students who described themselves as nerds did use some slang, particularly older terms. But these items were often marked in some way in their speech, as when Claire explained why she does not like many people:

> 3. Claire: When it seems to me that people are really young <i.e., immature>, it's like their emotional response to different things just seems [dʒʌst simz] really w-(.) wacked.

Claire's utterance of the slang term *wack(ed)* is preceded by a false start and a brief pause, both signals of some kind of production difficulty. Whether her hesitance is due to uncertainty about the term or simply its appropriateness in front of me, it highlights the word as unusual for Claire, at least in this context. Supporting this interpretation is her formal, careful language elsewhere in her turn (such as *emotional response* and the full articulation of *just seems*) and the standardized form of the slang term itself, which more usually occurred as *wack*. In adding a Standard English past participle marker to a word popularized by African American students, then, Claire reveals that she is not quite as cool as her use of the term might imply. (At the time of the study, Claire was deliberately trying to become cooler, mainly by smoking marijuana, while retaining her commitment to nerdy ideals like intelligence.) What is more, her standardization of African American Vernacular English grammar is not racially neutral: [. . .] the two variants Claire chooses between are linked to racial categories. Hence the supercorrect *wacked* is not only more standard but also whiter than the original term.

The Phonology of Superstandard English

[. . .]

Among European American students at Bay City High School, a three-way ideological division of English corresponded to similarly ideologically based social divisions: most students of color were thought to speak nonstandard English, most white students were thought to speak colloquial Standard English, and nerds, who did not always incorporate colloquial forms into their speech, were heard to speak an exaggeratedly formal version of Standard English; that is, superstandard English. Superstandard English, unlike Standard English, was a marked linguistic variety among European American students at Bay City High School. Evoking the registers of scholarship and science, nerds' use of superstandard English produced a very different kind of identity than did the colloquial Standard English used by cooler students. And as noted above, because of the ideological force of Standard English, even the slightest use of marked linguistic forms could be sufficient to produce a semiotic distinction. Thus, in nerds' speech, colloquial forms were juxtaposed with superstandard varieties (a violation of Ervin-Tripp's [1973] 'co-occurrence rules'). As with most linguistic variables, the use of superstandard features was not categorical.

One linguistic strategy that nerds used to make their speech distinctive was to imbue it with a measured quality, which lent a certain *gravitas* to their words, particularly as a result of resistance to phonological processes characteristic of colloquial speech, such as consonant-cluster simplification and the phonological reduction of unstressed vowels. Claire's pronunciation in Example 3 above illustrates the former pattern; Example 4 exemplifies the latter. In 4a, Erich describes his difficulties with another student in the school's computer club; in 4b he talks about construction problems in his neighborhood.

> 4a. He made up all these rules that he sort o- we sort of voted on and I didn't vote on them [ðɛm] because I wasn't there that day, and I have to abide by them [ðɛm].
>
> 4b. They're going to [goiŋ tu] have to [hæv tu] change-close off streets...

Erich's careful pronunciation in these examples is all the more remarkable given that the items in Example 4 occur in linguistic contexts that favor the phonological reduction of these words to '*em*, *goin*' or *gonna*, and *hafta*. The lack of stress on both tokens of *them* in 4a, the nasal of *on* preceding the first token, and the grammaticalized function of *going (to)* and *have (to)* in 4b all promote reduced phonological forms, but Erich resists the effects of linguistic environment on his speech.

This precisely enunciated speech style has semiotic connections to literacy: nerdy teenagers frequently used something akin to 'reading style' (Labov 1972) even in their spontaneous conversations. Indeed, nerdy students occasionally employed pronunciations based on spelling rather than speech, such as [folk] for *folk* and [həŋ kəŋg] for *Hong Kong*, as well as noncustomary pronunciations of words they encountered in their extensive reading but had not heard uttered aloud: for example, Loden pronounced her pseudonym as [lɑdn̩] rather than the more usual [lodn̩]; the name came from a class assignment. Here again iconization is at work. Nerds' careful speech style approximates in the spoken channel the linguistic forms as they would be written (this is especially clear in the use of spelling pronunciation).

This iconic link between careful speech and reading, moreover, forms the basis of a secondary link between careful speech and intelligence, via the (ideological) indexical association of advanced literacy, extensive education, and high intelligence. And intelligence in turn was associated, at least by nerds, with independent thought: a refusal to go along with the crowd whether in fashion or in phonology. The iconicity between resisting phonological pressure and resisting peer pressure is a shortcut through the chain of semiotic links already established. Erich invokes this association in Example 5, in which he explains why he thinks the term *sophisticated* applies to himself and his best friend, Micah:

> 5. Erich: We're not sophisticated in a bad sense, we just have uh much we're much more advanced (.) in terms of uh (.) (xxx) in terms of the our- our ways of perceiving things, at least (.) myself and Micah. <*Mary: What do you mean by that?*> We don't think- I don't think of anything in a no:rmal way:, <*Mary: Mm.*> like uh and I don't-I use much more, I don't know how to describe it. I don't use all the abbreviations for words? <*Mary: Hm.*> Like most people abbreviate-cut off half the words? For no particular reason? And I don't do that. hhh <*Mary: Like, do you have an example of that?*> Uh uh they they they they cut off the 'g' on the end of 'tripping' [tripiŋ:] <*Mary: Mm. Right.*> (and end,) N apostrophe. It makes it makes no sense to me.

Erich connects sophistication, in its positive (i.e., nontrendy) sense, both to 'advanced' and unconventional perspectives and to careful pronunciation. From the more elevated position that sophistication affords, the colloquial style of youth culture (and of U.S. culture more widely) simply 'makes no sense.' Here again Erich displays his rather clinical knowledge of slang even as he distances himself from it. His fastidious pronunciation of the slang word *tripping*, with a full superstandard [ŋ], is the linguistic equivalent of holding a particularly distasteful scientific specimen between thumb and forefinger for inspection before it is discarded. This blending of casual and formal language allows Erich to display knowledge without embracing the identity usually associated with such knowledge. Aware of my interest in language, Erich takes a researcherly analytic stance toward his own linguistic style.

Superstandard Grammar and Lexis

Related to the phonological formality of nerdy speech is its lexical formality. Nerds often chose formal-register polysyllabic variants of Greco-Latinate origin over more colloquial Germanic monosyllables, a longstanding stylistic distinction based on ideologies in the history of the English language. But where in Standard English these lexical items are associated with different registers, in superstandard English they were used across registers. Such lexical items therefore had the indexical effect of making speakers sound smart or learned. In Examples 6a and 6b, Erich discusses how he is different from other students at Bay City High:

6a. I Just can't stand people who have all the outward signs of being an extremely stupid person.

6b. My observation is that other people think we're kind of foolish and crazy for the way we do things.

Erich's choice of the Latinate intensifier *extremely* and the nominalized form *observation* invests his discourse with a formal, literate tone; additionally, as in Example 5 both examples invoke a stance of scientific objectivity and detached empiricism, here achieved through such collocations as *all the outward signs* and *My observation* is. In Example 7 Claire takes a similar stance in responding to a question from me about what term she uses for male high-school students:

7. Claire: I-I.I tend to-to refer to (.) the whole (.) um Y chromosome (.) as a guy.

Claire's lexical choices are formal: *tend, refer*. And in invoking the register of biology (*the whole (.) um Y chromosome (.)*) she participates in the same nerdy practice of scientific discourse already exemplified by Erich. The deliberateness of Claire's choice is suggested by the brief pauses that bracket and highlight the term. Like Erich, Claire understands our interaction to be a shared intellectual enterprise, and she repeatedly demonstrates her ability to engage in the scientific discourse of research. Where her use of slang in Example 3 above showed a similar linguistic self-awareness, the effect of this awareness is quite different in each case. The hesitancy in the earlier example is not in evidence here. Instead, the pauses preceding and following the phrase *Y chromosome* operate like quotation marks, not only emphasizing the term but also displaying Claire's consciousness of its markedness. Her utterance thus also illustrates the process of erasure: in highlighting her use of superstandard lexis, she implies the existence of an unmarked (standard) norm. It is at such moments that nerdiness moves from practice to performance, a move that is partly explicable in light of Claire's identity change-in-progress.

Undoubtedly, my role as a researcher triggered this analytic style in some students, and in fact all the teenagers I interviewed engaged in style-shifting to some degree, as compared with their interactions with their friends. However, although all the teenagers I interviewed adjusted their speech to the situation, only those who engaged in other nerdy practices, and often adopted the nerd label as well, used superstandard English. Moreover, such teenagers employed this style even in interaction with their friends, a practice that I witnessed among no other teenagers.

Hyperwhiteness and the Rejection of Cool

By distancing themselves from their cool white peers, nerds at Bay City High School created an even greater distance between themselves and their cool black peers. Although nerds did not necessarily understand their linguistic and other social practices in particularly racialized terms, these practices could take on racialized meaning in the context of the ideological black-white dichotomy that shaped whiteness for European American students at Bay City High. Nerdy teenagers' deliberate avoidance of slang, for example, indexically displayed their remoteness from the trends not only of white youth culture but of black youth culture as well, since African American slang was a primary source of European American slang. While this was not necessarily an intended consequence, Example 1 provides evidence that nerds defined themselves in opposition to both coolness and blackness. Bob first utters the word *blood* (a term used by many African American boys at Bay City High) with stereotyped African American Vernacular English phonology and exaggerated intonation: [bləd] Her marking of AAVE speakers in this example expresses the ideological distance between her identity and that of African American youth. Her return to her normal pronunciation in the second utterance of this word ([blʌd]) coincides with her attempt to provide a nonslang definition for the term. With this switch, coolness and blackness are recursively linked to each other and separated from the world of nerds.

Likewise, if the use of superstandard English worked to separate nerdy teenagers from their trendy white counterparts who generally spoke a more colloquial variety of Standard English, it also enforced a division between white nerds and most black students at Bay City High, who tended to use AAVE as their primary linguistic variety. The colloquial Standard English favored by cool white teenagers elided to some extent the structural differences between itself and AAVE (thereby allowing them a greater linguistic claim to coolness). Superstandard English, however, reinforced this racialized linguistic divide by exaggerating and highlighting the semiotic elements of Standard English that distinguish it from nonstandard forms of African American English.

Nerdy performances of intellectual ability also produced racialized difference, as suggested by Signithia Fordham's (1996) ethnographic study of academically successful students in a black high school. Fordham notes that some high achieving African American students were accused by their black peers of 'acting white' precisely because of their intellectual performance. This charge was often accompanied by the pejorative epithet *brainiac*, a term that, as Fordham makes clear, is racialized as black in much the same way that the analogous but not synonymous term *nerd* is racialized as white (1996: 361, n. 2). At its most negative, the term *brainiac* refers to an African American whose display of intellectual ability indicates a capitulation to European American cultural values. To avoid being labeled *brainiacs*, black students in Fordham's study often hid or downplayed their academic accomplishments and demonstrated their engagement with the concerns of African American youth culture. By contrast, nerdy white teenagers at Bay City High presented themselves as fully engaged in academic endeavors and other intellectual work and showed their indifference toward the youth culture that surrounded them. Such practices constituted a counter-hegemonic erasure of the devaluation of academic achievement, but they also erased recognition of accomplished black (and white) students who chose not to openly display their abilities.

Through the use of superstandard English and the semiotic work it performed, nerds at Bay City High were classifiable not simply as white but as hyperwhite. As the most extreme form of whiteness, nerds might be expected to be the best—that is, most unmarked—example of that racial category. But it was precisely the hyperwhiteness of nerds that marked them as atypically white. In U.S. culture generally, the ideological norm of whiteness needs blackness to operate, not only to establish an Other against which to measure itself, but to provide cultural forms for whiteness to appropriate and re-racialize. As groundbreaking scholarship in other disciplines has shown (e.g., Lott 1993; Roediger 1991; Rogin 1996), whiteness is separated from blackness in ideology but inextricable from it in practice. White nerds at Bay City High violated this practice by refusing to appropriate African American cultural and linguistic forms.

Besides expressing their distance from African Americans symbolically and implicitly through linguistic and other social practices, some nerdy students also explicitly stated this ideology of identity. Thus Christine in Example 8 provides an overt statement that African American students are at best useful to know, but only as protection against other African Americans (see also Bucholtz 1999):

8. <In response to my question about whether she knows people in the 'hip-hop crowd,' a term she takes to mean 'black students.'>
   Christine: Well I know them
                 I know (.) I know some people.
                 Which helps to alleviate situations sometimes.

Such sentiments insert a racialized subtext into the linguistic practices and ideologies that separated nerds from African American youth language and culture. Nerds' dismissal of black cultural practices often led them to discount the possibility of friendship with black students. In this sense, nerdy teenagers' social freedom in rejecting normative youth identities was constrained by their acceptance of normative, ideologically rooted views of their African American schoolmates.

The adoption of a cultural identity that could be read as hyperwhite did not guarantee, however, that nerds promoted what were viewed as 'white' interests. During the time I was conducting fieldwork, a great deal of political debate in Bay City centered on the dismantling of affirmative action in California's higher education system. Erich was among the Bay City High School students who organized large-scale protests against these measures; meanwhile, many European American students who drew heavily upon African American youth language and culture did not participate. The wholehearted, or even halfhearted, appropriation of black cultural forms did not ensure that trend-conscious white teenagers would also adopt a political perspective that was sensitive to African American concerns. By the same token, the rejection of the identity associated with trendy white youth as it emerged from and reworked African American cultural practices did not necessarily entail that nerds were similarly disengaged from the politics of race. In challenging dominant ideologies of youth culture, nerds both reinscribed and revised prevailing models of whiteness.

Conclusion

White nerds inhabited an ambiguous racial position at Bay City High: they were the whitest group but not the prototypical representatives of whiteness. It is likewise difficult to disambiguate nerds' relationship to white domination. In refusing to exercise the racial privilege upon which white youth cultures are founded, nerds may be viewed as traitors to whiteness. But engaging in nerdy practices may itself be a form of white privilege, since these practices were not as readily available to teenagers of color and the consequences of their use more severe. The use of superstandard English is thus both a rejection of the cool white local norm and an investment in a wider institutional and cultural norm.

[...] Nerds at Bay City High were not normal because they were too normal, not (unmarkedly) white because they were too white. [...] Thus although the marked hyperwhiteness of nerds undermines the racial project of whiteness as a normative and unmarked construct, it may also shore up racial ideologies of difference and division.

REFERENCES

Bucholtz, Mary 1998 'Geek the Girl: Language, Femininity and Female Nerds'. In *Gender and Belief Systems: Proceedings of the Fourth Berkeley Women and Language Conference*. Natasha Warner, Jocelyn Ablers Leela Bilmes, Monica Oliver, Suzanne Wertheim, and Melinda Chen, eds. pp. 119–131. Berkeley, CA: Berkeley Women and Language Group.

Bucholtz, Mary 1999 '"Why Be Normal?"': Language and Identity Practices in a Community of Nerd Girls'. *Language in Society* 28(2): 203–223.

Ervin-Tripp, Susan 1973 'The Structure of Communicative Choice'. In *Language Acquisition and Communicative Choice*. Anwar S. Dil, ed. pp. 302–373. Stanford, CA: Stanford University Press.

Fordham, Signithia 1996 *Blacked Out: Dilemmas of Race, Identity, and Success at Capital High*. Chicago: University of Chicago Press.

Lippi-Green, Rosina 1997 *English with an Accent: Language, Ideology, and Discrimination in the United States*. New York: Routledge.

Lott, Eric 1993 *Love and Theft: Blackface Minstrelsy and the American Working Class*. New York: Oxford University Press.

Morgan, Marcyllena 1998 'More than a Mood or an Attitude: Discourse and Verbal Genre in African American Culture'. In *The Structure of African American English*. Salikeke Mufwene, John R. Richford, Guy Bailey, and John Baugh, eds. pp. 251–281. New York: Routledge.

Roediger, David R. 1991 *The Wages of Whiteness: Race and the Making of the American Working Class*. London: Verso.

Rogin, Michael 1996 *Blackface, White Noise: Jewish Immigrants in the Hollywood Melting Pot*. Berkeley: University of California Press.

Solomon, R. Patrick 1988 'Black Cultural Forms in Schools: A Cross National Comparison'. In *Class Race, and Gender in American Education*. Lois Weis, ed. pp. 249–265. New York: SUNY Press.

NOTE

Transcription conventions are as follows: a period indicates falling intonation; a question mark indicates rising intonation; a comma indicates fall-rise intonation; a hyphen indicates a self-interruption that breaks the intonation unit; a dash indicates a self-interruption that breaks a word; between words, a hyphen indicates rapid speech; a (.) indicates a pause of less than one-tenth of a second; ellipses indicates deleted text; (xxx) indicates unintelligible speech; hhh indicates laughter; angled brackets indicate transcriber comments or turns that are not the focus of analysis; and phonetic transcription appears in square brackets.

5

MULTILINGUALISM, ETHNICITY AND IDENTITY

The world is frequently portrayed as an increasingly uniform place from the point of view of the number of languages used on our planet, not least by some of the media in Western countries where English is the dominant language. Despite this portrayal, however, its population continues to use a huge, if diminishing, variety of languages – most estimates are of around 6,000 living languages (a figure inevitably highly dependent on the definition of 'a language' used – see, for example, Crystal 1997: Chapter 47, for a discussion). Nevertheless, whatever the real figure, languages are certainly disappearing all the time and this process seems to be accelerating.

The main purpose of this chapter is to encourage you to reflect on and discuss multilingualism and its links with questions of power, identity and ethnicity, at every level from the global to the interpersonal. We begin by considering the phenomenon of English as a global language and then move on to a discussion of some of the ethnic and ideological issues which underlie controversy over the role of English and other languages in the USA. Following this, we deal briefly with the importance of questions of power and identity in language planning and language policy. Finally, we look at a case study of the complexities of language use in a bilingual setting.

ENGLISH IN THE WORLD TODAY

The language question in Hong Kong

Reading 5.1 has been chosen not only as it focuses on a highly topical and internationally important case – that of Hong Kong – but also because it highlights a number of issues to do both with language and attempts made to legislate regarding the roles of particular languages. These questions are of fundamental importance to the subject of this chapter. Morrison and Lui's discussion makes clear that the theoretical basis of language planning and policy decisions is diverse and contested and that the practical benefits or disadvantages of particular policies for particular groups or individuals are often of vital importance. Their analysis shows that the background to and implications of language policies can only be fully understood in their historical context and through the application of appropriate theoretical insights, in particular from sociology and psychology.

What also emerges clearly is that language is often central to questions of identity and ethnicity and that **linguistic capital**, as described by Morrison and Lui, can bring both cultural and economic advantage. For this reason, intervention in language issues is a highly sensitive process. The Chinese government's willingness to threaten school principals with fines or imprisonment for failing to follow medium of instruction guidelines and the decision of teachers to demonstrate in the streets against aspects of language policy in education are an example of the seriousness of the issues at stake and of the strength of feelings involved, as is, in a different context, the controversy over ebonics discussed in Chapter 4. Nevertheless, in reality such examples are not at all unusual from the point of view of the frequent capacity of power struggles played out through language controversies to give rise to conflict and, often, bloodshed. Above all, the article makes clear that although power relations are central to the dynamics of policy development and implementation it's often inadequate to attempt to account for the promotion or power of a particular language purely on the basis of a model of **linguistic imperialism**.

A number of the issues raised by Morrison and Lui will be taken up in the course of this chapter, but we shall focus first on a wider discussion of the phenomenon of the role of English in the world today. Much of what Morrison and Lui say is applicable to other situations, but it's also true that a key factor in the situation in Hong Kong is the presence of the English language in particular and, for example, the fact that it's widely perceived there to be of greater instrumental 'value' than the other languages involved or, indeed, any other language in the world.

The unique position of English in the world and the background to it
There is considerable disagreement as to whether the unique position of English in the world today is a positive thing, but few dispute the extent of the language's dominance. Having said that, reliable data concerning use of particular languages are notoriously hard to come by. Figures will inevitably vary, according to factors such as the ideological bias of those doing the counting, but by any standards English currently holds a uniquely influential position in the world. Some brief examples, quoted in Crystal (1997), will demonstrate this. According to Crystal:

- approximately 85 per cent of international organisations in the world use English as an official language and among this proportion are a full third which use it as their only official language;
- about one-third of newspapers are published in countries where English has some type of special status (see Crystal 1997: Chapter 2) and almost half of the world's radio receivers are located in such countries;
- the USA controls around 85 per cent of the world film market and the international trend being driven by its film industry is towards production of a restricted number of Hollywood blockbusters each year designed to 'serve' cinemas worldwide, albeit in dubbed form;
- English is the language of international air traffic control;
- at least three-quarters of international academic journals are published in English.

Whatever criteria we use, the picture is one of a pre-eminent role of English in the international arena and a huge demand for and promotion of access to the language (some estimates, for example that of the admittedly partisan British Council, are as high as 1,000 million people worldwide learning English [Crystal 1997: 103]). Equally clear is the fact that although the rise of English has a long history which can be traced back at least as far as the further development of the British Empire's markets in the mid-eighteenth century (for example, Bailey 1991), its post-1945 expansion has been closely linked to the increasing economic, military and cultural dominance of the USA on the world scene and that country is the clear 'epicentre' of the phenomenon of English as a global language. In one sense the spread of English over the past fifty years and the huge demand for access to its 'capital', exemplified in Morrison and Lui's article, is an accident of history in that it's partly a by-product of the way in which the USA has come to dominate international capitalism in the post-war era. It's worth noting, however, that the extent to which people's access to English is increasing in reality isn't as clear as it might seem at first sight, because such access is highly dependent on socio-economic status in a highly unequal world. 'The spread of English has been as uneven as the spread of the global economy', as Holborow puts it (1999: 58) in an analysis which illustrates the extent to which access to the language is often largely dependent on social class and socio-economic status. It would be simplistic to say that the current status of English is the result of some sort of 'grand conspiracy' theory, if nothing else because it would suggest an implausible degree of planning and rationality in the process of the consolidation of international capital. However, it's certainly true that considerable effort and resources have been devoted to promoting the rise of the language since World War II. Phillipson (1992: 7), for example, quotes a former Director of the Centre for Applied Linguistics in Washington as follows: 'The process was also greatly abetted by the expenditure of large amounts of government and private foundation funds in the period 1950–1970, perhaps the most ever spent in history in support of the propagation of a language.'

The effects of the dominance of English

As Morrison and Lui (Reading 5.1) show in the context of Hong Kong, and as other writers such as Pennycook (1994) demonstrate at a global level, the explanation for the status of English in the world today is hardly a linguistic one. All the same, it's worth bearing in mind that although the smug triumphalism of the imperial period concerning the supposed superiority of English is found much less frequently nowadays, variations on a belief that the language has intrinsic qualities of resources or expression which stand it above other languages are still surprisingly common. Such supposed 'advantages' are said either to be helpful in explaining the spread of English and/or to be one of the benefits of knowing the language (these are sometimes referred to as the 'language of Shakespeare' types of argument), despite the fact that they are easily and consistently refuted by linguists (see, for example, Holborow 1999: Chapter 3).

A more commonly voiced view nowadays is that English is a means of fostering international understanding and 'bringing the world together'. However, this 'detribalisation' argument is based on the dual misconception that the linguistic 'capital' of English has spread around the world in an even and equitable way, which it clearly hasn't, and that there is a simple causal relationship between linguistic diversity and conflict. Essentially, the problem is seen as being diversity itself rather than the combination of negative attitudes towards diversity (racism, bigotry, etc.) and issues of inequality and exploitation. One conspicuous example of the weakness of the 'detribalisation' argument is the well-documented fact that in the case of post-colonial Africa there is, as Phillipson puts it, 'no causal relationship between lack of ability to speak African languages and the presence or absence of "tribalism"' (1992: 281) (see also Phillipson and Skutnabb-Kangas 1995).

While arguments of the type described above for the intrinsic or extrinsic value of English are unconvincing, its cultural and socio-economic appeal cannot be simply explained away in terms of crude notions of **linguistic imperialism**, as Morrison and Lui show (see also Holborow 1999: Chapter 3 for a critique of Phillipson's model based on this concept). All the same, it's certainly true that English, like any other language, can be used to further the interests of ruling minorities and there are numerous examples of precisely this to be found in the post-independence contexts of the territories which belonged to the British Empire (see Phillipson 1992: Chapter 5 for a discussion of specific examples). In addition to and linked to directly political effects of this kind, the promotion of English can also have severely detrimental educational and psychological effects, which may include the **subtractive bilingualism** and lack of appropriate knowledge of core curricular subjects described by Morrison and Lui, as well as severe cultural disenfranchisement and related problems connected with **ethnolinguistic identity** and other factors related to self-esteem.

We shall now move on to look at a rather different example of controversy over the position of English, namely, that of the highly linguistically diverse setting of the USA.

'ENGLISH ONLY'? ENGLISH IN THE USA

'Why in the world anyone in America is allowing another language (other than English) to be his first ... I don't know.' (Quotation attributed to Margaret Thatcher and prominently displayed on the web site of the organisation 'U.S. English' in early 2002)

What is the promotion of English really about?

Reading 5.2 is an extract from Ronald Schmidt Sr.'s book, *Language Policy and Identity Politics in the United States*. It's included here in order to highlight further the extent to which debates about the status of languages in particular societies, in this case English in the USA, are very much influenced and often dominated by considerations of identity, ethnicity, class and 'race' and, by implication, power – see also the discussions of ebonics and of 'white' English in Chapter 4. It's important to bear in mind that, as Schmidt indicates, these categories, although enormously influential, are complex and in many ways highly subjective. Ethnic identities, for example, are multifaceted, the features which define them for people can change over time (see Schmidt's example of religious affiliation) and language is often, although not always, the single most important marker of ethnic difference – hence the term 'ethnolinguistic identity'. As writers such as Amado Padilla have pointed out, perceptions of one's own and others' ethnicity is closely linked to socialisation processes and this means that, as well as language often being a key factor in constituting ethnicity, 'the language of socialization becomes part of the core of ethnicity and is highly valued as a critical element in the meaning of identifying oneself as a member of an ethnic group' (1999: 115–16). Similarly, the concept of 'race' is based on 'commonsense' types of categorisation which are socially and ideologically constructed rather than having any basis in some 'objective' reality (which, as Schmidt emphasises in Reading 5.2, does not prevent them from having very real social and socio-economic consequences).

The background to the 'English only' lobby

All of this is very important in current debates about the role of English and other languages in US society, which in recent years have tended to focus on the demands and the ideology of the powerful 'English Only' or 'official English' lobby. The political impetus to promote English in the US has a long history and its supposed linguistic opponents have changed according to circumstances; both German and French, for example, have been targeted by 'English Only' advocates in earlier periods (see, for example, Bourhis and Marshall 1999). However, when in 1981 a Republican senator in California named Hayakawa proposed an English Language Amendment to the US Constitution there was no doubt that the language clearly in the sights of his attack was Spanish. Hayakawa's initiative was designed both to encourage and harness a growing perception that, in some areas of the country at least, the dominance of English was under threat from Spanish. The specific arguments which he put forward focused more on the ideas that English is or should be the unifying 'glue' of American society, that it is the 'task' of immigrants to learn English and that 'only by learning English can an immigrant participate in our democracy' (quoted in Bourhis and Marshall 1999: 248), a clear appeal to the sorts of nativist and ethno-ascriptive ideologies described in the extract by Schmidt. Such arguments are of course still highly topical in many countries, not least the UK. *The Guardian* newspaper of 7 February 2002, for example, began an article as follows:

> People wanting to become UK citizens will have to take compulsory English language tests and an exam on the ways of British life, the home secretary, David Blunkett, announced today.
> Immigrants will also face on oath or 'citizen's pledge' to help them embrace British values, laws and customs.

Hayakawa's proposed amendment to make English the official language of the USA, which was unsuccessful, was followed by a sustained campaign by the organisation 'US English' of similar proposals at both Congressional and state level, some of which had significant effects such as the weakening or ending of bilingual education programmes in some states, notably California. Interestingly, the welter of such legislative initiatives took place at exactly the same time that Congress was passing legislation designed supposedly to protect Native American languages (for example, in 1990 and 1992), leaving legislators to 'find a compromise between those two essentially contradictory objectives' (Kaplan and Baldauf Jr. 1997: 27). This is perhaps a telling sign of how attitudes towards ethnolinguistic 'minorities' can be swayed by the extent to which such 'minorities' are perceived to be a threat to more powerful groups at a given time. 'US English', which by 1999 claimed over 1.3 million members (Schmidt 2000: 31) managed successfully to coordinate the introduction of legislation in the 1980s making English the official language of California, Arizona, Colorado and Texas, all states with relatively significant linguistic 'minorities'. However, what's perhaps more striking is that this was increased to a total of more than 20 states in the course of the 1990s (Schmidt 2000: 29), few of which in fact have either a recent history of immigration or any sizeable 'non-home English' groups. On this basis Crawford contends that ' "English Only" flows from feelings of insecurity. Now that demographic changes of all kinds – greater mobility, non-traditional families, mass culture – are disrupting Americans' sense of community, there is a renewed search for unifying institutions' (quoted in McKay 1997: 251).

How threatened is English?

In the appeal of 'English Only', however implicitly, to the types of ideology described by Schmidt, it's hardly surprising that some of the relevant facts get lost, particularly regarding the key assumption that English is increasingly endangered by other languages, especially Spanish. McKay (1997) points out that while data collected by the US Census and Current Population Survey are subject to the same potential for inaccuracy as other census mechanisms they do produce results which can be taken to be a reasonably accurate picture of broad trends. It's certainly true that of those residents of the USA who speak a language other than English at home, by far the greatest proportion are speakers of Spanish and this proportion grew significantly in the period 1980–90 (from 48% to 54%). But, as McKay shows, it's also the case that in 1990 only 13 per cent of the population of the country overall fell into the 'home language other than English' category. Furthermore, although the dogma of the 'English Only' lobby has tended to focus on the issue of 'foreigners', in fact more than half of the 13 per cent of the population in question had been born in the US and less than a quarter of them had entered the country in the preceding ten years, a statistic which obviously begs the question of the definition of 'foreigner' being used. Similarly, the racism and fear behind the 'English Only' claim that immigration into the US has reached historically unprecedented levels is shown to be based on supposition and innuendo rather than fact – in reality immigrants constituted approximately 3.6 per cent of the population in the 1990s compared with between 5 per cent and up to nearly 10 per cent in the period 1860–1920.

Clearly English is far from being threatened in numerical terms. McKay goes on to point out that another myth propagated by the same lobby is the idea that 'immigrants' do not want to learn English. In fact, not only are the majority of non-home English speakers not 'immigrants', as already noted, but only 5.8 per cent of those who belong to linguistic minorities in the US (some of whom speak indigenous American languages) are unable to speak English. In fact McKay cites one study which showed clearly a problem of lack of teaching capacity rather than a lack of learner motivation. Given the linguistic 'capital' enjoyed by English in the US it would be strange indeed if there were widespread reluctance to learn the language. Nevertheless, in a clear current parallel with racist discourse in the Western European context, a belief to the contrary remains influential in a variety of sectors of US society. As McKay puts it, 'what may be fueling "English Only" sentiments are issues of race and ethnicity' (1997: 248). Studies such as that of Huddy and Sears (1990) tend to support this view – their research suggests that opposition towards bilingual education tends to be strongest among home-language English American citizens who demonstrate generally unfavourable attitudes towards 'immigrants' and speakers of languages other than English. Overall it seems quite clear that movements such as 'English Only' are not mainly about language itself at all, but rather about language as a token of power in the context of socio-economic and ethnolinguistic power struggles in the USA. As Padilla says:

> The fact of the matter is that ethnicity and language would not be an issue in the United States if groups such as Hispanics maintained their lowly status and did not challenge the status quo of prejudice and discrimination by calling for fair treatment in education, employment and housing as

mandated by civil rights legislation. It is when challenges to the status quo are presented to the dominant social (ethnic) group by lower status groups that ethnic competition and rivalry begin. It is this ecological constraint then that gives meaning to ethnicity. (1999: 117)

We have seen then that in the USA, as in many other places, multilingualism is often viewed as a threat, at least when it's convenient for those who hold power to see it as such. For this reason it tends to be portrayed by vested interests as being, among other things, cognitively, politically and culturally undesirable. Lobbies such as the 'English Plus' movement, set up in the USA in part to counter the successes of 'English Only', have attempted to switch the focus of the public debate towards a view which sees bilingualism more as a resource than a problem. This difference in perspective is crucial as it emphasises how uninformed criticism of individual and societal multilingualism tends to be composed of little more than prejudice and xenophobia, particularly as a wealth of research evidence exists which demonstrates the potential value of multi-lingualism to both the individual and society (see, for example, Baetens Beard-smore 1986; Baker 2001).

Clearly, however, any serious attempt, at local, national or global level, to slow the current trend whereby so many languages are disappearing forever needs systematic ways of assessing the strengths and weaknesses of a given language in a particular place at a particular time and of establishing how to safeguard linguistic diversity in a given society. In this sense it's perhaps ironic that so much energy and so many resources seem to be devoted to the 'protection' of English when this is clearly the most powerful language in the world, in an era when languages are vanishing around us all the time. The issues of bilingualism as a resource and the protection of languages bring us to language policy and language planning, the topic of the next section.

LANGUAGE POLICY AND LANGUAGE PLANNING

Language policy and planning are usually seen as a sub-discipline of the sociology of language and many introductory sociolinguistics textbooks contain definitions and descriptions of this field. Readers for whom 'language planning and policy' are new terms should see, for example, Mesthrie et al. 2000: Chapter 12, for an overview. The concerns of language planning and policy can be summarised briefly as follows, following Haugen's (1966 and Haugen, McClare and Thomson 1987) classic model:

1. Selection: the process of choosing languages to fulfil particular roles, especially in key areas such as education and the infrastructure of the society. For example, the choice of the 'standard' variety of a language as the one to be used in the written work of school pupils.
2. Codification: identification (and legislation on) the grammatical, lexical, etc. characteristics of that variety.

3. Implementation. The process of establishing, by legal and/or persuasive means, the particular variety in its roles and the production of necessary resources, for example, textbooks, etc.
4. Elaboration. The development of a chosen variety to deal with new technology and concepts, using strategies such as the creation of neologisms.

Reading 5.3 is an extract from an article entitled 'Language policy, language education, language rights: indigenous, immigrant, and international perspectives'. It emphasises the importance for language planning and policy considerations of the sociolinguistic distinction between 'minority' languages which are indigenous and those belonging to immigrant communities. In addition to this, in discussing the study of the acquisition of English by female Cambodian refugees in the USA, the author emphasises the crucial roles of psychological and cultural factors in this process and the fact that socioculturally imperialistic approaches in second-language teaching programmes tend to be unhelpful and counterproductive. Another reason for including this article is that it encourages the reader to reflect on the factors which affect the future of threatened languages and the circumstances in which their fortunes might improve.

The scale of the problem

As well as a passionate defender of threatened languages, Hornberger is perhaps an optimist. In her article she makes claims such as that there is 'consistent and compelling evidence that language policy and language education serve as vehicles for promoting the vitality, versatility and stability' of the languages which she discusses. This repetition, which is accompanied by quotations of act-of-faith declarations such as 'There is a way out' and 'How can it be hopeless when there is so much hope?' suggest that the optimistic tone of the article is in itself largely an act of faith. In one sense this is perfectly appropriate to discussions of language survival as, ultimately, languages disappear because their speakers take a decision to stop using them. They may do so in situations of extreme cultural or even physical coercion but the final nail in the coffin of a given language remains the point at which intergenerational transmission of a language by parents to their children ceases, hence the importance of the types of quotations cited above. Nevertheless, although Hornberger does not set out to obscure or underplay the difficulties and challenges facing threatened languages, it's worth considering that her optimism is arguably at odds with the weight of evidence which she discusses. Almost all of the examples that she gives which involve any type of quantification are in fact of attrition and decline rather than maintenance or revival. The one exception is that of Maori-medium education, although even here the figures deal with pre-school and school enrolments which in itself tells us little about even acquisition and competence, let alone use. A common problem in sociolinguistics is of course assessing

accurately whether and how a language is in decline, but the fact remains t'
the evidence which Hornberger claims supports her position is difficult to find
in the article. Indeed, she describes a number of cases of clear decline and '
acknowledges earlier in the article that even Quechua, with over 10 million
speakers, is under serious threat. The crucial question, then, for those of us who
share Hornberger's view that linguistic diversity is an invaluable aspect of the
cultural resources of the human race, is why such diversity appears to be in
continuing decline rather than flourishing. Obviously, there's no simple answer
to the question as the variables are complex and multifaceted. Furthermore, as
Hornberger argues, while theorisation of the issues is essential, assessment of
any particular situation requires an in-depth understanding of its particular,
often unique, characteristics. The 'force of history' that she refers to is not for
most observers a uniform one. What is certainly the case, however, is that issues
of power are at the heart of these matters. No analysis or explanation of the
sociolinguistic realities of, for example, Quechua could possibly ignore the
dynamics in the Andean countries in which it is spoken, of the relationships
between language and social class, ethnicity, the state and other groups who
understand the inextricable nature of language and power and have an interest
in exerting influence. As Kaplan and Baldauf put it in discussing the problems of
professional language planners:

> Those interested in working in language planning may find themselves
> under significant pressure to produce policies and programs, grounded
> not on the best available theoretical and practical knowledge about the
> issues, but based solely on agency preconceptions of what is politically or
> economically feasible. (1997: 210)

Macro and micro approaches

Hornberger's article is of interest also because it highlights on the one hand
'macro' issues of ideology and policy, which is what most of this chapter has
been about so far, but also more **micro** approaches. Hornberger emphasises the
value of **ethnographic** perspectives and methods in understanding language
issues from the point of view of those directly affected (such as the Cambodian
women in the study that she describes). In addition to this, she also draws
attention (453) to the significance of the **micro-interactionist** approach in
research which investigates the symbolic meanings of languages for their users
and the implications of these for planners and policy makers. A study carried
out using this type of approach is the topic of the final reading in this chapter.

A CASE STUDY: CATALAN IN CATALONIA

Joan Pujolar's book *Gender, Heteroglossia and Power: A Sociolinguistic Study
of Youth Culture*, from which Reading 5.4 is taken, is an intriguing exploration
of how the complexities of language choice and use relate to issues of gender,
ethnicity, class and power. The focus of Pujolar's study is the ways in which two

groups of young people use Spanish and Catalan in the bilingual city of Barcelona.

The historical background

For readers who know little about the history and contemporary characteristics of Catalonia and the Catalan language, these are summarised in a variety of books (for example, Pujolar 2000 [from which Reading 5.4 is taken]; Woolard 1989; Hoffmann 1991). However, we will now provide a few essential facts in order to contextualise Pujolar's work.

Catalonia, whose capital is Barcelona, is a semi-autonomous region in north-east Spain. Catalan, a member of the Romance family of languages, has much in common with both French and Spanish. It also has a long history of being put under great pressure by the Spanish and the Spanish state. This was particularly true from about the beginning of the eighteenth century and especially from the end of the Spanish civil war in 1939 up to 1975, during which time General Franco's dictatorship set out with a vengeance to eradicate the languages other than Spanish spoken within the boundaries of the Spanish state.

Nevertheless, although it emerged from nearly three centuries of repression severely debilitated, the language managed to survive and today it is usually estimated to have between six and nine million speakers. This is a far greater number than any of the other languages in western Europe which do not have the status of the (main) official language of a nation state, and the successful survival of Catalan is one of the reasons why it has attracted a lot of interest from sociolinguists and others in the past few decades. The Catalans did not stop speaking Catalan en masse, in the way that speakers of many other repressed and stigmatised languages did during the process of consolidation of nation states in Europe. On the contrary, even in the most extreme years of the Franco regime, when Catalan had virtually no public profile and the level of repression was so great that parents were prohibited from baptising their children with Catalan names, very few families made the crucial, and often final, step of switching from using the stigmatised language (Catalan) with their children to using the dominant one (Spanish). The reasons for this unusual case of survival have been the subject of much interest and debate, but most researchers agree that it was partly to do with the emergence of a Catalan industrial bourgeoisie in the nineteenth century who gradually came to see their class interests as favoured by both cultural and also politico-linguistic Catalan nationalism.

The Franco regime certainly threatened and weakened Catalan, but it can also be argued that the sheer crudeness of the repression did much to strengthen the resolve of many Catalans to maintain and promote their language. A factor which it is sometimes argued has been an even greater threat to Catalan in the longer term and which is part of the essential background of Pujolar's work, however, is that of the effects of migration during the same period. Catalonia's economic success, combined with an extraordinary degree of neglect of some of

Spain's poorer regions by the Franco regime, led between the 1950s and the 1970s to massive migration of poor Spanish speakers to Catalonia, mainly from the southern regions of Andalusia and Murcia, and on a scale which completely transformed the ethnolinguistic composition of Catalonia. One result of this was that after Franco's death, when pro-Catalan language policies came to be implemented in the early 1980s, the issue was no longer simply the reversal of the damage of the Franco years and beyond, which had resulted for example in widespread illiteracy in Catalan among Catalans. As well as this, there was now the fact that a significant proportion of the population were first- or second-generation immigrants who might not necessarily see a role for themselves in the re-establishment of Catalan as the 'language of the (Catalan) nation'. This was especially true in industrial areas such as Barcelona. As Pujolar describes in other parts of his book, this produced an unusual state of affairs. In effect the case of Catalonia became that of a partially bilingual, prosperous, peripheral region (or nation) within the Spanish state, in which the group whose first language is not that of the state (the Catalans) hold the socioeconomic power balance over an almost equally large 'outgroup' of quasi-immigrants and their descendants (the first-language Spanish speakers). As Pujolar describes, this latter group are traditionally of low social status but at the same time their language, Spanish, is the only official language of the whole state of which Catalonia is a part (that is, Spain) and is therefore the language of, for example, political, administrative and military power at national level. Not surprisingly, this has created a situation in Catalonia in which, at the level of everyday interaction, who speaks which language to whom and for what purposes is a complex and highly politicised issue.

The limits of language planning and policy

One of Pujolar's starting points was the now generally recognised fact that language planning and language policy initiatives implemented in Catalonia since it acquired the status of an 'autonomous region' in 1979 have not been as successful as some of their proponents would have liked them to be. In the aftermath of the Franco regime, the languages of Spain other than Spanish had for many people become powerful symbols of resistance to Franco's brutal totalitarianism. In this climate there was a widespread feeling that it was both proper and necessary that Catalan should replace Spanish as the first language of Catalonia as quickly as possible, not just in the public and administrative arenas but at the level of day-to-day interaction too. For many sociolinguists, particularly those in the 'periphery' tradition referred to in the introduction to this book, one of the key factors was the linguistic behaviour of the 'immigrants' from other parts of Spain, as the following quote suggests: 'Unless integration takes place, Catalonia will lose its national identity within a generation' (Termes 1984: 188, author's translation).

In this sense 'integration' was often taken to mean a partial, if not wholesale, switch of language loyalty – the adoption of Catalan as one's main or only language. With hindsight, it is not too much of an exaggeration to say that the powerful combination of a sense of urgency and, perhaps, a feeling of right-eousness led to a tendency to avoid focusing on other aspects of the nature of language use in bilingual societies which might influence the process of what is often referred to as the 'normalisation' of Catalan. In any event, by the time that Pujolar began his research in the early 1990s it was clearly the case, more than twenty years after Franco's death, that large numbers of young as well as older people in Catalonia were using Spanish as their dominant language of everyday interaction. Pujolar's interest was in exploring why this was the case.

The Rambleros and the Trepas: youth, gender and ethnicity in Barcelona
Pujolar was guided by the intuition that all language use is ideologically **marked** and that the implications of this fact might prove useful in explaining more about people's language choices and the purposes for which they used Catalan and Spanish. He set out to do so through examining closely actual language use, particularly the voices and characters dramatised in his informants' interac-tions, as he was convinced that 'Such an approach may provide unique insights that may not be accessible by just asking fuzzy or untactful questions to informants on attitudes and perceived connotations' (Pujolar 2000: 175–6). In this way the core of his methodology was close analysis of actual language use and his book contains almost 100 extracts of mainly spontaneous speech of the type seen in the examples in the reading.

In order to obtain the data, Pujolar used an ethnographic approach which involved mainly the technique of **participant observation**, supplemented by group discussions and interviews. His respondents were two groups of young people, the *Rambleros* and the *Trepas*. The *Rambleros* were a closely knit group of six women and five men who lived in a working-class neighbourhood on the outskirts of Barcelona. The members of the group used Spanish almost exclu-sively among themselves although some of them made some use of Catalan at work and/or in the family environment. The *Trepas* were based in a marginally less disadvantaged neighbourhood than the *Rambleros* and their group was centred around a training school for young unemployed people with which most of them were involved. There were around fourteen members of the *Trepas*, but the group had a less stable composition than the *Rambleros*. Some of the *Trepas* had Catalan as their first language and the group's language use was characterised by a complex mixture of Spanish and Catalan.

Pujolar spent several months 'hanging around' with both groups during their leisure activities, which were centred mainly around pubs, bars, concerts and discos. He deliberately set out to create a close relationship with their members, rather than to maintain a supposedly 'scientific' detachment, so that he could gradually develop as clear a picture as possible of how they went about constructing their own social world, particularly through language. He was convinced that each of the two groups 'saw each language and language variety as associated with particular situations, social groups and ways of thinking and acting' (2000: 128). He felt that this could tell him a lot about what motivated the participants to use a particular language on a particular occasion and that to understand this it was necessary to treat the groups' culture on their own terms – to explore how their language behaviour made sense to the users themselves.

The focus of the research was threefold and relates centrally to some of the main concerns of this book, namely, language and youth, gender and other aspects of identity. Pujolar was interested in exploring three central issues:

- the reasons why youth cultures are sometimes characterised by high-risk behaviour such as hard drug use, dangerous driving and aggressive behaviour
- the ways in which gender relations among young people help to reproduce inequalities between the sexes
- the reasons for the reluctance of some young people in Barcelona to use Catalan.

For this purpose, he brought to bear a rich mix of theoretical perspectives from a variety of disciplines in order to examine in detail how language choice and use relates to fundamental questions about identity, power and culture. In order to do this, he made use of work from a variety of traditions, in particular critical discourse analysis and sociolinguistics.

As Pujolar's research progressed, some key insights arose, related to particular theoretical concepts. These are closely connected to some of the main themes of this book and we will now summarise briefly two of the most important ones.

1. Language use is more complicated than some of the earlier work on bilingualism suggested. People do not simply use one language or another, or one style or another, according to the situation or 'domain' in which they find themselves.

This had already been demonstrated some time ago by studies such as that of Susan Gal, referred to in the introduction to this book. Following on from Gal's later work (for example, 1989), Pujolar's point is that far from merely responding to a particular context, speakers *create* and *constitute* identities, roles, power relationships and indeed situations through the linguistic strategies which they use.

In this respect, he draws on the Russian linguist Mikhail Bakhtin's concept of **heteroglossia**. This is the idea that all languages are stratified into particular **speech genres**. These genres are appropriated and used by speakers in their negotiation of their own and others' identities. In this sense, for Bakhtin, all language use is **dialogical**. This means that everything that we say necessarily relates to previous utterances and anticipates future ones:

> Each utterance is filled with echoes and reverberations of other utterances to which it is related by the communality of the sphere of speech communication.

... Each utterance refutes, affirms, supplements, and relies on the others, presupposes them to be known. (Bakhtin 1986: 9; quoted in Pujolar 2000: 30)

Language use in this sense is fundamentally about voices and, as Reading 5.4 describes, a basic discoursal strategy that people employ is to refer to and appropriate a variety of voices relevant to their lives. In the first sample of data, for example, Ayats's ironical use of 'school teacher' language is a case of **double voicing** – he uses the voice of another person (a 'stereotypical' teacher) for his own expressive purposes. There are, of course, clear links here with the discussion of Les Back's work in Chapter 4.

For Pujolar, these concepts are essential to explaining *how* we go about constructing reality through language in a number of areas related to identity, gender being central among these. Pujolar quickly arrived at the conclusion in his research that expression and negotiation of gender identity was a central element in accounting for the ways in which the two groups used language. As our chapter on language and gender shows, ambiguity and ambivalence are essential concepts in avoiding simplistic description and analysis. This view is very much taken up by Pujolar in a Bakhtinian mode through the concept of **polyvalence,** the idea that the meaning of an utterance is never predetermined in advance – its voices are negotiable. In this respect, polyvalence is also a resource which allows what is another important concept for Pujolar and which has already arisen in this book – the possibility of resistance through strategies of language use. His description in Reading 5.4 of Clara's use of switching between Spanish and Catalan is a good example of how individuals draw on polyvalence to negotiate identity and relationships.

2.   Our dialogical use of language is operationalised, that is, put into practice, partly through the use of a number of techniques identified in particular in the work of sociologists such as Erving Goffman.

Goffman was sometimes referred to as a 'microsociologist' because, anticipating the interests of researchers such as Pujolar, his focus was the ways in which the 'macro' structures and institutions of society affect the manner in which people present and negotiate their identities in the routine interaction of day-to-day life. Some of his key concepts are used extensively in Pujolar's work. Goffman sees theatrical performance as at the heart of interaction (how aware people are generally of their theatricality is a question not dealt with by Pujolar). According to Goffman, we use **frames** of various types in order to make sense of events in our daily lives and these tell us, for example, whether we should interpret something which happens as real or as 'a joke, or a dream, or an accident, or a mistake, or a misunderstanding, or a deception, or a theatrical performance, and so forth' (Goffman 1974: 10, quoted in Pujolar 2000: 34). Frames can be **keyed,** that is, they can be transformed and used as a resource to indicate what is taking place in a particular situation; for example, in play activities where we want the other person to understand that what we are saying is somehow 'not serious'. In the reading this is why Pujolar describes the *Rambleros'* use of Catalan in greetings and organisational talk as a 'keyed frame' activity.

Overall this discussion has brought us back to some of the central concepts developed in this book. Pujolar's research reminds us that power is pervasive in questions of language and in ways which are sometimes but not always obvious to its users, that language creates as well as reflecting our social worlds and that it is fundamental to crucial aspects of identity such as gender, ethnicity and age. Perhaps most importantly, and as we've set out to illustrate in this book, it also emphasises that language is both a site and a tool of struggle – that people are not automata who blindly use particular language varieties in given ways. Linguistic contestation, in all its different and many forms, clearly plays a crucial role in the negotiation of identity, in the articulation of power and in the shaping of our modern world.

ACTIVITIES

- Considering the points made in Reading 5.1 about language in Hong Kong and **linguistic capital,** assess and compare the amounts of linguistic capital which the language varieties used in your own situation have. Discuss with other students and/or find out what people in your local community think and see whether you can agree on the reasons for the amount of 'capital' which each variety has. Consider also the types of 'voices', or polyvalence, which different languages, dialects or styles are typically associated with in your community.

- 'It is extremely difficult for a society to practise free flow of media and enjoy a national culture at the same time – unless it happens to be the United States of America' (Smith 1980: 53, quoted in Pennycook 1994: 38).
  Consider the above quotation in the light of what you know about the phenomenon of 'English as a world language'. Do you agree that the dominance of English and the USA is so great that a 'free flow of media' is incompatible with a 'national culture' for all other countries? If so, what are the implications of this?

- Immigrants will be made to learn English so they can feel more British under radical government plans announced yesterday. Home Secretary David Blunkett warned that it was time that ethnic minorities adopted British 'norms of acceptability' following last summer's race riots. (*Daily Express* 10 December 2001)

  > The Home Office defended remarks by David Blunkett today that immigrants should speak English in their homes. The home secretary, in an essay for *Reclaiming Britishness,* a book published today, said speaking English at home would help immigrants 'overcome the schizophrenia which bedevils intergenerational relationships . . . speaking

English enables parents to converse with their children in English, as well as their historic mothertongue, at home and to participate in wider modern culture ... In as many as 30% of Asian British households, according to a recent citizenship survey, English is not spoken at home'. (*Guardian* 16 September 2002)

What sort of assumptions about connections between factors such as language, identity, community, culture and conflict underlie the comments attributed to the Home Secretary here? How might a policy of 'making immigrants learn English', for use outside and/or inside the home, be implemented and what would be its likely effects?

READINGS

Reading 5.1
Introduction: ideology and linguistic imperialism

In 1971 Bernstein wrote that 'how a society selects, classifies, distributes, transmits and evaluates the educational knowledge it considers to be public, reflects both the distribution of power and the principles of social control' (p. 47). This was, perhaps, a prescient remark for the medium of instruction (MOI) issue in Hong Kong, which carries strong ideological overtones. Ideology here is taken to be the values of dominant groups in society which permeate (maybe consensually) the social structure, to the advantage of the already dominant groups and to the disadvantage of the already disadvantaged (Eagleton, 1991: 29–30).

In a linguistic turn, Habermas's early work (1970a, 1970b) regarded ideology as 'systematically distorted communication' and the 'suppression of generalizable interests' (Habermas, 1976: 113), where structural features in communities (including language communities) and societies operate to the advantage of the dominant and the disadvantage of subordinate groups. Ideology and communication are closely coupled; the MOI issue in Hong Kong is bound up with issues of power, domination, legitimacy and social stratification. Power, through ideology, is omnipresent in language; language is a principal means for the operation of power (Fairclough, 1989: 2). Indeed, adopting Gramsci's notion of hegemony (domination by consent of all parties, including the dominated), he suggests (Fairclough, 1989: 4) that language is intimately involved in the manufacture of ideological consent.

That ideology operates in and through communication is, by no means, a novel idea. At its limits, Phillipson's theory of linguistic imperialism (1992, 1998) suggests that language – particularly English – is the means *par excellence* for economic and political domination by the West. Boyle (1997: 169) comments that 'English, under the innocuous guise of a helpful language for

From: Keith Morrison and Icy Lui (2000), 'Ideology, linguistic capital and the medium of instruction in Hong Kong', *Journal of Multilingual and Multicultural Development*, 21: 6, 471–86.

business and travel, has become a potent weapon for cultural and economic domination'. Phillipson (1998: 104), in developing his view of linguistic imperialism, uses Skuttnab-Kangas's definition of *linguicism* as ideologies and practices which legitimate and reproduce asymmetries of power and resources (physical and immaterial) between groups 'which are defined on the basis of language' (Skuttnab-Kangas, 1988: 13), and argues that the dominance and promotion of English are a form of linguicism.

Phillipson's views are not without their critics. Davies (1996: 495) provides a withering critique of Phillipson's thesis, arguing that, amongst other aspects, it (1) is naive; (2) focuses on negative rather positive aspects of ideology; (3) is ahistorical and non-dynamic. Linguistic imperialism is also limited where it provides an almost monocausal account of the complex use of English in societies across the world. Similarly Cherrington (forthcoming) suggests that the notion of linguistic imperialism leaves little room for deliberate, free choice of language in former colonised countries. Notions of linguicism and linguistic imperialism understate agency, rendering participants cultural dupes or passive puppets of an ideological order, or cogs in a mechanistic universe (see also Eagleton, 1991; Giroux, 1983). As Davies (1996: 488) remarks, Phillipson's thesis 'leaves no room for disagreement'.

People seek and use English, not because they are ideological stooges or unenlightened victims of ideological and cultural hegemony, but, as this paper argues, for a variety of reasons; for example, economic and political, to achieve necessary fluency in a world-wide lingua franca, and, thereby, to survive in a world-wide market and diverse culture (see also Rassool, 1998: 89–90). English is not a necessary passport to success, but, like other non-ideological passports, it helps.

This paper suggests that linguistic imperialism might be a useful concept in denoting the language situation in the earlier days of the colonial administration of Hong Kong, but it provides an inadequate account of the role of English in its more recent and post-colonial situation. In so doing, this paper attempts to situate the notion of linguistic imperialism, to show where it might be a useful analytical tool, and to show the limits of that utility.

This is not to suggest, of course, that the concept of linguistic imperialism could ever entirely account for the complexity of the MOI issue in Hong Kong; the situation is much more multi-layered, complicated and multi-factorial than this. To assert that MOI policies and practices in Hong Kong are – or ever were – somehow simply a manifestation of linguistic imperialism is to construct a 'straw man', as linguistic imperialism is unable to account for the multiple motives, purposes, uses and issues in the MOI issue in Hong Kong. Linguistic imperialism cannot provide a full explanation for English as the MOI in Hong Kong, as 'Hong Kong Chinese have always *wanted* English' (Boyle (1997: 176) (his italics). In this sense linguistic imperialism concerns the *intention* to dominate, which does not fit the recent or contemporary situation of English in Hong Kong. Rather, the construct may have some heuristic value in providing a partial historical explanation for certain important aspects of the MOI issue in Hong Kong, and it is this which the paper explores.

In discussing the contemporary situation of English as the MOI in Hong Kong, this paper suggests that a more useful account is provided by the notion of 'linguistic capital'. This is not to suggest that the twin notions of 'linguistic imperialism' and 'linguistic capital' are discrete, mutually exclusive or polar opposites to each other; that is a false dichotomy. Linguistic imperialism embraces aspects of linguistic capital and linguistic capital owes some of its origins and contemporary power to linguistic imperialism. Nor can they, separately or together, provide a total analysis of the MOI issue in Hong Kong. Rather, the issue is one of emphasis and comprehensiveness: the notion of linguistic capital may possess more comprehensive explanatory potential of the recent and contemporary MOI issue. If this is so, then the concept of linguistic imperialism might apply only in uncomplicated situations or early stages of a country's colonial development, and linguistic capital might be more apposite in accounting for complex situations. This is not to suggest that linguistic capital alone will provide a complete account of the MOI issue in Hong Kong; rather it might simply catch more of the relevant issues than linguistic imperialism.

The Linguistic Capital Thesis

The notion of 'linguistic capital' is related to Bourdieu's view of cultural capital (Bourdieu, 1976, 1997; Bourdieu & Passeron, 1990). In educational terms the cultural capital thesis argues that some students possess the cultural background ('habitus') and dispositions (e.g. a positive attitude to school, motivation, parental support, social advantage, ease in dealing with authority, high culture, linguistic facility) so that when they meet school knowledge they can engage it comfortably and take advantage of it (Morrison, 1995: 438). This advantages the life chances of those who already possess cultural capital, as their uptake of education is high. Those with less of the valued cultural capital have a lower uptake of the same school knowledge as it is culturally alien to them and, thereby, their life chances are reduced. Thus social stratification and patterns of domination and subordination, are *reproduced*, albeit by a school system benignly intended to provide equal opportunity to all. Schools also *produce* cultural capital, and parents deliberately send their children to certain schools in the pursuit of cultural capital to enhance their life chances.

The same holds true for linguistic capital. Linguistic capital can be defined as fluency in, and comfort with, a high-status, world-wide language which is used by groups who possess economic, social, cultural and political power and status in local and global society. The linguistic capital thesis, then, states that students who possess, have access to, or develop linguistic capital, thereby have access to better life chances. Schools which offer access to a high-status language, in effect, offer better life chances for those who can take up that language; the offer is open to all, though only a small sector possess the linguistic (or its related economic, social and cultural) capital to be able to take advantage of it. Those without linguistic capital (present before school or acquired during school), have fewer opportunities for such enhanced life chances. Schools, through their MOI, are implicated in the reproduction and production of advantage in society; linguistic capital is both the medium and outcome of the pursuit of enhanced life chances.

It is a truism that parents in Hong Kong send their children to English medium of instruction (EMI) schools in the pursuit of enhanced life chances for them in a market-driven society that is part of the world economy. Linguistic capital, like other forms of capital (e.g. cultural, human, economic, political) has exchange value in a market economy. The issue is less about being part of a linguistically imperialist order and more about the real, pragmatic world, and Hong Kong thrives on pragmatism.

It is also commonplace, of course, to suggest that English in Hong Kong is one passport, amongst many, to success in Hong Kong (e.g. Boyle, 1997), and that English has been instrumental in the prosperity of Hong Kong. English provides entry into lucrative careers in an increasingly competitive jobs market (at a time when unemployment is relatively high in Hong Kong). It does this, Boyle suggests, without risking loss of the Chinese culture and language. English can be regarded as the neutral language of international trade and markets, economics, technology, science, travel and tourism (Pennycook, 1994, forthcoming; Cherrington, forthcoming). It provides access to cultural and economic capital; this ensures the economic survival of Hong Kong and its citizens, and, as Bourdieu (1997: 54) suggests, economic capital is at the root of *all* the other types of capital (his italics).

The language policy in Hong Kong was, and is, a deliberate action on the part of the ruling class (formerly the British administration and latterly the Chinese government respectively) to perpetuate its power in Hong Kong. In the early days considerably before 1997, the language policy was aligned with the notion of colonial domination. Since 1997, the language policy is part of the concern for restoration of the power and status of the Chinese government and the Chinese language in the community.

Linguistic Imperialism and Linguistic Capital in Hong Kong before 1984

English was the sole language of the British administration and legislature; in the 1970s and early 1980s English enjoyed a higher status than Chinese. To have a well-paid job or climb the social ladder required proficiency in English. As So (1984) observes, the infrastructural changes in Hong Kong in the post-1949 era consolidated the status of English. Before 1949, when the size of both the government and the English proportion of the private sector was small, the demand for bilinguals who could act as interpreters and facilitators of trade between the Chinese-speaking and English-speaking communities was limited, and the impact of English on the majority of the population in Hong Kong was slight (So, 1984).

After 1949, the colonial administration developed into the largest and predominant employer. The English proportion of the private sector also increased in size and dominance. Leading corporations like the Hong Kong and Shanghai Bank, the Hong Kong Telephone Company Ltd., the Swire Company Ltd. and the Jardine and Matheson companies were all English-managed and the people in charge spoke English. As Fishman et al. (1979) suggest, with the rapid growth of trade and the development of Hong Kong into an international manufacturing and financial centre, English became the predominant medium for trade. This, coupled with advances in science and technology, created many opportunities for educated workers who possessed a knowledge of English. Already, here, the notion of linguistic imperialism was being superseded by the notion of linguistic capital.

The British administration's concern was to use the schooling system to select a local elite to work for the colonial government so that these government officials who could speak good English would act as mediators between the British and the local population (Boyle, 1995). In this sense the notion of linguistic imperialism, in using English in the service of colonial domination, is perhaps useful. One can suggest that the language policy was ideological – imperialist – in that the British colonial power was striving for control of all aspects of trade and business. This reinforces Eagleton's (1991: 16) view of ideology as powered by motives that are bound up with the legitimation of dominatory interests. Knowledge of English was a prerequisite for joining the elite class in the colony. Those without English were screened out.

Before 1997, almost all interviews for government or large business corporations were conducted in English; applicants for Chinese departments of tertiary institutions were usually interviewed in English as well as in Chinese. Indeed senior academic positions were filled by expatriate British (Altbach, 2000: 16). The ability to speak and write English to serve the British colonial rule was also a means to climb the social ladder for a small minority of the local populace who possessed English. Linguistic capital developed out of linguistic imperialism.

Before 1997, the popularity of EMI schools was secure and was unrivalled by the Chinese medium of instruction (CMI) schools. Parents saw a rosy future for their children in EMI schools, as here they were provided with access to desirable, prestigious jobs in the managerial, administrative, financial and high-technology sectors; the seeds of linguistic capital are clear here. Such prestigious jobs required qualifications from universities, whose MOI was English, and a good pass in English was essential for university entrance.

The practice in Hong Kong exemplifies exactly Bourdieu's and Passeron's (1990: 73) view that students had (and still have) to achieve a successful level of acculturation with regard to language. Working-class students had to compete with privileged students who had made the most of their linguistic, cultural and economic capital (as Bourdieu (1997: 50, 83) remarks, economic capital can be converted into cultural capital and, indeed, linguistic capital). That this situation continues is suggested in Krashen's (1996) comment that middle-class students from a print-rich environment will continue to develop higher literacy levels than their working-class counterparts in their mother tongue, which advantages their learning of a second language.

The post-1945 economic transformation of Hong Kong contributed to the popularity of EMI schools because of the opportunity for upward mobility that they provided. In the 1980s the prestigious Carmel Secondary School changed from EMI to CMI and parents withdrew their children. As a result, it became a Band 5 (lower status) school instead of maintaining its former Band 1 position. (Hong Kong schools are classified into five bands on the basis of academic results, the 'top' 20 per cent of schools being Band 1, and the lowest 20 per cent Band 5).

It is simplistic, of course, to suggest that, by attending an EMI school, one was subscribing to the ideology of the supremacy of British culture. Economics rather than ideology were at stake, and students had to acquire the cultural and linguistic capital of the English language rather than the ideology of English domination. Hong Kong Chinese were not wishing to become anglicized, only to learn English for the rewards that it brought to them (not particularly to the British colonial administration). The provision of schools by the Christian church (the largest single provider of education in Hong Kong (Leung, 1999a)), was motivated by a concern for education rather than linguistic imperialism.

That said, the language policy helped to perpetuate British power in society at the expense of the quality of education of large sections of the local population. Despite the popularity of EMI schools, there were several problems caused by the fact that nearly 80 per cent of school children were educated in EMI schools. Still today, although Hong Kong is a diglossia in which both Chinese and English are used, the English and Chinese-speaking communities largely live apart. There is no need for most Hong Kong Chinese children to use English out of school. They attend their own concerts, watch locally-made films and Cantonese television, listen to local Chinese radio, and read Chinese newspapers. The typical Hong Kong child does not speak English at home, read English books, or watch English television (the City University of Hong Kong (1999) gives a figure of 97 per cent of children speaking Cantonese at home). English is confined to work, and children's exposure to English is largely confined to school.

Kvan (1969) pointed out that the preponderance of EMI schools posed serious learning problems for children. The Chinese University of Hong Kong in 1976 found that students could not express themselves in English and were at a loss for ideas when trying to communicate in Chinese or English. Cheng (1973) indicated that 73 per cent of students felt that using English as the MOI placed a huge strain on learning. The situation worsened in the 1980s and 1990s; with the continuous expansion of secondary education, more school-children were being educated using English and were often taught by teachers whose own English was poor.

The undesirable backwash effects of this practice were numerous, the most notable being the detrimental effect on students' development, especially those with less ability in English (Education Department, 1994). Kvan (1969) pointed out that students who were educated in CMI schools were more mature, responsive and interested in their environment than were their counterparts in EMI schools. In the classroom, both teachers and pupils were confronted with language problems, the students' pidgin impeded understanding and discouraged independent, deep learning.

The alarm that this caused amongst educationalists, representatives of business and legal professions was voiced by Fishman et al. (1979: 125), who argued that there was little justification for the widespread use of English, and none at all for its increase. Yet the use of English, however poor, *was* widespread, and, in this respect its predominance can be regarded as imperialist, in that the standard and quality of education for the majority of the local population was being deliberately neglected by the ruling class. The colonial education system produced a largely disempowered populace who simply could not find their voice in English and whose voice (Aronowitz & Giroux, 1986) in Chinese was denied. As a result, the British administration faced little challenge from the governed and little threat to its established power, as opposition literally was silenced, incapable of voicing discontent. The language policy advantaged an elite minority and relied on the disempowering of other groups (i.e. Habermas's 'suppression of generalizable interests'), i.e. it was ideological. That this was a manifestation of linguistic imperialism, of course, is not to deny the significance of English as a form of linguistic capital which was linked to economic capital.

The MOI Issue from 1984 to 1997: The Rise of Linguistic Capital

From 1984, the Education Commission (e.g. Education Commission, 1984, 1986, 1990) made several recommendations on language policies for schools and tertiary institutions. Gibbon (1982) suggests that parents, educators and policy makers were aware of the serious educational and social implications of the language policy and although the Education Commission Report (1986) stated that more than 90 per cent of students would achieve better academic results through CMI, parents did not accept this (they recognized the significance of English linguistic capital). The *Education Commission Report No. 4* (1990) stated that 70 per cent of schools should adopt the mother tongue as the MOI while 30 per cent should use English, in order to maximize the effectiveness of EMI education for those students identified as capable of benefiting from it (para. 6.4.1). EMI schools would become high-status schools and CMI schools would be lower status.

That this proposal, in effect for streaming, would exert a far-reaching undesirable effect in the schooling system of Hong Kong was attested to by the Linguistic Society of Hong Kong (1992: 111), which argued that it would stigmatize mother-tongue education and would be socially divisive (see also Lo, 1999: 142). EMI schools would recruit academically able students whose parents were well educated, while CMI schools would become second-class institutions, recruiting less able children from less educated parents. Students from EMI schools would constitute the elite. Linguistic capital, both produced and reproduced in English, would exert a powerful and long-lasting effect on future careers.

This parallels exactly Bourdieu's cultural capital thesis (Bourdieu, 1976: 112), which suggests that students from 'lower' social classes are eliminated at successive stages of education (e.g. primary, then secondary, then higher education). Social and economic origins, advantages or disadvantages are transformed into educational destinations, advantages and disadvantages as a result of early decisions on students' schools. Echoing Boudon (1973), Bourdieu (1976) argues that such social advantages and disadvantages are cumulative, because initial choices of school determine future education irreversibly.

Bourdieu and Passeron (1990: 73) argue that the influence of linguistic capital is especially manifested in the early years of schooling, yet continues to be felt throughout schooling, and that educational career prospects (e.g. choice of secondary school) are more strongly linked to language performance than to all other criteria (pp. 81–2). Indeed they argue (p. 99) that educational systems frequently address themselves only to students who possess particular (high-status) linguistic and cultural capital and who are able to take up, and profit from, particular – selected – forms of education (pp. 115–16). Linguistic capital translates into educational capital, thence into the reproduction of cultural capital, and, beyond, into economic capital.

Linguistic capital reproduces the societal status quo of inequality and differential status and life chances, privileging minorities at the expense of the majority. Such a description could be tailor-made to the Hong Kong streaming proposals. Small wonder it is that EMI schools, as deliverers as well as receivers of cultural capital, were – and are – massively oversubscribed. In 1994–95, 223 out of 392 secondary schools opted to be EMI schools; in 1995–96, 231 out of 393 opted to be EMI schools. This scramble to remain EMI schools is unsurprising, because (1) schools sought to avoid being negatively labelled as 'lower band' schools; (2) principals and parents did not wish to deny students the opportunity to enter universities which used English as the MOI; (3) principals and parents were aware of the life-long consequences of decisions about the MOI.

Similarly, when the Education Commission Report (1994) recommended that, for some students, English language instruction should be started at the Primary Four level (i.e. with eight-year-old children) (para. 3.39), parents and schoolteachers objected, although the report asserted that the recommendation was based on educational grounds (para. 3.44).

The policy for EMI and CMI schools was not just a matter of linguistic capital; it embraced cultural and ideological factors as much as educational factors. Indeed Tung (1992: 121) suggested that the system being used by the Education Department to classify EMI and CMI schools (informed by Cummins's (1979) Threshold Hypothesis) was, itself, neither accurate nor free of ideology, owing much to Western ideas and practices and selecting ideas that would serve the interests of the (then) British administration in perpetuating its influence and power.

Cummins's (1979) 'Threshold Hypothesis' sought to explain relationships between children's use of two languages and their intellectual abilities, e.g. the differences in academic outcomes of bilingual children (those who had to use a second language as well as a first). Bilingual pupils who did well in school tended to be those whose proficiencies in both their first and second languages had reached a high level for their age, whereas pupils who did not do well academically tended to be those whose proficiency in both their first and second languages were beneath a low level. Cummins labelled the high level of languages proficiency that should be attained by bilingual pupils before they could benefit from being educated in both languages as the 'higher threshold'. Bilingual proficiency associated with low academic performance was one in which pupils were proficient in neither their first nor second language. The level of competence, below which academic progress could be hampered, was labelled the 'lower threshold'.

Tung (1992) argues that the Education Commission in Hong Kong mis-interpreted the Threshold Hypothesis, and that the criteria used by the Education Department for classifying students into different categories in the Threshold Hypothesis were questionable, the threshold levels of students being determined by their scores on vocabulary and reading comprehension rather than a full range of linguistic tasks.

Whilst this may be true and, thus, provides evidence of the linguistic imperialist thesis, the broadening of the scope of the MOI issue traced here suggests that it is linguistic capital rather than linguistic imperialism which was the major explanatory variable here.

Developments in the MOI issue after 1997

In the run-up to, and since, the return of Hong Kong to China in 1997, the language debate was, and continues to be, intensely controversial. Hong Kong citizens had been expecting changes in the language issue after 1997; the Basic Law stated that Chinese would be the official language of Hong Kong and that English 'may also be used by the executive authorities, legislative and judicial organs of the Hong Kong Special Administrative Region' (Article 9).

In 1997, the Education Department's 'Arrangements for Firm Guidance in Secondary Schools' MOI' stated that the number of secondary schools using English as the MOI would drop by half, to fewer than 100 (some 20% of the total). From 1998, schools would be given a profile of their student intake's language abilities and told whether they were to be EMI or CMI. Only schools with 85 per cent of students assessed as capable of learning in English in the previous three years, as assessed by the Medium of Instruction Grouping Assessment (Wan, 1998), would be able to use English as the MOI. Teachers' abilities in English, and school-based support and assistance, would also be used in categorizing schools. Schools had to apply before 22 October 1997, with results published in April, 1998. Those breaking the advice on the MOI would be penalized, with principals facing a maximum fine of $25,000 and two years in jail, and the replacement of the school management committee. The announcement caused surprise in many quarters because of the severity of these measures.

The issue was that people in Hong Kong should know their mother tongue and reaffirm their allegiance to the motherland. The Chinese language was to be given due weight, power and status. All expatriate civil servants would have to take a Chinese language test to demonstrate their proficiency in both languages in order to be able to transfer to permanent work contracts. Consequently, the number of overseas officers has dropped by 56 per cent to 1089 at the time of writing. Linguistic capital in English was being added to or, in some cases, replaced by linguistic capital in Chinese, including Putonghua.

The Education Commission Report of 1996 (p. 14) advocated Putonghua as part of the core curriculum for all primary and secondary students (with the necessary recruitment of teachers), and the Education Department (1997: 1) recognized that 'our community is essentially Chinese' and that the mother tongue must be encouraged. This can be interpreted as a recognition of the true Chinese parentage of Hong Kong, a reassertion of power by the Chinese government, a new version of Chinese linguistic imperialism, and a response to a hundred years of western ideological domination.

Erbaugh (City University of Hong Kong, 1999: 3) compares the situation in post-colonial Hong Kong to the successful, if sometimes difficult, transition in other decolonized countries (e.g. Korea switching from Japanese to Korean; Vietnam switching from French to Vietnamese). In a nutshell, the policy changes can be seen as motivated towards ensuring the reproduction of the power of the Chinese government and the Chinese identity. Indeed Wen (1999) asserts that the general perception of the imposition of the mother tongue was that it was more political than pedagogical. It is, perhaps, an open question whether one is seeing a new form of linguistic imperialism (Cantonese and Putonghua) in Hong Kong or a recognition that cultural capital in Hong Kong is truly Chinese and that this must be reflected in its MOI and investment in, and elevation of, Chinese linguistic capital.

At the time of writing there are 114 schools using English as the MOI. From 1960 to 1997 between 60 per cent and 90 per cent of secondary schools were EMI and from 10 to 40 per cent were CMI; after 1997 25 per cent were EMI schools and 75 per cent were CMI schools. At university level the pre-1997 figure of 86 per cent EMI universities in Hong Kong remains unchanged after 1997 (Pan, 1999).

The issue of MOI is still hotly contested, and continues to provoke wide-spread educational debate that reaches to the heart of the purposes of education (e.g. Yau (1998: 18) comments that some students want English as the MOI merely because they are money-minded, and that education has a much wider brief than this). There is a recognition that the system that came into effect in 1998 was flawed (Young, 1999: 16), as there was no objective or rigorous mechanism to assess teachers' capabilities in English. The government now is introducing procedures for benchmarking the language abilities of 14,400 English teachers and 4300 Putonghua teachers, a move which has brought demonstrations in the streets of Hong Kong in 2000 by teachers who feel insulted and scapegoated by such a move (Wan, 2000: 4). It is envisaged that by 2006 all teachers will be benchmarked and only those who meet the required English standard will be able to continue teaching in EMI schools. Increasing mother-tongue teaching from 2001 is on the agenda, as it manifestly has improved student performance (Leung, 1999b: 8).

The Education Department (1997: 2) and the Chief Information Officer (To, 1998: 14) made it clear that using Chinese as the MOI would enable students to learn more effectively. Their linguistic capital would increase their educational capital. By lifting the language barrier students would be 'better able to understand what is taught, analyse problems, express views, develop an enquiring mind and cultivate critical thinking' (To, 1998), i.e. higher-order thinking would be facilitated through mother-tongue teaching. Indeed, the Education Department (1994) reported research which showed that in a language environment which was more Chinese than English, the 'students were generally more "deeply" or academically motivated' and committed to learning and understanding.

In 1997, the Education Department (1997: 1) reported that educational research both worldwide and in Hong Kong demonstrated that (1) students learn better through their mother tongue; (2) they are more motivated to learn in their mother tongue; (3) those who learn in the mother tongue generally achieve better than their counterparts who use English as the MOI (e.g. in the Hong Kong Certificate of Education examinations). Lao and Krashen (1999: 3) report research which contrasts an EMI student who was 'very unhappy' and 'felt very pitiful' because she or he did not understand the teacher with a CMI student who reports a 'happy learning atmosphere' with a lot of discussions.

The Director of Education (Law, 1999: 8) commented that CMI schools reported 'more active discussion in class, a quicker pace of learning, and improved examination results'. Lao and Krashen (1999: 2) suggest that students in CMI schools were more active and creative than similar students in EMI, who were more passive and limited in their verbal responses (frequently uttering only short phrases or single words). They cite research by Tsui (1992) which stated that after one year of mother-tongue teaching, 80 per cent of CMI school principals and 70 per cent of CMI teachers believed that mother-tongue teaching facilitated higher-level learning by students. The Education Department research report of 1994 had found that children in CMI schools used high-level cognitive strategies, whereas those in EMI schools relied on rote memorizing, superficial learning strategies, and were more anxious in their work. The way forward, the report claimed, was to use Chinese medium.

What is being argued here is that 'purely on educational grounds' (Education Department, 1994: 8 and cf. Education Department, 1997: 5), with 'no hidden agenda; no political motive' (Law, 1999: 8), there are powerful reasons for the increase in CMI schools coupled with extensive teaching of English as a second language. Linguistic capital, social and educational advantage, therefore, is accrued in CMI rather than in EMI schools; it is being redefined as Chinese linguistic capital. The Education Commission (1996: 4) also argued that there was a 'strong body of opinion' on educational grounds (though this is contested) to suggest that it is better for students to start learning English *after* (our italics) developing an aptitude for learning in the mother tongue.

As the results over time of the comparative performance of EMI and CMI schools become available (and the Hong Kong SAR is developing projects on 'value-added' indicators and benefits of schools), then data will be forthcoming to substantiate these claims further. These will build on the existing data (Education Department, 1998) which show that mother-tongue teaching helps pupils achieve high value-added performance and that the general belief that attending an EMI school raises proficiency overall as well as in the English Language, is largely unfounded.

The Chief Information Officer (To, 1998) also recognized the *realpolitik* of Hong Kong's international status, stating that the government would attach *equal* importance (our italics) to English. Wong (City University of Hong Kong, 1999: 3) regards English proficiency as vital for internationalism, an internationalism which is central if Hong Kong is to avoid being just another city of China and 'of no importance'. This echoes the Education Department's (1997: 1) view that 'Hong Kong is an international business, financial and trading centre, and English is the language of business worldwide ... [and is] crucial to our economic competitiveness'. Statements like these reveal the distance that has been travelled from the early days of regarding English merely as a form of linguistic imperialism.

By the mid-1990s Hong Kong had the highest GDP in Asia, was Asia's financial and banking centre, and was the second busiest container port in the world. It was China's largest trading partner and employed three million workers in southern China alone, and was the world's tenth largest trading economy (Institute of International Education, 2000). Hong Kong survives on its human – and linguistic – capital, as, like Singapore, it has few natural resources.

Conclusion and Prospect

The recent debate on the MOI is separating out several pressures. On the one hand, the *educational*, *pedagogical* and *psychological* arguments appear to support the use of CMI, and linguistic capital, it seems, should be reinterpreted as Chinese. On the other hand, *economic* and *technological* arguments appear to support both the use of English as the MOI together with an increase in Putonghua as the sources of linguistic capital (e.g. the perpetuation of the bilingual and trilingual elite in Hong Kong). One can suggest, perhaps crudely, that several micro-level factors seem to push towards CMI whilst macro-level factors push towards EMI. Agreement between pressures is rare (Morrison & Ridley, 1988: 32, 63); education is an 'essentially contested concept' (Hartnett & Naish, 1976).

However, overriding this is the macro-level *political* factor, which seems to be winning the day, in which CMI serves a political agenda, redefining linguistic capital in Chinese terms whilst recognizing the global significance of English. As this is aligned powerfully to the educational argument which points to evidence of increased student performance in CMI schools, it is almost unassailable.

The nagging problem is that currently the practice in Hong Kong is still for the most academically able students to seek to attend EMI schools; here English linguistic capital continues to be linked to cultural and economic capital and to reproduce the existing stratification of society and schooling. As long as this practice is sustained then English will continue, perhaps, to function as one sorting mechanism for life chances for many students in Hong Kong. However, there are some signs that the practice may not be exerting such power: as student achievement in CMI schools increases and, hence, as CMI schools become more popular, then the perception of English as the sole route to cultural capital may diminish.

This is not to say that the linguistic capital of English will diminish greatly, as it will still be essential for trade, travel, business, economics, and access to science and technology. Significantly, also, Hong Kong employers value an overseas education from students, as it purports to give them a competitive edge (Institute of International Education, 2000: 14). Indeed Lau (1998) comments on the desperate need for improved English in the worlds of business, the professions, and government in Hong Kong. Though the impetus to learning English for economic purposes appears unstoppable, one has to be mindful of the powerful moves that are being made in East Asia for a Chinese version of the Internet to be extended as an alternative to the English-medium Internet for trade, commerce and business.

English will continue to be a necessary passport for students wishing to study in Hong Kong and the West, with over 10,000 Hong Kong students studying in the US alone, and some 10,000 others studying in the UK, Canada and Australia (Institute of International Education, 2000). Lin (City University of Hong Kong, 1999: 3) recognizes that, as long as the universities and elite schools in Hong Kong continue to be EMI, then parents will not be willing to admit that their children are not part of the elite. This resonates with the speech by the Secretary for Education and Manpower to the Legislative Council of Hong Kong on 26 May 1999 which states that if students are to enter the Universities then they will need to switch to English sooner rather than later. Learning English continues to be a form of capital investment. Maybe until the universities in Hong Kong and overseas offer and recognize CMI as much as EMI this problem will not diminish, i.e. it is structural (McCarty, 1999: 6). Even though the benefits of CMI teaching are manifest, the problem is to persuade 'pragmatic, aspiring, socially mobile parents' that this is preferable to EMI (McCarty, 1999: 3).

Linguistic capital can account for the relationship between individual advancement and the structural location of those individuals within a global and local market economy; it links micro- and macro-analysis (individuals' action within a particular social structure, akin to Bourdieu's view of 'habitus'), and it addresses social and cultural production and reproduction. Linguistic capital is both the medium and outcome of social production and reproduction; indeed the MOI issue in Hong Kong, as interpreted through the lens of linguistic capital, is an instance of Giddens's structuration theory (Giddens, 1976, 1984) where agency (e.g. parental aspiration) combines with structure (e.g. parents' cultural background and the school system) to produce and reproduce social structures and behaviour. Linguistic capital indicates how schools, through the choice of MOI, might be agents of social, cultural and linguistic legitimation, social reproduction and production.

Linguistic capital, it has been suggested, is able to render a more comprehensive account of the MOI issue in Hong Kong than linguistic imperialism, and amends the limitations of linguistic imperialism, in (1) focusing on the positive aspects of ideology; (2) allowing for agency, intentionality and informed choice; (3) being historical and dynamic; (4) embracing a much wider range of issues than merely domination and suppression, that more closely captures the multi-layered nature of the MOI issue in Hong Kong; (5) providing a more fitting account of the post-colonial situation and its more immediate antecedents; (6) embracing multi-causality, rather than the mono-causality of linguistic imperialism; (7) offering a theory of social, cultural and economic production and reproduction through education that resonates with a theory of structuration; and (8) indicating the role for education in social and cultural production and reproduction.

Clearly one cannot pin too much on linguistic capital as a sole explanatory factor in the MOI issues in Hong Kong as, like linguistic imperialism, it is largely a single construct in a multi-constructed society. This paper has suggested that, under colonial rule, English in Hong Kong performed a strong ideological role and that, within this, the seeds were sown of linguistic capital. In the post-colonial era English is a matter of linguistic capital rather than ideological hegemony. That English continues to be linked to economic advantage for Hong Kong citizens is less an ideological matter and more a signification of its global importance. For an ideological reading of the MOI issue in Hong Kong now, one perhaps has to turn to the rise of Putonghua in Hong Kong schools. Whether this will turn out to be a new version of linguistic imperialism or simply an affirmation of affinity with the motherland is an open question.

REFERENCES

Altbach, P. (2000) 'The worldwide threats to academic freedom'. *South China Morning Post*, 18 August, p. 16.

Aronowitz, S. and Giroux, H. (1986) *Education under Siege*. London: Routledge and Kegan Paul.

Bernstein, B. (1971) 'On the classification and framing of educational knowledge'. In M. F. D. Young (ed.) *Knowledge and Control*. London: Collier-Macmillan.

Boudon, R. (1973) *Education, Opportunity and Social Inequality*. New York: John Wiley and Sons.

Bourdieu, P. (1976) 'The school as a conservative force: Scholastic and cultural inequalities'. In R. Dale, G. Esland and M. MacDonald (eds) *Schooling and Capitalism*. London: Routledge and Kegan Paul.

Bourdieu, P. (1997) 'The forms of capital'. In A. H. Halsey, H. Lauder, P. Brown and A. S. Wells (eds) *Education: Culture, Economy, Society*. Oxford: Oxford University Press.

Bourdieu, P. and Passeron, J.-C. (1990) *Reproduction in Education, Society and Culture* (2nd edn). London: Sage.

Boyle, J. (1995) 'Hong Kong's educational system: English or Chinese?' *Language, Culture and Curriculum* 8 (3), 291–304.

Boyle, J. (1997) 'Imperialism and the English language in Hong Kong'. *Journal of Multilingual and Multicultural Development* 18 (3), 169–81.

Cheng N. L. (1973) 'Questionnaire findings of 170 university students' language abilities and attitudes towards the Chinese and English languages'. In K. K. Luke (ed.) *Into the Twenty-First Century: Issues of Language in Education in Hong Kong* (pp. 110–15). Hong Kong: Linguistic Society of Hong Kong.

Cherrington, R. (forthcoming) 'Linguistic imperialism'. In M. S. Byram (ed.) *Encyclopedia of Language Teaching and Learning*. London: Routledge.

City University of Hong Kong (1999) 'What medium of instruction for Hong Kong?' *Bulletin*, Issue 19, September. University Publications Office: City University of Hong Kong.

Cummins, J. (1979) *Cognitive/Academic Language Proficiency, Linguistic Interdependence, the Optimal Age Question, and Some Other Matters*. Working Papers on Bilingualism. ERIC Document Reproduction Service No. ED 184334.

Davies, A. (1996) 'Ironising the myth of linguicism'. Review article. *Journal of Multilingual and Multicultural Development* 17 (6), 485–96.

Eagleton, T. (1991) *Ideology*. London: Verso.

Education Commission (1984) *Education Commission Report No. 1*. Hong Kong: Government Printer.

Education Commission (1986) *Education Commission Report No. 2*. Hong Kong: Government Printer.

Education Commission (1990) *Education Commission Report No. 4*. Hong Kong: Government Printer.

Education Commission (1994) *Report of the Working Group on Language Proficiency*. Hong Kong: Government Printer.

Education Commission (1996) *Education Commission Report No. 6. Enhancing Language Proficiency: A Comprehensive Strategy*. Hong Kong: Government Printer.

Education Department (1994) *Research on Change of Medium of Instruction in Secondary Schools*. Hong Kong: Government Printer.

Education Department (1997) *Medium on Instruction Guidance for Secondary Schools*. Hong Kong: Government Printer.

Education Department (1998) *Evaluation Study on the Implementation of Medium of Instruction Grouping in Secondary Schools (1994/5–1996/7)*. Hong Kong: Government Printer.

Fairclough, N. (1989) *Language and Power*. Harlow: Longman.

Fishman, J. A., Cooper, R. and Conrad, A. (1979). 'The spread of English'. In K. K. Luke (ed.) *Into the Twenty-first Century: Issues of Language in Education in Hong Kong*. Hong Kong: Linguistic Society of Hong Kong.

Gibbon, J. (1982) 'The issue of the language of instruction in the lower forms of Hong Kong secondary schools'. *Journal of Multilingual and Multicultural Development* 3 (2), 117–28.

Giddens, A. (1976) *New Rules of Sociological Method*. London: Hutchinson.

Giddens, A. (1984) *The Constitution of Society*. Cambridge: Polity Press.

Giroux, H. A. (1983) *Theory and Resistance in Education*. London: Heinemann.

Habermas, J. (1970a) 'On systematically distorted communication'. *Inquiry* 13, 205–18.

Habermas, J. (1970b) 'Towards a theory of communicative competence'. *Inquiry* 13, 360–75.

Habermas, J. (1976) *Legitimation Crisis*. London: Heinemann.

Hartnett, A. and Naish, M. (1976) *Theory and Practice of Education (Vol. 1)*. London: Heinemann.

Institute of International Education (2000) *Hong Kong: Local and International Education*. http://home.school.net.hk/~iie/info/hked/hkeducation.htm (10 August).

Krashen, S. (1996) *Under Attack: The Case against Bilingual Education*. Culver City: Language Education Associates.

Kvan, E. (1969) 'Problems of bilingual milieu in Hong Kong: Strain of the two-language system'. In D. C. Jarvie and J. Agassi (eds) *Hong Kong: A Society in Transition*. London: Routledge and Kegan Paul.

Lao, C. Y. and Krashen, S. (1999) 'Implementation of mother-tongue teaching in Hong Kong Secondary Schools: Some recent reports'. *Discovery*, 18 October. http://www.ncbe.gwu.edu/ncbepubs/discover/05hongkong.htm.

Lau, E. (1998) 'Medium of instruction a hot potato (15 April)'. *Hong Kong Voice of Democracy*. http://www.democracy.org.hk/pastweek/mar15_21/instruction.htm

Law, F. (1999) 'In pursuit of excellence: Challenges and changes for the Hong Kong Special Administrative Region'. Paper presented at the International Congress for School Effectiveness and Improvement, Hong Kong, 5 January.

Leung, K. F. (1999a) 'Church, state and education during the colonial period'. In M. Bray and R. Koo (eds) *Education and Society in Hong Kong and Macau: Comparative Persepctives on Continuity and Change*. Hong Kong: Comparative Education Research Centre, University of Hong Kong.

Leung, T. S. (1999b) 'Mother-tongue teaching may be expanded'. *South China Morning Post*, 16 December, p. 6.

Linguistic Society of Hong Kong (1992) 'The mixed-code and bilingual education'. In K. K. Luke (ed.) *Into the Twenty-first Century: Issues of Language in Education in Hong Kong*. (pp. 110–15). Hong Kong: Linguistic Society of Hong Kong.

Lo, Y. C. (1999) 'Curriculum reform' In M. Bray and R. Koo (eds) *Education and Society in Hong Kong and Macau: Comparative Perspectives on Continuity and Change*. CERC Studies in Comparative Education 7. Hong Kong: University of Hong Kong, Comparative Education Research Centre.

McCarty, S. (1999) 'East Meets West and South in Hong Kong'. First published in the Asia-Pacific Exchange (Electronic) Journal 3 (1), 1996, and subsequently available on the web site http://kagawa-jc.ac.jp/~steve_mc/hongkong.html.

Morrison, K. R. B. (1995) 'Habermas and the school curriculum'. Unpublished PhD thesis, University of Durham.

Morrison, K. R. B. and Ridley, K. (1988) *Curriculum Planning and the Primary School*. London: Paul Chapman Publishing.

Pan, S. (1999) 'Bilingual policy change in Hong Kong and its impact on bilingual education'. Paper presented at the Symposium on Bilingualism and Biliteracy through Schooling, Long Island University, Brooklyn, NY.

Pennycook, A. (1994) 'The worldliness of English in Singapore'. *The Cultural Politics of English as an International Language*. Harlow: Longman.

Pennycook, A. (forthcoming) 'History of language teaching: 1945 to the present'. In M. S. Byram (ed.) *Encyclopedia of Language Teaching and Learning*. London: Routledge.

Phillipson, R. (1992) *Linguistic Imperialism*. Oxford: Oxford University Press.

Phillipson, R. (1998) 'Globalizing English: Are linguistic human rights an alternative to linguistic imperialism?' *Language Sciences*, 20 (1), 101–12.

Rassool, N. (1998) 'Postmodernity, cultural pluralism and the nation-state: Problems of language rights, human rights, identity and power'. *Language Sciences* 20 (1), 89–99.

Skuttnab-Kangas, T. (1988) 'Multilingualism and the education of minority children'. In T. Skuttnab-Kangas and J. Cummins (eds) *Minority Education: From Shame to Struggle* (pp. 9–44). Clevedon: Multilingual Matters.

So, W. C. (1984) 'The social selection of an English-dominant bilingual education system in Hong Kong: An ecolinguistic analysis'. Unpublished PhD thesis, University of Hawaii.

To, D. (1998) 'Careful vetting'. *South China Morning Post*, 16 May, p. 14.

Tsui, A. (1992) 'Using English as a medium of instruction and English language acquisition'. In K. K. Luke (ed.) *Into the Twenty-first Century: Issues of Language in Education in Hong Kong*. Hong Kong: Linguistic Society of Hong Kong.

Tung, P. C. S. (1992) 'Learning from the West: The MOI in Hong Kong schools'. In K. K. Luke (ed.) *Into the Twenty-first Century: Issues of Language in Education in Hong Kong*. Hong Kong: Linguistic Society of Hong Kong.

Wan, C. (1998) 'Goal posts moved on "student ability"'. *Hong Kong Standard*, 14 March. In Dow Jones Interactive Publication Library (on-line). http://nrstq2p.djnr.com/cgi-bin/DJInteractive.

Wan, C. (2000) 'Course mix to placate teachers on tests'. *South China Morning Post*, 17 August, p. 4.

Wen, W. P. (1999) 'Mother-tongue teaching must be accomplished consistently (in Chinese'. Cited in Y. C. Lo (1999) 'Curriculum reform'. In M. Bray and R. Koo (eds) *Education and Society in Hong Kong and Macau: Comparative Perspectives on Continuity and Change*. CERC Studies in Comparative Education 7. Hong Kong: University of Hong Kong, Comparative Education Research Centre.

Yau, C. (1998) 'Some pupils could struggle'. *South China Morning Post*, 11 June, p. 18.

Young, R. L. M. (1999) 'No wholesale switch to mother tongue'. *South China Morning Post*, 1 December, p. 16.

Reading 5.2
Fuels for the Fire: Identity Politics and Ethnolinguistic Inequality in the United States

[...] political conflict over language policy requires more than the preconditions of language diversity, contact, and perceived competition. Language policy conflict erupts most forcefully when competing concerns over the relationship between language and group identity, fueled by anxieties over national unity and drives for greater ethnic equality, are expressed politically in the form of demands for state action. Because every country's historical experience is unique, each has a singular (albeit contested) understanding of its national identity and its internal ethnic composition. The United States is no exception, having its own particular tradition of discourse on these matters that has helped to set the stage for the recent debates over language policy in this country.

From: R. Schmidt Sr (2000), *Language Policy and Identity Politics in the United States*, Philadelphia: Temple University Press.

[. . .]

National and ethnic identity in the United States

At least since the war for independence from Great Britain in the eighteenth century, there has been near unanimity among U.S. political elites—and among foreign commentators on the United States as well—that that there is a distinctively *American* national identity. Few have doubted that Americans have a character unto themselves, constituting a national community unique in the world.

At the same time the substantive content of what exactly constitutes the American national identity has been contested throughout our history. This is hardly surprising since nationalism is an ideology and the terms of any particular version are inherently contestable. The debates over what constitutes the American national character have proceeded along many tributaries during our history, and it is impossible and unnecessary to summarize them here. [. . .] At this point, it will suffice to present some basic facts about the origins of the American people and the terms of several debates over the core of U.S. national identity that are signficant for the language policy conflict.

The intricacy of U.S. debates over the national character is attributable, in part, to the complexity of the country's origins. Americans can trace their roots to a uniquely diverse range of ancestors. There is virtually no place on earth that has not contributed to the flow of people who eventually became citizens of the United States. And the diversity of means to becoming American may be uniquely complex as well. While our dominant myth is surely that we are a nation of immigrants, immigration is only the most common among several ways in which we have become a people. In addition to voluntary immigration and colonization by several European powers (Great Britain, Spain, France, the Netherlands, Sweden, and Russia), some peoples became part of the United States not by choice but by purchase (e.g., through the Louisiana Purchase in 1803) or by violence (e.g., through the infamous Middle Passage from Africa to enslavement; and through the military conquest and annexation of native peoples' lands, nearly one-half of Mexico's territory in 1846–48, and Puerto Rico in 1898). [. . .] these divergent paths to becoming American continue to reverberate in our understandings of both the stakes and the appropriate course of action to follow in relation to our linguistic diversity.

A second source of complexity in understanding the American national character is attributable to the fact that the United States became an independent country through a series of contested political acts by a particular set of political actors. Most of the political actors who gave birth to an independent United States had British roots, and understood their political actions in terms of English political beliefs that have been characterized by recent scholars as either 'liberal' or 'republican,' or a unique combination of both. Among the consequences is that one of the most powerful claimants for core status in the

American national identity is a kind of political volunteerism that remains unusual in the contemporary world. From the beginning of our national independence, that is, Americans have been asked to choose their nationality through a political act. This, in turn, gives rise to a kind of universalism that makes it possible for any human being—no matter what her or his original nationality—to be an American through an act of choice. But this has also made possible a kind of political exclusivity rarely found in other countries, symbolized in the mid-twentieth century by legislative committees established to investigate '*un*American' activities and beliefs. Thus while it is possible for anyone in the world to become an American, it is also possible for one's fellow citizens to declare that—based on your actions and beliefs—you are not really an 'American' after all. Another example could be found in popular automobile bumper stickers of the late 1960s/early 1970s that read, 'America—love it or leave it!' This was understood by all to signify that if one did not support the U.S. war effort in Vietnam, one should—by rights—forfeit one's citizenship and go elsewhere. Few other countries, if any, understand their national identities in this way.

At the same time that this ideological tension between universalism and exclusivity has operated on one plane, another tension, between the potential universalism of American political beliefs and their decidedly British roots, has existed on a different plane. That is, the fact that nearly all the political elites who founded the United States as an independent country were British in origin has given to the American national identity a strong ethno-ascriptive character of Anglo origin that has existed in tension with the universalism of the country's official political ideology. While all might become Americans, some have been perceived as more 'American' than others, by virtue not of their political beliefs and actions but of their blood roots. The word 'nation,' after all, has its origins in the Latin *natal*, or 'birth.'

The result of these complex and conflicting realities is what Rogers Smith (1997) has aptly termed 'multiple traditions' of membership in the American political community. One tradition strains toward the volunteeristic universalism of a political definition of American national identity, while another stands firmly rooted in an ascriptive hierarchy of ethno-Americanism.

Within that ascriptive hierarchy of Americanism exist a myriad of ever-changing, but never absent, ethnic groupings. [. . .] ethnic identities—like national identities—are socially constructed through the delineation of boundaries, using comparisons of origin narratives, cultural practices and beliefs, religious traditions, beliefs in inherently distinctive or biological characteristics (e.g., race), and the like. In the United States, some of the ethnic boundaries that matter most have changed dramatically over time. Prior to the 1960s, for example, religious affiliation was a centrally important ethnic boundary, with certain branches of Protestantism at the top of the hierarchy as the norm against which all others were measured, with Roman Catholicism marked as decidedly inferior, and Judaism even more severely marked. A half-century later, these distinctions matter much less to the life chances and social standing of most Americans.

Similarly, national-origin distinctions between European Americans were once much more important in American life than they are at present. The prospect of a marriage between the daughter of English-origin parents and the son of an Italian American couple once brought a level of dismay almost incomprehensible to Americans who have come of age since the 1960s. Both national-origin and religious identities remain extant in the United States at the end of the twentieth century, but these boundaries are far less rigid and pronounced than they were several generations ago.

Nevertheless, one ethnic boundary that has remained highly significant in American life, from the country's origins to the present, is that of race. As noted, the concept of race is based on perceived distinctions understood as inherent or essential to the nature of different peoples (i.e., as biological). As such, the concept of race challenges the assertion made above that all ethnic boundaries are socially constructed. Because these perceived essential differences, moreover, are used to establish a hierarchy of worth and values among peoples, race becomes a 'sign of privilege and honor' on one side, and a sign of eligibility for 'policies of discrimination and control' on the other (Montejano, 1987: 4–5).

Belying their own assumptions, however, racial boundaries have assumed a variety of forms, as those making the racial categorizations have relied upon an ever-changing multiplicity of characteristics signifying essentially different peoples (e.g., cultural beliefs and practices, national origins, skin color and other physical characteristics, languages, and so on). It was common, for example, for early twentieth-century writers to discourse with great confidence about the inherent differences between the English, French, and German 'races'. Nevertheless, these inconsistencies, together with the denial by most social and physical scientists of any natural or biological foundations for the ethnic boundaries creating the racial groupings of the United States, have had little effect on the reality of these boundaries in the experienced lives of most contemporary Americans. Indeed, racial groupings continue to be the most important ethnic boundaries in American public life.

In recent decades, in virtually all arenas of life (e.g., among academicians, the media, political actors, and government officials, as well as in the civil and private niches of daily living), most Americans have come to understand their most significant ethnic divisions in terms of five primary groups—each of which has a racial connotation. The largest group is composed (for the most part) of European-origin Americans, variously termed 'white,' 'Anglo,' and 'Euro-American.' The second largest of these racialized groupings is that of African-origin Americans, described as 'black,' 'Afro-American,' and 'African American.' Third, and rapidly growing toward becoming the second largest of the groups, are those of Latin American origin (including those from Spanish-speaking Caribbean islands), most frequently designated as 'Latinos' or

'Hispanics.' The fourth-largest group comprises those Americans with roots in Asia and the Pacific Islands, typically called 'Asian Americans' or 'Asian/Pacific Islanders.' The smallest group, finally, is composed of those whose ancestors were most native to the territory of the United States, who did not migrate to the 'New World' following the 'Age of Discovery,' and who include those described as 'Native Americans,' 'American Indians,' 'Inuits,' 'Aleuts,' 'Eskimos,' and 'Native Hawaiians.' As well as having geographic origins, each of these racialized groups has been color-coded in U.S. cultural discourse: white, black, brown, yellow, or red.

As social constructs, each of these groups is subject to boundary-definition controversies and to internal division. Each of them is an 'imagined community' not existing in nature, and each is a meta-ethnic grouping composed of highly diverse peoples sometimes characterized by long-standing conflicts with each other. Many Irish-, French-, or German-origin Americans, for example, find it extremely offensive to be called 'Anglo' (with its so clearly British roots). Similar internal divisions can be found among members of each of the other U.S. meta-ethnic communities (e.g., descendants of African American slaves versus recent migrants from Africa or the Caribbean; Chinese versus Japanese versus Filipino versus Vietnamese versus Cambodian versus Indian Americans; Mexican versus Cuban versus Puerto Rican versus Nicaraguan Americans; Navajo versus Hopi versus Lakota Sioux versus Hawaiian Natives).

Despite this range of diversity and the problematic nature of each group's boundaries, American public and private life in the late twentieth century has been suffused with these racialized ethnic groupings. In informal social discourse, as well as in more formal public discussion, Americans habitually take cognizance of and refer to each other's ethnic identities in terms of these five primary categories. And yet it also remains true that there is widespread agreement around the globe and within the country that there is a distinctively 'American' national character.

As noted, the significance of our ethnic group memberships in relation to language policy is highly contested. What remains to be sketched here in terms of the context for the language policy debate in the United States are the facts that (1) the problematic relationship between national and ethnic group identities has given rise to a set of debates often termed 'culture wars' among the country's intellectual and political elites in recent years, and (2) this politics of identity in the United States is also fueled by long-standing inequalities between our racialized ethnic groups.

Ethnicity, Nationality, and the U.S. 'Culture Wars'
To understand language policy conflict in the United States, it is important to recognize that these debates over language have become intertwined with a larger set of conflicts often described as 'culture wars.' The core of the debate, while raging along many fronts, has been over how to appropriately understand

the relationship between culture and our identity as a national people. And the central terms of the debate have been set by the question of whether the United States is best understood as a multicultural nation or as a country with one singular and unifying American culture. Its battle fields have included preschools, postgraduate schools, college and university campuses, academic professional associations, a large number of published books, academic journals as well as more popular journals of public affairs and news magazines, national political conventions, legislative bodies at all levels of government, and, of course, the expansive air waves of radio, television, and cyberspace.

The most prominent supporters of a multicultural understanding of the United States in these debates have been college professors and teachers, as well as some political activists from among peoples of color. The Reverend Jesse Jackson, for example, has frequently spoken out in favor of a 'rainbow coalition' that will promote a multicultural understanding of American society. Similarly, opponents have included both intellectuals and political leaders, from all parts of the political spectrum, including conservative Republicans (e.g., Patrick Buchanan and William Bennett), liberal Democrats (e.g., Arthur Schlesinger), and those farther left (e.g., Todd Gitlin).

It is not necessary or desirable to summarize this debate in any detail here, but several points deserve articulation. First, this debate is highly symbolic in nature, being centrally concerned with the symbols through which Americans understand themselves to be a people. A good metaphor for understanding this is the Latin phrase enshrined on our money—'E pluribus unum'—which translates as 'Out of many, one.' An ambiguous phrase, it can be understood—and has been defended in the culture wars—as either supporting or opposing a multicultural understanding of the American people. What is often forgotten, however, is that the phrase is purely symbolic, a talisman of no material significance in that the value of the money on which it is emblazoned is not affected by its interpretation.

Second, as David A. Hollinger (1995) has rightly pointed out, it is important to understand that these often vitriolic 'culture wars' are not really about a multicultural understanding of American life at all. They are about 'culture' to be sure, in that their subject is most frequently the appropriate cultural education for Americans. Virtually no proponent of multicultural education, however, has argued that American education should import and incorporate as its own a non-American cultural edifice from another country. Rather, the debate concerns the national educational significance of cultural contributions by Americans whose origins are not European, and especially not Anglo European. Should we understand our national cultural heritage as one that has developed from British roots, elaborated and dialectically expanded by Americans, but still an extension of an inherited British culture to which all previous newcomers have adapted? Or should American culture be understood, in addition, in terms of oppositions and tensions emanating from the fact that the British colonization of, and subsequent U.S. expansion over, much of the North American continent had opponents and victims who drew upon a vast array of cultural materials (including, sometimes, British and other European materials) to fashion and articulate their own understanding of what it meant— for them—to be Americans and human beings? Until recently, U.S. education at all levels has been unaware of the very existence of this wide range of American voices and cultural contributions, much less attempting to incorporate it in the teaching of who we are as a people. Put differently, then, the 'culture wars' debates are most centrally about the national cultural significance of the voices of those who have been excluded from elite status and high-level power positions by virtue of their ascribed characteristics (e.g., race, gender, religion, national origin, etc.).

Seen in this way, the 'culture wars' of the late twentieth century are best understood as a debate over the significance of our meta-ethnic identities in relation to our national identity. Are we a people with one, coherent European-origin (especially Anglo-origin) culture that should be passed along as a precious heritage to all Americans as their own; or, should the racialized ethnic experiences and the multiple articulations of the American experience deriving from our often violent history of ethnic conflicts be prominently incorporated into our understanding of our national identity and culture? More personally, should all Americans understand their past and culture from the point of view of, say, George Washington and Thomas Jefferson; or should they understand themselves as including also the experiences and worldviews of Nat Turner, Sojourner Truth, and César Chávez—*in addition to* those of Washington and Jefferson? And more tritely, the question is often formulated as: Should we understand ourselves in terms of a melting pot or a stew pot or a salad bowl? As might be self-evident by now, these questions are closely intertwined with the debates over language policy, as the identity politics concerns of both sets of political argument are virtually identical. In that sense, the analysis in this book should contribute to a better understanding of these other 'culture wars' as well as to the debate over language policy.

Racialized Ethnicity and Social Inequality

[...] the quest for equality between ethnolinguistic groups is one of the two primary fuels driving language policy conflict around the world. In the United States, moreover, our history of racialized ethnicity and discrimination on the basis of ascribed ethnic identities forms an important backdrop for the language policy debate. As a closer look at the non-English-language data from the 1990 Census reveals, many of the persons making up the largest and fastest-growing minority language groups are categorized as members of the non-white, non-European-origin racialized ethnic groups outlined above (e.g., Latinos or Hispanics, or Asian/Pacific Islander peoples). As such, they are members of minority ethnic communities with long histories of exclusion and domination in the United States. This confluence of memberships in U.S. language minorities and racial minorities has given particular impetus to the argument for a pluralist language policy in this country [...] Both this argument and the response by assimilationist leaders, in turn, place the debate firmly in the territory of identity politics.

Helping to fuel the debate of both the 'culture wars' and of language policy is the persistent social stratification among the primary U.S. ethnic communities, and therefore among ethnolinguistic communities as well. This is not the place to explain the origins or consequences of U.S. ethnic inequalities. Those aspects of this issue intertwined with the U.S. language policy debate will be prominently discussed in chapters to come. Here, rather, the discussion and tables that follow simply illustrate that on several quantitative measures of social well-being, the United States can be characterized as having a pattern of social inequality along ethnic lines.

In particular, the United States, as well as virtually every other country in the contemporary world, is ethnically stratified in relation to wealth, income, occupational status, educational attainment, and social prestige. And, with few exceptions, status on the lower rungs of this stratification system is disproportionately related to membership in U.S. racial minority groups. Thus, Latinos, Native Americans, African Americans, and members of some Asian/ Pacific American groups have a greater chance of being poor, underemployed, undereducated, and socially despised than do European-origin Americans or members of certain other Asian American communities, as demonstrated in Tables 5.1–5.4, each of which is based on analysis of the 1990 U.S. Census.

A 1996 Census Bureau update of the figures on those living in poverty revealed minor changes, but the overall pattern remained the same: The poverty rate among non-Latino whites was 8.6 percent; among blacks, 28.4 percent; among Asian Americans, 14.5 percent; among Latinos, 30.3 percent; and among American Indians, 31.2 percent (McClain and Stewart, 1998: Tables 5.1, 5.2).

Each of these U.S. ethnic groups has considerable internal variation, but in view of the widespread perception of Asian/Pacific Americans as a 'model

Table 5.1 Education Attainment of Young Adults by Race and Ethnicity, 1992

Ethnic Group	Percent High School Graduates	Percent with Some College	Percent College Graduates
Anglo/white	91	27	28
African American	81	26	14
Latino	60	20	10
Asian	92	20	47
American Indian	78	30	11

Source: O'Hare, 1992: 29.

Table 5.2 Median Household Income by Race and Ethnicity, 1979 and 1989

Ethnic Group	1979 Household Income	1989 Household Income
Anglo/white	$30,200	$31,400
African American	$18,700	$19,800
Latino	$23,100	$24,200
Asian	$34,100	$34,800

Source: O'Hare, p. 34.

minority,' it is especially important to note that this category includes groups that are experiencing considerable poverty and low social and educational mobility. This is particularly true among certain refugee populations from Southeast Asia (e.g., Cambodians and the Hmong) and some Pacific Islander groups. Paul Ong (1993), for example, reported 1990 Census data for Southern California indicating a 25 percent poverty rate for Vietnamese Americans and 45 percent rate for other Southeast Asian-origin peoples (p. 15). Paula D. McClain and Joseph Stewart, Jr. (1998), moreover, cite 1990 Census data indicating that 14 percent of Chinese-origin Americans and 13.7 percent of Korean-origin Americans live in poverty (p. 32).

Placement on these vertical rungs on the U.S. status structure, it should be noted, is not just a function of educational attainment, despite the general correlation between educational level and social and occupational standing. Rather, when educational levels are controlled for analysis, European-origin Americans (especially males) still enjoy quite favorable occupational placement, wealth, and income in comparison with African Americans, Latinos, and Asian/Pacific Americans. Even highly educated Asian Americans, for example, appear to experience a 'glass ceiling' that limits their proportionate representation among higher levels of the U.S. managerial and techno-institutional social structure (Hubler and Silverstein, 1993).

What role, if any, does language play in the construction and maintenance of this ethnic stratification system? [...] two points may be made here. First, the ability to use English is highly correlated with occupational standing, wealth, and income in the United States. That is, those individuals who are unable to use

Table 5.3 Median Net Worth of Households by Race and Ethnicity, 1988

Household Type	White	African American	Latino
All households	$44,400	$3,800	$5,500
Married-couple households	$61,400	$14,900	$12,300
Female households	$25,500	$700	$500

Source: O'Hare, 1992: 36.

Table 5.4 Poverty and Welfare Receipt by Race and Ethnicity, 1991

Income Category	Anglo/ White	African American	Asian	American Indian	Latino
Percent in poverty	9	33	14	32	29
Percent in deep poverty	3	16	7	14	10
Percent receiving welfare	13	47	19	51	44
Percent of poor receiving welfare	61	85	62	87	79
Numbers (in 1,000s)	188,667	30,758	7,065	1,730	22,039

Source: O'Hare, 1992: 38.

English at all are disproportionately found at the lower end of the U.S. social structure. Second, however, the use of a language other than English is *not* correlated with low economic standing, provided that the individuals are able to speak English fluently. In other words, non-English monolinguals in the United States do pay a price for not being able to use the dominant language. Bilinguals who know English well, however, are not penalized in the occupational structure for their knowledge and use of a language other than English (see, Tienda and Neidert, 1985). In any case, there is ample fuel for the conflict over language policy in the United States in the convergence of our highly racialized ethnic stratification system and the immigration-fed growth of NEL [non-English language] monolingualism.

Summary and conclusion

To summarize, then, it is evident that the U.S. political conflict over language policy does have social foundations. Multiple language groups coexist in the country, and there are contact and some sense of competition among them. The two principal fuels igniting language policy conflict throughout the world—ethnolinguistic inequality and an identity politics that is connected with language diversity and is centered on the relationship between national and ethnic identities—also exist to some degree in U.S. society. Activists and political leaders involved in U.S. language politics, moreover, have made conflicting claims upon the state for public policies addressing certain aspects of this linguistic diversity, contact, and competition. The particular claims made by these political activists in relation to both identity politics and U.S. ethnolinguistic stratification remain to be discussed.

REFERENCES

Hollinger, David A. (1995), *Postethnic America*. New York: Basic Books.
Hubler, Shawn and Stuart Silverstein (1993), 'Schooling doesn't close minority earning gap', *Los Angeles Times* (January 10), p. A1.

McClain, Paula D. and Joseph Stewart Jr. (1998), *Can We All Get Along? Racial and Ethnic Minorities in American Politics*, 2nd ed., Boulder, CO: Westview Press.

Montejano, David. (1987), *Anglos and Mexicans in the Making of Texas, 1836–1986*, Austin: University of Texas Press.

Ong, Paul, research director (1993), *Beyond Asian American Poverty*, Los Angeles LEAP Asian Pacific American Public Policy Institute and UCLA Center for Asian/Pacific American Studies.

Smith, Rogers (1997), *Civic Ideals: Conflicting Visions of Citizenship in U.S. History*, New Haven: Yale University Press.

O'Hare, William P. (1992), 'America's Minorities – the Demographics of Diversity', *Population Bulletin* 47: 4 (December), pp. 2–47.

Tienda, Marta and Lisa J. Neidert (1985), 'Language, education and the socio-economic achievement of Hispanic-origin men', in Rodolfo O. de la Garza, Frank D. Bean, Charles M. Bonjean, Ricardo Romo and Rodolfo Alvarez (eds.) *The Mexican American Experience: an Interdisciplinary Anthology* (Austin: University of Texas Press, pp. 359–76.

Reading 5.3

[...]

Richard Ruiz (1996) points out that 'movements toward the officialization of English in the United States are consistent with the tendency in large multi-national states to promote a transethnified public culture.' He differentiates 'transethnification' from assimilation, in that in transethnification, 'It is not necessary to lose one's ethnicity to be useful to the state, . . . nor is it necessary . . . that one's attachment to the state have any sentimental aspect (in Kelman's [1971] sense of historicity and authenticity).' In the US, Ruiz argues, languages other than English are 'perfectly acceptable . . . [but only] as long as they are mediated through individuals and not communities; [however,] if they are community languages, they should be confined to the private sector and not make demands for public subsidy; [and] if there is to be public subsidy, their use should be for the common public good, and not signal competing allegiances.'

In a language ideology built on the promotion of transethnification, instrumentalism, and nationism, as Ruiz suggests that US and other multinational states language ideologies are, it is difficult to find room for state-supported programs of language education that would promote the full use and development of two or more languages in school, and that would lead to the kind of bilingual/biliterate/bicultural versatility encapsulated in the immigrants' twin plea to learn the new and keep the old. The case of Israel offers an example of a state that has in the past been characterized by such a monolingual ideology, geared toward the revitalization of Hebrew and bolstered by a series of myths and assumptions; however, new multilingual language education policies of 1995 and 1996 offer promise for indigenous and immigrant languages including

From: Nancy Hornberger (1998), 'Language policy, language education, language rights: indigenous, immigrant, and international perspectives', *Language in Society*, 27: 439–58.

Arabic, the Jewish heritage languages, and more recent immigrant languages such as Russian and Amharic (Shohamy 1994, Spolsky & Shohamy 1998). My own work, along with my reading of others' work on language and education policy and practice for immigrant (and other) language minorities in the US and elsewhere, has led me to formulate two principles that support such multilingual ideologies and policies.

The first principle, drawn as an implication from the continua model of biliteracy (Hornberger 1989), is that the more the contexts of their learning allow bilingual/biliterate learners to draw on all points of the continua of biliteracy, the greater are the chances for their full biliterate development. That is, the contexts of their learning must allow learners to draw on oral-to-literate, monolingual-to-bilingual, and micro-to-macro contexts; to use productive and receptive, oral and written, and L1 and L2 skills; and to receive both simultaneous and successive exposures, with attention to both similar and dissimilar aspects of language structure, and to convergent and divergent aspects of language scripts (Hornberger 1990, 1992).

In a multi-year ethnographic dissertation study of women and girls in several Cambodian refugee families in Philadelphia, Ellen Skilton Sylvester (1997:vii) notes: 'The challenges many [Cambodian] women and girls face in learning to read and write English are often seen in relation to short schooling histories in Cambodia, differences between Khmer and English, and little exposure to reading and writing in their first language.' Although her study addresses these issues, Skilton Sylvester places the onus of responsibility on 'educational policies and practices [that] often treat the Cambodian students' native language as a problem rather than a resource, and provide few opportunities for these students to practice and learn the literacy skills needed to become "literate insiders" in the United States' (1997:vii).

Using the continua model of biliteracy as a 'tool for uncovering the aspects of literacy that influence participation in educational programs by Cambodian women and girls,' Skilton Sylvester suggests that – in addition to the continua of biliterate contexts, development, and media – the continua of CONTENT, the meaning or 'inside' of literacy (as compared to media, the structure or 'outside' of literacy), constitute an additional key dimension, particularly so for an understanding of how it is that these Cambodian women and girls remain literate 'outsiders' rather than becoming 'insiders' (1997:187). By content, Skilton Sylvester refers to 'what is taught through and about reading and writing as well as what is read and written' (1997:242), and she defines it in terms of majority-minority, literary-vernacular, and parts-whole continua. For these Cambodian women and girls, being 'outsiders' has to do with whether, and to what degree, literacy contents to which they are introduced in their classes include serious attention to Asian voices and experience (i.e. a range of minority as well as majority contents); to the kinds of literacies they practice in their daily lives, e.g. the reading of romances; to the writing of letters, stories, and plays (i.e. a range of vernacular as well as literary contents); and to reading and constructing whole texts, as well as performing rote memorization, drills, and fill-in-the-blank exercises (i.e. a range of parts-to-whole language contents).

Skilton Sylvester applies micro-level understandings of the meanings and uses of literacy among these Cambodian women and girls to the analysis and critique of macro-level language and education policies for language minorities in schools and adult education classes. She shows how 'current practices often leave Cambodian women and girls "in-between," pulled in two directions by the home and the classroom'; and she points to 'a different possible kind of "in-between"' where schools and adult education programs would be '"in-between" sites that value and respond to learners' daily lives AND teach what they need to know to become insiders in the United States' (1997: vii).

What she is talking about is exactly the kind of support for bilingual/biliterate/bicultural versatility that is called for in pleas like Varija Prabhakaran's. With regard to mother-tongue literacy in the Cambodian community of Philadelphia, there is telling evidence that an interest in preserving Cambodian language and culture does not preclude the learning of English or acculturation to American ways: quite the contrary. It is precisely the individuals who practice Cambodian literacy, and who have a clear sense of specific functions for Khmer literacy – as an aid in learning English, as a skill for employment, as a vehicle to preserve Cambodian language and culture in a new land, or as an essential for going back to Cambodia to help people there – who also work hard to learn English, express a general appreciation for all languages, seek to negotiate a way of life that harmonizes their old and new cultures, and reach out to improve intercultural communication between Cambodians and Americans (Hornberger 1996:83). This kind of versatility is essential if immigrants and their languages are not only to survive but also to thrive and contribute in their new land.

The second principle with regard to educational policy and practice for immigrant (and other) language minority learners is that the specific characteristics of the optimal contexts for their learning can be defined only in each specific circumstance or case; there is no one 'program' – or even three programs, or ten, or twenty – that will necessarily provide the best learning context for all biliterate learners.

To be sure, there is accumulating consensus, in both research and practice, that enrichment models of bilingual education – those that 'aim toward not only maintenance but development and extension of the minority languages, [toward] cultural pluralism, and [toward] an integrated national society based on autonomy of cultural groups' (Hornberger 1991:222) – offer much potential for both majority and minority learners' academic success. Canadian French immersion programs are one example of such a model; two-way bilingual education is another. But there are certainly other program types that could embody an enrichment model of bilingual education, whose 'primary identifying characteristic is that the program structure incorporate a recognition that the minority language is not only a right of its speakers but a potential resource for majority language speakers' (Hornberger 1991:226).

Nevertheless, the specifics of how a program actually incorporates that recognition will vary greatly depending on context; and we need many more indepth studies and descriptions of such programs before we can begin to understand what works, what doesn't work, and why. One two-way bilingual education program for which we have a detailed description is the Oyster School in Washington, DC, one of the oldest two-way programs in the US. In the early 1990s, at the time of Rebecca Freeman's ethnographic/discourse-analytic study, the Oyster School's population was 58% Hispanic, 26% white, 12% black, and 4% Asian, representing more than 25 countries (Freeman 1996:558). The school's language plan, then as now, provided for instruction in Spanish and English for children speaking both majority and minority languages. Freeman began by looking at patterns of language use in this bilingual school, and she ended by discovering that curriculum organization, pedagogy, and social relations were shaped by a larger underlying identity plan.

Freeman's original intention was to study the two-way bilingual education language plan by triangulating classroom observations, the school's bilingual education policy, and conversations with principals, teachers, and students of the school. However, she began to find that there was not in fact strictly equal bilingualism in the school: Codeswitching to English in Spanish class was common, but not the reverse; there was district-wide testing in English, but not in Spanish; and the English-dominant students were not as competently bilingual in Spanish as the Spanish-dominant were in English. At that point, Freeman began a more open-ended search for 'what was going on.' What she found was that the success of the program resulted not so much from the school's language plan, but rather from its underlying identity plan, the school community's 'attempt to provide the students not only with the ability to speak a second language, but in the case of the minority students, techniques for asserting their right to speak and to be heard in a society that, at least in the Oyster School construction, regularly refuses minority populations such rights' (Freeman 1993:107).

Language rights, international perspectives, and stability

A vignette: *short sketch of person's character*

> Caernarvon, in North Wales on the Isle of Anglesey, is famous not only as the site of the castle where the Prince of Wales is traditionally crowned (an English, not a Welsh, event), but also as the place in the world where the most Welsh is spoken. Caernarvon is also the headquarters for CEFN, a Welsh non-party citizens' movement which seeks equality of citizenship and equality for Welsh people as a nation and for the Welsh language. Eleri Carrog, founder, tells how the organization grew out of a 1985 nationwide petition movement to combat the misuse of the Race Relations Act, and to

support the right of employers to recruit bilingual speakers to give service in a bilingual community. That petition drive was the original impetus for a movement that has grown far beyond the founder's expectations, with CEFN becoming an unofficial legal aid system for those wishing to fight authority to establish language rights. CEFN, with others engaged in the campaign for Welsh language rights, has met some success with the 1993 passage of the Welsh Language Act. (9/3/96)

It is not only Welsh speakers who have become activists for the right to use their own language. Language rights, or linguistic human rights, have taken on increasing urgency worldwide in the light of the twin threat posed by the loss of a vast proportion of the world's linguistic resources – the endangered languages – and by the growth of world languages like English.

This year marks 50 years since the Universal Declaration of Human Rights was adopted unanimously by the United Nations General Assembly in 1948. Within the last decade, two UNESCO-supported conferences (Recife, October 1987, and Paris, April 1989) have called for a Universal Declaration of Language Rights that would 'ensure the right to use the mother tongue in official situations, and to learn well both the mother tongue and the official language (or one of them) of the country of residence' (Phillipson 1992:96). Since 1985, the Working Group on Indigenous Populations of the UN Commission on Human Rights has been developing a draft Universal Declaration on Indigenous Rights, which includes, among 28 rights of indigenous peoples, 'the right to maintain and use their own languages, including for administrative, judicial, and other relevant purposes; [and] the right to all forms of education, including in particular the right of children to have access to education in their own languages, and to establish, structure, conduct, and control their own educational systems and institutions' (Alfredsson 1989:258).

In sum, these declarations call for the right to education in one's own language, and the right to a significant degree of control over the educational process as it affects one's children. Stephen May argues for both these rights for indigenous minorities, and he offers the case of Maori education in Aotearoa/New Zealand as an example where such rights have led to developments in which 'a long and debilitating history of colonization and marginalization for Maori is being contested, and Maori language and culture [is being] reasserted' (May 1996:154). In a situation where Maori language was 'all but ... banned from the precincts of the schools' from the turn of the twentieth century (1996:157), and was in rapid decline especially after World War II (1996:158), May notes, 'Two recent educational developments have begun to halt the process of language loss for Maori: first, the establishment of bilingual schools in the late 1970s; and second, and more significantly, the emergence of alternative Maori-medium (immersion), schools – initiated and administered by Maori – during the course of the 1980s' (1996:160).

Alternative, Maori-controlled, Maori-medium education began at the pre-school level in 1982 with the *Kohanga Reo* 'Language Nests'; it has grown to a movement including not only primary schooling in the *Kura Kaupapa Maori* 'Maori philosophy schools', but also secondary and tertiary-level institutions. Furthermore, since 1990 both Kohanga Reo and Kura Kaupapa Maori have been incorporated into the state educational system as recognized (and state-funded) alternative education options – a situation not without some contra-dictions with respect to the notion of relative autonomy that has been so fundamental to the movement (May 1996:164). As of 1991, 1% of Maori primary school students were enrolled in Kura Kaupapa Maori; as of 1993, 49.2% of Maori children enrolled in pre-school were at a Kohanga Reo. Comparing the case of Maori language revitalization to the Hebrew case, Spolsky suggests that, just as in the Hebrew case ideology played a crucial role in the success of language revitalization efforts, so too there are signs of the strength of ideology in the Maori case. Specifically, the Maori efforts (a) have been community-based, even shying away from government; (b) they are concerned not just with language, but with maintaining ethnic identity; and (c) they opt out from mainstream linguistic and cultural ideologies (Spolsky 1995).

McCarty et al. 1994 tell of similar success stories in American Indian/Alaska Native education, where local knowledge has successfully become a genuine foundation for indigenous schooling, as a result of decade-long, collaborative efforts by native speakers and non-native educators. In a concluding essay to that volume (Hornberger 1994), I suggest that the enabling conditions for such sustained and lasting improvements in indigenous schooling, as gleaned from the Native American experience as well as the case of the Puno bilingual education project I studied, include the following: a vital native language valued by the community; versatile bilingual/bicultural/biliterate personnel who take the lead in effecting change in their schools; and long-term stability of the change site – stability of site personnel, governance, and funding (Hornberger 1994:62).

'Language as resource' policy/language policy as a resource

The language as resource orientation in language planning, as first discussed by Ruiz 1984, is fundamental to the vision of language policy, language education, and language rights presented here; but in concluding, I should emphasize that it is not an uncomplicated, conflict-free vision of 'language as resource' that I have in mind.

Language policy with a 'language as resource' orientation can and does have an impact on efforts aimed at promoting the vitality and revitalization of endangered indigenous languages, and it is in this sense that we can speak of language policy itself as a resource. It is also true, however, that the force of history may overwhelm ANY policy attempt, even in the case of such a large indigenous language as Quechua.

Aodán Mac Póilin, writing about the Irish Language Movement in Northern Ireland (1996), has talked about this in terms of linguistic momentum, i.e. 'the forces which ensure that a language is used in society and passed on from one generation to the next.' He notes that the same linguistic momentum 'which allowed Irish to survive against enormous pressures in pockets of the country is now working in the other direction, in favor of English, and is, in spite of the best efforts of the revivalists, effectively inhibiting the development of Irish as a community language outside the Gaeltacht.'

After all, it is not the number of speakers of a language, but their positioning in society, that determines their patterns of language use. Mac Póilin refers to the relative linguistic significance of groups of speakers, which he says 'is related less to the number of speakers than to the degree to which the language is integrated into the daily life of its users; their social coherence; and most importantly if the language is to survive, the community's ability to successfully regenerate itself as a speech community' (1996:4).

The whole notion of language minority has more to do with power than with numbers, anyway. However, if it is true that our language and literacy practices position us in social and power hierarchies, it is also true that they may be sites of negotiation and transformation of those hierarchies. In a recent essay on research on bilingualism among linguistic minorities, Martin-Jones notes (1992:16) that the conflict research tradition seeks to explain how and why languages come to be functionally differentiated, in terms of a social history of inequality, while the micro-interactionist research tradition sees 'individuals within a bilingual community ... as actively contributing to the definition and redefinition of the symbolic value of the community's languages in daily conversational interactions'.

An example of the kind of negotiative and transformative action that individuals within a bilingual community can take is the bottom-up revitalization effort mentioned earlier. Of fundamental importance here is that such revitalization efforts are not about bringing the language back, but rather about bringing it forward:

> When we consider that reversing language shift entails altering not only the traditional language corpus but also how it is traditionally used, both at the micro level in terms of inter-personal discourse patterns, and at the macro level of societal distribution, the crucial importance of the involvement of speakers of the language becomes even more apparent. In a very real sense, revitalization initiatives ... are not so much about bringing a language back; but rather, bringing it forward; who better or more qualified to guide that process than the speakers of the language, who must and will be the ones taking it into the future? (Hornberger & King 1996:440)

May also emphasizes this point when he clarifies that the movement for alternative, Maori-medium education is 'neither separatist nor a simple retrenchment in the past' (1996:164); rather, he says, it revolves around a question of control, of having Maori-medium education available as a legitimate schooling choice. He reminds us that 'nothing in the assertion of indigenous rights – or minority rights more generally – precludes the possibilities of cultural change and adaptation' (1996:164).

Furthermore, it is not only members of language minority communities but also language education professionals who can be active contributors to negotiative, transformative processes of language revitalization, language maintenance, or indeed language shift. There is increasing recognition in our field of the role of language education professionals as language policy makers, whether they are classroom practitioners, program developers, materials and textbook writers, administrators, consultants, or academics (cf. Hornberger & Ricento 1996). McCarty has gone so far as to argue (1996) that 'while schools cannot in themselves "save" threatened indigenous languages, they and their personnel must be prominent in efforts to maintain and revitalize those languages.' In this regard, and again from a 'language as resource' perspective, key considerations for the education of indigenous, immigrant, and other language minorities are bilingual/bicultural/biliterate versatility, the continua of biliteracy, and enrichment-model bilingual education.

Once again, though, I do not mean to suggest that the implementation of a 'language as resource' perspective offers a conflict-free solution. In our finite world, the recognition and incorporation of multiple languages within any single educational system is bound occasionally to bring the language rights and needs of one group into conflict with those of another, not to mention the long-standing conflict between language and content priorities in the education of language minorities. A recent dissertation by Angela Creese (1997) looks at the limits and successes of a UK language policy that aims to provide for the language rights and needs of bilingual children in multicultural schools through mainstreaming the children while providing them with in-class language support – an approach also familiar in the US. Using an ethnographic interpretive methodology, Creese observed and audio-recorded Turkish bilingual teachers and Anglo teachers of English as a second language as well as the subject teachers they were working with in their classrooms. She looked at the relationships the teachers formed, the roles they played in class, and the language they used in playing these out; she found that, within the constraints imposed by the educational aims and reality of current policy, the language rights of the children rarely became a priority equal to the content-based aims of secondary education. The teachers showed great versatility in forming a range of collaborative relationships (which Creese calls support, partnership, and withdrawal); but if they attempted to change the hierarchy of educational aims, they were often challenged by the children they were helping. Further, teachers who worked outside this hierarchy of aims '[were] not only in danger of working themselves out onto the periphery in terms of their own status in the school, but [could] also be seen by the children they [were] targeting as providing a deficit form of education' (1997:2). Creese concludes that 'there is much more that can be done to celebrate rather than tolerate [the] diversity in British schools' (1997:322). This account is not intended to single out UK policy for criticism, but to illustrate a point that holds true for many language policies around the world: A serious commitment to provision of the rights for children to be educated in their own language requires a systemic and systematic effort, which cannot necessarily be handled by an add-on program or policy.

Language rights, then, from a 'language as resource' perspective, are not a question of automatic "concession on demand", but rather of control and choice among potential alternatives, in balanced consideration of other possibilities. Elsewhere I have argued (Hornberger 1997) that it is crucial that language minorities be empowered to make choices about which languages and which literacies to promote for which purposes; and that, in making those choices, the guiding principles must be to balance the counterpoised dimensions of language rights for the mutual protection of all. Among the balances that must be struck across competing language rights are those between tolerance-oriented and promotion-oriented rights (Kloss 1977), between individual and communal freedoms (Skutnabb-Kangas 1994), between freedom to use one's language and freedom from being discriminated against for doing so (Macías 1979), and between 'claims to something' and 'claims against someone else' (Ruiz 1984). These are difficult ethical choices, but they must be made; I am arguing here that those best qualified to make them are the language minority speakers themselves.

At a time when phrases like 'endangered languages' and 'linguicism' are invoked to describe the plight of the world's vanishing linguistic resources, in their encounter with the phenomenal growth of world languages such as English, I have argued here that there is also consistent and compelling evidence that language policy and language education serve as vehicles for promoting the vitality, versatility, and stability of these languages, and ultimately of the rights of their speakers to participate in the global community on, and IN, their own terms.

Leanne Hinton has reported on the 1992 Tribal Scholars Language Conference, a gathering of Native Californian language activists at Walker Creek Ranch in Marin County, one of the outcomes of which was the master-apprentice language program mentioned earlier. In conversation with L. Frank Manriquez, a Native Californian artist of Tongva and Ajachmen origins, Hinton commented on how inspiring the conference had been, even in the face of what appeared to be a hopeless situation for so many native Californian languages. To this Manriquez responded, 'Yes. How can it be hopeless when there is so much hope?' (Hinton 1994:233).

REFERENCES

Alfredsson, Gudmundur (1989). 'International discussion of the concerns of indigenous peoples'. *Current Anthropology* 30:255–59.

Creese, Angela (1997). 'Partnership teaching in mainstream British secondary school classrooms: A language policy for bilingual students'. Dissertation, University of Pennsylvania.

Freeman, Rebecca D. (1993). 'Language planning and identity planning for social change: Gaining the ability and the right to participate'. Dissertation, Georgetown University.

———— (1996). 'Dual-language planning at Oyster Bilingual School: "It's much more than language."' *TESOL Quarterly* 30:557–82.

Hinton, Leanne (1994). *Flutes of fire: Essays on California Indian languages.* Berkeley: Heyday.

Hornberger, Nancy H. (1989). 'Continua of biliteracy'. *Review of Educational Research* 59:271–96.

———— (1990). 'Creating successful contexts for bilingual literacy'. *Teachers College Record* 92:212–29.

———— (1991). 'Extending enrichment bilingual education: Revisiting typologies and redirecting policy'. In Ofelia Garcfa (ed.), *Bilingual education: Focusschrift in honor of Joshua A. Fishman on the occasion of his 65th birthday*, 215–34. Philadelphia: Benjamins.

———— (1992). 'Biliteracy contexts, continua, and contrasts: Policy and curriculum for Cambodian and Puerto Rican students in Philadelphia'. *Education and Urban Society* 24:196–211.

———— (1994). 'Synthesis and discussion – vitality, versatility, stability: Conditions for collaborative change'. *Journal of American Indian Education* 33:3.60–63.

———— (1996). 'Mother tongue literacy in the Cambodian community of Philadelphia'. *International Journal of the Sociology of Language* 119:69–86.

———— (1997). 'Literacy, language maintenance, and linguistic human rights: Three telling cases'. *International Journal of the Sociology of Language* 127:87–103.

————, and King, Kendall A. (1996). 'Language revitalisation in the Andes: Can the schools reverse language shift?' *'Journal of Multilingual and Multicultural Development* 17:427–41.

————, and Ricento, Thomas (1996), eds. 'Language planning and policy and the English language teaching profession'. Special issue of the *TESOL Quarterly* 30:3.

Kelman, Herbert C. (1971). 'Language as an aid and barrier to involvement to the national system'. In Joan Rubin and Bjorn Jernudd (eds.), *Can language be planned?* 21–51. Honolulu: University Press of Hawaii.

Kloss, Heinz (1977). *The American bilingual tradition.* Rowley, MA: Newbury.

Mac Póilin, Aodán (1996). 'Aspects of the Irish language movement in Northern Ireland'. Paper presented at the Canadian Association for Irish Studies, University of Prince Edward Island, June.

Macías, Reynaldo (1979). 'Language choice and human rights in the United States'. In James Alatis (ed.), *Georgetown University Round Table on Languages and Linguistics*, 86–101. Washington, DC: Georgetown University Press.

Martin-Jones, Marilyn (1992). 'Minorities and sociolinguistics'. In William Bright (ed.), *Oxford International Encyclopedia of Linguistics* 4:15–18. New York: Oxford University Press.

May, Stephen (1996). 'Indigenous language rights and education'. In John Lynch et al. (eds.), *Education and development: Tradition and innovation*, 1:149–71. London: Cassell.

McCarty, Teresa L. (1996). 'Schooling, resistance, and American Indian languages'. Paper presented at the Annual Meeting of the American Anthropological Association, San Francisco, November.

————, et al. (1994), eds. *Local knowledge in indigenous schooling: Case studies in American Indian/Alaska Native education.* Special issue of *Journal of American Indian Education*, 33:2.

Phillipson, Robert (1992). *Linguistic imperialism*. Oxford and New York: Oxford University Press.

Ruiz, Richard (1984). 'Orientations in language planning'. *NABE Journal* 8:15–34.

———— (1996). 'English officialization and transethnification in the USA'. Paper presented at the Annual Meeting of the American Anthropological Association, San Francisco, November.

Shohamy, Elana (1994). 'Issues of language planning in Israel: Language and ideology'. In Richard D. Lambert (ed.), *Language planning around the world: Contexts and systemic change*, 131–42. Washington, DC: National Foreign Language Center.

Skilton Sylvester, Ellen (1997). 'Inside, outside, and in-between: Identities, literacies and educational policies in the lives of Cambodian women and girls in Philadelphia'. Dissertation, University of Pennsylvania.

Skutnabb-Kangas, Tove (1994). 'The politics of language standards'. Paper presented at TESOL meeting, Baltimore.

Spolsky, Bernard (1995). 'Conditions for language revitalization: A comparison of the cases of Hebrew and Maor'. *Current Issues in Language and Society* 2:177–201.

————, and Shohamy, Elana (1998). 'Language in Israeli society and education'. *International Journal of the Sociology of Language*, to appear.

Reading 5.4

Extract 1 [Trepas]

Ayats was wearing a T-shirt featuring some hard rock group. Pepe initiated the sequence by telling Ayats that his shirt was ugly. He was probably representing a teacher censoring Ayats for being improperly dressed. Ayats, though, turned it into a pretend squabble amongst kids.[1]

Pepe: [amb èmfasi] quina samarreta <u>més Il- Il- Iletja</u> que portes nen
[With emphasis] What an <u>u- u- ugly</u> T-shirt you are wearing, kid.

Ayats: [Amb pronúncia exageradament acurada] la teva és una [Èmfasi]
[With exaggerated accuracy in pronunciation] yours is a [Emphasis]
<u>merda · així de >clar</u>
<u>shit! That's >plain</u>

Pepe: <sí · sí · ja ho sé
<Yeah yeah, I know.

Ayats: així de clar · no no <u>josep</u> així de clar
That's plain. No, no Josep. That's plain.

Pepe: sí sí · ja ho sé · però jo no dic que no
Yeah yeah. I know. But I am not saying otherwise.

Ayats: [Veu molt baixa] <u>li diré al marcel</u> que m'ho has dit aixó eh[?] ·
[Low voice] <u>I will tell Marcel</u> that you said that to me, right?>(xxxx)

From: Joan Pujolar (2000), *Gender, Heteroglossia and Power: A Sociolinguistic Study of Youth Culture*, Berlin: Mouton de Gruyter.

Pepe: [Cridant] <marcel · miha què m'ra dit de la samarreta = [Shouting]
             <Marcel. Look what he said to me about the T-shirt=

Ayats: [Cridant]=marcel · <u>no potser no si aquí mano jo home</u> [Shouting]
             = Marcel. <u>'Oh no, that cannot be. I am the one in charge here, man!'</u>

This episode is a pretend game featuring two kids fighting over a T-shirt. The expression *lletja* 'ugly' sounded childish in this context, as well as *merda* 'shit', pronounced and treated as if it was a very strong word ('That's plain!'), which it was not (at least for Ayats and Pepe). Additionally, to name Pepe with his full name and in Catalan *josep* suggests that the school context was being evoked. Additionally, the line 'I will tell Marcel' reminds us of schoolboys betraying their companions to the teacher. The underlined stretch in the last line was probably the voice of a teacher.

These naive characters who did not speak in argot and did not drink were played out in a characteristic tone of voice, as if pronounced in the front of the mouth. It was the same voice used by Pepe and Ayats to produce the exclamation *Ospa!*, which was a euphemized form (and therefore not tough enough) of the swearword *hòstia*, which is of religious origin. On one occasion, Pepe said that the name of the hard-core group would not sound good if it was translated into Catalan, meaning it would not sound hard, tough enough. In order to illustrate this point, he produced the actual translation *with this same voice* as evidence that Catalan would not have provided the right tone. On another occasion, Pepe dramatized a Catalan singer of a concert with this voice, while he used stylized Spanish in the same narrative to animate the voices of the public.

Such voices point to a stereotype about the Catalans that was used in a similar way to the stylized Spanish characters, i.e. to dramatize figures who should be seen as *other*, to convey irony, distance or lack of seriousness. The Rambleros used plenty of these voices. For instance, after I explained to Irene and Alicia that I walked to the tube-station every day after I saw them, Alicia said to Irene '*és molt esportista*' 'he is quite a sportsman'. Although the voice was plain and the statement might have been taken as serious, the switch to Catalan indicated that she was exaggerating, that is, teasing. On another occasion, Irene, had an acute need to pass water and expressed it through a Catalan phrase. This allowed her to distance herself from what she was saying, thus diminishing the demeaning potential of using scatological expressions. With one of the Rambleros men, I had several short conversations in Catalan. This happened late at night and the point of it was that speaking Catalan was 'a laugh'. One of the couples in the Rambleros decided one day to have a conversation in Catalan, half to practice and half to have fun. The event was presented to others as great fun. Isolated harmless exclamations, some of which have already been shown, were often produced in Catalan, such as '*renoi!*' 'gosh!'. Such voices were also used in genres connected with out-of-frame activity or frame maintenance. These were interventions which had to do with the organisation of the groups, but not with the fun making: for instance, coordination work and greetings. Thus it was not uncommon amongst the Rambleros to produce moves in Catalan such as '*què fan?*' 'what are they doing', '*on anem?*' 'where are we going?', or '*nem?*' 'let's go?'. Such proposals for the group to take a course of action could be taken as mitigated (in Brown and Levinson's sense) if they were done in Catalan, as they could be understood potentially as a joke. Goodwin (1990) also reports on girls diminishing the force of commands through dramatizations of characters. In my fieldwork, it was not unusual for me to be greeted in Catalan, particularly by Spanish speakers, although this did not imply that the person wanted to engage in a lengthy conversation in this language. In greetings, it is also very typical to adopt a half serious half joking stance (i.e. a keyed frame), as if our showing concern for other people should not be carried too far or taken too seriously in the present situation. This is probably why we find abundant examples of codeswitching in the so-called conversational openings and closings in the literature (see Heller 1988; Codó 1998; Torras 1999).

If, instead of analyzing switches into Catalan, we focus on switches into Spanish in Catalan narratives, the asymmetrical position of the two languages amongst the Trepas becomes much clearer (it is not possible to explore this point with regard to the Rambleros, as they never spoke Catalan with each other). Spanish was the actual voice of the (Trepas) group. It was the voice in which their world was experienced and their views were constructed. The switches into Spanish were a constant reminder that the world outside the narrative was in this language:

Extract 2 [Trepas]

Jaume: ya · pero tu te'n recordes que · aquell dia que va haver aquell
Yeah, but you remember that · that day when there was that
pique no[?] dee ·· *que si los porros a fuera si los porros ad · pues*
row, right? over: 'Whether joints outside or joints insid-.

elles fan lo mateix ·· i no es donen compte no? · y nosatros [...]
Well, they [the women] do the same. · And they do not realise it, right? and we [men] [...]

Here Jaume referred to a conflict experienced by the group, whereby women had complained that men spent most of their time outside the premises of bars and left the women inside on their own. The switch did not actually reproduce anybody's intervention (additionally, part of the discussion had been in Catalan), but a particular representation of what the argument was about. A similar example was provided by Pepe when he described people's general reaction to the working conditions of the training school. There is also an equivalent example from Patrícia in the group discussion, as she was talking about the separation between the genders:

Extract 3 [Trepas]

Patrícia: també fumo · · i sí que ho veig el rotllo- no ho veig pel rotllo de
I also smoke. · And I do see it. The issue, I don't see it as a question of
gustos · ho veig pel rotllo de · *el corrillo de chicos el corrillo de chicas*
tastes, I see is as a question of · *the little ring of boys the little ring of girls*

Patrícia chose to depict a typical image of the group in Spanish. Congruently with this image, the *view* or *opinion* of the group or the penya was usually animated in this language. Therefore it is not a surprise that Jaume represented his thoughts in Spanish, although he considered himself to be a full bilingual and many saw him as a Catalan speaker:

Extract 4 [Trepas]

Jaume: vull llegir però ·· me costa un montón d'agafar un llibre i és que
I want to read, but ·· I its awfully difficult for me to pick up a book and it's that
es un- · si tingués molt més temps no[?] però és que ·· quan tinc
is a- ·· if I had much more time, right? But it is like this ·· When I can
algo que fer · penso · *me leo un libro · o me voy a la calle con los*
do something, I think: 'do I read a book . . . or do I go out in the street with my
colegas · prefereixo estar amb la gent no [?] la veritat · prefereixò
mates?' I prefer to be with these people, right? The truth is: I prefer
estar amb la gent que estar amb un llibre
to be with these people than to be with a book.

[. . .]

Additionally, many switches to Spanish appeared to be done simply to add dramatic effectiveness and liveliness to a narrative. In these cases, the Spanish voice took over parts of the narrative mode itself. It became a voice meant to display more involvement, accompanied by gestures and vocal effects. In a very long narrative produced by Aleix in which he was arguing that some young people also had sexist attitudes in the workplace, he would present the conceptual principles of his argument in Catalan while the examples he gave were in the form of scenes dramatized in Spanish. In these scenes, not only were the voices of the characters dramatized in Spanish: the narrative voice was in Spanish too. A simpler example came up in Patrícia's interview. She compared a debate on feminism given in a secondary school, where people were a bit passive, with one given at the university, where 't'empiezan con elucubraciones' 'they start with long-winded theoretizations'. Here the switch to Spanish is accompanied with a mimicking voice expressing scorn for such pretentious speculations. Of course, it is arguable that I could have counted this episode as a Spanish voice with a negative overtone. Nevertheless, I believe that Spanish was used here as a device to produce a more dramatic effect.

Other Spanish voices were of an even more subtle quality. Up to now I have presented switches which one would probably represent in written language between quotation marks, even though the exact meaning of some voices might be difficult to assess. Other types of voice, however, seem to have a much more ambivalent, skewed status. Clara's switches are a case in point. Her family language was Spanish and she could speak Catalan fluently. Nevertheless, she rarely spoke *only* in Catalan. When speaking with me, she would switch languages very often. Sometimes it was not clear to me whether there was actually a main or matrix language in her speech. Often, she would switch to Spanish for a quote, a dramatization, a joke, irony, and not come back when the purpose of the switch seemed to have ended. So I found myself, across several turns, responding in Catalan to her Spanish interventions and wondering if I should not accommodate to her. Sometimes I did so, but then she would often switch back to Catalan, which was all the more disorientating.

To interpret Clara's switching practices, more than just stylistic effects should be taken into consideration. Because of her political beliefs, Clara felt that she had to speak Catalan with me, or at least avoid prompting a switch to Spanish on my part. Thus, while her switches into Spanish generally followed the need to produce particular expressive effects, her switches into Catalan were done so that I would not feel obliged to speak in Spanish myself.

In her interview, she declared that she had some difficulties of expression in Catalan, which she solved by simply switching to Spanish. But, what could these 'difficulties of expression' consist of? I have located some examples which illustrate the difference between Clara's Catalan and Spanish voices:

Extract 5 [Trepas]

Clara: *no siempree* [Ella riu] · *te invito a comer* · *que*[?]
   Not always [She laughs]. *I invite you to eat. What?*
Joan: *brazo de gitano* [i li ensenyo el braç, ella riu fort]
   A 'Gypsy's arm' [I show her my arm; it is a pun, because a 'Gypsy's arm' is a type of cake; she laughs loudly].
Clara: <u>*ei pues el dimarts vens a casa*</u> · [assenteixo] · *qué te ha parecido mi*
   <u>Hey, then you come Tuesday to my place.</u> [I nod] *How did you find my*
   casa bonita > a fed [riu]
   house: beautiful > or ugly?
Joan: <*si* · *noo*
   <*yes* · *noo.*

After many turns of jokes, Clara switched to Catalan (underlined) probably to ensure that I took her invitation seriously. Her voice was now serious and flat. After a pause where I shyly accepted her invitation, Clara switched back to Spanish to ask my opinion about her flat, which I had already seen. This time, her voice (a soft, higher pitch) was half ironic and opened the possibility of joking again. Additionally, putting her question in terms of 'beautiful' or 'ugly' evoked the childish language analyzed in extract 1 above. The proper slang words would be *guai, chachi* 'great' or *cutre* 'crap'. As I see it, her ironic tone was meant to express role distance and was probably geared to avoid an embarrassing situation had I not liked her house.

So this ironic voice could have a very important role in managing relationships and communication. In my first nights out with the Trepas, Clara said to me various times things such as 'you will turn yourself into a cynical person' or 'you are very witty' through switches to Spanish. These were some of the skilful moves she performed so that we could get to know each other by talking half seriously and half jokingly about our personalities.

The importance of the expressive contrast between her Catalan and Spanish voices can be shown in the following extract, where she was explaining to me how she convinced a friend to start her studies again:

Extract 6 [Trepas]

Clara: estava al centre cívic · *comiendole la cabeza a la · a la natalia* ··
    I was in the Civic Centre *'nagging · Natalia*
    para que se matriculara [...] · *matriculaté · porque no sé qué.*
    so that she would register [...] : *'Do register, because I don't know,*
    porque con (xx) llegarás muy lejos
    because with (xx) you'll get very far'

The idea of *convincing Natalia* was expressed through the slang or colloquial phrase *comer la cabeza* (literally 'to eat someone's head'). Had this been expressed in a flat, standard voice, it might have sounded paternalistic of Clara to do this with a friend. Additionally, the cliché line 'you'll get very far' also conveyed irony.

Now it could be said that this was a Spanish *funny* voice comparable to the Catalan ones mentioned above. Nevertheless, it was a voice *of hers*, not a voice of *someone else*. This ironic tone was very common in peer-group talk. Probably everybody had such a register. Catalan voices tended to become a flat, dry, matter of fact, radio-weather-forecast kind of voice. Spanish could be used to produce teasing, affection, fun, lively tones, i.e. the tones of the everyday talk of the group. Spanish thus provided some symbolic means through which relationships were established and developed within the group. Because having fun was the main frame of activity, some otherwise serious issues could be talked about in the form of jokes. This voice was therefore fundamental to the identities of the group and this explains why Clara could not be brought to maintain Catalan throughout a whole conversation.

Concluding remarks

It is an established notion in sociolinguistics that the variety spoken by a given social group often becomes a symbol of the values and identities of the group, and that it may also be shaped and used in a way that conforms with the group's idea of itself. As such, speakers are encouraged to show loyalty to their own group's culture and way of speaking. This allegedly explains why peripheral or lower class communities often maintain their local varieties in the face of competition from more powerful linguistic forms such as standard or dominant languages. This is usually referred to as the status/solidarity dichotomy. According to this view, many speakers seek to find a balance between their desire for social advancement and the pressures to display solidarity towards their local variety (Woolard 1985). For the study of language choice and codeswitching, Gumperz (1982: 66, 73) proposes the categories of *we-code*, as 'associated with in-group and informal activities' (such as relationships with kin and friends) versus *they-code*, 'associated with the more formal, stiffer and less personal out-group relations.' He argues that speakers effectively interpret code-switches on the basis of this dichotomous association in combination with the subtle contextualizing functions that linguistic alternations perform in talk (ibid.: 91–95). In a way, this dichotomy can also be portrayed as an inside/outside, in-group/out-group symbolic contrast.

I think that something of this kind is happening to an extent in my data, although the complexities of the situation I studied require a more elaborated explanatory framework. What emerges from the analysis of the code-switching practices of the Rambleros and the Trepas is that the function of we-code was associated with Spanish, whereas Catalan was generally treated as a they-code. Spanish occupied most of the conversational space within the groups and it was the language in which the expressive recources (speech genres and styles) associated with peer-group values and identities were being developed. Spanish, to summarize, sounded tougher and cooler, and it was more appropriate to evoke transgressive characters and most of the groups' shared experiences. Catalan, on the other hand, was a language not mastered by everybody and only used in a restricted set of situations. The only shared experience of significance with Catalan had been at school and in other public domains, which means that it often evoked formal and submissive characters and situations.

However, some important qualifications need to be made in relation to how the we/they dichotomy is commonly portrayed in the literature. First, I believe that Catalan cannot really be portrayed as a dominant language or as a language of wider communication than Spanish even in that particular context. Spanish is, after all, the language of the state, the overwhelmingly predominant language of advertising and the media, and the main language spoken in the community. What we have here is that some of the processes of sociolinguistic identification that normally contribute to the maintenance of local varieties operate in favour of the dominant language precisely because the population of immigrant origin has been able to establish the use of its we-code at the local level and to benefit from its status as a dominant language within Spain.

Secondly, I do not really subscribe to the notion that the we/they dichotomy is somehow at the root of the interpretive devices that people use to produce and understand utterances. I have already argued that the production and interpretation of an utterance operate on the basis of the dialogical processes that connect the utterance with previous utterances and actions, and which rely on people's ability to identify the genres and voices that are being used. This means that the symbolic spaces associated with each language emerge as a *product* of these processes. They do not originate in a pre-determined identity or competence. I see the we/they dichotomy as a *social construct*, a product of the processes whereby groups establish dialogical relationships between different discourses and languages. This is why we can find situations such as this one, where Spanish was not only the we-code for Spanish speakers, but also for people who had Catalan as the family language.

NOTE

1. TRANCRIPTION CONVENTIONS (adapted)

Catalan utterances (including translations)	represented in roman type
Spanish utterances (including translations)	*represented in italics*
...	pauses
(xxx)	inaudible utterances
[ ]	contextual information
>	start of overlap with the following turn
<	start of overlap with previous turn
=	contiguous utterance
"xxx xxxx"	change of voice or character dramatizations
underlined text	elements of talk particularly pertinent to discussion

REFERENCES

Codó, Eva (1998), 'Analysis of language choice in intercultural service encounters', unpublished dissertation. Universitat Autónoma de Barcelona.

Goodwin, Marjorie H. (1990), *She-Said-He-Said: Talk as Social Organisation among Black Children*, Bloomington and Indianapolis: Indiana University Press.

Gumperz, John J. (1982), *Language and Social Identity*, Cambridge: Cambridge University Press.

Heller, Monica (1988) (ed.), *Codeswitching: Anthropological and Sociolinguistic Perspectives*, Berlin: Mouton de Gruyter.

Heller, Monica (1988), 'Strategic ambiguity: code-switching in the management of conflict', in Heller (ed.), 77–96.

Torras, Maria Carme (1999), 'Selection of medium in conversation: a study of trilingual service encounters', unpublished dissertation, Universitat Autónoma de Barcelona.

Woolard, Kathryn (1985), 'Catalonia: the dilemma of language rights', in Wolfson, N. and J. Manes (eds), *Language of Inequality*, Berlin: Mouton Publishers, 91–110.

GLOSSARY

alliteration Repetitious pattern of consonants; e.g., *Around the rugged rocks the ragged rascal ran*. Patterning of vowels is known as assonance.

ambiguity Double/multiple meaning. An ambiguous statement has more than one possible interpretation.

ambivalence Implies uncertainty in intention. In pragmatics, the function of an utterance is ambivalent if its illocutionary force is not explicit.

axiom markers Forceful emphasis added to an axiomatic statement such as *boys will be boys*, as in: *boys will be boys and that's all there is to it*.

conversationalisation Refers to the process by which the language associated with conversation in the private or personal sphere is appropriated for use in other more public, institutional domains such as advertising, public health and social welfare, management and so on. It is a recurrent theme of **discourse technologisation** (see below).

co-operative principle A term derived from Grice (1975), the 'co-operative principle' states that people will attempt to co-operate with each other when communicating. They will 'be informative', 'truthful', 'relevant' and 'clear'. Interaction proceeds on the assumption that these rules or 'maxims' will not be broken. Assuming co-operation, people can thus make sense of each other's communication even if it appears, on the surface, that their utterances are inappropriate Yule (1998: 145) analyses the following example:

Carol: Are you coming to the party?
Lara: I've got an exam tomorrow.

He notes that on the face of it, Lara's reply doesn't seem to answer Carol's question. Yet Carol will assume Lara is being 'co-operative' (informative and relevant) and will work out that an exam tomorrow means that Lara will be studying tonight and cannot make the party.

dialogical; dialogism The principle originating in Bakhtin's work (e.g. 1981, 1986) that all language is essentially structured as dialogue. Any text is produced in response to a previous one, anticipates future ones and only has meaning as such. One of the important implications of this view is that all language is rooted in its social context of use. From this perspective, as we use language in day-to-day interaction we appropriate utterances from all sorts of **speech genres**. In doing so, we portray these to our interlocutors as our 'own' voice or as **keyed** uses of the voices of others. For a synopsis of Bakhtin's ideas, see Marshall (2001).

diglossia A term originally coined by Ferguson (1959) to describe situations in which two substantially different varieties of a language exist in the same society and are used for different, strictly defined purposes and have very different status. A typical example would be the respective roles of Classical and colloquial Arabic in many Middle Eastern countries. Subsequently a broader use of the term developed in which diglossic relationships are seen as central to many communities in which more than one language exists. Proponents of this wider definition, however, continue to make a distinction between the concepts of diglossia and bilingualism (e.g., Fishman 1967).

discourse Variously understood to refer to connected stretches of language, to situated verbal interaction and to a specific domain of language use. In critical language study, the term generally encompasses the second and third of these usages; critical discourse analysis combines them explicitly (see e.g. Fairclough 1992, 2001; Talbot 1998). The third use is probably more common in cultural studies than the second; it views discourses as historically constituted social constructions that organise and distribute knowledge and relations of power.

discourse technologies/technologisation of discourse According to Fairclough and Wodak (1997: 260), the technologisation of discourse is a distinctive characteristic of the modern world: 'The increased importance of language in social life has led to a greater level of conscious intervention to control and shape language practices in accordance with economic, political and institutional objectives.' Fairclough (1992a: 215) points to conversation control skills, advertising and counselling as examples of discourse technologies. He (1996: 73) lists a number of defining features of discourse technologisation: the emergence of expert 'discourse technologists' such as 'communication specialists' who advise and instruct people in power how to use language for strategic ends; a shift in the 'policing' and standardising of discourse practices (for example, the prescriptive talk practices that call centre operators are advised to follow, and the subsequent surveillance of these workers to check that they are following the designated script); the design and projection of context-free discourse techniques so linguistic tools become transferable across different sorts of institutional and occupational settings; and the strategically motivated simulation in discourse where 'pretence' is employed for particular ends.

dominant dialect The term 'dominant dialect' refers to that variety which is usually used in print and which is normally taught in schools and to non-native speakers using the language. It is also the variety which is normally spoken by educated people and used in news broadcasts and other similar situations. It is more often known as the 'standard' variety of a language. This term is, however, problematic, since all other varieties are by implication non- or sub-standard. In very many languages, there is a particular relation between the dominant dialect and written forms. Its grammar and vocabulary have been codified. It is used extensively in education, including formal, public written examinations in all subjects. Beyond school it is used widely in public and professional life.

double-voicing; double-voiced A single discourse can contain a variety of voices, can include multiple layers of identity. Bakhtin explains how 'double-voiced discourse':

> Serves two speakers at the same time and expresses simultaneously two different intentions: the direct intention of the character who is speaking, and the refracted intention of the author. In such discourse there are two voices, two meanings and two expressions. (1981: 324–5)

In this way double-voicing is a powerful means by which speakers can use what they see as another group's discourse in order to communicate for example irony, ridicule or ambivalence. For a synopsis of Bakhtin's ideas, see Marshall (2001).

dysphemism Abusive terms, or 'bad-naming' (Bolinger 1980: 119). It is the inverse of euphemism, or 'good-naming'.

ebonics A combination of 'ebony' (black) and 'phonics' (sound). It refers to African American Vernacular English (AAVE) which is a rule-governed and systematic variety of English.

ethnography A method of social investigation which involves in-depth description and analysis of the characteristics of groups in society. The emphasis is often on understanding how the members of the group interpret and construct their relationships and their views of the world. Typically the researcher gathers data through **participant observation**.

ethnolinguistic identity Aspects of the ethnic identity of a person or a group which are seen to be constructed mainly by the language that they speak. In this sense language may be a fundamentally important marker of ethnicity (for example, in Catalonia) or not (for example, in northern Ireland where language is not a factor in distinguishing Protestant and Catholic ethnicities).

expressive Function of language focusing on speaker-state: conveying feelings, opinions, exclamations, likes and dislikes.

face Public self-image; what someone loses when they are embarrassed or humiliated. It has two aspects:

1. Negative face: the need to be left alone, to be independent and not imposed upon;
2. Positive face: the need to be liked, to be part of a social group.

frame Frames are, according to Goffman, the 'basic frameworks of understanding available in our society for making sense out of events' (1974: 10). As such they have the potential to be manipulated in order to engage in activities such as play. See **key** below.

generalisation Stereotyping in operation. Generalisation 'refers to the extension of the characteristics or activities of a specific and specifiable group of people to a much more general and open-ended set' (Teo 2000: 16); e.g., *Teenagers are up to no good; Black people have rhythm*.

hedging The softening or weakening of the force of an utterance. Some hedges are: *sort of, I think, a bit, as it were, kind of, isn't it?* They may be used to avoid appearing overbearingly dogmatic, or to soften criticism.

hegemony Control by consent; more fully, the attempt by dominant groups in society to win the consent of subordinate groups and to achieve a 'compromise equilibrium' in ruling over them (Gramsci 1971). This winning of consent is achieved when arrangements that suit a dominant group's own interests have come to be perceived as simply 'common sense'. For a clear account, see Storey (2001).

heteroglossia The idea, deriving from Bakhtin (e.g., 1981, 1986), that linguistic diversity is inherent in linguistic communities. This diversity, structured in terms of **speech genres**, serves to create and maintain the social stratification of language in society along the lines of class, gender, generation, etc. For a synopsis of Bakhtin's ideas, see Marshall (2001).

hip-hop Cutler (1999:*n*) quotes Rose (1994: 74) in explaining that 'hip hop culture emerged as a source of alternative identity formation and social status for youth' with origins in the South Bronx area of New York in the 1970s. Connected with graffiti, breakdancing and rap music, Rose describes how 'alternative local identities were formed in fashions and language, street names and most importantly, in establishing neighborhood crews or posses'.

hybridisation A 'mixture' or 'blend'. For instance, texts can be hybridised in containing features of two genres (e.g., advertising and welfare benefit information). As far as 'ethnicity' is concerned, 'hybridised' identities occur when speakers from one culture adopt practices from another.

indirect request A request that is not made explicitly, so that if challenged its utterer could deny making it. In asking his wife 'Is there any ketchup, Vera?', Vera's husband is not explicitly requesting her to perform the action of bringing ketchup to the table. A direct request would be, e.g., *Please bring me the ketchup*.

intertextuality; intertextual(ly) Refers to the way that a text echoes another text. Fairclough describes 'intertextuality' as 'basically the property texts have of being full of snatches of other texts ... which the text may assimilate, contradict, ironically echo, and so forth' (1992a: 84). In these ways, a text transforms prior texts. Those in charge of text production are usually in positions of authority and so intertextuality needs to be analysed critically in relation to social power and social change.

intransitive verbs Verbs which do not take a direct object. Verbs like *come, go, happen, die* do not need objects, in contrast with transitive verbs like *hit, make* (*He made the tea*) which do. There are many verbs which can function either way: *the palm is growing; the palm is growing a new leaf.*

introducer A narrative role specific to collaboratively produced narratives in conversation. The introducer is the co-narrator who opens the narrative, thereby choosing topic and **protagonist**. Introducers often nominate the **primary recipient** as well. You can see all three in this story elicitation: *You wanna tell Daddy what happened to you today?*

key Keying, a term coined by Goffman (1974), refers to the way in which speakers can exploit a **frame** in order to communicate play activities, jokes, irony, half-seriousness, ambivalence and so on. In bilingual communities a speaker may, for example, adopt the language not typically associated with their group, in order to distance themselves from what they're saying. The same effect can be achieved, of course, in a monolingual context by strategic use of **speech genres**, styles, etc. stereotypically associated with other groups.

linguistic capital A person who knows a language which has power and status in their community and/or the wider world has linguistic capital. Those in possession of linguistic capital are likely to have better life chances than those without it and, like economic capital, those who already have it are best placed to acquire more of it.

linguistic imperialism The idea, developed particularly by Phillipson (1992), that language is a primary means in the modern world whereby the West exerts political and economic domination over the rest of the world. The theory has been very influential but has also been widely criticised as too simplistic and, sometimes, as neo-colonial in its outlook.

marked Something which is marked, as opposed to unmarked, is considered to be in some way different from what is seen as natural, neutral or expected. It can be argued that all language use is by definition ideologically marked as choice is always involved in using language and ideological considerations inevitably influence our choices.

metaphor The attribution of a quality to something to which it is not literally applicable; e.g., *an icy stare*. 'The essence of metaphor is understanding and experiencing one kind of thing in terms of another' (Lakoff and Johnson 1980: 5). For critical language study, metaphors are important because they are ideologically loaded and can be powerful rhetorical devices, particularly when their metaphorical nature is not immediately obvious. Representations of refugees in the news provide clear examples. Refugees are individuals who have been forced, each in unique circumstances, to leave their homes and livelihoods and seek asylum in a foreign country. They are sometimes subjected to crude **dysphemism** involving use of metaphor (*dross, vermin, human sewage*). More

frequent, however, are less crudely obvious metaphorical expression/
nevertheless dehumanise their subject. For example, if the arrival of a /
people in the host country is reported in the news as a *wave* or *flc*
arrival is likened to the movement of a large body of water. They are ت
presented not as individuals but as a potentially dangerous mass or force. The
metaphor generates a way of talking and writing about people as if they were
not people at all; they can *erode*, require *floodgates*, etc.

metonymy One item standing in for another from the same context. A classic
example is a café customer being identified in terms of the food he ordered: *The
ham sandwich is waiting for his check* (Lakoff and Johnson 1980: 35). The key
thing about metonymy is contiguity, that is, occurring in the same context.

micro Micro methods and analysis in sociolinguistics are techniques which
focus on the details of phenomena such as actual language use and switching by
bilinguals, the norms governing the structure of conversation in a given society
or how ideology is communicated through the details of the ways in which
people speak. This fine-grained analysis contrasts with the more 'macro'
concerns of societal bilingualism, language planning, language policy and so
on. These latter areas are sometimes referred to as the sociology of language as
opposed to sociolinguistics as such.

micro-interactionism The detailed study of linguistic choices made and strategies adopted by speakers in, for example, conversation. See **micro** above.

minimal responses; minimal backchannelling These typically signal support for
the speaker and listener's active participation in a conversation, although this is
dependent on how they are said and where they are linguistically placed. Co-
operatively realised by such items as 'mhm', 'yeah', 'right', they provide
evidence of how a conversation is jointly produced.

modality Degree of speaker-commitment to what they say, conveyed by various
means including modal auxiliary verbs (e.g. *may*, *must*), related adverbs (e.g.,
possibly, *probably*) and **hedges**. There are two main kinds modality, relating to
truth and obligation:

1. Truth-modality. This relates to the degree of certainty about a statement,
    to the speaker's commitment to it as true. It therefore relates to **expres-
    sive** value. Consider the difference between *I think that may be mine* and
    That's mine. If someone speaks with the modality of categorical certainty
    they are trying to sound authoritative.
2. Obligation-modality. This relates to a person's commitment to a state-
    ment as necessary, as in *All coursework submitted must be type written
    and double spaced.*

multifunctionality Language has multiple functions at the same time. For
example, *it's freezing in here* may be simultaneously referential (conveying
information), **expressive** and directive (trying to get someone else to do something).

negative politeness Respect behaviour; signalling deference or consideration for others' independence. Negative politeness strategies are employed to avoid potential threats to negative **face**. A person wanting to borrow a pen from a stranger, for instance, might minimise the imposition involved in the request by **hedging** and prefacing it with an apology; *Sorry to bother you but could I just borrow your pen a moment?*

nominalisation A process represented in a noun or noun phrase; e.g., *the bombing of villages*. When processes are represented in this way (rather than in verbs, as in *X bombed villages*) they are mystified. In particular, it can be difficult to work out the agency involved: who or what is responsible for the process.

over-lexicalisation Where the same object, process or state is referred to by a variety of terms The use of an unusually high number of different words in the same general area of meaning (especially synonyms or near-synonyms). Over-lexicalisation indicates preoccupation with some aspect of reality.

parallelism Making connections by repeating patterns, often of phrases (*out of sight, out of mind*) or clauses (*we will find the scroungers, we will punish the scroungers*).

participant observation A research technique in which the researcher attempts to become part of a particular community for an extended period in order to study aspects of their (language) behaviour in as 'natural' a setting as possible. The technique is often considered to be a way of avoiding the distorting effect that experimental situations can have on people's behaviour, but it can also raise serious ethical issues. See also **ethnography** above.

passive A grammatical term. Contrasted with 'active', this term refers to the situation where the grammatical subject of any sentence or clause is the 'goal' of the action, e.g., *The burglar was apprehended by the police*. The agent performing the action (*the police*, in the example) may be deleted, as in *The burglar was apprehended*. This is known as an agentless passive.

poetic Function of language focusing on the playful use of language for its own sake. The term has a literary slant, but the poetic function of language is much more widespread.

polyvalence The Bakhtinian idea (e.g., 1981, 1986) that no linguistic practice has a universal significance in a particular language; that meaning is always dependent on context. See also **dialogism** and **double-voicing**. For a synopsis of Bakhtin's ideas, see Marshall (2001).

positive face The need to be approved of and/or seen as part of a group.

positive politeness Friendly behaviour; signalling closeness, similarity. Positive politeness strategies are employed to avoid potential threats to positive **face**. Someone requesting help from a fellow passenger, for example, might soften the imposition by using an affectionate term of address: *Help me with these bags, would you, love?*

presupposition 'Preconstructed' background knowledge. A 'classic' example from philosophy is that the statement *The King of France is bald* presupposes that *there is a King of France*. Presuppositions have 'constancy under negation', so that *The King of France isn't bald* would still presuppose that *there is a King of France*. For another example, take a handwritten notice on a coffee vending machine which read, *This coffee isn't free!* and deserved the graffiti response: *It isn't even coffee!* In these examples the presuppositions are 'triggered' by *the* and *this* respectively. Other triggers are iteratives like *again*: *They saw the flying saucer again* presupposes that *they saw a flying saucer before*; and factive verbs like *regret*: *Laura regrets drinking Sean's home brew* presupposes that *Laura drank Sean's home brew*. For a detailed account, see Levinson (1983).

primary recipient As a narrative role, this is specific to collaboratively produced narratives in conversation. The primary recipient of a conversational narrative is the main person it is being directed to. The role carries privileges, particularly an entitlement to criticise the **protagonist**.

problematiser In conversational narrative, this is the person who finds fault with it, 'who renders an action, condition, thought, or feeling of a protagonist or a co-narrator problematic' (Ochs and Taylor 1995: 108).

protagonist Principal character in a narrative. In a first-person narrative, the protagonist and the story's main teller are the same person.

reverse discourse (Foucault 1981) Subordinated or oppressed groups of people can employ a 'reverse discourse' where they draw on the language and categories of the dominant discourse and subvert their meaning. 'Reverse discourses' thus challenge authority and power and, in doing so, constitute resistance.

simultaneous speech At its most basic, this is where two or more speakers talk at the same time, although a more refined definition can be found in Coates (1988: 107–13). In contexts between friends, it often signals support and solidarity.

speech genre In Bakhtin's sense, linguistic speech genres are types of utterances which have typical forms and content and which are associated with and help to create contexts of communication. Examples of these in everyday action would be chatting, teasing and joking. For a synopsis of Bakhtin's ideas, see Marshall (2001).

Stylised Asian English A variety of adolescent talk described by Rampton (1995: 68) that includes a range of grammatical, prosodic and phonetic features different from those used by the local vernacular of English. For instance, verbal auxiliaries were rarely contracted ('I am not liking that one'); every syllable was usually stressed; and /w/ was sometimes changed to [v] or [b] ('vearing' for 'wearing'). It often functioned as a comment on Anglo-Asian relations of domination, particularly when young Asian people came up against 'white' institutional authority or power.

subtractive bilingualism A phenomenon which is said to come about when a second language is learned at the expense of the first language, or where acquiring a second language impoverishes a person's overall language competence rather than enhancing it.

symbolic capital Assets in the 'symbolic marketplace' (Bourdieu 1991). When the symbolic assets involve language, it is sometimes referred to as **linguistic**

capital. According to Bourdieu, people may have four kinds of resource available to them: economic capital (wealth), cultural capital (education, access to knowledge and skills), social capital (being 'well-connected') and symbolic capital (honour and prestige). For a clear, sociolinguistic account, see Mesthrie et al. (2000).

synecdoche A rhetorical device where the part stands for the whole; e.g., *All hands on deck*. In sexist talk about women, and in verbal abuse, women may be referred to in terms of body parts: e.g., *Did you see those tits walking by?* (Adams et al. 1995: 396). Synecdoche is not always easily distinguished from **metonymy**. The difference is that it depends on meaning relations (semantics) rather than context (contiguity).

synthetic personalisation Synthetic personalisation is the manipulation of interpersonal meanings and forms for strategic and instrumental purposes. Fairclough notes that this

> may be a matter of constructing fictitious individual persons, for instance as the addresser and addressee in an advertisement, or of manipulating the subject positions of, or the relationship between, actual individual persons (in the direction of equality, solidarity, intimacy or whatever), as in interviews. (2001: 179)

He further describes it as

> a compensatory tendency to give the impression of treating each of the people 'handled' *en masse* as an individual. Examples would be air travel (*have a nice day!*), restaurants (*welcome to Wimpy!*), and the simulated conversation (e.g. chat shows) and *bonhomie* which litter the media. (2001: 52)

In broadcast talk, it is through 'synthetic personalisation' that the presenter or host minimises distance between themselves and their audience, often through the creation of a 'likeable', 'down-to-earth' character or **synthetic personality**.

synthetic personality A constructed 'friendly', 'approachable' persona, often adopted in broadcast talk for public consumption (Tolson 1991).

upwardly converged Where speakers move towards the prestigious (usually standard) variety of speech

TRANSCRIPTION KEY

(.)	pause of up to half a second
(..)	pause of up to one second
(2.5)	approximate timing of longer pauses
=	latching (immediate follow-on)
heh heheh	laughter
(h)	laughter in speech
hhhhh	exhales
.hhh	inhales
(( ))	paralinguistic features and other business
(xx) (word)	indistinct utterances
>word<	more rapid than surrounding speech
[ ] or ⌈	simultaneous speech
CAPS	loud talk
wo:::d	extended sound
word	stress
wor-	incomplete utterance/cut-off
/or ?/	rising intonation

BIBLIOGRAPHY

Adams, K. and A. Winter (1997), 'Gang graffiti as a discourse genre', *Journal of Sociolinguistics*, 1: 3, 337–60.

Adams, Peter, Alison Towns and Nicola Gavey (1995), 'Dominance and entitlement: the rhetoric men use to discuss their violence towards women', *Discourse and Society* 6: 3, 387–406.

Allan, Stuart, Karen Atkinson and Martin Montgomery (1995), 'Time and the politics of nostalgia: an analysis of the Conservative party election broadcast "The Journey"', *Time and Society*, 4: 3, 365–95.

Atkinson, Karen (1993), 'Co-operativity in all-female intergenerational talk', unpublished PhD thesis, Cardiff.

Atkinson, Karen and Nikolas Coupland (1988), 'Accommodation as Ideology', *Language and Communication*, 8: 3/4, 321–7.

Atkinson, Karen and Shaun Moores (in press), ' "We all have bad bad days": attending to face in broadcast troubles-talk', *The Radio Journal*.

Atkinson, Karen and Sarah Oerton (1996), 'Benefit babes: young mothers and their discourses of identity', unpublished paper, Sociolinguistic Symposium 11, University of Cardiff, Wales, September.

Atkinson, Karen, Sarah Oerton and Diane Burns (1998), 'Happy families? Single mothers, the press and the politicians', *Capital & Class*, 64, 1–11.

Back, Les (1996), *New Ethnicities and Urban Culture: Racisms and Multiculture in Young Lives*, London: UCL Press.

Baetens Beardsmore, Hugo (1986), *Bilingualism: Basic Principles*, Clevedon: Multilingual Matters.

Bailey, Richard W. (1993), *Images of English: A Cultural History of the Language*, Ann Arbor: University of Michigan Press.

Baker, Colin (2001), *Foundations of Bilingual Education and Bilingualism*, Clevedon: Multilingual Matters.

Bakhtin, Mikhail M. (1981), *The Dialogic Imagination*, Austin: University of Texas Press.

Bakhtin, Mikhail M. (1986), *Speech Genres and Other Late Essays*, ed. M. Holquist, trans. C. Emerson and M. Holquist, Austin: University of Texas Press.

Baron, Dennis (2000), 'Ebonics and the politics of English', *World Englishes*, 19: 1, 15–19.

Baugh, John (2000), *Beyond Ebonics: Linguistic Pride and Prejudice*, New York: Oxford University Press.

Bell, Allan (1991), *The Language of News Media*, Oxford: Blackwell.

Bentham, Jeremy (1791), *Panopticon*, London: T. Payne.

Blum-Kulka, Shoshana (1993), ' "You gotta know how to tell a story": Telling, tales and tellers in American and Israeli narrative events at dinner', *Language in Society*, 22, 361–402.

Blum-Kulka, Shoshana (1997), *Dinner Talk: Cultural Patterns of Sociability and Socialization in Family Discourse*, Mahwah, NJ: Lawrence Erlbaum.

Blum-Kulka, Shoshana (2000), 'Gossipy events at family dinners: negotiating sociability, presence and the moral order', in Justine Coupland (ed.), *Small Talk*, Harlow: Pearson Education Ltd, pp. 209–12.

Boden, Deirdre (1994), *The Business of Talk: Organizations in Action*, Cambridge, MA: Polity Press.

Bolinger, Dwight (1980), *Language: The Loaded Weapon*, London: Longman.

Bourdieu, Pierre (1977), '*The Economics of Linguistic Exchanges*', trans. R. Nice, Cambridge: Cambridge University Press.

Bourdieu, Pierre (1990), *In Other Words: Essays towards a Reflexive Sociology*, Stanford, CA: Stanford University Press.

Bourdieu, Pierre (1991), *Language and Symbolic Power*, ed. J. B. Thompson, trans. G. Raymond and M. Adamson, Cambridge, MA: Harvard University Press.

Bourhis, Richard Y. and David F. Marshall (1999), 'The United States and Canada', in J. A. Fishman (ed.), *Handbook of Language and Ethnic Identity*, Oxford: Oxford University Press.

Brown, Penelope (1980), 'How and why are women more polite: Some evidence from a Mayan community', in S. McConnell-Ginet, R. Borker and N. Furman (eds), *Women and Language in Literature and Society*, New York: Praeger, pp. 111–36.

Brown, Penelope (1993), 'Gender, politeness and confrontation in Tenejapa', in Deborah Tannen (ed.), *Gender and Conversational Interaction*, Oxford: Oxford University Press, pp. 144–62.

Brown, Penelope and Stephen Levinson (1987), *Politeness: Some Universals in Language Usage*, Cambridge: Cambridge University Press.

Bucholtz, Mary (1998), 'Geek the girl: language, femininity and female nerds', in Natasha Warner et al. (eds), *Proceedings of the Fourth Berkeley Women and Language Conference*, Berkeley, CA: Berkeley Women and Language Group, pp. 119–31.

Bucholtz, Mary (1999a), ' "Why be normal?": language and identity practices in a community of nerd girls', *Language in Society*, 28: 2, 203–23.

Bucholtz, Mary (1999b), 'You da man: narrating the racial other in the linguistic production of white masculinity', *Journal of Sociolinguistics*, 3: 4, 443–60.

Bucholtz, Mary (2001), 'The whiteness of nerds: superstandard English and racial markedness', *Journal of Linguistic Anthropology*, 11: 1, 84–100.

Bucholtz, Mary (2002), 'Youth and cultural practice', *Annual Review of Anthropology*, 31, 525–52.

Cameron, Deborah (1992), Review of Tannen 1991, *Feminism and Psychology*, 2:3, 465–89.

Cameron, Deborah (1995), *Verbal Hygiene*, London: Routledge.

Cameron, Deborah (1997a), 'Demythologizing sociolinguistics' in Nikolas Coupland and Adam Jaworski (eds) (1997), *Sociolinguistics: A Reader and Coursebook*, Basingstoke: Macmillan.

Cameron, Deborah (1997b), 'Performing gender identity: young men's talk and the construction of heterosexual masculinity', in Sally Johnson and Ulrike Hanna Meinhof (eds)(1997), *Language and Masculinity*, Oxford: Blackwell, pp. 47–64.

Cameron, Deborah (1998), '"Is there any ketchup, Vera?": gender, power and pragmatics', *Discourse and Society*, 9: 4, 437–55.

Cameron, Deborah (1999), '"Communication skills" as a gendered discourse', *Proceedings of the 1998 Berkeley Women and Language Conference*, University of California at Berkeley: Berkeley Women and Language Group.

Cameron, Deborah (2000), *Good to Talk? Living and Working in a Communication Culture* London: Sage.

Cameron, Deborah, E. Frazer, P. Harvey, B. Rampton and K. Richardson (1992), *Researching Language: Issues of Power and Method*, London: Routledge.

Capps, Lisa (1999), 'Constructing the irrational woman: narrative interaction and agoraphobic identity', in M. Bucholtz, A. C. Liang and L. Sutton (eds), *Reinventing Identities: The Gendered Self in Discourse*, Oxford: Oxford University Press, pp. 83–100.

Cheshire, Jenny (1982), *Variation in an English Dialect*, Cambridge: Cambridge University Press.

Clarke, Joanna (1996), 'Rave talk as antilanguage', unpublished BA Dissertation, University of Glamorgan.

Coates, Jennifer (1989), 'Gossip revisited: language in all-female groups', in Jennifer Coates and Deborah Cameron (eds), *Women in Their Speech Communities*, London: Longman, pp. 94–122.

Coates, Jennifer (1996), *Women Talk*, Oxford: Blackwell.

Coates, Jennifer (2000), 'Small talk and subversion: female speakers backstage', in Justine Coupland (ed.), *Small Talk*, pp. 213–40.

Coates, Jennifer and Deborah Cameron (eds) (1989), *Women in Their Speech Communities*, London: Longman.

Coupland, Justine, Nik Coupland and J. D. Robinson (1992), 'How are you?: negotiating phatic communion', *Language in Society*, 21, 207–30.

Coupland, Justine (ed.) (2000), *Small Talk*, Harlow, Essex: Pearson Education Ltd.

Coupland, Nikolas and Adam Jaworski (eds) (1997), *Sociolinguistics: A Reader and Coursebook*, Basingstoke: Macmillan.

Coupland, Nikolas and Virpi Ylanne-McEwen (2000), 'Talk about the weather: small talk, leisure talk and the travel industry', in Justine Coupland (ed.), *Small Talk*, pp. 163–82.

Crisell, Andrew (1994), *Understanding Radio*, London: Routledge.

Crystal, David (1997), *English as a Global Language*, Cambridge: Cambridge University Press.

Cutler, Cecilia A. (1999), 'Yorkville crossing: white teens, hip hop and African American English', *Journal of Sociolinguistics*, 3: 4, 428–42.

Dorval, Bruce (ed.), *Conversational Organization and Its Development* (Advances in Discourse Processes, vol. 38), Norwood, NJ: Ablex.

Drew, Paul and John Heritage (eds) (1992), *Talk at Work: Interaction in Institutional Settings*, Cambridge: Cambridge University Press.

Durham, D. (2000), 'Youth and the social imagination in Africa: introduction to parts 1 and 2', *Anthropology Quarterly*, 73: 3, 113–20.

Dwyer, Claire (1998), 'Contested identities: challenging dominant representations of young British Muslim women', in Tracey Skelton and Gill Valentine (eds), *Cool Places: Geographies of Youth Cultures*, London: Routledge, pp. 50–65.

Edwards, Viv (1997), 'Patois and the politics of protest: black English in British classrooms', in Nikolas Coupland and Adam Jaworski (eds), *Sociolinguistics: A Reader and Coursebook*, London: Macmillan, pp. 408–15.

Ehrlich, Susan (2001), *Representing Rape: Language and Sexual Consent*, London: Routledge.

El Refaie, Elisabeth (2001), 'Metaphors we discriminate by', *Journal of Sociolinguistics*, 5:3, 352–71.

Eliasoph, Nina (1987), 'Politeness, power and women's language: rethinking study in language and gender', *Berkeley Journal of Sociology*, 32, 79–103.

Emihovich, Catherine (1998), 'Bodytalk: discourses of sexuality among adolescent African American girls', in Susan Hoyle and Carolyn Temple Adger (eds), *Kids Talk: Strategic Language Use in Later Childhood*, Oxford: Oxford University Press, pp. 113–33.

Ervin-Tripp, Susan (1973), 'The structure of communicative choice', in Anwar S. Dill (ed.), *Language Acquisition and Communicative Choice*, Stanford, CA: Stanford University Press, pp. 302–73.

Fairclough, Norman (1992a), *Discourse and Social Change*, Cambridge: Polity Press.

Fairclough, Norman (ed.), (1992b), *Critical Language Awareness*, Harlow: Longman.

Fairclough, Norman (1994), 'Conversationalization of public discourse and the authority of the consumer', in Russell Keat, Nigel Whiteley and Nicholas Abercrombie (eds), *The Authority of the Consumer*, London: Routledge, pp. 253–68.

Fairclough, Norman (1995), *Media Discourse*, London: Arnold.

Fairclough, Norman (1996), 'Technologisation of discourse', in Carmen Rosa Caldas-Coulthard and Malcolm Coulthard (eds), *Texts and Practices: Readings in Critical Discourse Analysis*, London: Routledge, pp. 71–83.

Fairclough, Norman (2000), *New Labour, New Language?*, London: Routledge.

Fairclough, Norman (2001), *Language and Power* (2nd edition), London: Longman.

Fairclough, Norman and Ruth Wodak (1997), 'Critical discourse analysis', in Teun A. van Dijk (ed.), *Discourse as Social Interaction*, Discourse Studies: A Multidisciplinary Introduction, Vol. 2, London: Sage, pp. 258–84.

Faith, Karlene (1994), 'Resistance: lessons from Foucault and feminism', in H. Lorraine Radtke and Henderikus J. Stem (eds), *Power/Gender: Social Relations in Theory and Practice*, London: Sage.

Ferguson, Charles (1959), 'Diglossia', *Word*, 15, 325–40.

Fishman, Joshua (1967), 'Bilingualism with and without diglossia: diglossia with and without bilingualism', *Journal of Social Issues*, 23: 2, 29–38.

Fishman, Pamela (1983), 'Interaction: the work women do', in Barrie Thorne, Barrie, Cheris Kramarae and Nancy Henley (eds), *Language, Gender and Society*, Rowley, MA: Newbury House, pp. 89–102.

Fordham, Signithia (1996), *Blacked Out: Dilemmas of Race, Identity and Success at Capitol High*, Chicago: University of Chicago Press.

Fordham, Signithia (1998), 'Speaking standard English from nine to three: language as guerilla warfare at Capital High', in Susan Hoyle and Carolyn Temple Adger (eds), *Kids Talk: Strategic Language Use in Later Childhood*, Oxford: Oxford University Press, pp. 205–16.

Fordham, Signithia (1999), 'Dissin' the "standard": ebonics as guerrilla warfare at Capital High', *Anthropology and Education Quarterly*, 30: 3, 272–93.

Forstorp, Per-Anders (1998), 'Reporting on the MS Estonia catastrophe: media-on media events and interprofessional boundary work', *Text*, 18: 2, 271–99.

Foucault, Michel (1979), *Discipline and Punish: The Birth of the Prison*, trans. A. Sheridan, New York: Random House.

Foucault, Michel (1980), *Power/Knowledge: Selected Interviews and Other Writings 1972–77*, ed. C. Gordon, Brighton: Harvester.

Foucault, Michel (1981), *The History of Sexuality, Vol. I: An Introduction*, New York: Vintage.

Frankenburg, R. (1993), *White Women, Race Matters: The Social Construction of Whiteness*, Minneapolis, MN: University of Minnesota Press.

Fraser, Nancy (1989), *Unruly Practices: Power, Discourse and Gender in Contemporary Social Theory*, Minneapolis: University of Minnesota Press.

Gal, Susan (1979), *Language Shift*, New York: Academic Press.

Gal, Susan (1989), 'Language and political economy', *ARA*, 18, 345–67.

Gal, Susan (1991), 'Between speech and silence: the problematics of research on language and gender', in M. di Leonardo (ed.), *Gender at the Crossroads of Knowledge: Feminist Anthropology in the Post-Modern Era*, Berkeley: University of California Press, pp. 175–203.

Gal, Susan (1998), 'Culture bases of language-use among German-speakers in Hungary', in P. Trudgill and J. Cheshire (eds), *The Sociolinguistics Reader*, Vol. 1, London: Arnold.

Gates, Henry Louis jnr (2000), 'A reporter at large: Black London', in Kwesi Owusu (ed.), *Black British Culture and Society: A Text Reader*, London: Routledge, pp. 169–80.

Getridge, Carolyn (1998), 'Linguistics society of America resolution on ebonics', in Theresa Perry and Lisa Delpitt (ed.), *The Real Ebonics Debate: Power, Language and the Education of African-American Children*, Boston: Beacon Press, pp. 160–1.

Giddens, Anthony (1989), *Sociology*, Cambridge: Polity Press.

Giddens, Anthony (1991), *Modernity and Self-Identity: Self and Society in the Late Modern Age*, Cambridge, UK: Polity Press.

Giles, Howard and Nikolas Coupland (1991), *Language: Contexts and Consequences*, Milton Keynes: Open University Press.

Gilroy, Paul (1993a), *The Black Atlantic: Modernity and Double Consciousness*, London: Verso.

Gilroy, Paul (1993b), *Small Acts: Thoughts on the Politics of Black Cultures*, London: Serpent's Tail.

Goffman, Erving (1959), *The Presentation of Self in Everyday Life*, Garden City, NY: Doubleday Anchor.

Goffman, Erving (1963), *Stigma: Notes on the Management of Spoiled Identity*, Englewood Cliffs, NJ: Prentice-Hall.

Goffman, Erving (1974), *Frame Analysis: An Essay on the Organisation of Experience*, Harmondsworth: Penguin Books.

Goffman, Erving (1981), *Forms of Talk*, Oxford: Blackwell.

Goodman, Sharon and David Graddol (1996), *Redesigning English: New Texts, New Identities*, London: Routledge.

Gramsci, Antonio (1971), *Selections from the Prison Notebooks*, ed. and trans. Q. Hoare and G. Norwell-Smith, London: Lawrence and Wishart.

Grice, H. P. (1975), 'Logic and Conversation', in Adam Jaworski and Nikolas Coupland (eds) (1999), *The Discourse Reader*, London: Routledge, pp. 76–88.

Grillo, Robert (ed.), *Social Anthropology and the Politics of Language*, London: Routledge.

Gumperz, John (ed.), *Language and Social Identity*, Cambridge: Cambridge University Press.

Gunnarsson, Britt-Louise, Per Linnell and Bengt Nordberg (eds) (1997), *The Construction of Professional Discourse*, Harlow, Essex: Longman.

Hall, Kira and Mary Bucholtz (eds), *Gender Articulated: Language and the Socially Constructed Self*, New York: Routledge.

Hall, Stuart (1992), 'New ethnicities', in James Donald and Ali Rattansi (eds), *'Race', Culture and Difference*, London: Sage, pp. 252–60.

Hall, Stuart and Tony Jefferson (eds) (1976), *Resistance through Rituals: Youth Subcultures in Post-war Britain*, London: Unwin Hyman.

Haugen, Einar (1966), *Language Conflict and Language Planning: The Case of Modern Norwegian*, Cambridge, MA: Harvard University Press.

Haugen, Einar, J. Derrick McClure and Derick S. Thomson (eds) (1990), *Minority Languages Today*, Edinburgh: Edinburgh University Press.

Hearn, Jeff (1998), *The Violences of Men*, London: Sage.

Hebdige, Dick (1979), *Subculture: The Meaning of Style*, London: Methuen.

Helms, J. (ed.), *Essays on the Verbal and Visual Arts*, Seattle: University of Washington Press.

Hemmings, Sue, Elizabeth B. Silva and Kenneth Thompson (2002), 'Accounting for the everyday', in Tony Bennet and Diane Watson (eds), *Understanding Everyday Life*, Oxford: Blackwell, pp. 272–313.

Hewitt, Roger (1982), 'White adolescent creole users and the politics of friendship', *Journal of Multilingual and Multicultural Development*, 3: 3, 217–32.

Hewitt, Roger (1986), *Whitetalk, Blacktalk*, Cambridge: Cambridge University Press.

Hill, Jane (1999), 'Styling locally, styling globally: what does it mean?', *Journal of Sociolinguistics*, 3: 4, 542–56.

Hochschild, Arlie Russell (1983), *The Managed Heart: Commercialization of Human Feeling*, Berkely, CA: University of California Press.

Hoffmann, Charlotte (1991), *An Introduction to Bilingualism*, London: Longman.

Holborow, M. (1999), *The Politics of English*, London: Sage.

Hollows, Joanne (2000), *Feminism, Femininity and Popular Culture*, Manchester: Manchester University Press.

Holmes, Janet (1995), *Women, Men and Politeness* London: Longman.

Holmes, Janet (2000), 'Doing collegiality and keeping control at work: small talk in government departments', in Justine Coupland (ed.), *Small Talk*, Harlow, Essex: Pearson Education Ltd, pp. 32–61.

Holt, Grace Sims (1972), ' "Inversion" in black communication', in Thomas Kochman (ed.), *Rappin' and Stylin' Out: Communication in Urban Black America*, Urbana: University of Illinois Press, pp. 152–9.

Hutchby, Ian (1991), 'The organisation of talk on radio', in Paddy Scannell (ed.), *Broadcast Talk*, London: Sage, pp. 119–37.

Houghton, Catherine (1995), 'Managing the body of labor: the treatment of reproduction and sexuality in a therapeutic institution', in Kira Hall and Mary Bucholtz (eds), *Gender Articulated: Language and the Socially Constructed Self*, New York: Routledge, pp. 121–41.

Huddy, Leonie and David Sears (1990), 'Qualified public support for bilingual education: some policy implications', *The Annals of the American Academy for Political and Social Science*, 508 (March), pp. 119–34.

Humm, Maggie (1989), *The Dictionary of Feminist Theory*, Hemel Hempstead: Harvester Wheatsheaf.

Hurtado, Aida (1989), 'Relating to privilege: seduction and rejection in the subordination of white women and women of color', *Signs*, 14: 4, 833–55.

Hornberger, Nancy (1998), 'Language policy, language education, language rights: indigenous, immigrant, and international perspectives', *Language in Society*, 27: 439–58.

Hutchby, Ian (1996), *Confrontation Talk: Arguments, Asymmetries and Power on Talk Radio*, Mahwah, NJ: Lawrence Erlbaum.

Iedema, Rick and Ruth Wodak (1999), 'Introduction: organisational discourses and practices', *Discourse & Society*, 10: 1, 5–19.

Jasinski, J. (2001), *Sourcebook on Rhetoric: Key Concepts in Contemporary Rhetorical Studies*, London: Sage.

Johnson, Sally (ed.) (2003), *Discourse and Society*, 14, 1.

Johnson, Sally and Ulrike Hanna Meinhof (eds) (1997), *Language and Masculinity*, Oxford: Blackwell.

Kaplan, Robert B. and Richard B. Baldauf Jr. (1997), *Language Planning: From Practice to Theory*, Clevedon: Multilingual Matters.

Kasesniemi, Eija-Liisa and Pirjo Rautiainen (2000), 'Mobile culture of children and teenagers in Finland', in James E. Katz and Mark Aakhus (ed.), *Perpetual Contact: Mobile Communication, Private Talk and Public Performance*, Cambridge: Cambridge University Press, pp. 170–92.

Kress, Gunther (1986), 'Language in the media: the construction of the domains of public and private', *Media, Culture and Society*, 8, 395–419.

Labov, William (1972a), 'The isolation of contextual styles', *Sociolinguistic Patterns*, Philadelphia: University of Pennsylvania Press, pp. 70–109.

Labov, William (1972b), *Language in the Inner City*, Philadelphia: University of Pennsylvania.

Labov, William (1972c), 'Rules for ritual insults', *Language in the Inner City: Studies in the Black English Vernacular*, Philadelphia: University of Pennsylvania Press.

Lakoff, George and M. Johnson (1980), *Metaphors We Live By*, Chicago: University of Chicago Press.

Lakoff, Robin Tolmach (2000), *The Language War*, California: University of California Press.

Leech, Geoffrey (1966), *English in Advertising*, London: Longman.

Leonard, Marion (1998), 'Paper planes: travelling the new grrrl geographies', in Tracey Skelton and Gill Valentine (eds), *Cool Places: Geographies of Youth Cultures*, London: Routledge, pp. 101–18.

Levinson, Stephen (1983), *Pragmatics*, Cambridge: Cambridge University Press.

LINC (1991), *Language in the National Curriculum: Materials for Professional Development*, LINC.

Linnell, Per and Srikant Sarangi (1998), 'Discourse across boundaries: on recontextualisations and the blending of voices in professional discourse', *Text*, 18: 2, 143–57.

Lippi-Green, Rosina (1997), *English with an Accent: Language, Ideology and Discrimination in the United States*, London: Routledge.

Lott, Eric (1993), *Love and Theft: Blackface Minstrelsy and the American Working Class*, New York: Oxford University Press.

Maltz, Daniel and Ruth Borker (1982), 'A cultural approach to male-female miscommunication', in John Gumperz (ed.), *Language and Social Identity*, Cambridge: Cambridge University Press, pp. 196–216.

Marshall, Tim A. (2001), 'Dialogism', in R. Mesthrie (ed.), *Concise Encyclopedia of Sociolinguistics*, Oxford: Elsevier Science.

Martin-Jones, Marilyn (1989), 'Language, power and linguistic minorities: the need for an alternative approach to bilingualism, language maintenance and shift', in Robert Grillo (ed.), *Social Anthropology and the Politics of Language*, London: Routledge, pp. 106–25.

Mary Kay Cosmetics (April 2002), http://www.mary kay.com.

Maybin, Janet and Neil Mercer (1996), *Using English: From Conversation to Canon*, London: Routledge.

McDonald, Kevin (1999), *Struggles for Subjectivity: Identity, Action and Youth Experience*, Cambridge: Cambridge University Press.

McElhinny, Bonnie (1997), 'Ideologies of public and private language in sociolinguistics', in Ruth Wodak (ed.), *Gender and Discourse*, London: Sage, pp. 106–39.

McKay, Sandra (1997), 'Multilingualism in the United States', *Annual Review of Applied Linguistics*, Vol. 17, pp. 242–62.

McRobbie, Angela (1991), 'Settling accounts with subculture: a feminist critique', *Feminism and Youth Culture: From 'Jackie' to 'Just Seventeen'*, London: Macmillan.

McRobbie, Angela (1994), *Postmodernism and Popular Culture*, London: Routledge.

Mesthrie, Rajend, Joan Swann, Andrea Deumert and William L. Leap (2000), *Introducing Sociolinguistics*, Edinburgh: Edinburgh University Press.

Mirrlees-Black, Catriona, Pat Mayhew and Andrew Percy (1996), *The 1996 British Crime Survey Home Office Statistical Bulletin*, 19/96.

Mirrlees-Black, Catriona, Tracey Budd, Sarah Partridge and Pat Mayhew (1998), *The 1998 British Crime Survey Home Office Statistical Bulletin*, 21/98.

Montgomery, Martin (1995), *An Introduction to Language and Society* (2nd edition), London: Routledge.

Moores, Shaun (1999), 'The mediated "interaction order"', in Jeff Hearn and S. Roseneil (eds), *Consuming Cultures: Power and Resistance*, London: Macmillan, pp. 221–40.

Morgan, Marcyliena (1998), 'More than a mood or an attitude: discourse and verbal genre in African American culture', in Salikoko Mufwene et al. (eds), *The Structure of African American English*, New York: Routledge, pp. 251–81.

Morrison, Keith and Icy Lui (2000), 'Ideology, linguistic capital and the medium of instruction in Hong Kong', *Journal of Multilingual and Multicultural Development*, 21: 6, 471–86.

Mumby, Dennis K. and Robin St Clair (1997), 'Organisational discourse', in Teun A. van Dijk (ed.), *Discourse as Social Interaction*, London: Sage, pp. 181–205.

O'Neil, Wayne (1998), 'If ebonics isn't a language, then tell me, what is?', in Theresa Perry and Lisa Delpitt (eds), *The Real Ebonics Debate: Power, Language and the Education of African-American Children*, Boston: Beacon Press, pp. 38–47.

Ochs, Elinor and Carolyn Taylor (1995), 'The "Father Knows Best" dynamic in dinnertime narratives', in Kiru Hall and Mary Bucholtz (eds), *Gender Articulated: Language and the Socially Constructed Self*, New York: Routledge.

Oerton, Sarah and Karen Atkinson (1997), 'Voices from the valleys: young "single" mother's talk', unpublished paper, BSA Annual Conference, University of York, April.

Oerton, Sarah and Karen Atkinson (1999), 'Voices from the valleys: researching lone mothers' talk', *Community, Work and Family*, 2: 2/3, 229–56.

Owusu, Kwesi (2000), *Black British Culture and Society: A Text Reader*, London: Routledge.

Padilla, Amado (1999), 'Psychology', in J. A. Fishman (ed.), *Handbook of Language and Ethnic Identity*, Oxford: Oxford University Press, pp. 109–21.

Pelissier Kingfisher, Catherine (1996a), *Women in the American Welfare Trap*, Philadelphia: University of Pennsylvania Press.

Pelissier Kingfisher, Catherine (1996b), 'Women on welfare: conversational sites of acquiescence and dissent', *Discourse and Society*, 7: 4, 531–57.

Pennycook, Alistair (1994), *The Cultural Politics of English as an International Language*, London: Longman.

Perry, Theresa (1998), 'I "on know why they be trippin": reflections on the ebonics debate', in Theresa Perry and Lisa Delpitt (eds), *The Real Ebonics Debate: Power, Language and the Education of African-American Children*, Boston: Beacon Press, pp. 3–16.

Perry, Theresa and Lisa Delpitt (1998), 'Preface and foreword', *The Real Ebonics Debate: Power, Language and the Education of African-American Children*, Boston: Beacon Press, pp. xi–xiv.

Phillipson, Robert (1992), *Linguistic Imperialism*, Oxford: Oxford University Press.

Phillipson, Robert and Tove Skutnabb-Kangas (1995), 'Linguistic rights and wrongs', *Applied Linguistics*, 16: 4, pp. 483–504.

Pujolar, Joan (2000) *Gender, Heteroglossia and Power: A Sociolinguistic Study of Youth Culture*, Berlin: Mouton de Gruyter.

Qureshi, Karen (2000), 'Limited talk', in Caroline Mitchell (ed.), *Women and Radio: Airing Differences*, London: Routledge, pp. 182–8.

Ragan, Sandy (2000), 'Sociable talk in women's health care contexts: two forms of non-medical talk', in Coupland (ed.) (2000), *Small Talk*, pp. 269–87.

Rampton, Ben (1992), 'Scope for empowerment in sociolinguistics', in Deborah Cameron et al., *Researching Language: Issues of Power and Method*, London: Routledge, pp. 29–64.

Rampton, Ben (1995), *Crossing: Language and Ethnicity among Adolescents*, Harlow: Longman.

Rampton, Ben (1999), 'Sociolinguistics and cultural studies: new ethnicities, liminality and interaction, *Social Semiotics*, 9: 3, 355–73.

Rankin, Maggie and Helen Karn (1999), 'Mock ebonics: linguistic racism in parodies of ebonics on the internet', *Journal of Sociolinguistics*, 3: 3, 360–80.

Rhodes Hoover, Mary (1998), 'Ebonics: myths and realities', in Theresa Perry and Lisa Delpitt (eds), *The Real Ebonics Debate: Power, Language and the Education of African-American Children*, Boston: Beacon Press, pp. 71–6.

Rickford, John (1999), 'The ebonics controversy in my backyard: a sociolinguist's experience and reflections', *Journal of Sociolinguistics*, 3: 2, 267–75.

Riggins, Stephen (1997), 'The rhetoric of othering', in Stephen Riggins (ed.), *The Language and Politics of Exclusion: Others in Discourse*, Thousand Oaks: Sage.

Roediger, David R. (1991), *The Wages of Whiteness: Race and the Making of the American Working Class*, London: Verso.

Rogin, Michael (1996), *Blackface, White Noise: Jewish Immigrants in the Hollywood Melting Pot*, Berkeley, CA: University of California Press.

Rose, Tricia (1994), 'A style nobody can deal with', in Andrew Ross and Tricia Rose (eds), *Microphone Fiends: Youth Music and Youth Culture*, New York: Routledge, pp. 71–8.

Sarangi, Srikant and Stefaan Slembrouck (1996), *Language, Bureaucracy and Control*, London: Longman.

Scannell, Paddy (ed.) (1991), *Broadcast Talk*, London: Sage.

Scannell, Paddy (1991), 'The relevance of talk', in P. Scannell (ed.), *Broadcast Talk*, London: Sage, pp. 1–13.

Schmidt, R. Sr. (2000), *Language Policy and Identity Politics in the United States*, Philadelphia: Temple University Press.

Scott, James C. (1986), 'Everyday forms of resistance', in James C. Scott and Benedict J. Tria Kerkvliet (eds), *Everyday Forms of Peasant Resistance in South-East Asia*, London: Frank Cass.

Sheldon, Amy (1996), 'You can be the baby brother, but you aren't born yet: preschool girls' negotiation for power and access in pretend play', *Research on Language and Social Interaction*, 29: 1, 57–80.

Sheldon, Amy (1997), 'Talking power: girls, gender enculturation and discourse', in Wodak (ed.), *Gender and Discourse*, pp. 225–44.

Smith, A. (1980), *The Geopolitics of Information: How Western Culture Dominates the World*, New York: Oxford University Press.

Smith, Ernie (1998), 'What is black English? What is ebonics?', in Theresa Perry and Lisa Delpitt (eds), *The Real Ebonics Debate: Power, Language and the Education of African-American Children*, Boston: Beacon Press, pp. 48–58.

Smitherman, Geneva (1998a), 'Black English/ebonics: what it be like?', in Theresa Perry and Lisa Delpitt (eds), *The Real Ebonics Debate: Power, Language and the Education of African-American Children*, Boston: Beacon Press, pp. 28–37.

Smitherman, Geneva (1998b), 'What go round come round: *King* in perspective', in Theresa Perry and Lisa Delpitt (eds), *The Real Ebonics Debate: Power, Language and the Education of African-American Children*, Boston: Beacon Press, pp. 162–71.

Smitherman, Geneva (2000), *Talkin That Talk: Language, Culture and Education in African America*, London: Routledge.

Smitherman, Geneva and S. Cunningham (1997) 'Moving beyond resistance: ebonics and African-American youth', *Journal of Black Psychology*, 23: 3, 227–32.

Soloman, R. Patrick (1998), 'Black cultural forms in schools: a cross national comparison', in Lois Weis (ed.), *Class, Race, and Gender in American Education*, New York: SUNY Press, pp. 249–65.

Spender, Dale (1980), *Man Made Language*, London/New York: Routledge & Kegan Paul.

Storey, John (2001), *Cultural Theory and Popular Culture* (3rd edition), London: Prentice Hall.

Swales, John and Priscilla S. Rogers (1995), 'Discourse and the projection of corporate culture: the mission statement', *Discourse & Society*, 6: 2, 223–42.

Talbot, Mary (1995), 'A synthetic sisterhood: false friends in a teenage magazine', in Hall and Bucholtz (eds), *Gender Articulated*, pp. 143–65.

Talbot, Mary (1995), 'Synthetic sisterhood': false friends in a teenage magazine', in K. Hall and M. Bucholtz (eds), *Gender Articulated: Language and the Socially Constructed Self*, New York: Routledge, pp. 143–65.

Talbot, Mary (1998), *Language and Gender: An Introduction*, Cambridge: Polity Press.

Talbot, Mary (2000), '"It's good to talk"?: the undermining of feminism in a British Telecom advertisement', *Journal of sociolinguistics*, 4: 1, 108–19.

Tannen, Deborah (1984), *Conversational Style: Analyzing Talk among Friends*, Norwood, NJ: Ablex.

Tannen, Deborah (1986), *That's Not What I Meant!*, New York: Dent.

Tannen, Deborah (1990), 'Gender differences in conversational coherence: physical alignment and topical cohesion', in Dorval (ed.), *Conversational Organization and Its Development*, pp. 167–206.

Tannen, Deborah (1991), *You Just Don't Understand*, London: Virago.

Tannen, Deborah (1995), *Talking from 9 to 5*, London: Virago.

Tannen, Deborah (ed.) (1993), *Gender and Conversational Interaction*, Oxford: Oxford University Press.

Teo, Peter (2000), 'Racism in the news: a Critical Discourse Analysis of news reporting in two Australian newspapers', *Discourse and Society*, 11: 1, 7–49.

Termes, Josep (1984), *La Immigració a Catalunya i Altres Estudis d'Història del Nacionalisme Català*, Barcelona: Empúries.

Thorne, Barrie, Cheris Kramarae and Nancy Henley (eds), *Language, Gender and Society*, Rowley, MA: Newbury House.

Thornborrow, Joanna (2002), *Power Talk: Language and Interaction in Institutional Discourse*, London: Longman.

Thornton, Sarah (1995), *Club Cultures: Music, Media and Subcultural Capital*, Cambridge: Polity Press.

Tifft, L. (1993), *Battering of Women: The Failure of Intervention and the Case for Prevention*, Oxford: Westview Press.

Tolson, Andrew (1991), 'Televised chat and the synthetic personality', in P. Scannell (ed.), *Broadcast Talk*, London: Sage, pp. 178–200.

Tyler, Melissa and Steve Taylor (1997), '"Come fly with us": emotional labour and the commodification of sexual difference in the airline industry', paper presented to the Annual International Labour Process Conference, Edinburgh.

Uchida, Aki (1992), 'When "difference" is "dominance": a critique of the "anti-power-based" cultural approach to sex differences', *Language in Society*, 21, 547–68.

van Dijk, Teun (1991), *Racism and the Press*, London: Routledge.

van Dijk, Teun, S. Ting-Toomey, G. Smitherman and D. Troutman (1997), 'Discourse, ethnicity, culture and racism', in Teun van Dijk (ed.), *Discourse as Social Interaction*, London: Sage, pp. 144–80.

Walsh, Clare (2001), *Gender and Discourse: Language and Power in Politics, the Church and Organisations*, London: Longman.

Wearside Domestic Violence Forum (2000), *Domestic Violence Fact Sheet*, Sunderland: Wearside Domestic Violence Forum.

Weedon, Chris (1997), *Feminist Practice and Poststructuralist Theory*, Oxford: Blackwell.

West, Candace (1984), 'When the doctor is a lady', *Symbolic Interaction*, 7: 1, 87–106.

West, Candace and Don Zimmerman (1983), 'Small insults: a study of interruptions in cross-sex conversations between unacquainted persons', in Barrie Thorne, Cheris Kramarae and Nancy Henley (eds), *Language, Gender and Society*, Rowley, MA: Newbury House, pp. 103–17.

White, Cynthia (1970), *Women's Magazines, 1694–1968*, London: Michael Joseph.

Willis, Paul (1977), *Learning to Labour*, London: Routledge & Kegan Paul.

Wodak, Ruth (1996), *Disorders of Discourse*, Harlow, Essex: Longman.

Wodak, Ruth (ed.) (1997), *Gender and Discourse*, London: Sage.

Woods, Nicola (1988), 'Talking shop: sex and status as determinants of floor apportionment in a work setting', in Jennifer Coates and Deborah Cameron (eds), *Women in Their Speech Communities*, London: Longman, pp. 141–57.

Woolard, Kathryn (1989), *Double Talk: Bilingualism and the Politics of Ethnicity in Catalonia*, California: Stanford University Press.

Yule, George (1998), *Pragmatics*, Oxford: Oxford University Press.

Zimmerman, Don and Candace West (1975), 'Sex roles, interruptions and silences in conversation', in Barrie Thorne and Nancy Henley (eds), *Language and Sex: Difference and Dominance*, Rowley, MA: Newbury House, pp. 105–29.

INDEX